THE RINK

Stories from Hockey's
Home Towns

Chris Cuthbert
Scott Russell

Penguin Books

PENGUIN BOOKS
Published by the Penguin Group
Penguin Books Canada Ltd, 10 Alcorn Avenue, Toronto, Ontario, Canada M4V 3B2
Penguin Books Ltd, 27 Wrights Lane, London W8 5TZ, England
Penguin Putnam Inc., 375 Hudson Street, New York, New York 10014, U.S.A.
Penguin Books Australia Ltd, Ringwood, Victoria, Australia
Penguin Books (NZ) Ltd, cnr Rosedale and Airborne Roads, Albany, Auckland 1310,
New Zealand

Penguin Books Ltd, Registered Offices: Harmondsworth, Middlesex, England

First published in Viking by Penguin Books Canada Limited, 1997
Published in Penguin Books, 1998
10 9 8 7 6 5 4 3 2 1

Manufactured in Canada

Canadian Cataloguing in Publication Data

Cuthbert, Chris, 1957–
    The rink: stories from hockey's home towns

ISBN 0-14-026602-X

1. Hockey – Canada – Anecdotes. I. Russell, Scott, 1958– . II. Title.

GV848.4.C3C87 1998   796.962'0971   C97-931662-6

Visit Penguin Canada's web site at **www.penguin.ca**

To Diane, Jennifer, Justin, Mom and Dad
–C.C.

For Catherine, Alex and Charlotte
While in our "little barn," I can always count on home ice advantage
–S.R.

Contents

If I were asked by some stranger to North American culture to show him the most important religious building in Canada, I would take him to Toronto's Maple Leaf Gardens.
—William Kilbourn, *Religion in Canada*

Introduction

Scott Russell

Some winters I felt as if I lived in the Forum. I knew every scratch on the paint along the boards. There was one long gash near the south penalty box I used to touch before every game and remember how it was made.
—Hugh MacLennan, *Two Solitudes*, 1945

ON MOST WINTER SATURDAYS we found ourselves at hockey's sacred rink. Over the years, the Montreal Forum had become something more than an arena to a pair of "Hockey Night in Canada" broadcasters. At first, it was enemy territory to us, one of whom had come from Brampton and the other from Oshawa, Ontario. As kids we had been Maple Leaf fans and in this game old loyalties die hard, especially when you're talking about an ancient rivalry involving storied teams in Toronto and Montreal. There is no question, the Forum came to represent the Habs and, as such, we had always despised it.

We had first entered the doors of the building at Atwater and Ste. Catherine Streets as sportscasters, and although our introductions to the place occurred at separate times, the effect was similar, we discovered, when we discussed it years later. The smell of the Forum was different from other rinks we had been in. The brilliance of the red, white and blue seats struck a chord with us, as did the immaculate presentation of the aging building. The Stanley Cup banners that hung from the ceiling were a wonder, something we had never seen the like of in our hockey travels. It goes without saying that the people of this rink were larger than life as they roamed the Forum early on a game day with the ease of common folks in a comfortable living room.

There was Red Fisher, the long-time hockey columnist for the *Montreal Gazette*, sharing a coffee and easy banter with his pal and broadcasting legend Dick Irvin. By the ice, Jean Béliveau sat and chatted with media members and kids. The great Hall of Famer was regal in his carriage but remarkably relaxed in the familiar surroundings of the hockey arena where he had left his mark so indelibly. Just in front of him, a two-man crew soaped and wiped the glass surrounding the ice surface until not one mark from the black rubber pucks remained. We became convinced that this was the perfect rink in a city devoted to hockey. It went against the grain, but we could not deny the fact that the Forum was someplace special, almost magical, and it captured our attention, not to mention our respect, immediately.

On one of our last trips to the Forum, before its closure on March 11, 1996, together we watched the Buffalo Sabres coach, Ted Nolan, skate alone on the early-morning ice. Whizzing up and down and slamming pucks into the empty net, Nolan would often glide between the blue and centre red lines while casting his glance up to the banners. He had played seventy-eight games in the National Hockey League and precious few at the Forum, but he was engrossed by its legendary charm and proud traditions. Nolan's team had played the night before and travelled to Montreal in the wee hours of the morning, so the game-day practice he had scheduled was optional for the players. When he skated over to us, his eyes were wide and he yelled over the glass. "I can't believe the whole team isn't out here," he shouted. "This is our last chance in this place. You'd think they'd all wanna touch the ice just so they could remember it."

The Forum was a place that hockey players aspired to. They held tremendous regard for the building and what it meant to the game. In a ceremony to mark the rink's closing, former members of the Canadiens carried a torch onto the ice surface and, in front of a weeping throng, passed it on to Montreal's hockey heroes of the day. It was a moving testament to a house that had been built in 1924 and which, in its seventy-two years of existence, had become a meeting place for a people who shared a common passion.

If the Forum was a rink that players worked extremely hard to get to, then the question becomes, where did they start out? Hockey is a game of the grass roots and its practitioners have an exceptional regard for their beginnings. Jean Béliveau is in his sixties now, but his recollections of the first indoor rink he played in are alarmingly clear. "We had an inside arena in Victoriaville because it was owned by the exhibition commission," he told us. "In the summer they used it to judge cattle. That was the main purpose of the building, but we used it to play hockey." Before that rink, Béliveau played on an outdoor ice surface at the Sacred Heart College in his home town. The Catholic brothers, who were his teachers, sent him out to prepare the ice late on Friday and Saturday evenings. "On a windy night the spray from the hose stuck to me," Béliveau recalled. "When I finally got home at midnight, I would look like an icicle."

The hockey rink is the place where many Canadians grow to maturity, and as much as the church or the school, it allows the people of communities to gather for entertainment and fellowship. There is no denying the fact that the most compelling reason for going to the rink is to watch the game that we have, as Canadians, become so attached to. Still, we are not all hockey fans in this country. One woman told us that she loathed going to the local arena in Kingston, Ontario, on Saturday mornings to watch her two brothers play in the house league. It was frigid and she felt that she and her sister had nothing to do with what was taking place on the ice. She even went as far as to say that she felt like a prisoner on most weekends. Now, many years later, the same woman reveals a deep understanding of what the rink can mean to the community in spite of one's apparent lack of connection to it. "Unlike the church I went to, the rink in Kingston was non-denominational," she said. "It excluded no one and was a place where everyone was welcome."

In the United States, sport appears to be quite regionalized, and in various parts of the country emphasis is placed on different games. Many inner cities are basketball territory with countless asphalt courts in evidence. Children play that game in that place and you can see it every day. The southwest, in particular the states of Oklahoma and Texas, is a hotbed of football. There, high school stadiums built for gridiron confrontations are magnificent and much larger than an observer from this country could imagine. The baseball parks that dominate the southern landscape of places like Florida demonstrate an obsession with the national pastime in those parts of the country.

The same is not true of Canada. Here, hockey is universal and the common building in most communities, whether urban or rural, is the local rink. Marc Crawford, coach of the 1996 Stanley Cup champion Colorado Avalanche, remembered scouting talent across Canada and finding a striking similarity wherever he went. "If I didn't know where the rink was, I looked for the city hall or the church. I knew if I found one of those, the rink was close by. Uniformly it worked out that way," he said. "I think that's important for towns and cities. They build it in the downtown core, in the heart of the city."

As we delved into the importance of the rink to Canadians, we were amazed at the associations people in this country have with these special buildings. In the Vancouver airport, we encountered Nelson and Jim Byford who were returning from Toronto after having seen the Leafs play the Canadiens at Maple Leaf Gardens the night before. The trip was a seventieth birthday present for Jim from his three sons, and they had all stayed in one room at a downtown hotel, sleeping two to a bed. "I knew Maple Leaf Gardens didn't have long left so we had to do this now. It was worth it," Nelson said. "We had red seats," said Jim. "It was beautiful and if we had them developed, I'd love to show you the pictures." The two hugged and then boarded separate flights, Jim on his way to Silverton, British Columbia, and his son Nelson bound for Victoria. For a couple of days, they had been closer, in a hockey rink, than they had been in years.

While fathers and sons have long been associated in the arena's confines, other hockey relationships are developing in this Canadian institution. On our way to Newfoundland, we ran into Martin Smith, a professional hockey player who had just returned to Canada after his team's last game. He played for the Manchester Storm in the English league and had made it home just in time to see his sister compete for Canada at the women's World Hockey Championships in Kitchener, Ontario. Fiona Smith had helped Canada win the gold medal and most likely will play for her country at the Olympic Games in Nagano, Japan, in February 1998. She and Martin are a couple of years apart, but they were defence partners as peewees when they played in the rink in North Battleford, Saskatchewan. As a spectator this time, the brother revelled in his sister's success.

The rink fosters connections of all kinds and it can also be a tremendous source of pride for various communities. In New Brunswick, for instance, the talk is not about some fabled arena full of great folklore, but instead of Harbour Station, a brand-new facility that has helped to rejuvenate industrial Saint John. On a chance meeting in Halifax, a jovial man named Gilbert Correia approached Scott, whom he recognized from "Hockey Night in Canada," and raved about the new rink in Canada's oldest city. Born in Bermuda and blessed with a Maritimer's friendliness, Correia insisted that we pay a visit to "the Station" and see "how fabulous it really is." We were not disappointed, particularly when we saw the size of the congregation and the jubilant nature of the place.

There are thousands of rinks in this country of various shapes and sizes and the importance of each can be judged only by the people who make use of them. In our attempt to tell the stories of these temples of hockey, it is a foregone conclusion that our efforts will be incomplete. Players and places of equal significance are inevitably left out, but in the telling of ten tales that we hope represent all parts of the country, there may be some similarities that extend throughout. The hockey rink, we believe, is important beyond the bricks and mortar and more striking than the architecture. The rinks are where the dreams of the players begin and end. They are structures that have shaped our nation since its infancy.

In the Edmonton Oilers' locker room, a collection of people reflects the extent of the game of hockey and how far reaching its effect can be. These are young players, for the most part, who are, in the spring of 1997, enjoying their first real taste of playoff success. It is supposed to be a pressure-filled time in one of Canada's bastions of the league, millions of dollars at stake with each game won or lost. In the room there are also parents. Bill deVries of Sundridge, Ontario; Bobby Grier of Boston, Massachusetts; and Peter Marchant of Williamsville, New York. The sons, Greg, Mike and Todd, respectively, go over their equipment with their dads or just sit and enjoy a morning cup of coffee knowing the game is hours away. A ping-pong table sits in the middle of the room where Jason Arnott and Louie Debrusk, two of the team's larger forwards, bang the little white ball back and forth with astounding grace. There is chatter and laughter and all the things we remember from the rinks we knew years ago.

The talk turns to the places these young men grew up in. Arnott shone at the Wasaga Star Arena on the shores of Georgian Bay. The team captain, Kelly Buchberger, played first at Langenburg Arena in rural Saskatchewan. "I lived about eighty yards from the place," Buchberger said. "I was over there just about all the time." To a man, they admit that the Edmonton Coliseum is not really that physically different from the rinks they first competed in. The tradition of the place is what impresses them. They know that Wayne Gretzky, Mark Messier and their current teammate, Kevin Lowe, have won numerous Stanley Cups here.

Ryan Smyth of Banff, Alberta, puts new laces in his well-worn skates before every game. One of the speedier young players in the league, Smyth puts a premium on what he can make his blades do. Earlier, by the boards, he had talked about how glad he was to be back in the Coliseum after having survived the slushy ice of Dallas. "This rink has the best ice in the league,"

Smyth said, matter-of-factly. "It's hard and fast and that's the way our team is built." In other words, the rink has shaped the way its resident team plays the game.

In the thousands of rinks across Canada, countless quirks and subtle characteristics make each unique. We interviewed nearly two hundred people as we visited and researched each of the twelve rinks we've written about. They told stories of arenas that made for rugged and physical play and others that favoured the swift and skilled players. Some rinks have produced world champions and some Stanley Cup winners. Others are notable because they welcome international tournaments and are the testing ground for the stars of the future. Each rink has something to give and, more importantly, a folklore attached to it. It is a shame there is not space for more of those stories in these pages. We are convinced that every rink has tremendous merit and the ones described here are only representative of the extensive treasures across the country.

They are not baseball parks in which spectators bask in the warmth of glorious sunshine nor are they the great cathedrals of football. Hockey rinks, in various parts of Canada, can be cold and forbidding places. Sometimes they are rudimentary aluminum buildings, where you cling to the warmth of a coffee cup in gloved hands, covered from the waist with a woollen blanket. These are extreme environments in which the people huddle to watch a favourite game unfold on a frozen and unforgiving surface. They welcome the hearty and the spirited and promise a sense of community—indeed, some would argue that Canadians are never more at home than when they gather in hockey's house.

Prologue
Windsor, Nova Scotia

Chris Cuthbert

Canada is the birthplace of this tremendous game. You invented it and you always want to be the best. Prove it, then, in honest battle.
—Anatoli Tarasov, 1969

"IF THAT BUILDING COULD talk it would tell a lot of stories." Frank Gallagher is referring to the aged Stannus Street rink in the heart of Windsor, Nova Scotia. It is believed to be the oldest standing rink in Canada, dating from 1897. A legacy of hockey lore from the Windsor Rink surrounds us at the Hockey Heritage Centre on Albert Street in this Maritime town that proclaims itself the Birthplace of Hockey.

The debate over hockey's origins has long been waged between Montreal and Kingston. Now some hockey historians are recognizing Windsor's claim—certainly its devotion to the game has never been in dispute.

Photos of Windsor's championship teams dating back to 1888 adorn the museum's walls. Among them is the 1919 Windsor Academy team, which was a perfect 22–0 en route to the provincial title. They were led by Ernie Mosher, the "Windsor Wizard," who later captained the Halifax Wolverines to Nova Scotia's only Allan Cup, in 1935. Another early star was "Doggie" Kuhn, who scored a goal in his first shift of his first NHL game for the New York Americans against the Ottawa Senators.

"There was a mystique about playing for Windsor and it always seemed to have a history of winning," says "Chook" Smith. Smith had been a local favourite for three decades and not only is he enshrined in Windsor's Hall of Fame but he's a regular visitor to the museum. "In Nova Scotia's small towns people knew all the players and went to all the games. There wasn't much else to do. There was no television. I've had people tell me that they lived forty miles away and would travel to Windsor in the back of a half-ton truck to watch the games."

Smith was captain of the 1964 Windsor Maple Leafs, champions of the Maritime Senior Amateur League. The team featured George Guilbault, who had broken Jean Béliveau's junior scoring records, along with another Quebec star, Simon Nolet, who later won a Stanley Cup with Philadelphia. "They made more playing for Windsor than they would have in the American Hockey League," says Chook.

"Didn't you say it was amateur hockey?" I ask. Smith laughs at the naïveté of the query.

Eric Stephens, manager of the local Chevrolet dealership, stores vehicles in the old rink. He is summoned to unlock the weathered edifice where generations of hockey memories are still housed. Chook Smith, who hasn't skated on the Windsor Rink's natural ice in fifty years, cannot resist. He follows us down to the rink to rediscover his past.

The Windsor Rink resembles a long wooden covered bridge with a steeple on its distinctive cupola. "They'd fly the Canadian Ensign from the flagpole there to signify that the ice was good enough for pleasure skating during the day and hockey at night," says Stephens. As a boy, Chook Smith peered out his dining-room window every winter's day hoping to see the flag flying. "It was the best sight you could imagine," Smith adds.

Dr. Garth Vaughn lives next door. A former general surgeon, Vaughn has become the driving force behind Windsor's assertion to being the birthplace of hockey. The author of *The Puck Starts Here*, Vaughn has chronicled the game's early days, emphasizing Windsor's hockey past.

"This was the second rink in town," Vaughn says. "The first rink burned down in the 'Great Windsor Fire' of 1897." That blaze destroyed most of the town. The inferno appeared under control until a strong wind off the Minas Basin fanned the destructive flames. "It was probably the Acadians who had been expelled out there blowing the wind in," Vaughn jokes.

"They built this structure to store lumber used to rebuild the town so it wouldn't be stolen," he continues. "Within three years the town was rebuilt. They used this as a natural ice rink until after the Second World War.

"It was the centre of my life. We could afford to go to a movie once a week but the rest of the time we were on the ice. The girls wore short skating skirts. Of course we followed them around. You had to get there early to see who had a new skirt."

Chook Smith scans the rink's rafters as if he's been unleashed in an old family attic laden with mystery and hidden treasure. He can almost smell the aroma of hot dogs that once wafted through the rink from his father's canteen. The consensus of rink patrons was that hot dogs never tasted better than here in the old rink. "This was the focal point of the winter around here," Smith says. "Every year I would get a season skating ticket for Christmas."

The massive cross-beams stretch across, less than ten feet overhead, above the intimate confines of the bandbox rink coined "the Icebox" in its day. "It's quite a piece of engineering," assesses Stephens, the car dealer. Above either side of the entrance are balconies where a live band or Victrola provided musical accompaniment for recreational skating. Occasionally music would be used to police on-ice activity. "Whenever a fight broke out that couldn't be controlled, they had a 78 record of 'God Save the King' that would be played," says Vaughn. "Everybody would stand at attention until it finished. Then the fight would resume. One night they had to play it three times before the fellas got finished."

During World War II, Windsor was an embarkation point for Canadian troops. Armed forces designated for assignment overseas were transferred through Windsor to Halifax onto the ships bound for Europe. The war years supplied high-profile talent to the area's armed forces teams. Just about everybody who frequented the Windsor Rink then remembers the night Bob Goldham played here for the Cornwallis Navy squad. A young Garth Vaughn raced to the train station to welcome the incoming hockey idol. "I was certain I was going to see Bob Goldham come off that train wearing his Toronto Maple Leafs uniform," Vaughn says. "I was so disappointed when he came off in his naval divvies with a kit bag over his shoulder."

On the ice, though, Goldham didn't disappoint, leading Cornwallis to a 10-1 rout of the local Army team. Chook Smith watched in awe. He remembers that only a few kids in the crowd were able to slow Cornwallis down. "Between periods the sticks disappeared from the Cornwallis bench," Smith recalls. "A few local kids took their sticks but didn't have anywhere to take them. Later, they found the sticks hidden in the beams overhead."

Despite the lopsided score, Bob Goldham suffered an embarrassing moment before the adoring Windsor crowd. The NHL star was sent sprawling head-first along the melting ice surface. "The ice was pretty soft that night," Vaughn recalls. "One of the drunks yelled out, 'Look, he's showing us how they do the breaststroke in the NHL.'"

Just over a mile away from the Windsor Rink lives the Wayne Gretzky of pumpkin growers, with the records to prove it. Howard Dill is the only competitor ever to win four consecutive world titles, from 1979 to 1982, for producing the heaviest pumpkins. His Atlantic Giant seeds have yielded world champions for the past seventeen years. Dill has been featured in *National Geographic, Ripley's Believe It or Not* and the *Guinness Book of World Records*. He was interviewed by Barbara Frum. His pumpkin seeds have been transported into space and studied as a possible cure for leukemia. One of his giants was flown to the Persian Gulf to inspire Allied troops.

Dill greets visitors to his thirty-six hectare farm on College Road inside Windsor's town limits with an affable smile and glistening blue eyes. Bus loads of tourists and dignitaries, from Joey Smallwood to Super Bowl-winning quarterback Earl Morrall, have come to marvel at the miracles of his pumpkin patch.

A few recognize Howard for his other passion, the game of hockey. "I can tell you Don Cherry's junior stats with Barrie," he says earnestly by way of welcome. "He had forty-six points in three years before going to Hershey. His brother Dick was a better player, you know." It's the first of many hockey references he drops into the conversation. "I've got fifty head of dairy cattle we milk by hand. I've never missed a shift underneath a cow," the sixty-three-year-old says laughing. "That's how Max Bentley developed his great shot. He had strong hands from milking cows."

Howard didn't get much of a shot at playing hockey. His mother died of tuberculosis when he was ten years old, bequeathing an adult's share of farm responsibilities to his wiry frame. "I didn't have the livelihood that most kids grew up with," Dill says. "I had a very strict father. I was up at five in the morning doing chores. I didn't have time to play the game like I wanted to at the pond or on the rink. So I turned my attention to excelling as a fan."

His hockey appetite was whetted at the Windsor Rink watching the home-town Maple Leafs play their provincial rivals in the Valley League. "I would go to every game in the winter. It cost a quarter," Dill says. "The rink manager was a poor man with a large family. He told me if I brought him a dozen eggs he'd let me in. He got the best of the deal because a dozen eggs were worth fifty cents."

Those games at the Windsor Rink provided refuge from the daily rigours of Howard's unrelenting farm life, but radio accounts of World War II reminded Dill that the world beyond the family farm was even more daunting. "We'd listen to the seven o'clock news and it didn't sound good. The only good news was when they announced that there would be a hockey game at the rink against Wolfville or Kentville. It gave you a contrast to the sadness of war."

The eggs that bought his entry to the Windsor Rink hatched another form of escape as a collector long before hockey memorabilia became the rage. "It was horse and wagon days," he says. "I would deliver eggs every Saturday. I'd put the touch on every lady on the route to save me all their Bee Hive corn syrup labels and box tops from Quaker Oats, Ivory Snow and St. Lawrence corn starch. I had everybody working for me. Some would even buy an extra can of corn syrup just to get me another label."

With his ingenuity and the co-operation of thirty customers along his route, Howard amassed an invaluable assortment of more than 2,500 glossy NHL photos issued by Bee Hive, beginning in 1936. Today in a cluttered bedroom of the family farmhouse are more than 20,000 items, including yearbooks from the 1930s and 1940s of his beloved Boston Bruins and a rare program from the 1928 Ottawa Senators. "It would take two years to catalogue everything," Dill boasts of the collection he shares with his son Danny. "Another collector came up here and said, 'I think I've seen them all, but this is heaven.'"

For the hockey purist, paradise isn't in Dill's farmhouse, but in his back pasture. On this property, first owned by Howard's great-grandfather, sits Long Pond, the reputed cradle of hockey. It is the place Thomas Chandler Haliburton, a graduate of King's College in Windsor, wrote of in 1844 providing the most compelling evidence for Windsor's claim to be the birthplace of hockey: "Boys let out racin', yelpin', hollerin', and whoopin' like mad with pleasure... hurley on the long pond on the ice."

Like Haliburton, over a century later Howard Dill delighted in the joy of playing on Long Pond, although no special privileges were accorded the owner of hockey's sacred rink. "Sunday afternoons as a boy you'd have to fight your way on it," Dill says. "There was quite a rivalry between the town boys and the King's College students. The bigger guys would push the younger guys off the ice. I couldn't come on and say I owned the pond. Someone might have whacked me and sent me home."

In his pumpkin patch, the monster crop is flourishing in the fertile Annapolis Valley soil. The pumpkins of Dill's boyhood grew to eighty pounds. Without any genetics training, Howard experimented, transferring the pollen of the heartiest pumpkins to create a super-heavyweight breed. In 1996, his seeds produced pumpkins tipping the scales at more than one thousand pounds. The Dill farm now supplies seeds to seven thousand individual growers and sixty seed companies. He has clients world-wide placing orders in seventeen languages. It's not hard to find the analogy here—like pumpkin growing, Dill's favourite winter sport has become a world-wide competition, and the seed is the home-town rink.

1 Brampton Memorial Arena
Brampton, Ontario

Chris Cuthbert

Everyone has deep in their heart the old town or community where they first went barefooted, got their first licking, traded the first pocket knife, grew up and finally went away thinking they were too big for that Burg. But that's where your old heart is.

—Will Rogers

THE THUNDER CLOUDS ROLL IN as the convoy of cars arrive from Ohsweken with the Six Nations Chiefs and their supporters. Summer's last gasp has produced a sweltering August day followed by an intense storm to wash away the heat. At other local rinks, hockey schools and all-star try-outs are already in full swing. Team Canada is completing final preparations for the World Cup of Hockey at its camp in Whistler, British Columbia. Tonight, the Brampton Memorial Arena will be packed, but the only ice will be used by team trainers. The home-town Excelsiors are set to battle Six Nations in the fourth game of the Eastern Canadian lacrosse championship.

Brampton Memorial Arena, circa 1965

Although I never mastered the sport, my roots are in a lacrosse town. They have been playing Canada's original game in Brampton for 125 years, initially on

9

the greensward that is now Rosalea Park, and currently at Memorial Arena.

The Excelsiors are Canada's most historic sports franchise. In 1926, George Lee, a local teacher, concluded an astonishing fifty-five-year reign as the team's first president. Upon his farewell, Lee reminded Brampton supporters of the origins of the team's distinguished name. "The name Excelsior proposed by me and chosen by the club was taken from Longfellow's beautiful poem of that title, and, as you probably know, means 'more lofty, still higher, ever upwards.'"

The loftiest achievements of the Excelsiors are six Mann Cup championships, symbolic of national senior lacrosse supremacy. Brampton won its last Mann Cup in 1993. Since then, tonight's opponents from Six Nations have been the sport's dominant power. The Chiefs lead this series 3–0, one victory away from another berth in the Mann Cup final.

My visits to the Memorial Arena have been infrequent since I left the city in the mid-seventies. The front steps have been replaced by a wheelchair ramp that leads to the arena entrance and into my past. An hour before game time, there is already a line-up at the ticket counter. For six dollars I can watch a playoff lacrosse game and turn back the clock.

Al Waxman plays Jack Adams on the set of CBC's docudrama "Net Worth" at Memorial Arena

Beyond the ticket booth is a staircase leading to the dressing rooms below where I would lug my hockey duffle bag every Saturday morning. This is where I learned to skate. From the cloudy recesses of distant memory I can still retrieve a few frames of those first uncertain steps on ice. This is

where I scored my first minor hockey league goal. There were so few that the first is not difficult to recall. As a child, I felt a wide range of emotions here: the passion and joy of play, butterflies of fear, exhilaration of winning, dejection of losing. Now, just breathing the heavy arena air brings back those sensations.

The rink itself is smaller than I remembered. Banners of past triumphs drape the building, lacrosse on the east side, hockey on the west. There are twice as many lacrosse banners. The green seats in either end are six rows deep. Within the bluelines are three rows of blue seats, two rows of reds behind the benches and penalty boxes at centre. The arena is crowned by a wooden barn-like Hipple roof, which gives Memorial much of its architectural flavour. It's a throwback to another era, which is why it was used as a stand-in for the Detroit Olympia in CBC's docudrama "Net Worth."

On the concrete floor the two combatants have begun their pre-game ritual. Six Nations is clad in aqua-coloured uniforms, the current preference of sports marketers. The Excelsiors wear traditional maroon and gold, which the club has sported since Canada's infancy. India rubber balls beat off the boards like drums signalling an impending battle. A few hundred early-

Opening ceremonies at Brampton Memorial Arena, January 14, 1950

arriving fans exchange waves across the building, but now is not the time to surrender a pre-ferred seat for a visit. Many of Brampton's "old guard" are present, as well as youngsters armed with sticks ready to field an errant ball. Once this was Canada's game. It still is Brampton's.

The Memorial Arena had been the dream of town fathers for twenty years but the Depression and World War II sidelined the project. Finally, twelve days after Newfoundland joined Confederation in 1949, Brampton-ians had another cause for celebration. The official sod-turning for the town's first artificial ice rink was preceded by a festive parade from Gage Park to the site, a parcel of land on the Fairgrounds deeded to the town by the Peel Agricultural Society. Nine months later, the gala opening of the Memorial Arena was staged with T.L. Kennedy, the premier of Ontario, as guest of honour.

The *Brampton Conservator* reported, "The premier reminded those in attendance that following the First World War, Peel Memorial Hospital was erected to the memory of those who had sacrificed their lives for King and Country, and expressed hope that the arena would be a living memorial and would also prove to be of great benefit to the town."

The new facility quickly became a political football. Within a week of its christening, controversy raged over whether it should open Sundays. Later, town council voted to allow "free skating on Sundays at times that would not conflict with Sunday school or church services." An amendment permitting hockey practices on the Sabbath was overturned.

There had been a similar tug of war between hockey and public skating at Brampton's first indoor rink years earlier. The George Street Arena, a turn-of-the-century structure that was recently demolished, was a natural-ice facility. Ice conditions and rink availability hinged on the weather. When conditions were good, public skaters and hockey players battled for priority. A compromise created what must have been the first multi-purpose rink in the country. The hockey ice surface was reduced, making room for a public skating track around the outside of the boards. It enabled both groups to use the rink simultaneously.

Despite the political wrangling, there was enormous pride in the new arena. There were those who wished to protect it with the zeal of a mother safeguarding new living-room furniture. In a 1950 editorial, the *Brampton Conservator* said, "It has already been suggested that watchmen be stationed throughout the arena to guard against the practice of some youngsters, and others, of climbing over seats and sitting on the backs of seats." Forty-six years later, a sign remains posted near the front entrance admonishing patrons, "Please do not stand on seats. Do not sit on back of seats. Thank you."

A former Excelsior star is the first face I recognize in the Memorial Arena seats. Bob Burke, a grade-school pal, became the highest-scoring player in the history of the junior and senior Excelsiors. Burke also played on Canada's world championship field lacrosse team in 1978, scoring two goals in the decisive game against the United States. He is a national sports hero few Canadians know. "When was the last time you saw a lacrosse game here?" he asks. Sheepishly, I admit it has been a while. "You're in for a treat," he promises.

From the opening face-off, the action rages. The standing-room-only crowd is in an uproar. Burke was right. This is a treat. I wonder, if they were playing this game at the CoreStates Center in Philadelphia or Chicago's United Center, how long it would be before lacrosse was drawing twenty thousand fans a game. The Excelsiors blitz Six Nations for three goals in the final seventy-three seconds. Brampton takes a 5–1 lead to the dressing room after one period. The Memorial Arena is buzzing.

During the first intermission I retreat to the lounge at the north end. The snack bar is located beneath a pair of crossed antique lacrosse sticks. To the left are pictures of storied Excelsiors teams dating back to the turn of the century. On the opposite wall are framed tributes to thirty-three members of the Brampton Sports Hall of Fame. Eighteen are former lacrosse stars, none more beloved than Mush Thompson.

I visited George "Mush" Thompson a few days later. He'd just returned from the funeral parlour where Pete Ella had been laid to rest. Ella was Thompson's teammate on the first Excelsiors team to win the Mann Cup, in 1930. With Ella's passing, Mush became the only living member of Brampton's first-ever national champions.

It come as no surprise that Mush outlived the others. Longevity was a trademark of his life pursuits. Thompson's lacrosse career spanned twenty years. He curled for fifty-two winters, resided in the same house a few blocks from Memorial Arena for fifty-nine years. The Gummed Papers plant was his workplace for forty-seven years. He served on town council for thirteen years. He still drove to another Brampton rink named in his honour. Mush was eighty-six.

"You're still driving?" I asked a little surprised. "For one more year," chimed his wife Marg. "And maybe more," chirped Mush.

"How long have you been married?" I asked. Mush looked across the room at Marg and said, "You tell him."

Marg hesitated. "We were married in, what was it, 1933?"

"I hope that's when I married you. If it's not, I want to find out who the hell I married back then," he kidded. They'd been firing back and forth like this as husband and wife for sixty-three years.

Mush Thompson is a lacrosse legend but he played a little hockey, too.

"In 1929, I was on a Brampton team that played against the Toronto Marlboros and Charlie Conacher," he said. "There was Charlie, Busher Jackson, Alex Levinsky, Jack McGill. I was the goaltender. Brampton needed a goaltender and I was it. They beat us 19–1 in Toronto."

"You must have had a rough night," I teased. "I'm surprised you'd admit the score."

"There's no use trying to deny it," replied Mush. "They won the Memorial Cup that year so you know how good they were. Our defence couldn't hold them."

Hockey couldn't hold Mush. Instead he embarked on a lacrosse career that led to the Canadian Lacrosse Hall of Fame. He was the youngest player on the Excelsiors' national championship teams of 1930 and '31.

Thompson grew up a block from the field where the Excelsiors played in the days when every Brampton boy dreamed of becoming an Excelsior. He captained the junior team to an Ontario championship in 1930, losing only once along the way. Later that summer his dream was realized when he got the call to join the seniors.

There are twelve men on a field lacrosse team. Mush was a fielder, a position that demanded running the length of the field as an attacker with defensive responsibilities as well. The team's souvenir program contained a scouting report of its youngest player: "He's an untiring worker in the field, a good stickhandler and delivers a snappy pass and a wicked shot."

Brampton wasn't the only lacrosse hotbed in those days. The deciding game of the 1930 Mann Cup was staged at Varsity Stadium in Toronto before more than twenty thousand fans. Mush Thompson and the Excelsiors beat the New Westminster Salmonbellies—who became the Excelsiors' arch-rivals for the next six decades—by a score of 4–1 for Brampton's first national title.

The Excelsiors repeated as Mann Cup winners in 1931. Not long after, the game was converted to box lacrosse, so there was less running and more body contact. It was lacrosse just the same for Mush and Brampton fans. "You had to go right after dinner to get a seat," Marg recalled. In a town of five thousand, crowds of two thousand would regularly jam Brampton's new outdoor stadium, the Rose Bowl.

Thompson won his third Mann Cup, his first in box lacrosse, in 1942. The combined team of players from Mimico and Brampton was assembled during the war years when neither centre had enough players to field a team of its own.

Mush retired in 1947 but his fondest lacrosse memories were still ahead. The following year, he founded the Brampton Minor Lacrosse Association and he ran it until 1956. The minor program raised a new generation of future Excelsiors, including his three sons.

By 1956, Jim, Gord and Wayne Thompson were ready to bolster the junior Excelsiors. The team's new coach was their father. The games moved to the Memorial Arena where the team still had a loyal following, but one fewer fan. Marg couldn't bear to watch. She fretted about her boys getting hurt and fighting. However, she was still able to monitor their progress without leaving home. "I would sit in the back yard and I'd know what the score was before they got home," she said. "I could hear the cheers from the arena. I could always tell the score."

Her boys gave Brampton fans plenty to cheer about. The first year together, father and sons won the Eastern Canadian title and were bound for the Minto Cup. That is, if they received Marg's permission. "They were building a back room for the house and hadn't put the windows in," Marg laughed. "I said, you're not leaving me without windows. So they hurried up, the four of them, to get the windows in before they left."

The Excelsiors didn't win the Minto Cup that year but it remains Mush Thompson's proudest moment. "I'm probably the only coach in any sport to take three sons to a national championship in the same year," he boasted.

Good things came in threes for Thompson. Although Jim left the team after 1956, Mush coached Wayne, Gord and the junior Excelsiors to three consecutive Minto Cup championships before retiring in 1959.

If the Patricks are hockey's first family, the Thompsons must surely be Canada's first family of lacrosse. Grandson Mark was a member of the 1980 Mann Cup Excelsiors, and Mush watched his five-year-old great-grandson play for Orangeville a week before my visit. Another family prospect is one-and-a-half-year-old Riley. "All he did was carry a lacrosse stick around the whole summer," Marg said, with what won't be the last scouting report on the youngest Thompson.

Barbara Jane was the only daughter in the Thompson household. "She was madder than heck they didn't have a girls' team," added Marg.

Before I departed there was one piece of unfinished business. He'd been called Mush for so long few people in town could recall the origins of his nickname. George explained it came from his childhood friend Les Ridley. "When we were playing in the winter in the snow drifts, I'd always go first," said Mush. "If you notice, I've got big feet. They were size twelves when I was twelve. I'd go first in the snow. He'd follow in my footprints yelling 'Mush.'"

Two days after my visit, Mush suffered a stroke and died a week later. He left giant footprints all across the Brampton sports scene.

Standing beneath Mush Thompson's picture in the arena lounge, during the first intermission, I gaze through the rink windows. The view is timeless. Little has changed since I frequented the Memorial Arena as a boy. It is still occupied by a legion of regulars who have been coming here since the arena first opened. They migrate to the same spot night after night, summer and winter, as if holding reserved tickets or an unspoken claim to a specific seat, like a church pew on a Sunday morning. Families and friends of the home team sit on the east side, visitors on the west. It's always been like that. Former

Excelsiors line the standing-room sections along the walls. It is one of a handful of facilities in Canada housing two sports the community is equally passionate about.

My eyes move from the action to a small press box that hangs over centre floor (ice). I recognize another familiar face. Ken Giles is in his customary chair chronicling another night at the Memorial Arena. "Ask Scoop Giles if his birth certificate reads Brampton Memorial Arena," prompt a few of the rink regulars.

Ken Giles wasn't born here, but he has lived in the Memorial Arena press box for more than forty years. He smiles at the wisecrack, admitting, "It's not far from the truth." There was more concern than smiles the day Giles entered the world in 1935. He was born with a form of cerebral palsy, and the right side of his brain was damaged, leaving him physically challenged.

Although his body couldn't fulfil his desire to play, it didn't stop him from trying, for he has the heart of a champion. He was a minor lacrosse goalkeeper, a position that allowed him to play with only his right hand on the stick. His father had a right-handed baseball glove custom-made. Giles developed a style of catching and throwing with the same hand a half century before Jim Abbott mastered the same technique in the majors. By the age of eighteen, Giles was also one of the youngest officials in the Ontario Lacrosse Association.

As a Grade 8 student at McHugh Public School, he watched construction of the arena take shape across the street. The giant Clydesdales, doing the work of today's heavy equipment, were stomping around in his back yard, building his new home. As the arena was raised, so were his career possibilities. A year later, he was a fledgling high school sports reporter. He hasn't stopped covering the local scene since.

Just about everybody who knows Giles calls him "Scoop," a nickname that has stuck since his high school days as a cub reporter. "Even my mother calls me Scoop," he laughs. "The only time she ever calls me Ken is when she's upset with me."

In his downtown apartment are the mementoes of a lifetime's work: a congratulatory letter from Prime Minister Brian Mulroney on his induction into the Brampton Sports Hall of Fame, a 125th anniversary commemorative Canada Medal awarded for community service in 1992 and a lifetime members' plaque from the Excelsiors lacrosse club. There is an old portrait of Ted Reeve, a member of the 1930 Mann Cup team, who later turned to sportswriting. Giles's pride and joy is the old Underwood portable type-writer that was standard equipment until computers finally forced it to the sidelines. Jimmy Burrell, his predecessor in the twenties, passed on his Underwood like a torch to Giles, to continue recording the glory of the local sports scene. It's just as well computers came along when they did. Scoop had virtually pounded the old portable into submission with the headline sports stories of four decades.

As we chat about "the good old days," his memories flash back to 1957. The junior Excelsiors were playing for the national title against New Westminster. Bob Pulford, now the general manager of the Chicago Blackhawks, was one of Brampton's star players, but he was unable to complete the series because he'd been summoned to his first NHL training camp with the Toronto Maple Leafs. "He was literally crying in the dressing room because he didn't want to go," Giles says. "The guys said, get out of here, you'll make more money playing hockey than you ever will playing lacrosse. Pulford wanted to stay until the end of the series but the Leafs said, no, you have to report to camp. In those days if you didn't report to Connie Smythe, you were drummed right out of the league.

"Jack Bionda was the greatest lacrosse player of his time," Giles continues. "He played with the '52 Minto Cup Excelsiors and stayed in Brampton to play hockey. At that time he could barely skate. Butch Keeling, a former New York Ranger, was coaching the Brampton Regents. He kept Jack and by the end of the year Bionda was good enough to go to the OHL. He never developed as a great skater but he did play with the Leafs and Boston."

Giles also had the "scoop" on Wayne Gretzky long before most reporters. Recognizing Gretzky's prodigious talent was easy, but few, if any, other reporters were afforded a half-hour exclusive with the eleven-year-old future "Great One." "I did the interview for Rogers Cable," Giles recalls. "He was quite adamant that he was going to be the next Gordie Howe. He wasn't a smart alec about it either. That's where his sights were set. That's where he was headed."

Thirty years after he watched Memorial Arena constructed across the street from his Grade 8 classroom, the city of Brampton erected another rink. They named it Ken Giles Arena. He occasionally receives early-morning calls about ice time availability, but the wrong numbers are never a bother. He keeps the rink number taped to the fridge door for quick reference.

On this nostalgic night, I realize something is missing from the Memorial Arena. Gone are the banners, of every colour imaginable, which hung in the rink to honour the communities that competed annually in the Brampton Novice Lions hockey tournament.

The novice tournament was just about the biggest thing that happened in town. It was my Easter vacation destination. For five dollars, I had a week-long holiday at the Memorial Arena, handicapping teams and their top players, tending a penalty box gate, running the clock or, if I was really fortunate, operating the public address system. Those banners were like an early geography lesson, representing teams from Port Huron, Michigan, to Pointe Claire, Quebec, Winnipeg to Windsor. My world was smaller then. Those were exotic locales.

It was billed as the largest novice hockey tournament in the world. Each spring, sixty teams with more than one thousand players participated. For most youngsters it was a once-in-a-lifetime hockey experience. For more than a hundred élite players such as Darryl Sittler, Bob Gainey, Denis Savard and Dale Hawerchuk, it was the beginning of the road to the NHL. Coaches

Young hot shot Ricky MacLeish, the top scorer at the 1960 Novice Lions tournament

Colin Campbell of the New York Rangers and Joel Quenneville of the St. Louis Blues are two other prominent tournament graduates.

Ricky MacLeish of Cannington, Ontario, was the first superstar of the Lions tournament. The future Philadelphia Flyer was the leading scorer in the inaugural event in 1960, and his brother Tom followed six years later as the tournament's sharpest shooter. Brampton fans came to expect a hot sniper in the Cannington line-up. In 1964, the tournament's highest point-getter was Dave Nicholson, a cousin of the MacLeishes. Four years later, Dave's brother Don was the dominant player, scoring eight goals in a single game.

Mark and Marty Howe attended in 1964 as members of the Detroit Rooster Tails, a team that also featured Bob Goodenow, now the executive director of the NHL Players' Association. Also in the spring of 1964, Gordie Howe and the Red Wings were tangling with Toronto in the Stanley Cup final. Between Stanley Cup games, the proud father cheered his youngsters at Memorial.

Howe's visit to the tournament was an unexpected surprise for his youngsters, who saw their father infrequently during hockey season. Mark corresponded with his dad by mail. He referred to their important hockey itinerary in a letter reprinted in Jim Vipond's book, *Gordie Howe, Number 9*.

Dear Daddy,

We had a practice at seven o'clock in the morning. We had practice from seven to eight thirty. Mrs. Vopni drove us to the skating club. Thursday we are going to Bramton [sic] with Mr. Chapman, Mike, Jack, Peter, Marty, and I. If you win the Stanley Cup we will win in Bramton... I hope you have a Happy Birthday,

Sincerely,
Mark Howe

Although Mark fulfilled the promise, leading the Detroit novices to a division title at the tournament, the Red Wings were beaten by the Maple Leafs in seven hard-fought games.

For each novice prodigy who advanced to the NHL, there were thousands of youngsters whose hockey highlight was simply competing in a tournament of the Novice Lions' magnitude. One player from 1967 recalls the adrenaline rush of charging up the incline runway to the ice surface—it was like taking off in an aircraft. The stands were packed with fans screaming for the home side, the Brampton B team that clashed with the team from Watford, Ontario. It was only an exhibition game but for him it could have been the Stanley Cup final. A stay-at-home defenceman with limited offensive skills, the youngster registered a rare assist and chalked up a penalty to ensure his name would blare over the public address system. It may have been a lopsided 8–0 victory, but it was one of the sweetest hockey experiences of my career.

"Mr. Hockey" Gordie Howe and two young Lions at the 1964 Novice Lions tournament

The Brampton tournament was one of the first on the hockey calendar that brought communities closer together. In its initial year, a bond developed between the host town and the team that had travelled the farthest to compete, the Winnipeg Colts. At the tournament's conclusion, a front-page story in the *Brampton Conservator* gave the Colts special attention: "The Winnipeg Colts, who were adopted by several Brampton families, earned the praises of the homes in which they were billeted. In fact when the Colts left Brampton's CNR station Sunday night, for many of the families it was like losing one of their own children."

The following week the *Conservator* published an open letter of gratitude from Winnipeg coach Stan Bradley, who concluded with a vow. "We intend to return next year to renew the friendship." Bradley was true to his word, and over the years, his Winnipeg contingent included future NHLers Chuck Lefley, Murray Bannerman, Kevin McCarthy, Brian Engblom and Paul Baxter. Following Bradley's death in 1974, the Lions tournament MVP award was named in his honour.

John Tavares has been called the Wayne Gretzky of lacrosse. He's back at the Memorial Arena floor living up to the billing. Tavares was Brampton's lethal scorer when the Excelsiors won the Mann Cup in 1992. Now he's one of many former Excelsiors playing for Six Nations. In a sport where most players are paid $25 a game to cover gas and meal expenses, Tavares collects a Gretzky-like stipend. It's estimated that the Mississauga native earns $15,000 for the twenty-four-game season. It's a salary Brampton could not afford to match.

Tavares is proof of the old adage that you get what you pay for. After three games of the Eastern Canadian final, he leads all scorers with eight goals and nine assists. He's working on a five-point night in Game 4. Six Nations has stormed back to tie the Excelsiors in the second period. Tavares's offensive prowess is reminiscent of the hockey whiz kid who was the marquee attraction at Memorial Arena twenty-four years earlier.

Greg Stefan has never forgotten the car ride to Brampton for that Novice Lions tournament. He sat alongside his best friend and teammate in the back seat. His friend's father, who was driving, turned around every few miles asking his son if he'd remembered his skates, his gloves, his mouth guard. Suddenly there was a grimace on the friend's face. He turned to Greg in a panic and said, "Uh-oh." They had reached Ancaster when Walter Gretzky swung the car around and drove son Wayne back to Brantford to retrieve the forgotten equipment.

As youngsters, Stefan and Gretzky were inseparable. They lived ten minutes apart in Brantford, playing hockey together in the winter, baseball in the summer. If they weren't at Greg's back-yard rink, they were at Wayne's. "Walter would have us doing drills," Stefan said. "Wayne would go around pylons. I was in net working on my angles. We were always learning but it was nonstop fun."

There were many advantages for a ten-year-old goaltender who called Wayne Gretzky his teammate. Stefan learned to play in front of big crowds at an early age. He didn't need to wear a face mask since Gretzky didn't share the puck with his opponents. Stefan wore a helmet but no face protection until peewee, when he finally submitted to the safety of a moulded mask. And with Gretzky on his side, Stefan was never overworked.

Wayne Gretzky and Greg Stefan enjoy a pre-game meal at the 1972 Novice Lions tournament

It was a different story for opposing goaltenders. In that 1972 Brampton Lions tournament, Gretzky scored nineteen goals in his first three games. He filled the scoresheet with nine goals and two assists in a 12–2 rout of Sault, Michigan. Local newspaper dispatches foreshadowed accounts written during his halcyon days with the Edmonton Oilers: "He completely dominated the game and left the Sault players bewildered by his prowess. He scored goals in every way from backhands, to slapshots, to fakes on the goalie, to tip-ins by the edge of the crease, and he made every one look easy… Gretzky is good enough to make the difference between a close game and a rout."

Near the end of the story was evidence that Stefan wasn't just a specta-tor in the Brantford goal: "At the other end Greg Stefan turned in one of the best netminding performances of the tournament."

Stefan didn't receive much publicity on a team overshadowed by its flashy star. It was all right with him. He saw the ugly side of the game that accom-panied the adulation. "I remember all the controversy with other parents about Wayne's ice time. The accusations that he was a puck hog," said Stefan, defending his boyhood chum. "He didn't hog the puck on purpose. If he passed it, we wouldn't score. He was so competitive. He'd hang on to the puck because he wanted to win so badly. I remember a lot of bitching around the dressing room from parents. That's why Wayne eventually had to leave Brantford."

If Gretzky was affected by griping parents, he never showed it to Stefan. The only hockey parent Wayne heeded was his father. "What made Wayne the great player he is was Walter," Stefan said. "He was loving, but hard on him at the same time. Even in a 12–2 game Walter would point out a missed play or a mistake. He'd give him shit about a certain play that wasn't made. Wayne took it all in. He wanted to be the best."

Gretzky was bound for NHL stardom. Two Brantford novice teammates followed him: Greg Stefan played nine years with Detroit, and forward Len Hachborn amassed more than 100 games with Philadelphia and Los Angeles.

Stefan is now an assistant coach with the Detroit Junior Whalers. His seven-year-old son Joseph just made his first AA travelling team. "He's a pretty good little hockey player," Stefan said proudly. "He's already asking me about tournaments and staying in motels. Funny, I was just reminiscing about the old minor hockey days with my dad the other day."

In 1972, I stashed away the program from the tournament as evidence that I had witnessed a future hockey legend. Fifteen years later, I dusted it off to show Wayne Gretzky in Edmonton as I prepared a feature on Minor Hockey Week in Canada. He recognized the program immediately. "After the Quebec peewee tournament, it was the best one I ever played in," he recalled.

It's beyond debate that he was the best player ever to play in Brampton. Gretzky was the only player to participate in six different Lions tournaments, beginning as a five-year-old who was not overmatched against boys twice his age. In his final year of novice eligibility, Gretzky was front-page news in Brampton each time his Brantford Nadrofsky Steelers played. Already, he was being linked to the NHL's dominant player of the day: "Some hockey authorities have said that Wayne is further advanced now than Bobby Orr at that age ... Two types of people go to the Arena to watch the amazing young player, those who want to see him score and those who want to see him fail," said the *Brampton Daily Times*.

Another headline story in the *Daily Times* that week involved Walter Gretzky and the first bidding war for his son's services. "A Peterborough group has offered Walter Gretzky, father of the Brantford novice scoring star, a good job if he would consent to move his family to Peterborough. The eleven-year-old centre is wanted by the Peterborough group so that he would be eligible for the midget draft in four years."

Although Wayne had scored 650 goals in a five-year novice career, Walter never appeared to look beyond the next game. "He may not develop any more," the senior Gretzky told a local reporter. "But I am very satisfied with the way things have turned out for him."

Despite Gretzky's gaudy stats and the fan frenzy he sparked, he was not Brampton's biggest hockey story of 1972. That occurred in September, when a home-town hero played in hockey's greatest showdown ever.

First impressions are lasting. Ron Ellis liked the Memorial Arena from his initial visit as a fifteen-year-old with the Weston Dukes. It didn't hurt, of course, that he fired a hat trick for the Toronto Marlies' farm club, which also featured former Leaf Brit Selby.

A decade later, Ellis was in the midst of a distinguished sixteen-year NHL career with the Toronto Maple Leafs, commuting from his new home in suburban Brampton.

Ellis was the son of an air force serviceman. That was apparent in the way he played—he was hard-nosed and honest, swooping up and down his wing, rarely straying off course. Ellis was a throwback to the days of the "Original Six," the era of hockey he most cherishes. "Playing against people like Béliveau and Howe was special," he said. "We all knew each other, had a book on each other. When we played Montreal, I knew we'd be against Backstrom, Larose and Ferguson. We took pride in playing both ways. Today if you win 9–8, it's okay. Back then, if we won 9–8, Punch Imlach would have skated us for hours. I wouldn't trade the three years I played before expansion for anything. The money they're making today would be nice, but those days I wouldn't trade."

Another untouchable is his Team Canada experience. Ellis was one of thirty-five players invited to participate in the 1972 Summit Series against the Soviets. It was intended to be a showcase of Canada's best hockey talent. Many were surprised that Ellis was included. "It's amazing how things come around. The selection committee was down to its last ten players," Ellis said. "John Ferguson was an assistant coach and he said, 'I think Ellis should be there.' We used to match lines with Montreal and I would play against John every night." Playing against Ferguson was a thankless task but Ellis has appreciated it ever since.

Ellis has vivid recollections of the first day of training camp in Montreal. There were so many great players on the ice together with so few full-time positions at stake. To ensure their participation, every player was guaranteed to play at least one game. Initially, Ellis thought that might be the extent of his involvement. His outlook changed when early line combinations were posted. "Paul Henderson and I played together in Toronto," Ellis said. "The first day we were on a line with Bobby Clarke. Paul said he played a lot like Normie Ullman. We had played with Normie for six years. Right there we felt we just might do something. Once we met Bobby we decided to work our butts off. We just clicked."

The line of Clarke, Ellis and Henderson gelled quickly. Henderson and Clarke both scored in the opening game of the series in Montreal. Unfortunately, the rest of Team Canada hadn't caught up to the Clarke trio. On that night Team Canada couldn't catch the Soviets. "It was devastating," Ellis recalled. "I was really disappointed for another reason, too. I hurt my neck badly that night and had to leave the ice. I was lying in the trainer's room in the third period thinking the series was over for me."

More than a few Canadian fans thought the series was over, too. It was only the beginning of the most incredible journey in our game's history. Ellis has replayed the series a million times for himself and inquisitive Canadian fans. It always has the same glorious conclusion with his linemate bagging the decisive goals in the last three games. "Paul was a great NHLer but he was known as a streak scorer. When he got hot, he got hot," Ellis said. "He certainly got hot at the right time for us. I think Paul scored seven goals in the series along with Phil Esposito. He scored some wonderful goals but he'll be remembered for the last one, which wasn't his best. On the actual winning goal our line wasn't on the ice. We had just come off and I remember Harry Sinden saying to us, 'Get ready, you're going back out.' To this day I don't know why, even Paul doesn't know why, but he stood up on the bench and called Peter Mahovlich off. He had never done it before, never did it again. Just as surprising is that Peter came off. When you watch highlights of the goal, you will see Paul streaking into the picture from the bench." Twenty-five years later, a replay of the Henderson goal still gives Canadian hockey fans—and Ellis—chills.

Team Canada returned home to a heroes' welcome. In Brampton, Ellis was feted by the city, which unveiled a new street name, Team Canada Drive. The following summer, he was grand marshal for the annual Flower Festival Parade. "It was all nice," Ellis recalled, although no honour or gift could be greater than the joy he brought back from Moscow. Currently, he's affiliated with the Hockey Hall of Fame working on a special commemoration of the twenty-fifth anniversary of Team Canada's '72 triumph.

Following his playing days, Ron opened a sporting goods store in

Brampton. He sponsored teams, conducted coaching clinics and became part of the community. The store was in business for five years, the same duration as an average pro hockey career. "We gave it our best shot," he said. "I had good people and I learned a lot. Unfortunately, our timing wasn't great and there was a downturn in the economy."

There was, however, an upswing in Brampton minor hockey. Ron's son R.J. followed in his father's footsteps to the Memorial Arena, where Ron offered guidance as a coach. The bottom line on the ice was much better than at the store: an Ontario bantam championship with R.J. scoring goals and Jamie Storr preventing them. Later, father and son celebrated again as Provincial Junior A League champions with the Brampton Capitals. "I told my son quite often that this is where I played at that level," Ellis said. "My father played in the same arena, so three generations have played at the Memorial Arena."

R.J. Ellis's grandfather was in the air force, his father an NHL star. He's combining the best of his family's worlds by studying to become a pilot at Royal Military College in Kingston and starring on the school hockey team. "He could have played pro at some level," assessed a proud father. "He's a good skater, big and strong, and when he's finished at R.M.C. he'll be stationed someplace where he can continue to play."

The temperature has been rising steadily on the floor throughout the hotly contested showdown between the Excelsiors and Chiefs. The sweltering heat in the arena makes it feel like a giant steam bath. The fans return after a brief second-intermission respite in the cool August night.

The Excelsiors carry an 11–8 lead into the third period, trying to stave off elimination. Nobody is celebrating yet. The game has resembled a fisherman's duel with a trophy catch. The Chiefs let out some line in the first period as the Excelsiors struck for a 5–1 lead. Six Nations, however, won't let Brampton wriggle off the hook. Each time the Excelsiors appear to be breaking free, the Chiefs reel them back with a couple of quick goals. Although they are still trailing by three, the Chiefs look poised to land the big one in the third.

Before the action resumes, I bump into former NHL referee Ron Wicks, a Brampton resident since the sixties. When I ask if he'd like to be officiating the game, Wicks cringes. "I call it controlled violence," he says.

Wicks speaks from experience. He was once coaxed into a few lacrosse assignments and found the transition from hockey difficult. "I'd call penalties for what I thought was rough play and the players would start to chuckle, even the victims," he says.

Wicks has become a fixture at Memorial, one of his favourite arenas. "Just the aroma," he says, not referring to a particular scent but the atmosphere of the old barn. "I was rehabbing from a back injury fifteen years ago. I'd come here and skate by myself in the morning. It's a tremendous old place."

Our attention returns to the game as some of the leather lungs nearby begin to bellow. Their target is veteran referee Don Brockie. For an instant, Six Nations has too many men on the floor. It goes undetected by the officials. "You can only count the money they give you for travelling expenses, Brockie," spouts a fan. "You must use it for dog food." Moments later, Brockie calls a penalty against Brampton. "You're making it close, Brockie, making it close," another heckles.

Like Wicks and other referees, Don Brockie is a lightning rod for the fans. He has developed the thick skin and sense of humour that are standard equipment for the occupation.

One of the loudest Memorial Arena regulars is Robin Sanderson, who doesn't miss many games from his wheelchair position in the stands. Recently, Brockie circled the floor during warm-up. Spotting Sanderson, Brockie scaled the boards to approach his loudest critic. With one arm around Sanderson, the referee leaned over to say, "Robin, if you see me making any mistakes out there tonight, be sure to let me know."

Bruce Hood, another former NHL referee and commissioner of the Ontario senior lacrosse loop, is in attendance. "Ask Hood why anybody in his right mind would take that job," Wicks says. Moments later, I confront Hood with Wicks's query. "You've been talking to Wicksy," he says with a smile. "Put your hand in a bucket of water and pull it out. That's the kind of impact I have as commissioner."

Bruce Hood officiated in the NHL for twenty-one years and was the first to referee more than one thousand games. He's not a stranger to Memorial Arena either. Before his NHL days, Hood played junior hockey for Brampton and refereed minor hockey games in the winter, lacrosse contests in the summer. "I never saw the hockey atmosphere as intense as I did in lacrosse," Hood says. "Brampton was kind of like the Philadelphia Flyers [of lacrosse]. They could play a nasty game. This building was known for that."

Bryan Lewis, the NHL's director of officials, also got his foot in the NHL door via the Memorial Arena. "When I was finished playing junior hockey here, I started officiating," Lewis recalls. "I was assigned to be a linesman in

Brampton one night. There was a blizzard and the referee didn't make it. I refereed. That was the turning point for me becoming a referee instead of a linesman. At the time, you were paid seven dollars to be a linesman, twenty as a referee. So it was exciting for two reasons. I was finally getting my chance to be a referee. And I was going to make twenty dollars instead of seven."

Brampton's most beloved official had his jersey retired in the Memorial Arena lounge. It isn't a striped referee's shirt but Excelsiors sweater number 8, worn by the late John McCauley.

"I was a Brampton rink rat. I grew up at the arena and cut my teeth on a lacrosse ball," McCauley told Don Cherry on his "Grapevine" television program in the mid-eighties.

"You were the best referee in the league," Cherry repeated throughout the interview, and he would not get an argument from anyone in Brampton about McCauley's status as an official. However, Grapes might be surprised to know that McCauley had rare talents as an athlete as well.

"He was a modern-day Lionel Conacher," declares Ken Giles, who covered McCauley's exploits in six different sports. McCauley excelled in everything from basketball to football, track to baseball, where his catching prowess earned him the nickname "Yogi." The two sports in which he was most gifted were hockey and lacrosse—indeed, he seemed to live at Memorial Arena year round.

From an early age, John dragged his equipment bag over a mile from his home on Sunset Boulevard to the rink, an athletic test in itself since his bag was stuffed with heavy goaltending gear. His father, Wes, believed the walks to the rink built character. He may have been right, because character and toughness were two qualities John always brought to any competition.

In 1962, as a junior lacrosse star, McCauley was embroiled in a highly charged game against the Alderwood Terriers. Early in the contest, John drove aggressively to the net, took his feared overhand bounce shot and scored. There was no celebration after the goal. In the act of shooting, McCauley had received a vicious slash across the face. The trainer collected seven bloody teeth off the arena floor and assisted his woozy star to the bench. John was urged to go directly to hospital for further examination. Heated words were exchanged at the bench. Moments later, he was back on the floor, his mouth crammed with cotton batting. He finished the night with seven goals. It's no wonder he had little difficulty distinguishing a dive from a serious injury during his refereeing career.

It didn't hurt that McCauley was also a physically gifted athlete. "At the age of twelve, he had an adult's physique," says Ken Giles. "You had to see his birth certificate to believe his age." McCauley never looked out of place as a peewee lacrosse player practising with the juniors or as a twelve-year-old netminder working out with the juvenile team.

Carl McCauley is the chief archivist of the McCauley clan. He has preserved his nephew's glorious past in ten scrapbooks bursting with pride and newspaper clippings. In the first scrapbook, an account of a minor lacrosse game catches my eye. "John McCauley paced the peewees with three goals… Ron Ellis caged three for Mimico." A few pages later is John's invitation on Detroit Red Wings letterhead to attend Hamilton Junior Red Wings training camp. He was fourteen.

At the same age, McCauley offered his services to Mush Thompson's junior Excelsiors. Although still bantam age, John contributed to Brampton's national junior championship team.

Three years later, legendary Oshawa coach Jim Bishop added McCauley to the Green Gaels' roster for the Canadian title. McCauley was such a hated adversary that Bishop's players opposed the move. "The other players didn't want me to pick him up," said Bishop at the time. "I told them we couldn't win the Minto Cup without him." McCauley paced Oshawa to its first of seven consecutive national titles.

Throughout his teenage years, participating in six sports wasn't enough to satisfy his appetite so he officiated minor hockey games every weekend as well. McCauley stood out as an official, too—he wore goal skates and an Udvari nameplate attached to his striped shirt. He was determined to make it, as a player or an official, like one of his role models, NHL referee Frank Udvari.

However, his playing ambitions were jeopardized by a knee injury suffered playing high school football, and the injury was exacerbated by the constant pounding up and down the cement floors during lacrosse season. Although McCauley backstopped Brampton to an Ontario juvenile hockey championship, scouts began to shy away from a goaltending prospect with a gimpy knee.

"At nineteen I made a decision that I liked refereeing better than playing goal," John told Don Cherry.

The same scouts and bird dogs who monitored his goaltending career recognized his potential as an NHL official. His baptism of fire as a pro hockey referee came in a whirlwind rookie year officiating Western, Central and

American league games. He sent Uncle Carl newspaper reports of games he'd worked from Portland, Oregon, to Portland, Maine. Usually the only mention of McCauley in the reports was criticism from one or both teams, but by 1973 John McCauley had become the most popular referee in the NHL. So popular, wrote Ken McKenzie in the *Hockey News*, that he was the only official with his own fan club. "It's located in Boston and they hang banners in his praise."

When the NHL seasons ended, John headed back to Memorial Arena to spend his summers coaching lacrosse. In 1980 alone, McCauley coached the Brampton Excelsiors to the Mann Cup title, his son Wes's peewee team to the nationals and a tyke squad with his younger son, Blaine, to the Ontario final.

Two years earlier, he had been the defensive coach for the Canadian field lacrosse team, which won the world championship in Manchester, England, when Canada defeated the United States 17–16. The Americans had never been beaten before and haven't been since, but in 1978 McCauley's aggressive defensive style put Canada over the top.

Surprisingly, McCauley had little empathy for officials when he coached. In fact, it was an extremely adversarial relationship. In a 1971 game, McCauley was slapped with one of his frequent ejections. "What kind of a call was that?" he ranted to a reporter after the game. "If I had made a call like that, it would have cost me a thousand dollars. That's the trouble with lacrosse. They've never been able to get any half decent refereeing."

He was even more outraged, and outrageous, during a playoff game coinciding with the start of the NHL officials' training camp. His colleagues travelled to the Memorial Arena to watch the Excelsiors in action. Instead, they witnessed McCauley making a mockery of the game and its officials. "The antics he went through on the bench were such that if he had been the referee, he would have given the coach a bench minor every time he made a move," recalls Bryan Lewis. The night climaxed with a patented McCauley ejection, his clipboard spiked into the floor with papers flying everywhere. His colleagues watched in bewilderment.

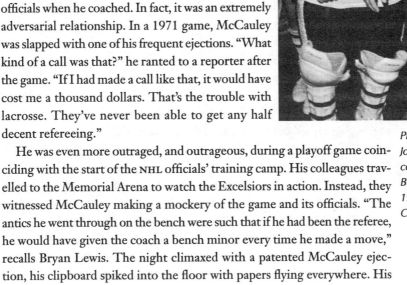

Proud coach John McCauley celebrates Brampton's 1980 Mann Cup victory

McCauley's philosophy was to read the rule book and then discard it, believing that 90 per cent of the job was judgment. John excelled in his field, because his judgment had been shaped by years of playing and coaching experience, most of it at the Memorial Arena. "We were exposed to a lot of situations in lacrosse," he told Cherry. "I knew how you felt and had a lot of empathy for you."

In fact, McCauley could have been successful behind an NHL bench, based on his coaching success and passion. "I think John could have coached in the NHL," confirms Ken Giles. "He knew the game, knew the players. He could get them to dig down that extra inch or two to make the difference. You'd see Excelsior teams go to the dressing room that you thought were beaten. John would take them in and they would come out completely revitalized."

Irene McCauley spent most of her married life separated from her husband by the demands of his NHL work. Every winter, they shared a long-distance relationship, but John called after every game to touch base and relate the adventures of life on the road. "This was a man who loved his job," Irene said. "Look at the abuse he took. But he always had a joke or a smile. He called one night after a woman had thrown beer all over him during a game. He looked up at her and said, 'Geez, couldn't you have warned me so I could have had a drink?' He used to call after games, which I really miss now. He never ever was down about a game."

Irene's support was never more critical than after an incident in 1979. The NHL's best were thrashed 6–0 by the Soviets in the deciding game of the Challenge Cup in New York. John, a standby official that night, and the game crew retreated to a tavern for a post-mortem. Assessing the night's result, John suggested that the defeat might be a valuable lesson for North American hockey. An inebriated fan, eavesdropping on the conversation, took exception and unloaded a sucker punch that landed heavily over John's left eye. "It's just as well I didn't referee that game. He would have shot me," McCauley said.

However, the injury he suffered that night was no laughing matter. McCauley underwent six operations to correct blurred vision caused by the blow. He didn't referee again for two years, but spent many days circling the Memorial Arena ice to keep his legs ready and praying his eyesight would return to normal. The NHL gave John off-ice duties during the recovery, and as a result of the skills he demonstrated as a supervisor and administrator, he was appointed director of officials in 1985.

His most poignant call home came during the 1988 Stanley Cup play-offs. NHL officials refused to work a playoff game between Boston and New Jersey, so amateur officials were recruited, with McCauley overseeing their work from the penalty box. It had the potential for disaster, but with McCauley's guiding hand the game proceeded without a serious hitch. Irene watched on television as her husband maintained his composure. Afterwards his call home told a different story. "Irene, I was never so nervous in my life," John told her. "I said, God, if you ever want to strike me down with a heart attack, do it now."

Only a year later, John McCauley was struck down at the age of forty-three. He died while undergoing surgery to remove his gall bladder. He is survived by Irene and three talented children. Eldest son Wes, a teammate of Eric Lindros at St. Michael's, is playing hockey in Italy. So influential was McCauley's hockey guidance to Lindros that Eric wished to wear McCauley's number 8 when he joined the OHL's Oshawa Generals. Since that number had been already taken, Lindros opted for the number that has become his signature, 88. Younger son Blaine is in his second year at Lake Superior State and is rated as a good NHL defensive prospect. Daughter Bridget works for the Toronto Separate School board as an educational assistant with special ed children. "They have so much of their father in them," Irene said fondly, and adds, in spite of her loss, "We're very, very lucky."

While Brendan Shanahan is skating with Team Canada, preparing for the World Cup of Hockey and the glare of the international spotlight, his brother Brian is toiling in relative anonymity as a lacrosse defenceman for Six Nations. Brian wards off Excelsior forwards as well as barbs fired his way by the Memorial Arena faithful. It's difficult for Brian to block out the fans because so many voices are recognizable. In 1992, they were cheering for him when he wore the Excelsiors' colours.

Fans like Robin Sanderson, who has muscular dystrophy, love to needle the former Brampton hero. "Robin's a die-hard. He's at every home game in his wheelchair," Brian says. "Every time I talk to him, I almost feel like crying. Those are the things I miss about Brampton. There's Butch Coates, the guy who sells 50–50 tickets. I remember playing junior lacrosse fifteen years ago and Butch was there. I still get along with those guys but there was some bad blood when I left."

Four years earlier, Brian, Robin and Butch shared a moment at the Memorial Arena they will never forget. The Mann Cup final returned to

Brampton in 1992. The New Westminster Salmonbellies, the Montreal Canadiens of lacrosse, invaded Brampton to clash with the Excelsiors, the Toronto Maple Leafs of the summer game. The championship series was a five-game war. Four games, including the clinching battle, were decided by a single goal.

"We had been trailing the fifth game by eight goals. The floor was so slippery they stopped the game to put rosin on the floor," Shanahan recalls. "It was so humid. If the arena holds 2,000, there were 2,800 people there. It was a sweatbox. It was like a dust bowl until the rosin settled. Then it was like playing sweaty lacrosse in the mud because the rosin was everywhere. The referees let everything go and it became knock-'em-down lacrosse. We won it in double overtime and the place just went crazy."

It's difficult to describe the euphoria of a championship, but Shanahan has a simple way of relating the experience to Canadian hockey fans. "I don't think I'd be any prouder if I'd won the Stanley Cup," he says. "I always said if I won the Mann Cup, I'd retire. But it gets in your blood and you want to keep going back. It's the greatest feeling!"

In the Mann Cup aftermath, the Excelsiors poured champagne into the cup before the celebration spilled into the city streets. "They had a big flat-bed truck waiting for us," Brian recalls. "Nobody showered. Guys just threw off their stuff and went running out to the truck. It was after midnight because the game had gone into double overtime. We drove through town drinking beer and screaming. Everywhere we went people honked their horns back at us. It was so spontaneous, it was great!"

It was the proudest night of Brian Shanahan's career, but he's even prouder of his kid brother. Although Brendan Shanahan ranks in the upper echelon of NHL stars, he might be a superior lacrosse player. "Brendan was a totally dominant player," Brian declares. "I have no doubt that if he had kept playing lacrosse, his name would rank with the best. I think he'd like to show how good he is. Believe it or not, [in 1991] he seriously considered playing for the Excelsiors when he was in New Jersey. In hindsight, I am glad he didn't. If he'd got hurt, I would have felt so guilty."

Lacrosse is a unique game that pays its players from petty cash but tugs at the heart of multimillion-dollar athletes like Brendan Shanahan. In lieu of financial rewards, it has provided his brother with priceless memories. Brian was the first of four Shanahan brothers to claim lacrosse's most coveted prize. "My older brother Davey played in the '81 Mann Cup final for Brampton, the year they lost," Brian says. "When we won the Mann Cup, he was happier than I was. He came running down to the dressing room, kissed me and said, 'You guys don't know what you've just done!' He was so thrilled. I was happy for him because he was so happy for me. He wanted to win one so badly."

There's an engraved plaque in the Memorial Arena lounge dedicated to the memory of Paul Derksen. It reads "In remembrance of a friend and team member who passed away while playing hockey at Memorial Arena." Twenty-nine names are inscribed below.

I asked a few people in the vicinity about the plaque, but no one was familiar with its story. In fact, few had even noticed it. A week later, I returned to Memorial Arena where rink attendants Vic Wright and Paul Deryck were "winterizing" the place for the upcoming hockey season.

Both have vivid recollections of the day Paul Derksen died. "They're the guys from Johnson Matthey who play here every Wednesday afternoon at five o'clock," said Wright. "I'm glad I wasn't here that day. I got to be pretty good friends with them."

Paul Deryck was on duty that day. He answered the panic-stricken pleas from the ice to call 911. Although Deryck responded immediately, the call was too late. To my surprise, Deryck said the Johnson Matthey crew had already booked for another season of Wednesday evening shinny.

Andy McCullough is the human resources manager at the Johnson Matthey plant in Brampton; the company refines precious metals. The events of November 23, 1994, are etched permanently in his mind. "It was a very traumatic evening," he recalled. "It affected me as much as, if not more than, when my mother passed away."

Paul Derksen was a respected fellow worker of McCullough's who had been employed with Johnson Matthey for nearly half his young life. The father of three girls under the age of five, Derksen, thirty-five years old, had just been named captain of the volunteer fire department in Hillsburgh. One of his responsibilities at Johnson Matthey was health and safety officer, training the staff in first aid and CPR.

The Wednesday afternoon games were a collective idea. A passion for hockey was a common thread that ran through the company. The weekly games were a fun diversion and morale booster for the staff. Derksen, McCullough's assistant, was in charge of ice rental and organizing the games. Every week they would play for an hour and laugh about it for the next seven days.

Andy's son Simon was one of the goaltenders. His presence stoked Derksen's competitive fires. "Paul used to try to score against Simon just to say he beat the boss's son," McCullough laughed. "Simon would always say if Paul scored on him he was having a bad night."

That evening at Memorial Arena was the worst night imaginable for everyone on the ice. Their hour had almost elapsed when Paul got a rare breakaway. He moved in alone on Simon, spotted an opening and fired the puck into the net. Usually when Paul scored, a friendly banter with the beaten goaltender would ensue. Not this time. "That day he just turned, skated away and went straight to the bench. He collapsed at the bench," said McCullough.

There were hysterical cries for help. Four colleagues applied the CPR training that Paul had organized. It was all in vain. Although he was not pronounced dead until he reached the hospital, Derksen's last breaths had been taken at the Memorial Arena.

The following Wednesday the group returned to the arena. "We held a service at centre ice," McCullough said. "We brought a video camera and each player skated up to the camera and said a few words about Paul. His family and two brothers were there."

The loss was devastating for the Derksen family. It also left a horrible scar on the men he worked and played alongside. Andy McCullough summoned a psychologist to deal with the trauma those on the ice had experienced. The healing process included the continuation of the weekly games and the institution of a memorial award in Derksen's name. It is given on an annual basis to the Johnson Matthey plant in North America with the best health and safety record. A facility in Seattle, Washington, was the proud recipient of the first Paul Derksen Memorial Award.

This winter the Johnson Matthey gang will return to the ice at Memorial Arena at five o'clock every Wednesday. Each player wears a memorial patch with Derksen's initials on his jersey. "We felt we owed it to him," said Andy of the decision to continue the weekly shinny, "since it was Paul who organized the ice time in the first place."

It's nail-biting time at the Memorial Arena. With sixty-eight seconds remaining in regulation time, Chris Driscoll sends the home-town fans into a frenzy with a power-play goal giving Brampton a 14–12 lead.

Again Six Nations storms back. With the Chiefs' netminder lifted for an extra attacker, Troy Cordingly, another former Excelsior, scores for the visitors with thirty-two seconds on the clock. Twice Six Nations has wiped out four-goal deficits. They appear poised to do it again. John Tavares, who already has twenty-two points in the series, is back on the floor. The crowd is hushed with anticipation—it's difficult to make noise when you're holding your breath. The Chiefs attack vigorously again but this time the Excelsiors' defence stiffens. Mercifully, the final horn sounds and the partisan crowd erupts. The home-town boys have salvaged one game in the Eastern Canadian final. "No sweep! The Excelsiors won't be swept," chants a relieved local fan.

The Brampton Novice Lions hockey tournament was terminated after its twenty-fifth anniversary in 1984, a victim of staggered spring vacation periods and myriad rival tournaments. Its place on the local hockey calendar was assumed by an even bigger event, the Brampton Canadettes' Dominion Ladies hockey tournament.

Billed as "The World's Largest," it began on a much smaller scale in 1967. "The Canadettes" has become one of the truest barometers of the astounding boom in Canadian women's hockey. Celebrating its thirtieth anniversary, the Easter weekend extravaganza features 340 teams of all ages and levels competing at thirteen different Brampton-area rinks.

On the eve of the Canadettes, three of the tournament's most prominent graduates, Cassie Campbell, Angela James and Leslie Reddon, were preparing with Team Canada for the Women's World Championships to be staged the following week in Kitchener. "It was definitely the defining feature of Easter weekend," recalled Reddon, who deposed Manon Rhéaume for a goaltending spot on the Canadian roster. "There was a mother who would dress up as the Easter Bunny and come around the rink that morning with Easter eggs. Even the last two years when I haven't played in it, I'd think about the Canadettes tournament around Easter."

Angela James has been described as the Wayne Gretzky and Bobby Orr of women's hockey at various stages of her career. James has participated in eighteen Brampton events in her twenty-five years at the rink. Like the novice boys' tournament, the Canadettes provided an early measuring stick for players. "It was where everybody could showcase their teams. It was actually bigger than provincials," she said. "Especially in the intermediate division. You could see who was up and coming."

Cassie Campbell was a home-grown Canadette starting at nine years of age. Campbell followed her older brother Jeff through minor hockey at

Memorial Arena. "I always watched my brother play there," she recalled. "Finally I got the opportunity to play there in bantam. I was so excited—the old dressing rooms and the 'ghosts' of Brampton hockey players that lived there."

Campbell resisted the lure of ringette, an alternative women's game that, in her childhood, attracted more female participants. "I never played ringette and never wanted to," she said. "I saw it as a feminization of hockey. I think it was an attempt to keep women out of such a masculine game."

The coaching guidance of her mother, Eunice, early-morning practices and an unforgettable winning shoot-out goal against rival Mississauga were all Memorial Arena memories that served as Cassie's stepping stones to the national team. Campbell continues to grow as a player, in step with the ascendancy of women's hockey. "I think the last two years it has totally changed—as soon as the kids found out it was going to be in the Olympics," Campbell said. "It's going to be huge in the next five years. If we don't have our own pro league [by then], we're going to be very close."

Seven months after the final lacrosse game of the season, I returned to the Memorial Arena to witness the Canadettes tournament first hand. The crowd was limited to only a handful of family, friends and organizers. It was an unfortunate contrast to the bedlam of the novice tournament.

A bantam game featuring Kitchener and Barrie was into the furious climactic minutes when I arrived. Barrie pulled its goaltender in desperation to overcome a two-goal deficit. A wild goal-mouth scramble ended with a Kitchener defender closing her hand on the puck. Barrie scored on the ensuing penalty shot to draw within a goal.

Before the face-off at centre ice, Pat Benatar's "Hit Me with Your Best Shot" blared from the P.A. system. With time slipping away, Barrie stormed the Kitchener net again. Remarkably, their last-ditch "shot" produced the equalizer. There was pandemonium on the ice and at the Barrie bench. It was the kind of finish we would have talked about for days at the novice tournament.

The national team of Kazakhstan was slated to play a senior squad from Simcoe County in the evening finale. Reports that Kazakhstan was coached by Alexander Maltsev of the '72 Soviet national team turned out to be untrue. As the visitors arrived, it was evident that something had been lost in the translation. This Maltsev was young enough to be the Soviet star's son.

Outside the dressing rooms, the Kazakhstan coach paced anxiously, recreating the cloak-and-dagger atmosphere that once pervaded Soviet hockey.

He forbade interviews or pictures until after the game. News that Simcoe County had only dark jerseys and his team must switch to white uniforms was greeted with dubious eyes.

There was nervous laughter from the Simcoe County Queens' room. The team comprised hockey enthusiasts ranging in age from nineteen to forty. This was only their twelfth game of the season. Unsuspecting, they had been thrust into the role of defending Canada's hockey honour. "I'm feeling good now," said Barb Burgess sarcastically, apprehensive of the talent level in the opponents' dressing room.

As the two teams hit the ice, Kazakhstan was bedecked in flashy Nike-sponsored uniforms. Each player sported brand-new Bauer skates. Simcoe County had hand-me-down jerseys furnished by a Barrie bar. There was no uniformity among their hockey pants and socks. But every player had a red maple leaf sewn on her sleeve.

The first period was dominated by Kazakhstan players who wove a splendid old Red Army tapestry on the ice. "For the first period I was sitting back thinking, let's watch," said Burgess after the game. "Then the coach said, no, let's play."

Simcoe survived the early Kazakhstan onslaught and the game remained scoreless. By the second period, the Canadians were out-muscling and out-hustling the visitors. Soon the "inevitable" Kazakhstan victory did not seem as certain.

A minute into the third period, Fiona McPhee broke loose down the right wing. The Simcoe County forward exploited a tiny opening inside the far post and fired the game's first goal. It would have put a lump in Don Cherry's throat. For the rest of the third period, the Simcoe County women summoned all the grit and heart they could muster to thwart Kazakhstan's attack. In the final minute, the visitors' frustration was painfully evident. A Simcoe player was writhing on the ice, the victim of a clandestine spear.

The final horn put an exclamation mark on an unexpected, glorious Simcoe County victory. Another night at Memorial Arena, where an ordinary game can magically become extraordinary.

In the victorious afterglow, the Queens turned their attention to Team Canada's hopes at the upcoming World Women's Championships. In three days, Memorial Arena would be the site of a world tournament game between Sweden and Finland. I asked Barb Burgess if she identified with today's female stars or NHL players as role models. "I guess I relate more to Wayne Gretzky, because I'm the same age as Gretzky," she said. "My daughter Krista is more interested in the women. In fact, I took her to the rink one day and she said, 'I didn't know boys played hockey.' I'd only taken her to girls' games."

The younger Alexander Maltsev was still reeling from the defeat, uncomfortably aware of the distance his country lagged behind in women's hockey. He fulfilled his commitment with an interview conducted through interpreter Svetlana Lapschina. "I liked very much the team we played against," he said graciously. "They were brave and straightforward, so different from our team."

Maltsev's sincere compliments were not limited to the victors. He had savoured the night's experience in a classic Canadian community rink. "We noticed right away the age of this building and the traditions that are behind it," he said in admiration. "It feels really good to be in an old building that has been nurtured, the beauty of its wooden construction, to be in something which is like a hockey cradle. Unfortunately, there's nothing like this at home."

Two days after their last stand at Memorial, the Brampton Excelsiors were defeated by Six Nations in the fifth and deciding game of the Eastern Canadian championship at Ohsweken.

I returned to the arena later that week to see if preparations had begun for the upcoming hockey season. Instead, the building was being groomed for the 143rd annual Brampton Fall Fair. It would be the last fall fair on these grounds, as organizers have decided to move the event back to its rural roots in nearby Caledon. Once a farming community itself, Brampton has expanded into a city of two hundred and seventy thousand.

Memorial is in its own battle against the clock. In the mid-seventies, many arenas like it across the country were demolished. The wooden Hipple truss roofs were collapsing, and a generation of these buildings was endangered. The Ontario government dictated new building standards to ensure the safety of arena patrons. On January 26, 1978, Memorial Arena was condemned because of suspected weakness in the roof structure.

The fate of Memorial was in the hands of city fathers. Other communities elected to tear their old arenas down. A few replaced the wooden barn roofs with modern bubble-type structures. Brampton chose to reinforce the existing roof.

Memorial was back in business the following autumn, but extra safety precautions had been instituted. If there was more than two inches of snow on the roof, rink attendants were obligated to go up top and shovel it clear.

In 1991, the provincial safety code became even more stringent. That prompted a second closing of the arena for repairs. "There's eighteen tons of steel up there now," points out rink manager Karl Benstead. The bill for the second renovation was $190,000, more than the original price tag for the building in 1950. Provincial inspectors also noted that Memorial was shifting, which suggested that further problems were just around the corner. Under the new code, old arenas in Ontario are to be inspected every five years. Memorial is due for another check-up soon.

Beyond the structural problems there are many questions about the long-term usefulness of Brampton's first artificial-ice facility. "It's small when you've gone from a town of five thousand and now you have over a quarter of a million people and it's still the main rink servicing the city," says Ken Giles. Recently, local politicians approved the construction of a $25-million state-of-the-art rink that will be home to a newly awarded Ontario Major Junior Hockey League franchise.

Where there was only the Memorial Arena in Brampton in 1950, there are twelve city rinks operating now. A new complex that has recently opened a few miles south of Memorial has four "pads," the new catchword in the rink business, a licensed restaurant and amenities never imagined fifty years ago. Two of the rinks are reserved exclusively for adult hockey year round.

I'm looking forward to donning the blades again, but I'll wait until the first week in October. That's when the ice goes back in at Memorial.

2 Cahill Stadium
Summerside, Prince Edward Island

Scott Russell

And the end of all our exploring
Will be to arrive where we started
And know the place for the first time.

—T.S. Eliot, *Four Quartets*

Cahill Stadium, the centrepiece of the local exhibition grounds, was completed in 1952

THE RED CLAY PARKING LOT is shared by the hockey rink and the track—harness horses have raced here for a hundred years. Off in the corner an old lobster boat, long since out of service, is suspended on huge saw-horses. On her stern is scrawled "Silver Clipper." I look back and see the line of cars forming and the families unloading from mini-vans and pick-up trucks. Others are already bustling through the doors of an ordinary brown building on a typically grey, Maritime, autumn afternoon. Slipping through the gate at

Cahill Stadium, I look up to see a huge sign that proclaims, "Can't Hide that Summerside Pride."

It is Thanksgiving Sunday and the rink's innards are as frosty as the giant icebox my mom kept the Butterball in. The East Hants Penguins from just outside Halifax and the Summerside Western

40

Capitals are warming up the ice. This is Maritime Junior A hockey on Prince Edward Island and the main attraction is this holiday matinée. Standing by the glass in a thick cable-knit sweater is the youthful coach of the home team. His nickname is "Turkey."

"Ever since I was six they called me that," recalls Gerard Gallant. "I think my older brother Blaine started it. I never minded but lately they've shortened it to 'Turk' and that's just fine with me."

Gallant played eleven seasons in the National Hockey League, mostly with the Detroit Red Wings. In all, he registered 480 points in 615 games and, along with Paul MacLean and Steve Yzerman, formed the most prolific forward line in Red Wing history. In 1988–89, the threesome scored 319 points, a record that eclipsed the mark set by the famed "Production Line" of Gordie Howe, Sid Abel and Ted Lindsay.

No son of hockey from Summerside can claim Gallant's respectable numbers. Not even Errol Thompson, who played for the Leafs alongside Hall of Famers Lanny McDonald and Darryl Sittler. Gerard Gallant is this town's icon—he made a name for the little island in the big cities of professional hockey. In returning to the place where he started, Gallant is rediscovering what he has known all along. The approval of the fans at Cahill Stadium is, to him, the most important thing of all.

Turk is a gentle and soft-spoken man who greets everyone with a smile, looking into their eyes with genuine interest as he shakes hands. His statistics are not quite as gentlemanly, as they include 1,674 penalty minutes accumulated during the course of a career—one less than his idol Gordie Howe. The Turk's one-time coach and now "Hockey Night in Canada" analyst, Harry Neale, tilted his head back and snickered at the thought of the irony. "Yes siree," said Neale. "Gerard was an awfully nice boy, but once he got on the ice he became one tough mother."

The Maritime Junior League is tough, and the way teams from tiny Prince Edward Island have survived is to be that much tougher than the rest. Cahill Stadium is designed to accommodate a certain way of playing the game. The ice surface is small and the corners sharp, meaning the rugged players do not ease into their clutches but instead take their opponents crashing to the rink's edges.

The seats are less comfortable than church pews. Wooden two-by-fours form the bleachers, painted grey and suspended over flooring that is almost turquoise. The stands rise sharply away from the ice in seven steps, so the fans seem to be right on top of the action. Capacity is not much more than two thousand, but when something is at stake, the faithful flock in far greater numbers. Gallant remembers his first year coaching the Capitals and facing the hated Charlottetown Abbies in the seventh game of a first-round play-off series. "As I walked out of the room, all I could see were heads. I couldn't hear myself think. I don't believe I've ever been so excited," he says.

Half-way through the warm-up, Gallant points in the direction of the glassed-in area perched above the home team's goalie. It is called the Nostalgia Room and is dedicated to a local sportswriter, John "The Realm" McNeil, who has covered hockey and everything else for the Summerside *Journal Pioneer* for fifty years. Inside the room are the relics of a people in love with the game and the heady days of this rink.

The centrepiece of the room is the likeness of the late Charles "Moose" Cahill, clad in a Philadelphia Arrows uniform. Cahill is the man after whom Civic Stadium was renamed in 1977. He spent most of his professional career in the American Hockey League but, as far as anyone around here can recall, he was the first Islander to play in the NHL. Cahill appeared in thirty-two games between 1925 and 1927, recording

Charles "Moose" Cahill of the Philadelphia Arrows. In 1925, with Boston, he became the first Prince Edward Islander to play in the NHL

one assist and four penalty minutes for the Boston Bruins. Still, he was the first from the Island to make it, and he returned home as a local hero at the end of his career "away."

Then there is the pugnacious visage of a fellow named Clarence "Windy" Steele. Gazing at me from the sepia tones that all ancient photographs become, he fills the uniform of the AHL Hershey Bears. It is said in these parts that Windy got his nickname because he was the fastest-skating forward anyone on the Island had ever seen in the 1930s. This right-winger did not graduate to the NHL; he was called to war instead. His son John, a thick and jolly man under a farm machinery cap, announces in Cahill Stadium's lobby that his dad was born on New Year's Day. "Yep, the story goes that one year

The Rink

on his birthday when he was playing with Providence, Dad flattened Eddie Shore more than once. Not many fellas can say that," claims Steele the younger. The modern addition to the recreational complex in Summerside was constructed in 1977 and is known as the Steele Arena. Windy would have beamed at the thought of it.

In the Nostalgia Room, countless articles, encased in ordinary-looking frames, document the triumphs of extraordinary teams from Summerside that played here. To an outsider, the teams and the names are unfamiliar, and one marvels at the grandiose telling of the stories in the local press. There is front-page coverage of the Freetown Royals and their captain Clayton Mill accepting a trophy emblematic of Prince County senior hockey supremacy in 1956. Prince County is the geographic designation for the western portion of the Island. Back then, Prince Edward Island had a population of 100,000, and it is safe to assume that Prince County's was about a third of that. The caption under Clayton Mill's beaming face reads, "... before a capacity crowd of 3,300 at Civic Stadium." The crowds, like the hockey heroes, seem out of proportion to the place.

The walls of the room are loaded with photographs. Here are the Maritime Intermediate Summerside Aces, complete with their championship banners from 1957–58 and 1958–59, and there are the Crystals, as every team in Summerside was called for so long, out of deference to the old Crystal Rink, the town's original ice facility. Civic Stadium replaced that arena in 1952 and was renamed Cahill Stadium a quarter of a century later.

In a glass case, off by itself at the back of the room, is a Florida Panthers jersey signed by each member of the team that went to the Stanley Cup Championship in the spring of 1996 (they lost valiantly to the Colorado Avalanche). The Panthers held part of their training camp the following season at Cahill Stadium, and the locals claimed them as their own.

There is a portrait of Errol Thompson, complete with a 1970s Afro haircut, in his Toronto Maple Leafs uniform. Now a travelling representative for a major brewery, Thompson also played for Detroit and Pittsburgh. His blue and white number 12 jersey, which he wore with the Leafs, is proudly displayed beside the picture.

Then there is the shrine: an enormous action photo of the assistant captain of the Detroit Red Wings alone on the ice at the Joe Louis Arena, no doubt looking for confrontation of some sort, his teeth clenched beneath the helmet that shrouds his beefy face. Gerard Gallant, the Turk, is the greatest memory Cahill Stadium has of itself.

Gerard Gallant of the Detroit Red Wings. The Summerside native, with Paul MacLean and Steve Yzerman, formed the most prolific scoring line in Red Wing history

"We're in our barn, play hard and take it to 'em," Gallant chants as he strides to the chalk board on the back of the dressing-room door. "Dump it in and go get it. It's a little ice surface for us, so play our game."

Cahill Stadium's dressing room for the home team is a far cry from the palatial setting Gerard Gallant knew at Joe Louis Arena in Detroit. There, he walked on plush, red carpet and gazed at the names of his predecessors on oak walls in the common area of the Red Wing digs. Here, Gallant's Western Capitals sit clustered in a narrow tunnel on red wooden benches underneath the buzz of harsh fluorescent lights. The place reeks of sweaty equipment as adolescents wait in a grey, spartan clubhouse where an old oil stove separates them from the coaches' quarters.

"Couple of you big pussies better get some hits today!" urges the Turk as he marches by the stalls. Above each is a picture of one of his former Red Wing teammates, which he hopes will inspire the boys. "Set the tone," his voice rises. "C'mon boys, let's go!"

As Gallant takes the team through the door and their skates dig defiantly into the black rubber pads on the way to the ice, a small blond-haired man in his early forties scurries around picking up loose equipment. With a chuckle, Blaine Gallant, Gerard's older brother and the Capitals' trainer, leans into my ear and whispers, "He's a legend. A frigging legend!" With a wink of mischief, the older Gallant follows out the last players as they prepare to face the mainlanders. On my way to the frigid bleachers, the dressing-room door swings shut behind me. I turn and read the freshly painted lettering meticuloulsy rendered by hand. It reads simply "The Doug MacLean Room."

Earlier that autumn, the Florida Panthers had danced to the early-morning rhythm of pucks and sticks at the game-day skate as Doug MacLean stood centre stage on top of a big, blue maple leaf in hockey's grand old house known only as the Gardens. Facing the players' bench, MacLean, working his gum, stared into the highest reaches of the grey seats scarcely believing he had come all this way.

At forty years of age, MacLean was about to embark on his second year of coaching one of the NHL's youngest franchises. He had already taken his team, a collection of youngsters and gritty grinders, to within an ace of the Stanley Cup. The club's base in South Florida is just about as far as you can get from his home in Summerside, Prince Edward Island, but MacLean maintains the connection religiously.

"I remember my first day on skates as clear as a bell," MacLean recalled, leaning on a net outside the visitors' locker room. "My mother took me to the stadium and reported back to my dad after it was over. She said, 'Jim, we don't have to worry about his involvement in hockey. He's absolutely no damn good at all!'" MacLean proved his mother wrong, as he went on to star throughout the minor system in Summerside and the rest of Prince Edward Island. Although he was never going to turn into an NHLer, he did go on to play for the University of Prince Edward Island, a team coincidentally nicknamed the Panthers. He also suited up for the Montreal Junior Canadiens and attended the St. Louis Blues training camp.

Even now, as one of the most colourful and energetic coaches at the highest level of pro hockey, MacLean looks back on his days at Cahill Stadium with not only fondness, but a genuine understanding of what the rink has meant to him. "No one could have greater memories of a place than I have of that rink," he said, with conviction. "Almost every good childhood memory I have comes from that rink." MacLean easily reached into the past to resurrect images of Friday nights spent watching his idols, the Intermediate Summerside Aces. His eyes lit up as the names tumbled out—names like Vance Harris and "Cokey" Grady, the stars of local teams who were worshipped by loyal fans like MacLean. He told of how he would lay out his equipment after the game on his bedroom floor, and of early-morning walks down Notre Dame Street to the stadium with his lifelong buddy Jim Clarke, all the while dreaming he was one of the Aces.

Doug MacLean grew up in a community where the hockey rink was the centre of activity for just about everyone in town. Another friend, Paul M. Schurman, broadcasts hockey games out of Cahill Stadium for the local radio station, CJRW. "Games never started at nine o'clock on Friday nights like they were supposed to," says Schurman. "That's because the stores were open until nine downtown. They'd delay the puck drop until everyone had a chance to get there. It said nine in the paper, but it ended up being a face-off at nine-fifteen—you could count on it."

MacLean's life in hockey has ultimately been connected to coaching. His first big assignment was behind the bench of the Summerside Western Capitals of the Island Junior Hockey League in the early 1980s. It was a loop that played its regular season games among provincial rivals, with the winner advancing to the playoffs to face mainland teams that formed the Maritime Junior A League. "I always said if you can coach in the Maritime Junior League, you can coach anywhere," MacLean said. "The rivalry between us and Charlottetown was terrible. They used to throw garbage cans on the ice."

His coaching days in his home town were satisfying. Of particular delight were the characters he encountered at Cahill Stadium. A favourite was "Speedy" Gallant (no relation to Gerard), the goal judge who had been a fixture at Cahill for a quarter of a century. With glee, MacLean acted out Gallant's mannerisms to a captive audience of his Panthers in the bowels of Maple Leaf Gardens. Speedy Gallant worked as a lineman for the local hydro company and had lost an arm in a work-related accident, but it didn't prevent

Doug MacLean, a Cahill Stadium graduate, took the Florida Panthers to the Stanley Cup final in 1996

him from putting on a show as the goal judge. He would gyrate with the play throughout the action and at the end of a period had built up more sweat than most of the players. Before every game his Capitals played, Doug MacLean would get the word from Speedy. "Dougie, if she's even close to the line I'm calling her in," Gallant would guarantee the coach. "But Charlottetown will have to use a cannon for it to count!" MacLean recalls that Gallant was usually true to his word.

In a golf shirt, the ice surface just a few feet away, MacLean basked in the relative warmth of Maple Leaf Gardens as he chatted easily of his home rink. "I always think now when I leave a rink that it should be cold." He suddenly shivered and rubbed his bare arms. "The stadium was so cold, but everybody smoked back then, which you were actually thankful for because the cigarette smoke sort of

The Rink

warmed you up." His eyes danced as he remembered a scene starring two regulars in the corner bleachers. "They'd bring a radio with them to every game and I supposed they were listening to play-by-play on CJRW," he said. "One day I asked to see the radio and started turning the dials which, of course, came off. I found out the radio was really a flask and these two old codgers had been drinking vodka just to keep warm."

MacLean had been a rink rat at the stadium. He tussled with his pals for the chance to sweep the ice with a corn broom and then drag the barrel around, flooding the frozen surface. "The big day was when we got the attachment for the back of the tractor to clean the ice. Not a Zamboni, mind you, but the cleaner they hitched to the back of the tractor." He grinned. To a small boy who grew up in the shadow of the stadium, it was, at times, larger than life. "It was big. When I was a kid, it was by far the biggest thing I'd ever seen," said MacLean, looking out towards the expanse of the great Gardens.

MacLean went on to coach at the University of New Brunswick and gradually found his way to the National Hockey League as an assistant with the St. Louis Blues under head coach Jacques Martin. In 1988, his long-time association with Bryan Murray began when MacLean accepted the assistant coaching job with Murray's Washington Capitals. He followed Murray to Detroit and on to Florida, where he got his chance to handle the Panthers at the beginning of the 1995–96 season.

Almost immediately after his appointment, the questions about Doug MacLean and his credentials started. Sceptics wondered who this guy from Prince Edward Island was, and whether he was qualified to coach in the big leagues. Although he still has critics on the Island, Doug MacLean has a devoted following that stems from growing up at Cahill Stadium. They jam the Summerside Firehall on Panther game nights to watch Doug on the satellite dish. In fact, MacLean found time to talk with old pals from the Island on a daily basis during the playoff run in the spring.

In the late summer, following Florida's appearance in the Stanley Cup final, MacLean convinced Bryan Murray to stage part of the Panthers training camp at Cahill Stadium. "I brought them to Summerside because it looks like the rink each of them grew up in," he said. "It's a real hockey rink and that's something they can all understand." The experience was a huge success. For seven days, Cahill's bleachers were packed for the twice-daily practices. Schools cancelled classes so youngsters could board buses to the rink and cheer for a team they had little knowledge of. What they were certain of was the coach. They knew he was an Islander who had not forgotten his home.

MacLean revelled in the attention because he was the talk of the town. Bryan Murray, a native of Shawville, Quebec, marvelled at the response of the people. "It was important for the guys to be close together in that situation," says Murray. "Seeing that rink every day, they were reminded of how much hockey means to a community."

As he led his team to the bus and back to the hotel to prepare for that night's game against the Leafs, Doug MacLean looked the part of the proud and confident NHL coach. With his suit on and his chest slightly puffed out, he made a detour to take another look at the empty Gardens. It is a rink he visited via television on Saturday nights as a kid from P.E.I. MacLean is amazed he has made it here, but as he turned to leave hockey's nearly extinct temple, his last words were about Summerside and Cahill Stadium. "When we were there in the summer, I'd look up in the stands and my heroes from the Aces were there. The guys I grew up idolizing were all still in that rink."

With the first period nearly done, Turk Gallant's Capitals are having a tough time against the mainland Penguins. Down by a couple of goals, the boys from Summerside have fallen victim to their own lack of discipline—or is it over-zealous refereeing? The Maritime League has recently adopted a zero-tolerance policy with regard to stick work and rough play. As well, obstruction fouls are called frequently, and Gallant's team has taken far too many.

Before the game, Turk, who was never noted for his diplomatic demeanour on the ice, complained about what he's seen unfolding. "It really bothers me the way the game is played now. These people are told to call everything they see, and it's not the way the game is meant to be played. The new rules are ruining the game." Gallant's fundamental approach to hockey was shaped growing up in this tiny arena where, by necessity, the game is very fast and hard-hitting. "I believe you should be able to play the game and play it rugged," he says.

Up in the third row of the bleachers just over Gallant's right shoulder, the fans are more than a little restless. Huddled close together, there are maybe a thousand of them in the chilly arena. Typically, the men are wearing hockey jackets and baseball caps and they sit silently, considering the action. The women have had the foresight to bring blankets to buffer themselves against the frozen boards that form the seats beneath them. There are at least as many women in the crowd as men and the females are by far the more vocal. When the Caps score, Gallant spits lustily over the boards and onto the ice. Beside me, Ruth Sudsbury leaps up, stamps her brown cowboy boots and chants, "Go you Caps, go!"

She has been coming to this place for forty years. Ruth Sudsbury is from a little place

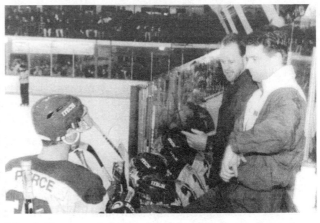

Gerard Gallant coaches the Western Capitals before a capacity crowd at Cahill Stadium

called Spring Brook up on the North Shore, and she just loves hockey. It helps that she is the wife of the Capitals' general manager, Clair Sudsbury, and the mother of a goalie and two defencemen who play in the minor system in Summerside. She tells the little girl sitting beside her to head down to the canteen during the intermission and get some french fries. "It's Thanksgiving—I'll bet they have good gravy today!"

She is a teacher, and over the years she and her husband have boarded dozens of hockey players from off the Island at their modest home in Summerside. At present it's a seventeen-year-old by the name of David Boeme, a native of rural Saskatchewan. "He's getting a little discouraged. Not getting many shifts and he's a long piece from home. I don't blame him. He's just a great kid," Ruth says, with more than a little concern. Her maternal instincts are strong, but Ruth fancies herself a learned observer of the game and likes to see the boys play it hard. She has left the rink only once before a game was over and that was when the Capitals and a team from Moncton cleared the benches in a brawl. Still, she knows and loves Island-style hockey. "I don't mind a fight. It's the best part of the game as long as it's not dirty," Ruth declares.

This hockey mother, who has spent much of her fifty years in Cahill Stadium, has great memories of the building. There have been dances and lobster suppers as well as other events surrounding the late-summer exhibition and carnival. It is, however, during hockey season that the place comes alive for her. There was the Centennial Cup final, emblematic of Junior A hockey supremacy in Canada, that Summerside hosted in 1989. Her Capitals made it all the way to the final game but lost to the mainlanders in front of a jammed Cahill Stadium frenzy.

Ruth brought her school kids here to see Doug MacLean's Florida Panthers. "Some of the kids had never heard tell of a Panther, didn't know what it was," she says. Like most in the rink, Ruth and her students were more attracted to the Island-born coach, a former neighbour, than they were to the million-dollar star players. "Everybody on the Island knows Doug MacLean. Whether they do or not—they do! He did more for this little province than anybody." She smiles broadly.

The little girl has returned with the french fries. Smothered in gravy, the contents of the cardboard box glisten and send steam into the rink's frigid air. With the second period about to begin, Ruth advises me she has got to turn her attention to the game. In watching four decades' worth of games at Cahill Stadium, Ruth Sudsbury will have seen what is about to happen many times before. The characters change but the attraction for her remains constant. It is what draws her to the rink. "When I'm here, I think of my kids. My attention is focused on them, the one in the stands with me or their ice time, if they are playing. To me this means family."

The puck is dropped and Ruth is on her feet hollering. Out on Summerside's frozen pond is her kid. He is number 20 for the Caps. David Boeme of Wolseley, Saskatchewan, is finally taking his first shift of the game. Ruth Sudsbury is absolutely delighted.

Visually, Cahill Stadium is not an impressive building. From the outside it might as well be an oversized storage shed for farm machinery, indistinguishable from a thousand other buildings in Prince Edward Island's agricultural landscape. It is not a feat of architectural grandeur, nor will it ever be declared an historic site. It will never attract a future generation of Islanders to stare in amazement at it. Cahill is a two-tone aluminum-sided building with a more modern arena attached to it, in the middle of the fairgrounds beside the Summerside Raceway. It was built in 1952, and it was done quickly. Nowadays it seems we wait forever for the monstrous new showcases of hockey to be constructed. The Molson Centre in Montreal, with part of historic Windsor Station as its exterior, took years to complete. From the time the shovels went in the ground until the moment the Canadiens' fabled torch arrived at centre ice at the new shrine seemed an eternity. Nearly five decades ago, in Summerside, it took a hundred men, most of them local fishermen, twenty-four working days to erect the frame and roof of what was called Civic Stadium. The thing that took time was getting the ice in. Then again, the ice was the most important element of the new building. On the Island, as it is everywhere else in Canada, the playing surface and not the surrounding building is the object of attention.

Prince Edward Island may be Canada's smallest province but the place they call the Cradle of Confederation nurtures hockey with great zeal. The provincial Department of Recreation lists thirty-seven hockey rinks or artificial ice surfaces on the Island. That's twenty-seven covered arenas and ten permanent outdoor rinks with ice plants in a province with a population of 135,000, about the same as the city of Oshawa, Ontario. Islanders proudly tell you that per capita, they have more hockey rinks here than anywhere in the world. Their boastful declarations, while not supported by any published statistic, seem plausible given the great desire each community has to have a rink as its centrepiece.

The range of facilities is as startling as the Island is gentle. In the bustling capital city of Charlottetown, the ultra-modern Civic Centre is the largest arena in the province and was home to the American Hockey League Prince Edward Island Senators for a couple of seasons. Built for the 1991 Canada Winter Games, the Civic Centre replaced the old Charlottetown Forum but attracted less than capacity houses for the Senators because ticket prices were too high. Many of the comfortable cushioned seats are left empty for today's junior and collegiate matches because, as many of the locals whisper, the ice is too far away from the stands and the atmosphere is just not the same.

At the other end of the spectrum is the dark and damp old shed at the University of Prince Edward Island. Jim Lawlor has been on the arena crew at the university for twenty years. On a visit to the arena, I opened the back door to the faceless hut made of concrete blocks and could just make him out through the dripping fog of the rink's interior. In overalls, Lawlor, armed with a paintbrush, was stooped over a half-finished blueline, stroking on the rink's markings by hand. The progress was obviously painfully slow. "If our floor was level, we could put tape down like everyone else," grunted Lawlor. "But our floor's not even close to being flat so we do this every frigging year."

I looked up and surveyed the ice surface to try to get the picture. The cap to the rink's boards looked like waves on the ocean, rising and falling in generous proportion as it surrounds the hockey-playing surface. At centre ice, the top of the boards is fully a foot higher than it is in the back corner or on the other side of the redline, which Jim had finished painting. The boards themselves are the originals from 1958, when the rink was first constructed. They are like no others I have ever seen—a thousand individual two-by-fours nailed vertically onto cross beams and bearing almost forty years of whitewash. There is absolutely no give to the rink's borders. Imagining bodychecks, I suddenly understood why players who graduated from this place were as tough or tougher than the nails that hold the boards in place.

Looking down at the ice, I noticed there were mushroom-like bumps in a few locations. Jim pointed up to the roof and said the water comes from the condensation because the metal ceiling is far too low. I shook my head and tried to visualize a cross-ice pass hitting one of the bumps and ending up in the bleachers or worse. Beyond the back boards was a brown and green Zamboni with a snow track over the top of its collection bin. It was brand spanking new in 1972. It had long since given up scraping the boils from the rink's complexion and now concentrated on surface makeovers.

Jim was still shuffling backwards, slapping on the blue paint while I made my way around the arena, and in spite of its obvious flaws, it looked pretty good. At the other end of the rink from where the Zamboni was parked there was a tiny scoreboard that said "Home" and "Guests." Not Visitors, but Guests. Very polite and somehow fitting for the Island, I thought. This three-hundred-seat shanty was once the proud home of the UPEI varsity hockey team. They now play downtown at the gleaming Civic Centre. As I bid farewell to Jim and pushed the back gate ajar, I was startled to recall that Summerside's Doug MacLean had played here. Somehow he had made it all the way to the NHL from this humble arena.

In the tiny fishing village of Rustico, the Stella Maris church stands as a beacon on the highest ground. Its twin steeples can be seen for miles around. Stella Maris means Star of the Sea, and the people who live here earn modest seasonal livings on the lobster boats. The off-season belongs to the children of the community and more importantly to the hockey players. In the church's back yard is the immaculate North Star Arena, and Freddy Doiron jumped at the chance to show it off.

Behind his aviator-style spectacles, the arena manager's eyes were alight as he waved towards the pride of the people. "It takes a week for us to get the ice in," he said, as he motioned to the two men dragging a huge hose across the arena floor. "They tell me at Madison Square Garden they can do it in a couple of hours." With that, he took me through the standard grey bleachers with bright yellow foot rails. The little wooden structure is like something I made with Popsicle sticks once, only this one is life-size. Perfectly proportioned and beautifully simple, it is a tiny house for hockey, with three rows of seats. The locals put the structure up in 1970, Fred told me, and the materials cost $51,000. He said he still has the bill somewhere in his office.

Freddy slipped through the back door and into the shed behind the far net, beaming as he flicked the switch and lit the room that houses the Sabroe ice-making machine. It was built in Arhus, Denmark, in 1985 and is a priceless piece of equipment to the folks of Rustico. It looked shiny and new, and it was obvious that the apparatus is doted on, its whirring belts like music to Freddy's ears.

Until 1985, the North Star Arena was an indoor facility with a natural-ice surface constructed during a rink-building boom on the Island. Soon it became apparent that the occasional mild winter would create a problem. Even with the windows left open all day and all night, the ice could not be kept for more than six or seven weeks a year. "Our kids didn't get enough ice time to get any better," Freddy explained. For a hamlet with perhaps four hundred residents and meagre financial resources, the prospects for the North Star Arena were not bright.

Freddy took my arm and marched me over to the other end of the rink by his office. There, encased in an elaborate glass display, are thousands of family names. Many of them are Gallants, Gauthiers and Doucettes, the traditional surnames of the people who have lived in Rustico since it was settled. Each had put up money to buy a square foot of artificial ice. The legion of names represents an entire community's effort to make its backyard rink a lasting thing. Freddy ran a forearm over his moustache and said, "When I first heard of it, I was living in Edmonton but I sent back a cheque for a hundred bucks quick as I could."

The man behind the artificial ice and the born-again rink in Rustico was the parish priest in 1984, a man named Art Pendergast. Hearing of his congregation's discontent with the dwindling hockey season, Pendergast knew there was a role the church could play. Freddy Doiron is delighted by the story, and as he told it, he embellished what must have been the simple act of a priest who knew where his flock's happines resided. "Father Art got up one day in church and shouted out from the pulpit," said Freddy. "'No act of God will bring us more than seven weeks of ice a year. If you want artificial ice then let's go get 'er!'" Freddy roared with laughter as he thought about the parishioners in their Sunday best plunking bits of change and dollar bills into the collection plate so the senior league teams from

Rustico and their western rivals in Tignish could battle for a few more Friday nights each year.

The fund-raising campaign gathered steam under Father Art's guidance, and soon Rustico natives living off the Island were being contacted for donations. The result was an effort that raised $145,000 dollars in order to purchase an artificial ice plant. The church was behind the survival of a rink whose most hallowed night came in 1993—but not because of the quality of hockey that was played.

The despised Tignish Aces were the guests when the home-town White-caps decided not to be accommodating. A full-scale, bench-clearing rumble ensued in front of a crowd far too large for the little building. No one has an accurate count of how many there were in the North Star Arena that Friday evening. Freddy Doiron rubbed his chin and said he reckoned it was well over a thousand. "I figure that's correct because the fire marshall was at the game that night and he sent me a letter the next day saying capacity was now 970 by law."

I watched as the little rink readied itself for the coming season. The two men sprayed water in a sweeping motion, back and forth, and it reminded me of the way my father used to do it in our back yard thirty years ago. This miniature wooden arena took me back in time, and its calm simplicity—a county rink unspoiled by corporate boxes and video scoreboards—hinted that what goes on here is sacred to the people. Then Freddy Doiron's jacket started ringing. He reached for his cell phone and I was yanked out of this house of hockey and into the reality of Rustico's driving rain.

With a blast of his whistle, Brian Carragher continues the penalty procession at Cahill Stadium on Thanksgiving Sunday. As he circles the Western Capitals net, he turns to see a scuffle break out and his mind is made up in an instant. Carragher, a referee for eighteen years in this part of the country, plays it by the book and the zero-tolerance policy means the two combatants must go. With Gerard Gallant yapping at his belligerent best, and the crowd chanting Carragher's nickname, "Bucky," he dispatches a fan favourite, Steve Dyer, to the showers.

Dyer is a hulking left-winger, twenty years old from Warsaw, Ontario, who is playing his last season of junior hockey and likely his last seriously competitive year in the game. In the room, bathed in sweat and with most of his equipment peeled off, Dyer relishes the rink he has just departed. "It's a small barn and I'm a grinder. I love the fact you don't have to skate far to get into the corners," he says, smirking. Then the perfect way to describe the exhilaration of Cahill Stadium flashes into his head. "The boards shake when you get a big hit!"

Like many of the players and fans at the stadium for this game, Dyer deplores what is happening to the style of hockey native to the Maritimes— the hard-hitting, back-alley kind of game where toughness and character mean survival and, ultimately, victory. Dyer hates all the whistles and the constant traffic jam in the penalty box. He has a hunch the all-too-frequent stoppages have driven loyal Summerside fans away from the arena. "There were fifty-four minutes in minor penalties called last Sunday. Our game took three and a half hours to play. This new policy means you can't shake your head without something happening," Dyer laments.

There is no question he places the blame for what is happening squarely on the shoulders of the rule-makers and, more specifically, on those who enforce them. Steve Dyer is not a big fan of referees like Bucky Carragher. In disgust, he flings a sopping glove in the general direction of the equipment room. When asked what he will do after the season, after his career is surely over, Dyer says with no hesitation, "Maybe I'll hit the real world just as hard."

Bucky Carragher is not a big man, but he is able to carry the big stick a referee needs to in this country rink. He has officiated at most levels of hockey throughout his career and across Atlantic Canada. Carragher called American Hockey League games in Charlottetown when the Senators were still around. He still does major junior games on the mainland as well as the Maritime Junior League and plenty of university matches.

It is in small rinks like Cahill Stadium that Carragher feels the most pressure. It is also here that he feels the genuine thrill of the action and the intense scrutiny of his critics. "I can tell in the stands if they've got ketchup on the fries. They're pretty close to me," he says.

Even Carragher is uncertain about the way things are going, given the new emphasis on zero tolerance. There is a reluctance in his voice as he recites the good intentions of the officials to eliminate thuggery and replace it with skilled play in rinks like this. "If you'd seen me referee eight or ten years ago, I was the kind of guy who would let them rock and roll. Now it's really hard to get a flow to the game," Carragher says, with genuine regret. He is bound and determined, though, to survive the changing trends that he must help to establish. He is a resilient character who has stubbornly held his ground in order to pursue his love of refereeing. While making a delicate overtime judgment in an Atlantic Universities Athletic Association (A.U.A.A.)

game between the University of Prince Edward Island and the University of Moncton in the spring of 1996, Bucky faced a referee's worst nightmare.

A goal scored by the UPEI Panthers at home in Charlottetown had eliminated the Blue Eagles of Moncton and sent the Island squad to the next round of the post-season. It was Carragher's decision that the shot, missed by the goal judge and not signalled by the red light, was in and out of the net very quickly. After indicating to the official scorer that the goal was to stand, Carragher was attacked by members of the Moncton team. Three players from the Blue Eagles shoved and punched Carragher in a display of violence against an official rarely witnessed. Before a more than capacity crowd at the emotionally charged Civic Centre in Charlottetown, the Island-born referee was at the mercy of the incensed players from "away." The miracle is that a full-scale donnybrook did not follow.

The incident received national attention and the future of the hockey program at the University of Moncton was doubtful as the entire team was indefinitely suspended by the A.U.A.A. Each of the three players who had battered Carragher was suspended for five years, and the university commissioned a study of the case by former Montreal Canadiens great Ken Dryden. In his recommendations, Dryden wrote, "The incident in Charlottetown has offered a defining moment for many players, coaches and officials. In a stunning, unfortunate way, it has redefined the possible."

To Brian Carragher, the victim of the attack, it had seemed unthinkable that he could be beaten up during the course of performing his duties as a referee. After all, Carragher has a fundamental belief in the fairness of the game. When the match is on, in any rink across the country, the referee is in charge and therefore untouchable. In reluctantly going over the event at the Civic Centre, Carragher resolutely says, "That doesn't have to happen to anyone, whether it's me or an official refereeing his first game. I don't think it will ever happen again."

Although the Canadian Hockey Association upheld the five-year suspensions for the players who attacked Carragher, Ken Dryden cautioned against such drastic action in his report's recommendations. Dryden called such suspensions the equivalent of "locking someone up and throwing away the key." Instead, the Hall of Famer advocated a one-year ban for each player, as well as strictly enforced community service. Dryden wrote, "Why not use sports, from which they have learned all their lives, to allow them to learn again?"

Carragher no longer cares to discuss most of what happened. Instead, he gets back on the ice and continues to do what he knows best. With his whistle firmly planted on the tops of his right hand's first two fingers, Carragher patrols Cahill Stadium as an enforcer. He refuses to be intimidated. "You have to look at it like being in a car accident. You have to get back in and drive again," he says. "I'm back enjoying what I'm doing. It's behind me now and I think people respect the fact that I'm back."

"Summerside was a bad-ass place," Bobby MacMillan was saying as he sat behind the bar of the Sport Page Club in downtown Charlottetown. "Trying to get a win outta there was tough." On the other side of the counter, Forbes Kennedy nodded his bulldog-like head in complete agreement. Talking out of the side of his mouth in deference to a well-chewed cigar butt, Kennedy almost spat out his view of the Island's greatest rivalry. "When you were playing the guys from Summerside and you were from Charlottetown, the game was all about hate. Geez! You just hated that team from up there."

The scene in the empty Charlottetown club early in the morning was almost too far-fetched to believe. Bobby MacMillan, a handsome forty-three-year-old with friendly eyes and a full mane of hair, won the Lady Byng Trophy with the Atlanta Flames in 1979. The Island gentleman scored 37 goals and 108 points that year to endear himself forever to the folks back home. MacMillan now owns the Sport Page, which serves as a gathering spot and watering hole for the local sports enthusiasts.

Forbes Kennedy, on the other hand, is remembered as one of pro hockey's notorious outlaws. Bald and bow-legged, with a hockey jacket draped over his sturdy frame, Kennedy owns one NHL record. While playing for the Toronto Maple Leafs in a 1969 playoff game against Boston, Kennedy collected eight separate penalties in a fighting frenzy. It is a Stanley Cup playoff record that still stands. In the presence of his pal the Lady Byng winner, Kennedy wore it like a badge.

MacMillan grew up in Charlottetown's minor hockey system and starred as a skilled forward. Elite players in the Island's capital city wore the uniform of the Abegweit Athletic Association, or the Abbies, as they came to be known. Whenever travelling to play their fierce rivals in Summerside, the Abbies knew they would have their hands full with the Crystals at Cahill Stadium. "When you went up to Summerside as a kid, it was like going on a road trip to Boston or New York if you played for the Hawks like I once did," recalled MacMillan. "It was always tough against them. You just knew the gloves were coming off at some point. That's what made it so special."

In his eleven big-league seasons, MacMillan accumulated 577 points with seven different clubs before calling it quits with Chicago at the end of the 1984–85 campaign. He was a talented player with an ability to put the puck in the net as well as create scoring chances. Being an Islander, he also knew the value of toughness. MacMillan is modest to the point of being bashful concerning his accomplishments, and credits others for his success the year he won the Lady Byng. In particular, he recalls two of the Flames' tougher players, Harold Phillipoff and Willi Plett, as being directly responsible for his stardom.

After scoring a couple of goals in his first outing with Atlanta, MacMillan was approached by Phillipoff and Plett in the locker room following the game. They advised the sniper that he should concentrate on scoring while they took care of any monkey business. All they asked in return was to have their names appear in the newspapers every once in a while, as MacMillan was surely going to be the interview subject after most matches. "From then on I'd start every chat with a reporter by saying, 'Who cares about what I did? Harold Phillipoff and Willi Plett played one helluva game,'" MacMillan chuckled.

The Sport Page where MacMillan and Kennedy comfortably chatted about careers long gone is a monument to Island sports heroes. The sweaters of Prince Edward Islanders who played in the NHL are all there: Gerard Gallant, Errol Thompson, Alan MacAdam, Rick Vaive, Summerside's Dave Cameron, Forbes Kennedy and MacMillan's own number 11 of the Flames. There are others as well. On the Wall of Fame there are dozens of engraved plaques paying tribute to all kinds of athletes from Prince Edward Island who have gained notoriety in their various sports.

As he referred to the pictures of Johnny "Snags" Squarebriggs, James "Fiddler" Macdonald and Frank "Duck" Acorn, among others, MacMillan gushed with anecdotes of a rich and mystical understanding of what it means to be an Island boy who made good. "I think there's a pride in going away and doing something special," mused the one-time NHL star. "The most important thing, though, is for people back on the Island to be proud of you when you come back home."

As I scanned the walls of the Sport Page Club, my eye fell on a yellowed copy of the *Charlottetown Evening Patriot* from Monday, April 4, 1966. Staring back at me was a cocky-looking young man with a brush cut. The caption under the photo read: "The third period was marred by a brawl between Boston's Forbes Kennedy and Doug Jarrett of Chicago who left the ice for repairs." It was a succinct summing up of one of Prince Edward Island's enduring characters of hockey's good old days.

Forbes Kennedy, or Forbie as he is known to just about everyone, coached the Summerside Crystals for half a dozen years. His home is in Charlotte-town now, and at sixty-one years of age he still coaches in the Maritime Junior League. The Abbies are his team, and much of the time he is suspended by the league because—well, just because he is cantankerous old Forbie. Even though he guided those teams at Cahill Stadium, he will admit to a certain distaste for Summerside. "There's all this talk of a rivalry between Montreal and Toronto. I agree. But Summerside and Charlottetown! There's nothing like that. It's war!" After making that declaration, he squinted wickedly and allowed the cigar smoke to drift lazily from the corner of his mouth.

Forbes Kennedy was not born on Prince Edward Island. His father worked at the correctional facility in Dorchester, New Brunswick, and the young Kennedy came into this world on the mainland. Two weeks after his birth, Forbie's family moved back to Prince Edward Island, creating a long-held morsel of Island folklore. "Everyone always claimed when I was born, my mother was doing time," guffawed Kennedy.

In spite of his NHL reputation as an enforcer, Kennedy had great skill. With the Montreal Junior Canadiens, his teammates included Henri Richard and goaltending great Eddie Johnston. "Forbie was a great skater and he was tough as nuts," Johnston recalled, when asked about Kennedy. A long-time NHL coach—formerly the head man in Pittsburgh—Johnston liked the fiery little Islander from the word go and understood what moti-vated Kennedy. "His motto was, if you came from out of Prince Edward Island and you didn't fight, you were gonna get your ass kicked when you went home."

The 1968–69 season was a landmark one for the National Hockey League with regard to the number of records set. In that campaign, Bobby Hull of Chicago set the league record for the number of goals in a single season: 58. Phil Esposito, the exceptional centre with the Boston Bruins, established NHL records for both assists and total points in one hockey year with 77 and 126 respectively. That same season, Forbes Kennedy led the league in penalty minutes with 219. "You always had to be tough to survive as an Islander in hockey. That's the way we've always played it. We always will," said Kennedy.

The most memorable night of Forbes Kennedy's NHL career was his last.

Almost three decades after April 2, 1969, the gnarled but resolute little fighter savoured the memory of the proceedings at the Boston Garden as a gourmet would haute cuisine. The first round of the playoffs and the first game of the series had the Bruins up 10–0 on Kennedy's Toronto Maple Leafs. The coach of the Leafs, George "Punch" Imlach, disgusted at his team's lack of backbone, approached Kennedy, who was languishing on the bench. "We're down by ten so you knew we weren't going to tie it," said Forbie. "Punch told me to go out there and get something going."

The result was one of the most frenetic episodes in playoff history. Kennedy planted himself in front of the Bruins net and claimed he took a slash across the ankles from the Boston goalie, Gerry Cheevers. From there the gloves came off and Kennedy fought most of the Bruins, including tough guy Ted Green and the irascible Johnny "Pie" McKenzie. Boston was his former club, and one-time teammate Eddie Johnston escorted the blood-ied Kennedy from the ice after he had amassed four minor penalties, two majors, one ten-minute misconduct and a game misconduct—eight penalties in all. "The fans, well, they threw beer on me. Threw bottles at my head and spit on me. I used to play for the Bruins, you know. They forgot that pretty quick," said Kennedy, shaking his head.

Back in the Leafs room, Pat Quinn was marching up and down still seething at having been ejected for smashing the Bruins' Bobby Orr into the boards. It was a hit that would keep Orr from the rest of that game and all of the next. Quinn, now the president and general manager of the Vancouver Canucks, has that night at the Boston Garden burned in his memory. Much of what he recalls had to do with Forbes Kennedy. "He was tough and skilled. An undisciplined player but he had talent for sure," remembered Quinn. "For Forbes, fighting the other team's tough guy was just as important as scoring a big goal. It was all the same value to him."

Kennedy was exhausted and soaked in sweat and blood as he slumped on the old dressing-room bench in Boston. He can recall what happened next as if it were yesterday. "My head's hanging between my legs because I can't lift it—I'm so tired. Imlach leaves the bench and comes to the room. He leans down and whispers in my ear, 'Forbie, when I said get something going, I didn't mean World War III!'" Kennedy erupted in laughter at the memory.

Forbes Kennedy never played another game. At thirty-three years of age, his knees were shot—he had both of them operated on almost immediately—but his legacy as a fighter has endured and his pugnacious nature is still evident. As a coach, back on the Island, he threatens defiantly to light up his cigar in rinks that forbid smoking when he is disgusted by a referee's call.

His teams have always believed in toughness first. It is something Kennedy respects even in fierce rivals from Summerside. "I think even though you hated the guys from Summerside when you were playing them, you respected them later. That's because they were just as tough as you and you have to respect that," he said, nodding as if trying to convince himself.

Like most of the Island boys who have gone to the NHL, Kennedy is only comfortable at home with pals and complete opposites like Bobby MacMillan, the Lady Byng Trophy winner. That day, across the bar counter in the Sport Page Club, the roles reversed and he sought approval from his colleague. Kennedy suddenly softened and his eyes solicited affirmation from MacMillan, who had been patiently listening to his tall tales. "One thing about that rink up Summerside way—it is cold. And I think it may have the best sheet of ice in the Maritimes. Right, Bobby?"

With Turkey Gallant's team down by two and going into the third period, there is a hush at Cahill Stadium disturbed only by the Olympia ice machine as it resurfaces the rink for the final twenty minutes. Clarence Wedge is at the controls. Sitting in the driver's seat, proud as a peacock, Wedge is forty-four years old and, as his former teammate Doug MacLean calls him, the ultimate rink rat.

"You got no judgment... you can't be an ice maker," Wedge snuffles as he lowers his tiny frame from the parked machine. "I take pride in my ice. You have to use lots of judgment when you're cutting it. Be careful not to get any ridges. If you do, boy... a guy can snap his leg just like that!"

No one has ever snapped a leg on ice that Clarence Wedge has made. He has been working here, officially, since he was twelve years old, and his understanding of the rink is beyond question. "I never went to school. Couldn't read or write, so I said, frig this and came and spent all my time here," declares Wedge.

In the beginning, the smallest kid around these parts had an enormous desire to be at the stadium. He recalls never being at his home, which is just across the street from Cahill, but instead spending eighty to ninety hours a week at the rink and taking home the sum total of $47 for his labours.

Clarence has had a fascination with the ice since he can remember. When he was eight, the Boston Bruins came to play an exhibition game in Summerside, and he was on the crew that cleaned the ice surface without the help of a Zamboni. "We'd sweep it with corn brooms—fifteen rink rats. We'd line up across from one side to the other and it would take us an hour to get to the other end. She was like glass!"

Sitting in his cluttered little office behind the net at one end, Clarence smokes a cigarette, rocking back and forth in a swivel chair befitting the rink foreman. This is the rink rat's territory, and he serves up his rise to prominence as a politician would recite a memoir. "In the old days, we could never cut the ice down, we'd have to melt it," Wedge says. He tells of the rink being so cold that nine or twelve inches of ice would build up after repeated floodings with the old forty-five-gallon barrels. Clarence was part of an eighteen-man crew that pushed and pulled a burner on a sled in order to turn the excess ice to water. Two more followed behind with a huge wet vacuum to suck up the residue. "It would take us twenty-four hours to do the whole slab, to burn it down to an inch," he says.

Wedge played junior hockey with the Summerside Crystals for a season and was a teammate of Doug MacLean's. The picture on the Nostalgia Room wall bears this out. There he is in the middle row, tiny Clarence, the smallest man on the squad by far.

Early in life, Clarence decided his pride was not in playing but in making it right for other, bigger kids to wage hockey's battles. He was the first to drive the Massey-Ferguson when the ice-cleaning attachment for the back arrived. Adventurous days were spent learning to operate the rigid clutch without skidding and smashing right through the end boards. On Sunday nights, Wedge would feverishly sharpen blades for three or four hundred people who came to the stadium to pleasure skate. His is a life lived in the rink.

The rink rat's reward is a notoriety that few in the community can claim. When questions are asked concerning the stadium's history, Clarence Wedge is deferred to. In the western part of the Island, he is as recognizable as the most revered players in the province. In the far reaches of Tignish, O'Leary and Alberton, the folks stop him in the street and say they know exactly who he is.

On his ice machine, touring Cahill Stadium, the fans all understand how important Clarence Wedge is. "Everybody acts like I'm the mayor of the town. When I go out driving the ice machine, they're all waving at me and I don't know who half of them are!" he says, with a twinkle of pride in his eyes.

Not long after Bucky Carragher has called the final penalty, the siren abruptly halts the Western Capitals' third-period comeback. The scoreboard at each end reads: HOME 5... GUESTS 6, confirming victory by the mainland East Hants Penguins. Gerard Gallant lowers his head and strolls along his deserted bench to the gate before hopping down to the dressing-room runway.

As the goalie comes off, Turk puts an enormous arm around the boy and leads him to the safety of the Doug MacLean Room. Ruth Sudsbury gathers her blanket and, in saying her goodbyes, blurts out one final gem. "You know, Gerard won't accept any pay for coaching this team. You should ask him about that," she says, and then bustles away.

I walk in on a meeting between Gerard and his assistant coaches, Jeff Squires and Ivan Baglole. Clair Sudsbury, the general manager, is there, too, in an effort to deduce the reason for the defeat. It is a holiday and the mood is reflective. In spite of the fact that most of the others are eager to get home for Thanksgiving supper, Turk is anxious to talk and directs me to the bleachers.

"We played tag around these old beams—or hide and seek. As long as you weren't causing trouble, Clarence wouldn't kick you out," Gerard says, as he gestures to the upper reaches of the little barn.

Gallant grew up two minutes' walk from Cahill Stadium and spent the years of his childhood here. From the time he was eight until he went away to play major junior hockey in Verdun, Quebec, at the age of sixteen, Turkey was either at this rink or at the Summerside Boys and Girls Club just up the road. He remembers it being the first rink he ever played in—remembers a group of eight or ten buddies watching junior games on Sunday afternoons and sweeping the stands when the match was over. In return, Clarence Wedge would let the boys skate for three or four hours after the game. It was a thrill. "My parents didn't always know where I was but they had a hunch I wasn't in trouble," says Gallant, with a fleeting grin.

Playing for the Crystals, Turkey won an Island Bantam championship and finished second in the Maritime League one year. Somehow that was not the most important thing to him. He talks more willingly about the character the rink helped him build than the championship teams it produced. He becomes more forceful when declaring the rink so cold "you pretty well have to wear a Ski-Doo suit in here in January and February."

Gallant's game in the NHL was built on being rugged. He credits his success with the Detroit Red Wings to two things. "It made my career to be able to play with Steve Yzerman," he says. On the Red Wing captain's line and as his assistant, Turk's impact on the league was far greater than he had ever anticipated. But in hunting for the roots of his success, Gerard Gallant goes all the way back to the rink he grew up in. He is convinced Cahill Stadium was instrumental in shaping his future. "Small little arena and the corners are narrow. Not a lot of room out there. That's my type of game. I'm not a swift skater like a lot of guys were and this was a perfect barn for that type of hockey," he explains. The type of hockey he refers to was one where players fought as a matter of course. It is a rugged theme that serves as the lifeblood of the game's mystique in this little province. In the final analysis, however, Turk echoes the words of Forbes Kennedy when he says there was a respect that existed between the players. Respect is a word Gallant uses over and over again.

Most vividly entrenched in his memory are Sunday afternoons when the Charlottetown juniors came to visit the Crystals. The central characters were the Abbies' Stevie Gallant and a fellow named Mike "Pinky" Gallant from Summerside. They are no relation to Turk, aside from the fact that all of them were as tough as nails. He recalls they would fight three times at centre ice on each occasion the two teams met. "I often told the boys in Detroit that Joey Kocur and Bob Probert are pretty tough, but these guys were incredible!" he says. Then, losing his easy smile, Gallant grimaces at the changing times in hockey. "They used to respect each other. They knew they'd fight even before the game started. Nowadays one guy would just as soon hack another. No respect."

Two rows up, Bucky Carragher and his officiating partner march by on their way back to Charlottetown. "Good game, Bucky," calls out a surprisingly generous Gallant. Carragher stops and turns to acknowledge the Summerside coach in amazement. "I'd take 'em all like that," says the Turk. "Happy Thanksgiving!"

"When I come back here, I'm just 'Turk.' That's the way I always wanted it. I have my buddies and I didn't want people saying, 'There's the guy that played in the NHL.' I'm happy I've had a great life. Feeling above other people just isn't me," he says. His NHL career was marked by grit and, at times, great play. Still, Gallant thinks more about the way he is perceived by the people he feels closest to. "It's not so important that people are proud of what I've done. What's important to me is that people respect how I've handled myself away from the game," he says. "I always thought about home before I did anything. I didn't want to be in the spotlight for the wrong reasons."

In the gathering cool of the rink that warms him most, Gallant considers his newest role as a coach. He claims he never thought about it as a career option. After his last days in the NHL with Tampa Bay and a brief fling in the International Hockey League with the Detroit Vipers, he felt like he needed something to do. None of the motivation was financial. "Money was never a big thing for me. Even when I was in Detroit. It was always respect that I wanted," he reiterates.

In Cahill Stadium, Gerard Gallant is still learning the game he loves. The rink teaches him more each time he comes to its shivering severity. Recognizing the value of this place, Turk cannot justify receiving a salary just to be here. "This organization is $50,000 in the hole. To look at this community and for me to be paid by a team in this financial difficulty—well, I'd feel ashamed. I see it as a learning experience for me, so maybe I should pay them!"

As we make our way out of the rink, the minor hockey kids are taking to Cahill Stadium's ice. Turk is stopped by several of them and asked to sign his autograph. Gerard knows most of them by name and it is likely that all of them have his signature already. They never tire of letting him know how much he means to them. He never tires of receiving the attention.

Of all the players who came from this rink, perhaps the entire province, Gerard Gallant is held in the highest regard. Unassuming and gracious, he embodies what many see as the Island spirit. The thing that he takes most pride in is his home. He learned to be tough at Cahill Stadium, but now he looks gently back at the extreme environment that has moulded his life. With careful hands, he lifts the rusted latch to the side door and motions me through.

In the dusk of Thanksgiving Sunday, Turkey shakes my hand and says, "Tell Yzerman hello when you see him." He calls to his brother Blaine, "I'll catch up with you at Mom's house for supper in a couple of minutes." Looking in the rear-view mirror, I see the greatest hockey player Summerside has ever produced waving to me. The plain brown building he stands in front of is suddenly extraordinary.

3 Notre Dame College
Wilcox, Saskatchewan

Chris Cuthbert

To keep a boy out of hot water, put him on ice.
—Paul Quarrington, *King Leary*

FROM REGINA IT'S FORTY-THREE kilometres south and a nine-kilometre jog west into the breadbasket of the country. Wilcox, Saskatchewan, is like any of the countless farm communities that dot the plains and yet unlike any other. Here the grassroots of hockey have been planted deeply in the rich prairie gumbo to yield an impressive annual harvest of young talent. Here, hockey rests not only close to the heart but in the soul as well.

The Paterson, Pioneer and Saskatchewan Pool grain elevators stand sentry in this three-elevator, two-rink town. The only red lights in Wilcox are located behind the hockey nets. On the right side of the road entering town is a sign that reads "Home of the Hounds, Athol Murray College of Notre Dame." A few yards farther on the left is another signpost, "Welcome to Wilcox, Canadian Champions Midget AAA 1980, 1986, Juvenile AA 1983, Jr. A 1988."

I turn right off Highway 39 onto Main Street into this town of 230 residents and 400 students, driving along the street where Wendel Clark won the 100- and 200-metre sprints at the school track meet, the same street swept clean by James Patrick and Gord Kluzak as punishment for their role in a school prank. I drive past the post office and the school tuck shop to St. Augustine's Church, Canada Park and the monument to Athol Murray, the legendary priest who was affectionately known here as "Père." Beyond the park is the Metz family farmstead, where Nick and Don Metz were raised before leaving for Toronto to help the Maple Leafs win five Stanley Cups in the forties. On the west side of the church, beside the blue spruce planted by Princess Anne, is the burial place of Murray. The gravestone reads:

Luctor et Emergo
Monsignor Athol Murray
Jan. 9 1892–Dec. 15 1975
Canadian Extraordinaire
Priest Teacher Humanist Sportsman Philosopher
Founder of Notre Dame College

In scale, Wilcox isn't much bigger than when Father Athol Murray first arrived here in 1927. In scope, the town has grown exponentially. It wouldn't be accurate to suggest Murray put Wilcox on the map, but his work and vision made Wilcox jump off the map for all to notice. More than twenty years after his death, Murray has an ethereal presence here, inspiring another generation of students not yet born when he died.

Born into an affluent Toronto family, Athol Murray was sent to the Jesuits of Loyola College in Montreal at the age of eight, following his mother's death. Subsequently, he embraced the classics at Laval University and studied law at Osgoode Hall. After a brief career in journalism, Murray entered the priesthood and was dispatched to Regina in 1922.

There, he established an athletic club for disadvantaged boys that he christened the Argos after the famed Toronto rowing club his father had co-founded.

Five years later, Athol Murray arrived in Wilcox in a cloud of dust during the Great Depression. Murray brought not only the word of God, but hope of better times and shelter from the dust-bowl storms. Young

Coach Athol Murray with the Senior A western champion Notre Dame Hounds in 1947. Extreme left is Frank Germann; beside him is Jackie McLeod

men riding the rails of the Soo Line in search of jobs found refuge at this prairie whistle-stop. Murray provided them not with employment but with the opportunity to further their education in this unlikely setting with ramshackle bunk-house residences and optional tuition. By 1933, Murray had forged an affiliation with the University of Ottawa, establishing Notre Dame as the smallest university college in the world.

Sport played a critical role at Notre Dame, both ideologically and practically. It was Murray's belief that "sport brings together opportunity and adversity and in this moment the best in an individual expresses itself. It is these moments that give a community great warmth, vigour and flash." The Notre Dame teams, nicknamed the Hounds, also played a more pragmatic role by raising money from gate receipts that provided financial support for the impoverished school.

Besides teaching courses in the Liberal Arts program, Murray coached the Hounds until 1947. Among his protégés were NHLers Garth Boesch and the Metz brothers of the Maple Leafs as well as Gus Kyle and Jackie McLeod of the New York Rangers.

Père's hockey passion extended beyond his tenure behind the bench. In the sixties, he shared the vision of a Canadian National Team program for élite amateur players with his close friend Father David Bauer and recommended Jackie McLeod as coach. By 1968, the year he received the Order of Canada, Murray had successfully spearheaded a funding drive to build the first Olympic-sized rink in Saskatchewan. Later, he recruited former National Team players Barry MacKenzie and Terry O'Malley to continue the tradition of hockey excellence at the school that has become a feeder to Canada's Olympic hockey program. More than a dozen Notre Dame graduates have represented Canada at the Winter Olympics, including Russ Courtnall, James Patrick, Kent Manderville and, more recently, Dwayne Norris and Derek Mayer.

For the many contributions Father Athol Murray made to Canadian sport, he was inducted into the Canadian Sports Hall of Fame in 1972. Murray has also been nominated for membership in the Builders category of the Hockey Hall of Fame.

Just to the east of the rink is Notre Dame's new archives building, dubbed "the Pizza Hut" by students because of its geometric shape and crimson roof. Inside is a classical feast of food for thought and insight about the college's founder. Archivist Neta Monson welcomes me. Like many at

Notre Dame, Monson has a hockey connection. She is a distant cousin of Garth Boesch, a Wilcox product who made his way to the NHL. On display here is an eclectic array of memorabilia, from the RCMP buffalo coat Murray wore to ward off the fierce Saskatchewan winters to the correspondence sent to him by national and world leaders. The Underwood typewriter he used daily to write up to a dozen letters to notables such as Mackenzie King, Dwight Eisenhower and Winston Churchill regarding the issues of the day is here. There is an original copy of the Act of Confederation, which Murray acquired from his uncle, Hugh John Macdonald, the son of Canada's first prime minister, Sir John A. Macdonald. In keeping with his family background, Murray was a staunch patriot and comfortable in the company of Canada's leaders.

The archives' walls are decorated with the second-largest private collection of Nicholas de Grandmaison works. Murray commissioned the Banff-based artist to paint portraits of great Canadians he believed were suitable role models for his students. Jean Béliveau, Lester Patrick and Ron Lancaster are among the legendary subjects.

Neta draws my attention to the ceiling, to sixteen plaster tablets that are moulded copies of the Parthenon frieze removed from the interior wall of the Athenian temple in the 1830s. The work, stretching more than sixty feet across, depicts the ancient Greek devotion to the gods. This reproduction was purchased by Murray in the 1940s from a New York auction house for the breathtaking sum of $10,000 (U.S.). The idealistic prairie priest wanted his students to be touched by the influences of ancient Greece and the roots of democracy. "Père believed in the Greek philosophy of developing the mind, body and soul," Monson says.

Then she unlocks the book vault to reveal a remarkable collection of ancient literature from the thirteenth to seventeenth centuries, something you might expect to find in Rome or Athens but not on the Canadian prairie. Although many of the texts were used by Murray in his daily teachings, few of the rare books are accessible to Notre Dame students today because they are written in Latin, Greek and an early French dialect. The collection includes handwritten manuscripts on goatskin or sheepskin produced prior to the invention of the printing press. Among the titles are St. Thomas Aquinas on the Epistles of St. Paul, 1481; the Chronicles 1515, printed on the original Gutenberg press; and Erasmus's Dedication to Henry VIII. A handwritten letter is visible inside the frayed binding of the Erasmus work, which, if from the author's hand, would be priceless in its own right.

I find it difficult to fathom how this treasure trove found its way to such a remote literary outpost. Neta explains that Murray befriended Father Alfred Bacciochi, a grand-nephew of Napoleon who came to North America at the turn of the century with many of the scholarly works once possessed by his great-uncle. Father Bacciochi was posted at Gull Lake, Saskatchewan, and entrusted the books to Père Murray upon his death.

It is clear that Père Murray was not just another parish priest and that there is much more to Notre Dame College than its rich hockey heritage. As the archives tour concludes, Terry O'Malley, Notre Dame's Dean of Spiritual Development, arrives.

Entrance to Notre Dame Rink and Kenney Hall

Terry O'Malley is one of those magical names from my radio when he wore the red maple leaf thirty years ago. He was a defensive stalwart on Canada's national team trying to stem the advancing European hockey tide. Believing it was the divine right of the Canadian team to triumph, I listened intently to those games on CBC radio beaming from the mysterious new hockey outposts of Prague and Moscow. When Canada was defeated, the experts at home said it was because we hadn't sent our best. We were conditioned to believe that a team of NHL players would crush the Europeans and never seemed to give O'Malley, Fran Huck, Morris Mott and company due credit.

O'Malley, like Notre Dame president Barry Mackenzie, went from the National Team program to Notre Dame; from National Team mentor Father David Bauer to Bauer's dear friend Père Murray. His first encounter with Murray was on a date frozen in time. O'Malley and the "Nats" were scheduled to play an exhibition game in Regina on November 22, 1963, the day John F. Kennedy was assassinated. "We got to Regina that night and we were all abuzz with the Kennedy news," O'Malley recalls. "We ended up losing the game to the Saskatchewan All Stars. Our heads weren't in it. That was my introduction to Athol Murray. He came in between periods and gave us a thousand dollars to support the team. Back then we ran the national team on $25,000 and the gates we received from exhibition games. 'So you're the

Canadian bastards,' he said. 'You're representing your country—what a great honour! We're banking on you.' All the Hounds came in with their red jackets on. They had raised money collecting pop bottles and whatever to help us out. This from a school which did not yet have running water. I remember Father David Bauer had tears in his eyes."

O'Malley's initial visit to Wilcox came in Canada's centennial year of 1967. Murray had invited the National Team to officially open a new Notre Dame rink that boasted an Olympic-sized ice surface. In typical Père Murray style, there were dignitaries, fanfare, pomp and ceremony. At a banquet to christen the rink, and likely to help pay some of the bills, O'Malley, one of the National Team captains, was seated beside Newfoundland premier Joey Smallwood. "Athol Murray had a sense of drama," says O'Malley. "He loved to call Smallwood one of the founding fathers of Canada. He would always bring people to the college who he thought were great Canadians."

Seven years later, another visit to Wilcox, when O'Malley was passing through Saskatchewan, laid the foundation for his second career as a teacher and coach at Notre Dame. Over a few mid-morning scotches, Père Murray regaled O'Malley with his life story, then made a pitch for his guest to make himself more at home and teach at Notre Dame. Terry thanked Père for the offer and promised to give it some consideration after his playing days. "At lunch he introduces me to the kids." O'Malley converts to his best Père Murray impersonation. "'Gang, I want to introduce you to a great Canadian.' No one looked up. He went on about my career and

The Olympic-sized ice surface at Notre Dame College

finally he said, 'Not only that but he's going to come here to teach.' Then all the heads turned and looked up. This was 1974. It was prophetic because I came in 1978."

Before putting down roots in Saskatchewan, O'Malley continued to scratch his hockey itch for seven years in Japan. There are few more divergent places in the sports world than Tokyo and Wilcox. O'Malley, a hockey mercenary, admits to experiencing culture shock in his early days in Japan, so he can empathize with the seven Japanese students enrolled at Notre Dame this year. "I'm kind of their guardian angel because I speak Japanese," O'Malley says.

The Japanese students, however, make the transition much more easily than their parents do. "A fellow by the name of Tomita, the president of the Japanese Ice Hockey Federation, sent his son here. He came out in the spring and I was showing him around." He points out the window. "We went into a field out here. It had been a wet spring and there was every imaginable kind of wildlife. We're right on one of the flyways to the Arctic. I honked the horn and the sky turned black, literally black, that's how many birds there were.

"Ten years later we all went out for dinner when we were visiting in Japan. The father said to me, 'Remember when I brought my wife to Wilcox? When we left, she started to cry and never stopped crying until we got to Vancouver. Where, she said, are you leaving my first-born son?'

"He did well here, went to the University of San Diego, played hockey there and got a degree in interior design," O'Malley concludes.

The hockey cycle has come full circle for O'Malley. He travelled the world representing Canada on a national team supported by Père Murray. Now O'Malley continues Murray's work at Notre Dame, where students from around the world flock to learn the Canadian game.

In the early years, the Notre Dame student body dined in the church basement on the slim pickings of the day or, at times, on what some of the more industrious students "borrowed" from local farmers. It was easier for Père Murray to look the other way than turn his students away hungry.

Tonight beef Stroganoff is the pre-game meal at Varsity Hall before the Hounds entertain North Battleford in Saskatchewan Junior Hockey League action. The food is good, the company is even better. Terry O'Malley has asked a few of the students to drop by for a chat. They arrive in regular shifts as if being sent over the boards in a fast-paced scrimmage.

Deana Huyghebaert and Cheryl Schurman are the first to visit. Deana is from Glenworth, Saskatchewan, in her final year at Notre Dame. "It will be emotional to leave after four years," she admits. Cheryl, from Kensington, Prince Edward Island, has been here two weeks. "It already feels like home," she says. Both have a common passion for the game, both possess hockey potential that outgrew their small home towns. Their goal is to play for Canada at the Winter Olympics in either 2002 or 2006. The conviction in their words and eyes leaves little doubt that I will be hearing their names again.

Next is Dominic Lacasse of Shediac, New Brunswick, "the lobster capital of the world," he proclaims. Lacasse came to Notre Dame on the recommendation of alumnus Scott Pellerin, a Shediac native who plays for the St. Louis Blues. Kim Kee Yong is from Seoul, Korea. In his second year, Kim is a member of the school football team and aspires to play for the Korean national hockey team. Marcel Tuma, from Switzerland, is the son of a European hockey agent. "I'm not here for hockey but because of school," says Marcel, who is still wearing an apron from kitchen duty tonight. "I want to work in a bank."

Like most of his schoolmates, Kevin Lapointe of Quebec City has his priorities in order. The Grade 10 student is in his second year at Notre Dame. He came to learn English, "because we can't get a good job without it." His goal is a scholarship to an American university and perhaps a hockey career in Europe.

Varsity Hall clears out as quickly as the students filled it up. It's game night, and the mess hall crowd will regroup shortly at the rink.

Appropriately, the gleaming Notre Dame rink is housed under the same roof as Kenney Hall, a modern educational facility that contains classrooms, science and computer labs, a library and a gymnasium. It is representative of how Notre Dame athletics and scholastics have been interwoven since the college's formative years under Père Murray.

In large red letters at the far end of the rink is the slogan "Never Lose Heart Hounds." Both inspiration and perspiration come in large measures here. The Hounds are warming up in their home whites with red trim, an oversized ND with "Hounds" printed underneath on the front of their jerseys, red maple leafs on the shoulders. At the other end of the hundred-by-two-hundred-foot Olympic-sized ice surface are the North Battleford North Stars, sporting black, green and gold uniforms, replicas of those worn by the NHL's Dallas Stars.

Rookie Brad MacEwan is behind the Notre Dame bench. It's the same position Terry O'Malley, Barry MacKenzie and Père Murray, in other eras and rinks, have occupied. The Hounds have split their first two league games, and although they're young and talented, it's not yet clear how much potential these Hounds possess. The youthful coach must step cautiously in the early weeks of the season, as if walking over a prairie slough not yet frozen solid. "It's not fair to jump all over the kids early in the year," he explains.

"They're already adjusting to dorm life and the process of a new school. We don't have a huge fan base to rally the team around, so twenty-two people have to believe in each other and build it themselves."

The camaraderie MacEwan seeks for his team is already evident in the stands along the rink's western flank. At least three-quarters of the student population is present to cheer on their schoolmates, many living vicariously through these games until it's their turn to represent Notre Dame.

Wilcox is too small to have the season ticket support of other Saskatchewan junior franchises, which can draw more than a thousand fans per night. The Hounds, however, have their share of regulars. A band of scouts from the NHL, U.S. colleges and the Western Hockey League take up residence here each winter. Lorne Davis of Edmonton, Larry Hornung of Phoenix and Jim Bzdel of Calgary have good attendance records at the school.

University of Regina coach Kevin Dickie is also monitoring the proceedings, but he is at a distinct disadvantage recruiting players. Dickie knows he can't compete with the lure of U.S. scholarships and the opportunity to turn pro. "Notre Dame has a reputation of producing not only good hockey players but good people," says Dickie, a Notre Dame graduate. "The NCAA almost looks upon this as a junior college. The dormitory life, the reputations of Barry MacKenzie and Terry O'Malley make these players more desirable."

Dickie advanced from the hockey program in his hometown of Lafleche, Saskatchewan, and thrived in the hockey environment of Notre Dame. "Every Tuesday and Thursday Terry O'Malley took two different players out at 6:30 in the morning to scrimmage with him and his little boy, who was about seven or eight. It meant a lot to me as a player that he took that extra time for personal attention. I can still visualize those mornings and how badly I didn't want to get up, and how much it had meant to me when the day was over."

O'Malley's leadership left a lasting impression on Dickie, who coached for five years with Melfort in the Saskatchewan Junior League, leading his team to three provincial titles. Proudly he boasts of never having lost a game as a visiting coach at Notre Dame.

Tonight the Hounds surrender a 4–1 loss to the visiting North Stars. Yet the consensus of the Notre Dame staff and the assembled scouts is that the young Hounds have promise and will improve with time. As we leave, Kevin is informed that curfew has been delayed until eleven o'clock tonight and classes won't begin until noon tomorrow because of a staff meeting in the morning. "There will be beer in the fields tonight," Dickie says with a knowing smile.

About an hour later, I make my way back to the Wilcox Motor Inn just across the road from the grain elevators. Already there's frost on the windshield and a harvest moon is beaming on this crisp prairie night. Suddenly the silence is shattered by hoots and hollers from the nearby fields. Kevin Dickie had the night well scouted.

The following morning, Johnny Weisshaar, his brother Carl and Maurice Metz, cousin of Nick and Don Metz of Maple Leaf fame, gather around Johnny's kitchen table to feast on a smorgasbord of hockey memories dating back six decades. They're Notre Dame graduates, home-town boys, farmers and former teammates. While Nick and Don Metz were winning Stanley Cups in Toronto, this troika was bringing hockey glory closer to home with Soo Line Intermediate titles. Johnny appears as energetic as the kid who never wants to leave the ice, Carl's face has a boyish charm, and Maurice is still the physical presence he was patrolling the Wilcox blueline a half century ago.

It doesn't take long for this Hot Stove League to heat up, but the easiest ice-breaker is to discuss Père Murray. "Père was an enthusiast but he definitely wasn't a coach," says Metz, espousing an opinion shared by most Wilcox hockey people. "Father Murray believed the three best coaches in Canada were Al Ritchie [coach of hockey's Regina Pats and the CFL's Saskatchewan Roughriders], Lester Patrick, and you can guess the third, he used to say. He was also the physician of the team. If anybody had a broken arm, he'd give them an aspirin and send them back out. Aspirin cured everything."

"There was a game when most of the team had German measles," adds Johnny. "They were getting whipped 9–0 by Regina, and in the dressing room after the second period, Père said, 'Goddamit, guys, if you can't beat them at least give them the measles.'"

Perhaps Père Murray didn't know hockey strategy or basic first aid, but his strength as a motivator was unchallenged. "It took me a couple of games to see I wasn't good enough to play for the Hounds," says Carl, "although Père would tell me Lester Patrick wanted me in the NHL. He would do a real sales job on you."

The sales pitch worked for Garth Boesch, a native of nearby Riceton who later joined the Metz brothers in Toronto, where he won three Stanley Cups. "He was a defenceman and Turk Broda was the goaltender at the time," says Carl. "He probably stopped more shots than Broda because he'd get right down in front of the fellow shooting. As a result, he broke both knees, one of the reasons he's in a wheelchair today."

"Another thing about Garth is that they called him 'Baron' Boesch when he was playing," adds Johnny. "The reason was that he was the first guy who ever wore a moustache playing NHL hockey. Some people liked it, some people didn't at the time. Now look at them!"

The premier player of their era at Notre Dame was Jackie McLeod, who went on to play five years with the New York Rangers and later coached Canada's National Team on the recommendation of Père Murray. "I coached him," says Carl. "But what could we tell him about hockey? He was fourteen and destined for the NHL."

The longer these weathered farmers talk hockey, the younger they appear. There's a sparkle in their eyes as they turn back the clock to their childhood. "The golden days of the rink were during the Depression years," Maurice proclaims. "It was the only entertainment you had. Most of the rinks were curling rinks and skating rinks side by side. Ours was wide open in between. The curlers were hit with pucks more than a few times."

"That was the hub of the town in the winter-time," continues Johnny. "The colder it got, the more the ice cracked. There were a few broken limbs since a lot of guys caught their blades in those cracks."

"The biggest danger back then was freezing your lungs because it was as cold inside as it was outside," says Maurice. That prompts a laugh from Carl. "I used to play the game and then cough until about three in the morning," Carl recalls. "They'd generally have a little pot-bellied stove or some kind of heater, but the rinks were so drafty it was pretty near a lost cause to warm up an old hockey rink."

Johnny, Carl and Maurice anchored a local hockey squad that was a force in the Soo Line loop from 1947 to '51. "We won a few championships," Johnny reports with pride. "Another year we couldn't finish the final. It was all natural ice and we ran out in Weyburn. The series was tied 2–2 in the best of five. We let them have their names on the Cup that year. It was no good if ours was the only name on it."

Maurice claims that the games between Weyburn and Wilcox were so well played that in one season not a single penalty was called in five meetings between the two rivals. It was a different story when Wilcox travelled to Yellow Grass. "Anytime you went by the boards there, somebody would reach out and grab you by the hair," Maurice says with a chuckle. "One night the place is absolutely crowded. I'm on defence and I happen to look over into the stands and the first thing I see is a purse come up and go down. This fellow from Yellow Grass had been jawing with two hockey mothers from Wilcox. They'd all been into the sauce. He evidently went to push one of the women. The other woman swung her purse and nailed him right over the head. Down he goes like he's been hit with a club. What she forgot is that she had a full flask in her purse. She knocked him colder than a mackerel. It stopped the game for about five minutes until he came to."

After the Hot Stove session in Johnny's kitchen, we head to the old Wilcox rink to meet "Mr. Notre Dame," Frank Germann. Germann arrived from nearby Pitman in 1936 to begin Grade 9 classes at Notre Dame. After high school, Germann graduated to the position of hockey coach at the age of twenty-one, succeeding Père Murray. He's been a teacher and administrator ever since.

The Wilcox rink is a vintage prairie Quonset design. Inside it resembles a dark, wooden tunnel. The light at the end is an open door to the fields outside where the snow that is scraped manually from the ice is dumped. Frank and Johnny explain that the Quonset is easy to erect and throughout the prairies is often used initially for grain storage—the Wilcox rink can hold up to 120,000 bushels of wheat. The rink on this site isn't the original one. The first, raised in the twenties, was torched in 1961. "Kids playing with matches," Johnny explains. "It got away on them. We lost three elevators, the rink, four annexes of grain and some horses. The rink roof took off like it was gasoline." The fire was in July, and a new rink was erected before the first winter storm. Unlike the modern arena alongside, the town rink is still a natural-ice facility. "You're lucky to be on by December 1 and to have ice until March 15," forecasts Frank. "Three or four years ago, we had such a mild winter there was no ice at all."

I search one of the side walls looking for an etching that Wayne Morrison, one of Notre Dame's teachers, had told me about. One night at the rink he scraped away the frost to discover a message scratched into the wood. It read, "Allan Karlander, 7 goals vs Shaunavon, March 1965." Karlander was another Hounds graduate who made it to the NHL with the Detroit Red Wings. I can't find the etching in the darkened rink but I feel sure it's there.

Next door, but under the same roof, is a three-sheet curling rink, where legendary curler Bob Pickering honed his game. On the wall of honour is a picture of the 1929–30 Wilcox senior hockey club that featured fourteen-year-old Nick Metz. "He was half the team," Johnny recalls. Nearby is a picture of the Wilcox squad that won the Soo Line championship in 1949–50. It features a beaming Johnny Weisshaar. He is even prouder of a pennant acknowledging the 1969 Wilcox peewee provincial champions that he coached. "We only had eleven kids. Everybody who tried out made it. The next year we had a whole bunch more. There were thirteen on that team," he laughs.

As Weisshaar locks up the old town rink, Frank leads me to the Notre Dame facility where the Hounds are working out. Germann has seen sixty different Notre Dame teams, and one player stands out among them all. "I always looked upon Cy Huck as the best natural athlete we ever had, certainly our best goaltender," Germann declares. It's a surprising statement considering Curtis Joseph was a star goaltender for Notre Dame when the Hounds won their national junior championship in 1988. "Cy went to work out with the Maple Leafs under Turk Broda. He was doing well but along the way he came up with a back injury. The Leafs were leery about a goaltender with a bad back and moved him out until he got healthy. He was very much like Joseph because he was so quick, particularly in 1947, when he was outstanding. He came back from Toronto to practise. I had the juniors at the time. I told them to try to score on Cy in a breakaway drill. They went for a half hour and couldn't score on him. They never saw anything like it. He was a natural."

Huck, however, became a tragic figure of Notre Dame hockey. The back injury robbed him of his dream of playing in the NHL and made daily life a state of constant discomfort. He began studies to enter the priesthood but his life spiralled downward into a state of depression. In 1961, Cy Huck was found dead alongside the railway tracks in his home town of St. Lazar, Manitoba. Père Murray arranged to have Huck's body returned to Wilcox, where he was laid to rest in the cemetery on the outskirts of town.

Another natural was Frank Germann himself, a modest man who was one of Notre Dame's most gifted athletes. With a little prodding, he details the day he shut out the barnstorming Kansas City Monarchs of the Negro Baseball Leagues. "I figured you had to throw off speed pitches to them, otherwise they were going to hit me hard," he relates. "I had a fairly good knuckle ball, which I used a lot. I had a slider and good control. If the catcher wanted it on the inside or outside corner, I could do it. Whatever, it worked because they were cursing me, swinging at the wind before the ball ever got there." The result was the stuff of legend. Frank Germann and his Wilcox team-mates blanked the famed Monarchs 1–0.

Germann's athletic prowess was in his bloodlines. His sister was a fast-ball pitcher of rare talent. "Flingin'" Frankie Germann graduated from the Wilcox sandlots to play pro ball in Chicago. His brother Vince was an NHL prospect who lost his life as a paratrooper in World War II. Frank, however, did not have professional sports ambitions, but found his niche as a teacher at Notre Dame. "I had a place I liked and wasn't anxious to give it up. I was teaching and coaching, doing the work I wanted to do."

For ten months of the year, Notre Dame College becomes home to students from across Canada and around the world, and the rink lobby is their rumpus room. Behind the end-zone view of the rink, two pool tables are in constant use, arcade video games are perpetually blinking, while a big-screen televi-sion goes largely ignored. There aren't any malls to hang out in in Wilcox so the rink becomes a meeting place and community centre. Here, even at play, students are subjected to subtle reinforcement of the high expectations that come with the territory.

Wall of Fame in the Notre Dame rink lobby

The Wall of Fame is a photo gallery of graduates proudly displayed like a family album. The focal point of the wall is a large Maple Leaf with dedi-cations to Father David Bauer, the Canadian National Team and Père Murray. On its left wing are more than one hundred freeze-frames of Notre Dame alumni who ad-

vanced to university glory, most with full U.S. scholarships. Pictured on the right side are more than fifty grads who proceeded to professional careers, from the Metz brothers to the Maple Leafs' "Hound Line" of the mid-eighties that featured Russ Courtnall, Wendel Clark and Gary Leeman. Another role model smiling from the wall is fourteen-year NHL veteran James Patrick.

Two weeks after my visit to Wilcox, Patrick and the Calgary Flames were preparing to open the NHL season on "Hockey Night in Canada" against the Canucks in Vancouver. Three former Hounds would be in action at G.M. Place: Patrick and Todd Hlushko of the Flames, and Russ Courtnall of the Canucks. I approached Patrick, the former Olympian and New York Ranger, as he put the finishing touches on his game sticks prior to the morning skate. When I requested a convenient time to discuss his Notre Dame experience, Patrick set the sticks aside and fired away.

The Calgary Flames' blueliner was encouraged to attend Notre Dame by his father. It seemed like a great idea to Patrick until the autumn day in 1979 when his parents stopped at the dorm, took his luggage up to the room and departed ten minutes later. "Here I am in the middle of nowhere," recalled Patrick, a Winnipeg native. "The first couple of months I was so homesick. I resented my parents for sending me there." The resentment festered in the initial weeks as the sixteen-year-old wrestled with pangs of self-doubt as he found himself suddenly surrounded by peers with similar, and in some cases superior, skills. "I was frustrated because I didn't feel I was playing good hockey, almost jealous of other players because of how good they were," Patrick said.

The talent was imposing. Gord Kluzak, who was chosen first overall in the 1982 NHL entry draft, was a nimble six-foot three-inch two-hundred-pound defenceman who intimidated opponents with size and his teammates with raw talent. The 1979–80 Notre Dame midgets produced four other NHL

1980 Air Canada midget champions. Front row, Johnny Weisshaar (third from left), Barry MacKenzie (third from right), James Patrick (second from right); middle row, Gord Kluzak (fourth from right), Lyndon Byers (second from right); top row, Gary Leeman (third from right), Gord Sherven (second from right)

players: Brian Curran, Lyndon Byers, Gary Leeman and Gord Sherven, who would also star on Canada's National Team.

Gradually, Patrick overcame his insecurities and began to blossom in this hockey hothouse. "I still feel to this day I was a better backward skater then than I am now, because of the skills we worked on," Patrick said. "It was the first year that I had big-league coaching. Barry MacKenzie stressed the fundamentals, especially for defencemen.

The Rink

One-on-one skills, agility drills, we worked on it every day. Physically, I know I learned more than any other year playing. Mentally, it was such a growing-up experience."

There were more growing pains, such as the game in Yorkton where four future NHL players sat in the stands wearing full equipment as punishment for having beer in their room. "It was the first road trip of the year," Patrick recalled with a sheepish grin. "Three of us, Gord Kluzak, Gord Sherven and I, went to a junior game. The rest of the team got together with a couple of cases of beer. We came back to the hotel room and someone had saved us a half dozen beers. We opened them but hadn't even taken a sip when our manager, Johnny Weisshaar, walked into the room. We haven't even had a drink but we're the ones who get caught. Johnny gave us a pep talk on what a bad path we were heading down. The funny thing was we were the good ones compared to the rest of the team. The next day we played a game in Melville with two defencemen. The worst part of it was Gord Kluzak's parents and grandparents had come in for the game. We had to tell them why we weren't playing. There's no excuses or lying about something like that. I felt bad for him and I wasn't too proud of myself. Barry MacKenzie was a tough coach, especially for that age. The next day in practice, he lined up the whole team on the blueline. He'd yell, 'Patrick and Kluzak to the other end and back! Kluzak and Sherven to the other end and back! Patrick and Sherven!' This went on for twenty-five minutes while the rest of the team watched."

The combination of talent and strict discipline was almost unbeatable for the 1979–80 edition of the Hounds. Notre Dame lost only once in the entire season, against North York, at the Mac's midget tournament during the Christmas holidays. The solitary defeat, however, sounded alarm bells in the Hounds' camp. "It was the best thing possible for us," recalled Patrick. "We had a closed-door meeting. Publicly we were taking a beating because everyone said we were an all-star team from across the country. Everybody there was happy that we had lost. If a loss could be good, that was certainly one. We got a lot of things off our chest. The first half of the year we played on skill. The second half we gelled as a team… The first half I was so home-sick. The second half of the year I developed these friendships and bonds with teammates, and I look back on it now as one of the best years of my life."

Even work duty became a source of pride and team unity. The Hounds were not only in charge of defending home ice but maintaining it as well. "Each week about six guys were assigned to rink-rat duty," Patrick explained.

"There was at least one and sometimes two games a night at Notre Dame, and you had to shovel the ice between periods. There would be six guys out there with these big shovels and it would take them about two minutes to clean the ice. Then a guy would come out with a barrel and flood it. It almost got competitive. They used to time guys to see how fast they could do it. After practice, the team would have to do the ice. At the time you didn't feel like shovelling the ice, but now I look back on it as one of the truly unique experiences about the place and just one more thing that brought the team together."

Sixteen years after arriving in Wilcox as an uncertain sixteen-year-old, James Patrick still reflects a boyish enthusiasm for the institution that was a major catalyst in his hockey career. As he departed for the Flames' dressing room, Patrick recited the school mantra that the Hounds would chant while huddled around their goaltender at the outset of each game. "God of the Notre Dame clan, grant that the mother who bore me suffered to suckle a man! So help me God, no mistakes, let's go!"

In the same studio where I chatted with James Patrick, Russ Courtnall had joined Scott Russell a year earlier for a "Hockey Night in Canada" between-periods interview. In attendance that night was Courtnall's former Notre Dame coach, Barry MacKenzie. When asked about MacKenzie's influence on his hockey career, Courtnall responded with an impassioned testimonial that transcended the usual intermission fare and spoke volumes about both Courtnall and MacKenzie.

Shortly after speaking with Patrick, I reminded Courtnall of that night and how much it sounded as if MacKenzie were a father figure in his life. "My dad passed away when I was thirteen," Courtnall reflected. "I was kind of lost without him. He was not only my father but my coach. When I had Barry as a coach, it really filled a void in my life. Not that he replaced my father, but he was the closest thing that came along that was like my dad giving me confidence and encouragement. He had that effect on people."

Courtnall's father had always wanted Russ to attend Notre Dame. He'd been impressed with the development of another local player from Duncan, British Columbia, who had experienced problems in and out of the classroom before his enrolment at Notre Dame. When that youngster returned after a year in Wilcox, Courtnall's father was struck by his growth as a player and a person. "Before my dad died, he looked me in the eye and said, 'I promise you will go to Notre Dame,'" Russ recalls.

Two months later, Courtnall received a call from Notre Dame and the offer of a bursary. To this day, he is not certain if his father had laid the groundwork for the opportunity or whether it was simply a wondrous coincidence. He was only fourteen, entering Grade 9, and his mother was hesitant of now losing her son too, albeit for only the school year. They agreed to postpone his move to Notre Dame for a year, but when the school called back a few weeks later, Russ accepted. "The thing I remember most is that every time I left the rink, I felt like I needed about fifteen minutes more to get a little better. I always left the rink thinking, tomorrow I'm going to work a little harder. I just drove myself."

Despite thriving in the Notre Dame environment, Courtnall elected not to return the following year. A local coach convinced him to remain in Duncan to play for his home town. "I should have gone back and I was really thankful that I did return the year after," said Courtnall, an NHL veteran of more than nine hundred games. "I was at Medicine Hat training camp in Grade 11 and they were going to send me down to Tier II in Drumheller. My roommate was an ex-Hound, Jim Appleby, a goaltender on the national midget champions with James Patrick and Gord Kluzak. He said, 'There's no way you're going to Tier II, you're going back to school.' He dialled Notre Dame and said, 'Tell them that you want to come back.' It was the best thing that ever happened. I had a great year and learned a lot from Barry. The following year I played junior and then I was drafted in the first round."

Even after Courtnall had made it to the NHL with the Toronto Maple Leafs, he hadn't made his final visit to Notre Dame. "When Russ was with Toronto and his brother Geoff was in Washington, they both missed the playoffs," recalled Dennis Ulmer, a teacher at the school. "Just before Easter they both came back and practised with the team in the old rink. They slept on the floor in the dorm. They were like little kids happy to be home. You can imagine the impact that has on your kids"—much like the impact Barry Mackenzie had on Russ. "He was probably the best coach I ever had, along with my dad."

Wendel Clark was a product of prairie hockey long before he arrived in Wilcox. His game was cultivated over endless hours at the town rink in Kelvington, Saskatchewan, under the tutelage of his father. Les Clark is the backbone of grass-roots hockey, a convenor, coach, a jack of all trades around the local rink, which became an extension of the Clark home. Wendel was on the ice daily with his brothers Don and Kerry, bosom buddies Joe and Kory Kocur, Barry Melrose's younger brother Warren and three other Clark cousins, Neil, Rory and Darrel—nine youngsters sharing the same rink and passion for the game.

When the old rink in Kelvington was condemned, the Clarks led the community in an effort to erect a new facility. "I can remember driving the tractor as a twelve-year-old, going round and round packing the ground at the new rink site," Clark recalled. "Everything in winter revolved around the rink."

By the time Clark enrolled at Notre Dame, he had been schooled in just about every rink across Saskatchewan. "The coldest rink ever was Invermay," he laughed. "We changed lines from the dressing room. It was minus forty outside, minus forty or colder in the rink. We were too young to sit on the bench, so every two minutes they would blow a whistle so we could change. Five in and five out of the dressing room. It was just too cold to sit out there."

As a Grade 9 student at Notre Dame, Clark came in from the cold and into the intense heat of competition. "I went from a great hockey environment where we got a lot of ice time, to Notre Dame, where you got to play competitively against city kids, the best in the province. That's why I went to Notre Dame," Clark said. "That was probably the most nervous I ever was at a training camp. There were 140 guys trying out. I'd never had to try out for a team before, and the others weren't just from Saskatchewan but right across the country."

Clark survived the try-out and the trials that come with being away from home, on your own for the first time. "You learn to solve your own problems," he declared. "If you're getting picked on by one guy, you can't go home and tell your mom or have your mom visit the teacher. You learn to settle it on your own, whether you get in a fight or discuss it. One time I was walking in the dorm and a Grade 12 guy says, 'New boys aren't supposed to be in the halls during dorm jobs [housekeeping duties].' He caught me and said he was going to beat me up. We had a wrestling match and I pinned him. After that I was allowed to walk in the hallways."

There was, however, no escaping the rigid discipline and demands of coaches O'Malley and MacKenzie. "After a loss to Moose Jaw, we were riding the bus home," Clark continued. "The coaches stopped the bus about fifteen minutes away from Notre Dame. We had to take our sticks and equipment off the bus and walk the rest of the way. It was about minus twenty. It didn't really matter who we were playing because we only lost three or four times a year. Barry really judged us on our potential and how we played, not whether we won or lost. That's the way my dad was."

Coach O'Malley tried a different tactic to make an impression on Clark. "Wendel could dominate a game but he wouldn't head man the puck," O'Malley recalled. "In a playoff game in Swift Current, I gave him hell for not moving the puck. I said, you're like that guy for the Globetrotters [Meadowlark Lemon] who dribbles the ball behind his back and through his legs while his teammates are standing around reading the newspaper. I gave him the nickname 'Meadowlark' Clark."

Wendel barely recalled the moniker but his Notre Dame coaches made a lasting impression. "I think the world of both of them. I think they both could have been NHL coaches, but they're also ideal for the level they are at. For midget or junior hockey, you can't get a better coach than Barry MacKenzie because he teaches the basics. At that level, that's where you need to learn it, at fifteen or sixteen."

On my initial tour of the Notre Dame rink, Barry MacKenzie had opened the door to the weight room and said, "This is where Rod Brind'amour lived." Stories of Brind'amour's weight room exploits are legend. Teacher Wayne Morrison remembered Brind'amour returning from the Western Canadian championships and heading directly to the gym. The team departed for the Centennial Cup the following day, and on their return a week later, Brind'amour disembarked from the bus and went straight to baseball try-outs. After the workout he went back to the weight room.

Notre Dame built a Tier II national champion on the foundation of Brind'amour's indefatigable spirit. "He was team captain, on the honour roll, a 90 per cent student," former teammate Kent Manderville recalled. "He'd always be in the weight room. He still is. Everybody in the NHL knows about his work ethic. He was a house leader in the dorm, a student leader. He was the cat's ass."

Rod Brind'amour was fifteen when he left Campbell River, British Columbia, in 1985 to advance his hockey career at Notre Dame, one of the first from his home town to go that route. Since then, more than thirty Campbell River players have followed in his footsteps. "It's a small town," said Brind'amour, now an integral member of the Philadelphia Flyers. "Once you have played bantam hockey there, you have to look for somewhere else to continue to progress. You're not just going to Notre Dame to make the NHL, although that's always in the back of your mind. You're hoping for a hockey scholarship."

Although remembered for his weight-training regimen, Rod had more vivid recollections of domestic duties that became part of his daily routine. "I'll be honest, it's tough going from home where your mother cooks your meals, does the laundry and cleans up, to a school where you have to do the chores. It was our job to keep the new rink clean. The walkway from the dorms to the rink was full of mud before that area was paved. I remember watching guys track in all that mud on their shoes knowing I was the one that was going to clean it up."

Curtis Joseph also played a starring role on the 1988 Hounds as an over-age player. "Martin Kenney, the school president, said, 'If you come out here you'll get a scholarship, I guarantee it,'" related Joseph, a teammate of Brind'amour on Canada's 1996 World Cup entry as well. "I'd played three years of Tier II hockey in Ontario without a sniff. It was the best move of my hockey career. Martin Kenney didn't lie. The first exhibition game in Minot, North Dakota, I was offered a scholarship. If I hadn't gone west to Notre Dame and got that scholarship, I would have ended up as one of the better goaltenders in the beer leagues."

Scholarships aside, the 1987–88 hockey season provided a magical ride. The Hounds dominated the Saskatchewan Junior League in their inaugural season. Joseph was the league's premier goaltender, Brind'amour the Hounds' only 100-point man. Despite fourteen midget-age players on the roster, and only Joseph over eighteen years of age, Notre Dame advanced to the Western Canadian championships against the Calgary Canucks for an unforgettable seven-game series.

The Canucks won three of the first four games and seemed to have Notre Dame on the ropes. *Luctor et Emergo.* The Hounds summoned strength from Père Murray's school motto to mount a comeback. In dramatic fashion, the Hounds rebounded to tie the series, forcing a seventh game in Calgary. In the process, they had chased the Canucks' starting goaltender who seemed to buckle under the persistent heckling of the Notre Dame student body. Corey Hirsch, now a Vancouver Canuck, was called upon in relief for Calgary. "It was the first great series I was a part of," recalled Hirsch.

The prospect of completing the comeback against Hirsch and the Canucks was still daunting. "They had been 43–3 at home that year," said Joseph. "The final game was during the week. The whole school signed a petition to take the day off, teachers too, and to go to school on the weekend. They bused the entire school from Wilcox to Calgary. They took up one end of the rink. It was impressive."

The students were boisterous, but well-behaved, faces painted with red Maple Leafs. In the heat of this torrid series, Notre Dame had been dubbed a "reform school" by the Calgary coach, and "a bunch of snot-nosed punks" by Calgary players, but Père Murray's barrel chest would have swelled with pride if he had heard them bellow the national anthem prior to the seventh game. With their schoolmates roaring approval, Notre Dame took a 3–2 lead into the final minute, but there would be one final moment of reckoning for the Hounds and Curtis Joseph. In a last-ditch Canucks' flurry to tie the game, the Hounds' net was intentionally dislodged. A penalty shot was awarded to Calgary.

During the Saskatchewan Hockey League's regular season, shoot-outs had been implemented to break ties. Joseph had posted a remarkable stretch of allowing one goal in twenty-five attempts. So the odds were with Notre Dame—and perhaps divine support, too. As Joseph prepared for the oncoming shooter, the Notre Dame fans began to chant, "Père be there." It was as if the spirit of Père Murray was alongside him in the net. Joseph turned back the Calgary shooter to preserve the victory and provide the climactic moment of a championship season. "Somebody was on our side for sure that day," reflected Joseph, who backstopped Notre Dame to the Centennial Cup title the following week.

Like Terry O'Malley, Barry MacKenzie was a member of Father David Bauer's National Team program in the sixties. "I'm an idealist, that's why I went with Bauer in the first place," says the former Canadian defenceman. However, his memories of the National Team are bittersweet, such as the 1964 Olympic medal lost not on the ice but in the boardroom. "I remember going to the rink in Innsbruck to get our medal. There had been a three-way tie for second place. The tie-breaking rule was goals for and against among the final four teams. That was the rule before the Olympics and since, but somehow during those games the rules changed. We had only lost 3–2 to Russia and thought we had won silver, at least bronze. We sat outside the rink on the bus for a half hour before Father Bauer came out to tell us we were fourth."

MacKenzie had a brief NHL career totalling six games with the Minnesota North Stars during the 1968–69 season. "I tried to play in the

NHL because that's the dream of every Canadian youngster who laces on skates," MacKenzie says. "The North Stars had a lot of good defencemen at the time. I had told Wren Blair [North Stars general manager] that I would rather be down in the minors for a year to establish myself than bounce back and forth, but that's exactly what happened the first year. Finally, I met Blair late in the season and asked him what was going on. He snapped, saying, 'You guys with an education are a pain in the ass. You'll never play another game here as long as I'm in charge.' Quite frankly, I don't sit around worrying about it. You have to get on with your life. I felt I was capable of playing longer but I don't have a lot of regrets."

His hockey experiences shaped the philosophy of education at Notre Dame, a school that features hockey but is not simply a hockey school. "Hockey is a teaching tool, another place to learn about life," says Mac-Kenzie, who has been at Notre Dame for nineteen years, the last five as president. "You can develop your hockey talents and get an education at the same time. Despite our success, there are only forty or fifty kids making a living out of the game who have graduated from the school. So the message is, make sure you have something else. Hockey is great, pursue the dream, but you have to have your character and work ethic to fall back on."

Tacked onto MacKenzie's bulletin board, above his desk, is an inspirational message entitled the "Road of Life." His road of life was not expected to pass through Wilcox. In fact, he used to tease his former National teammate Terry O'Malley about his commitment to the little school on the prairie. In 1966, that all changed when MacKenzie was driving across the country and stopped in Wilcox for a visit with Père Murray. "Talk about God's hand leading you," MacKenzie says. "I told my wife we should stop by the school with the old priest. We pulled into town on a Sunday morning and parked outside the church. Père was giving his sermon. Fifteen minutes after mass, Père introduced us in the dining hall. Then we spent time in his office. He poured glasses of scotch with no water and just kept telling stories. As we were leaving Wilcox, my wife went silent and then I noticed a tear coming down her cheek. When I asked what was wrong she said, 'I have never met such a beautiful person in my life.' At the time we had a house in Sudbury and a cottage on Manitoulin Island. She never would have agreed to come to Wilcox had it not been for that meeting."

For nearly two decades, MacKenzie has sustained Père Murray's dream. He is not a Father in the sense Athol Murray was, but he has adopted the mantle of surrogate father at a school run like a large family. "*In loco parentis*, in place of parent," he says, evoking a theme of his leadership. "So many kids don't get the parenting they need."

Also on the tackboard is a memorial card for Jeff Batters, a Notre Dame graduate who died in a car accident only weeks earlier. "When he played for me in Grade 11, everybody thought I was nuts, but I saw something in him I liked. He became a good player. When I heard of his death, there was no question that someone from Notre Dame should be there." MacKenzie not only attended the funeral but delivered the eulogy. He has become a father figure, drill sergeant, teacher, mentor and, to many Notre Dame players who graduated to professional hockey, still the finest coach they have ever had. Russ Courtnall's rich endorsement of his leadership is the best reward for his life's work, although he freely admits, "We never know how we impact on the kids." Nevertheless, MacKenzie has walked the road of life with purpose and in Notre Dame has reached a destination with special meaning. "The place consumes you," he says proudly.

Before leaving Wilcox, I inspect the greying, weathered Metz farmhouse that has been boarded up since Nick Metz died in 1991. Earlier in the day, I had spoken with eighty-year-old Don Metz from his home in Regina, but his hockey memories were locked up almost as tightly as the old family homestead.

I tried to rekindle his recollections of the Maple Leafs' 1942 Stanley Cup victory in which Toronto rallied from a three-game deficit to defeat the Detroit Red Wings. "I only played in four games in that series," he said modestly, overlooking the fact that those were the four games the Leafs won. "I played on a line with [Syl] Apps and [Bob] Davidson."

"Do you have a personal highlight from the series?" I asked. After a brief pause, Metz replied, "Just that we won." With prompting he volunteers another minor detail. "I guess I scored a hat trick in Game 5." Not only did Metz fire three goals, but he assisted on two others to pace Toronto in a 9–3 rout. The series turned around on Toronto coach Hap Day's controversial decision to replace Gordie Drillon, his leading goal-scorer, with Metz. Day's move looked even more astute in the sixth game when Metz opened the scoring with a goal that represented the game-winner in a 3–0 victory to tie the series. Two nights later Toronto beat Detroit 3–1, capping the greatest comeback in Stanley Cup history. It was the first of five Stanley Cup triumphs for Don Metz. Brother Nick was also a valuable member of four Cup-winning Maple Leaf teams.

Success for this hockey foot soldier came under the leadership of two dynamic commanders. "Both Père Murray and Conn Smythe were strong personalities," Metz said. "They had strong ideas and always followed through. They were also great army men."

Metz served a seven-year tour of duty with the Maple Leafs before returning to Wilcox. "There was nothing else for me in Toronto," he said. Fellow Maple Leaf and Notre Dame graduate Garth Boesch followed suit, informing Smythe, "I'm going back to the family farm in Saskatchewan where I can make some real money."

A few years ago, a handful of Notre Dame students broke into the old farmhouse as a prank. Terry O'Malley summoned Metz. "I told Don we had the culprits and they were going to apologize," O'Malley told me. "One of the kids was admiring a 1931 NHL rulebook he had found in the house. Don started to chastise them but then he stopped to ask the kid if he wanted to keep the book. He didn't give them hell like I was hoping he would. Instead he let the kid keep the rulebook and gave the farm lot to the school."

Barry MacKenzie, Terry O'Malley and the Tower of God

Just across Canada Park from the Metz homestead, adjacent to St. Augustine's Church, is the Tower of God, my final stop in Wilcox. It is a sixty-foot landmark conceived by Père Murray to honour the great religions of the world and to reflect his conviction that these faiths worship the same God. Within the fifteen-by-fifteen-foot chamber at the base of the Tower are walls dedicated to the Moslem, Christian and Hebrew creeds. Each wall is decorated with articles of faith and sacred quotations. The fourth wall is the "Wall of Great Affirmations," with passages from the world's greatest leaders and philosophers, from Plato and Aristotle to Lincoln and Churchill, acknowledging the presence of God.

It is a place for thoughtful deliberation, self-examination and escape, not only for the most devout but for young minds seeking direction. University of Regina coach Kevin Dickie is still drawn to it. "Before each of the ten games I coached here, I would go to the Tower of God," he says. "It was a superstition but I did it for the right reasons. I would spend ten minutes there thinking about life in general. If I ever have ten minutes before coming to one of Notre Dame's games, I'll go there."

For Kent Manderville, it was a sanctuary. "You're in a dorm room that's not very big, sharing with three other people," Manderville explains. "There were times you needed space. I'd go to the Tower of God or into St. Augustine's just to get away. It was another aspect of life I had never considered until I went to Notre Dame."

Rod Brind'amour still carries inspiration garnered from his visits to the Tower of God. One quote in particular has given him guidance and motivation in his hockey career and life. "Every human life is insignificant unless you, yourself make it great." The quotation is displayed in his home, on the wall of his "hockey room," alongside photographs of Barry MacKenzie and another man Brind'amour has never met, but who has had a profound impact on his life and hockey career—Father Athol Murray.

4 Harbour Station
Saint John, New Brunswick

Scott Russell

It eluded us then, but that's no matter—tomorrow we will run faster, stretch out our arms further . . . And one fine morning—
—F. Scott Fitzgerald, *The Great Gatsby*

IT IS A STRANGE PARADOX that presents itself as soon as the puck is dropped on a Tuesday night at Harbour Station. The American Hockey League Binghamton Rangers face the Saint John Flames in Canada's oldest incorporated city in a rink that is brand spanking new. The fans do not seem to notice. The arena is packed, nearly six thousand strong, and three hours of hockey celebration are about to unfold, something that will not be taken for granted in New Brunswick's largest city. This place is something they have waited for, it seems, forever.

Harbour Station, completed in 1993, is a state-of-the-art hockey rink and the pride of historic Saint John

Elsie Wayne is six rows up just to the left of the home team Flames' bench. This grey-haired human dynamo is the Progressive Conservative member of Parliament for Saint John and was for a dozen years before that the most popular mayor the city has ever known. She has a nine-year-old hockey-playing grandson who scored four goals the other night, but currently Elsie is engrossed in the fortunes of the Flames.

"C'mon, c'mon!" she

barks as the home team ventures into the Binghamton zone. Wayne is wearing a Flames white and red jersey with the number 93 embroidered on the back to recall the year of the team's inception. The jersey has pinks cuffs and just above the number on the reverse side, her name is emblazoned in bold red letters: ELSIE. She is a season ticket-holder and comes home from Ottawa as often as she can to see Saint John play. It is somewhat of a patriotic duty for her. "I get worried about what's happening to our game when we see so much of it going to our competitiors south of the border. It's a Canadian game. Something that we as a people have supported over the last centuries and we are going to do it again," she says.

This rink is making that possible in Saint John. Until 1993 and the AHL's arrival, the city had no professional hockey team and nothing like the splendour of Harbour Station. The colours are pleasing, with the dark green seats of the upper bowl mixing with the blues of the lower level in subdued tones. The concourse is open behind the stands, and thousands of conversations are going on at once as folks of all ages meet. The glass sparkles like the ice, and it strikes me that this is a smaller version of the Saddledome in Calgary, where the parent club of the Flames franchise plays its games.

Elsie winks and jabs me with her elbow following a goal by Jarrod Skalde, the Saint John captain. After she leads the crowd in a celebratory dance to mark her team's success, Wayne sits down, spreads out her arms and exclaims, "We used to have to play hockey on an outdoor rink. Now we've got the luxury of this indoor palace. God in Heaven!"

The first officially recognized hockey league game played in Saint John took place exactly a century before the Flames arrived. In 1893, a four-team association involving Maritime cities was launched and games were contested in the Singer Arena. Saint John claimed its first championship in 1897–98 when the Canadian Winter Port team was victorious over its competitors in the region. The advent of the Maritime Professional League in the early 1900s proved to be a turning point in the city's hockey history. Local officials opted not to join the pro ranks, preferring the intensity of local rivalries even though the games were often reduced to exhibition status.

Rick Bowness, the coach of the New York Islanders, is painfully aware of how slight Saint John's connection to professional hockey is. Bowness was born in Moncton, New Brunswick, and his father, Bob, played in the Maritime Senior League in the 1940s and '50s, when games were more like wars at the old Saint John Forum. "Every night was fights. On the ice and in the stands. And the boys on top would bring their rum. They supported the hell out of it."

By his own admission, Bowness is one of the few Maritimers who made it out of the area to the National Hockey League. In parts of seven seasons with four teams, he played just under two hundred games and boasts a modest fifty-five points scored. After his playing career was over, Bowness found that coaching was his future. Before graduating to guide NHL teams in Winnipeg, Boston, Ottawa and New York, he was the bench boss of the AHL Moncton Hawks, a team that has since folded.

Standing near the boards at the Molson Centre in Montreal, Bowness put the Islanders through their paces in preparation for their game with the Canadiens, which was to be seen coast to coast on "Hockey Night in Canada." "Make sure you say hello to all the good Maritimers out there," he said over his shoulder. Considering the late acquisition of pro hockey in Saint John, Bowness quickly arrived at a logical conclusion. "They wanted to see their own. They'd support minor hockey, junior hockey, college hockey and senior hockey. They did not want to pay to see outsiders play pro hockey," he said.

This may partly explain why Saint John attached itself to local senior teams throughout its rich history in the game. The Fusiliers won provincial titles in the 1920s and were led by Jackie Keating, who spent some time with the old New York Americans of the NHL. Keating turned to coaching and helped fashion a Maritime senior championship with the Saint John Beavers in 1946. Six years later, the Beavers challenged for the Alexander Cup, emblematic of Canadian senior hockey supremacy. They advanced to the national final only to be denied by the powerful Quebec Aces, a squad coached by the feisty George "Punch" Imlach and whose star player was future Hall of Famer Jean Béliveau.

Home-town boys who played amateur hockey moved to the newly built Lord Beaverbrook Rink in 1960, and success for local teams soon followed. The intermediate Mooseheads were the talk of the town in the late sixties and early seventies. The year 1973 holds a special meaning for the people of Saint John. That season the LBR, as the rink came to be called, was packed well beyond its fire limit of 2,800 many nights as the Mooseheads skated to the national title and claimed a Hardy Cup Championship by defeating the team from Rosetown, Saskatchewan. The entire squad, made up almost exclusively of local players, is honoured in the Saint John Sports Hall of Fame.

Although there was a fascination with amateur hockey in Saint John, a jealousy was developing as local fans saw the growth in cities nearby. Halifax was awarded a franchise in the American Hockey League in 1971–72 and in its first season of operation, the club, known as the Nova Scotia Voyageurs, won the Calder Cup Championship with Larry Robinson on defence and Al MacNeil as coach. The professional game made further inroads into the Maritimes when another AHL operation in Moncton began play in 1978–79 bearing the name the New Brunswick Hawks.

In the stands at the Molson Centre, not far behind Rick Bowness, was his pal Neil MacNeil, who had brought his two kids to Montreal to see the Islanders play the Canadiens. The ulterior motive was to catch up on old times with Bowness and engage in the blarney typical of Maritimers when they are reunited. "Saint John is a blue-collar town. It has the shipyard and the pulp mills, and hockey was always a big draw. The thing is, it never had the big club that Moncton and Fredericton did over the eighties and nineties. They wanted it big," MacNeil was saying. "There was a real fierce rivalry between Moncton and Saint John but it was all at the amateur level."

MacNeil was the director of Economic Development for Saint John when it decided to take its first stab at getting a professional team in 1980. In the summer of that year, the Quebec Nordiques had just completed their first season in the NHL and were looking for a suitable location for their AHL farm club. Saint John was the perfect choice for two reasons: it was close to the team's Quebec base, and a fierce rivalry with the team in Moncton would guarantee solid attendance. Although it wasn't as large and modern as the Nordiques would have liked, the Lord Beaverbrook Rink would be acceptable as a venue for the club's first few seasons if some minor improvements were made.

What Gilles Leger, the Nordiques' general manager, and Jacques Demers, the head coach, had not anticipated was the Lord Beaverbrook Rink Trust. When the rink was built in 1960, the newspaper magnate had covered the construction cost of more than $2 million. But there were some conditions: 2,300 hours of ice time were available, 1,157 of which were to be given free to the children of the city. In addition, the rink was to be administered by a board of directors that included the mayor, school principals, the Bishop of Saint John and the city's leading industrialist, oil baron K.C. Irving. The trust made it clear that the LBR was for the youth of the area and it stipulated, "The rink is not to be used for professional hockey."

The Nordiques, eager to prove they would be a boost to Saint John's fragile economy as well as a team that young hockey players could look up to, sought a variance to the Lord Beaverbrook Rink Trust. In presenting their case to the New Brunswick Court of Queen's Bench, the team allied itself with the City of Saint John and the Attorney General of the province. They promised better lighting and seating in the arena and also stated that, should they be allowed to move in, the rink would be functional for one additional month per year. The Nordiques also hoped to sway the court by emphasizing the benefits of having a pro hockey club in the city. They cited "the presence of the Nordique organization and players in the community who would take an interest in the community, hold coaching schools and generally give an example to the youth."

The court did not side with the Nordiques, although it would have been popular for Mr. Justice Higgins to have done so. He worried about ice time being taken away from amateur players in the community and a loss in the consistency of minor league scheduling. In short, he feared the professional team would dictate to the amateur and public-school skaters when and how often they would be allowed to play. The decision of the court on July 29, 1980, was worded this way: "Permitting a professional hockey team to operate in the rink would not be in the best interest of the children of the City, who were the beneficiaries of the trust."

Neil MacNeil looked out at the Islanders buzzing around the Molson Centre ice and shook his head at the thought of the whole ordeal. "In the end, the judge ruled no way would he overturn the Trust. So the first American Hockey League franchise of the Quebec Nordiques went to Fredericton instead." It was likely the first time professional hockey had been declared illegal in a Canadian city. More importantly, it made it abundantly clear that the ancient city of Saint John desperately needed a new rink if its hockey dreams were to be fulfilled.

Underneath the stands at Harbour Station, coach Paul Baxter strides out of the Saint John dressing room and makes his way to the workbench where a few of his players are fine-tuning their sticks between periods. He grabs one of the acetylene torches, fires it up and lights a cigarette. After exhaling, he says to his Flames, "We are trying to earn their respect." It's obvious Baxter is referring to the fans who have come to see his team perform.

Baxter played with the Quebec Nordiques when they located their AHL farm team in Fredericton because of the rink problem in Saint John. He knows the people here have been patient. He also knows there is a responsibility to do well because the new Harbour Station has created huge expectations in a revitalized city. "They've waited a long time. It's the oldest city in Canada and they've got a professional team that's in the second-best professional league in the world. They take tremendous pride in the house that they built and they expect things in the house to be of value," he says.

The walls of the Flames' dressing room are decorated by Baxter's persistent message. In startling signs posted above the lockers, on doors and bulletin boards, the coach's philosophy is omnipresent. "Much has been given to you and much is expected. You have advantages that others do not. We are here to work," one sign says. Another, just beyond the entry door, carries the same sentiment in slightly different prose. "Remember your advantages and your responsibilities. You are obligated to do your best in everything you endeavour. You are further obligated to give back much more than you take."

Baxter grew up in a place called Charleswood, just outside Winnipeg. He remembers playing minor hockey outdoors because only the Winnipeg Arena and the St. James Civic Centre offered the comfort of indoor artificial ice. "It was simple, warmer than thirty below you played, colder than thirty below you didn't and we're not talking wind chill," he chuckles. Baxter came out of Charleswood to distinguish himself as a rugged grinder in the World Hockey Association and later in the NHL with Quebec, Pittsburgh and Calgary. Along the way, he believes, the most valuable lesson he learned was the value of an honest day's work.

Now coaching in the AHL's state-of-the-art arena that has been painstakingly designed for his team and carrying the hopes of the community in which it plays, Baxter is moved by the similarities between the fans and the young ambitious athletes. He relies on a description of Saint John and its people that strikes an increasingly familiar chord. "They're a blue-collar town and I say that in a very positive way. They know how to work, they know how to battle, and they do a lot of the things we want our players to learn to do. It's a great fit because the people in Saint John know how to put in a strong day's work."

Until the arrival of the Flames in 1993, the most important achievement in the history of Saint John hockey was the triumph of the Senior Vitos in the Allan Cup final of 1992. Playing in the aging and inadequate Lord Beaverbrook Rink, the Vitos were owned by local restaurateurs Nick and Peter Georgoudis. They had a roster heavily laden with imported talent. Still, the team was followed closely by local fans, and before a jubilant crowd at

the LBR they captured the Canadian Senior AAA Championship over the Stony Plain Eagles of Alberta. It was the last season the Vitos played because, as an amateur operation, the club was finding it increasingly difficult to finance a competitive line-up.

The Saint John Vitos won the 1991–92 Allan Cup at the Lord Beaverbrook Rink

Paul Baxter extinguishes his cigarette with a swift twist of the sole of his shoe. Before making his way back to the Flames' locker room, intent on making a short but inspirational address to his players, he states what is becoming obvious. "This city supported senior hockey very well. But that wasn't what they wanted. They wanted a professional hockey club."

Attracting a professional team was the key if Saint John was going to have a brand-new arena. Without a permanent hockey tenant, any new sports facility in Saint John was sure to be a flop, and yet the rink had to be multipurpose because the city of 125,000 had no place to house the other concerts and events that might normally be expected to come to a centre this size. With the LBR already in place and the capital cost taken care of, justifying a modern rink in tough economic times was difficult.

Gord Thorne has been around hockey in Saint John for half a century and is the president of the Flames. He remembers following the Senior Beavers when he was a kid as they played in the old Forum against the likes of the Quebec Aces. "We didn't always have the money to go to the games because it was fifty cents or a dollar, but it was as exciting as hell to listen to them on radio."

Thorne, like most other hockey fans in Saint John, grew up waiting and hoping for the arrival of the pro game in his city. He recalls a blitz put on by radio station CFBC that attempted to raise money for a feasibility study into a new arena. In one day in 1978, callers pledged $30,000, revealing the ravenous appetite of locals for a new rink. The study was never undertaken and the faithful, like Gord Thorne, were devastated. "It got to one point in the 1980s when we thought we'd never get a rink in Saint John," he says.

This is where Elsie Wayne comes in. Brash and outspoken, she was elected mayor in 1983 and almost immediately revealed an ability to be both outrageous and courageous in defence of her city. Wayne is a civic booster, a hockey fanatic who is an even bigger fan of Saint John. It rankled the aggressive mayor and other city councillors that Moncton and Fredericton had professional hockey teams but their community did not. The problem was obviously the lack of an appropriate rink, but that was about to change.

In the mid-eighties, city council decided it was time to act and commissioned Market Square Corporation to continue the renaissance of the city's downtown core with a first-class sports and entertainment facility in mind. Harbour Station was designed by PBK, a company from Burlington, Ontario, that had overseen the construction of new arenas in Red Deer, Alberta, and Kamloops, British Columbia. This is the same outfit that designed larger buildings such as Sask Place in Saskatoon and the Edmonton Coliseum, home to the NHL Oilers.

The result was a project that required $16 million of taxpayers' money and an additional $6 million for the infrastructure, including enclosed pedestrian walkways that connect the rink to office buildings and hotels in the urban centre. In 1991, the municipality, the province and the federal government agreed the project was worthwhile and had Harbour Station built at the threshold of historic Saint John. It was a risk, and if it failed, the financially strapped citizenry would foot a huge bill they could scarcely afford.

Looking back, Elsie Wayne has no regrets and says she never doubted the ability of Harbour Station to succeed. "Everybody loves it, I wanna tell you," she says, hardly taking her eyes away from the ice. "We were looking at the time at a deficit of about $800,000 a year. It never reached that whatsoever. Last year we had a deficit of some $200,000 that had to be picked up by the city, and I think you'll find that it will break even pretty soon."

Since it was built, Harbour Station has attracted Garth Brooks, the Tragically Hip and the Lipizanner Stallions and has become the most popular entertainment facility in the Maritime region. It was, however, constructed to be the perfect hockey rink, with six thousand seats, and it needed a professional team to fulfil that ambition.

Al Coates leaned out of a private box at the Saddledome in Calgary and drew on the contents of a huge paper coffee cup. Down below, his team was carving up the ice under the direction of head coach Pierre Page. The general manager of the NHL Flames appeared more than a touch uneasy in the morning hours of game day. His low-scoring and injured troop had been struggling of late and they were about to face the Stanley Cup champion Colorado Avalanche in just a few hours.

"We led the charge back to the AHL as a place to develop young players," Coates was saying as he pointed to goalie Dwayne Roloson. The native of Simcoe, Ontario, played last year in Saint John with Calgary's minor league affiliate. The parent club has an abundance of youngsters on its current roster who started the present season in New Brunswick. It gives Al Coates both concern and comfort. American Hockey League players are generally youthful and inexperienced, and too many of them on one NHL team can mean trouble. On the other hand, if they can find a way to be competitive, there is tremendous hope for the future.

Coates was the assistant general manager of the Flames when the club decided to move its farm team from Salt Lake City in the International Hockey League to Saint John before the 1993–94 season. At the time, there were American Hockey League teams in Halifax, Moncton, Fredericton and St. John's, Newfoundland. They were the minor league operations of Quebec, Winnipeg, Montreal and Toronto respectively. Coates and the Flames were attracted by the new rink and the potential for rivalry in the one major Maritime centre that did not have pro hockey. "All of the teams were directly affiliated with National League partners, all wearing the parent team's logos, so it was a miniature version of the National Hockey League centrally located in the Maritimes. It was perfect."

Elsie Wayne had recounted sending Al Coates through a series of hoops before putting a stamp of approval on Calgary's professional hockey organization for her city. "When Al came to see me about bringing the Flames here, I said we want a team that is going to go out in the community, work with it and do things. He said, 'Elsie, in Calgary we gave $6 million to minor hockey. How's that?' I said, 'Well, that's a start!'"

Coates smiled broadly as he remembered his dealings with the protective mayor of Saint John, as she was then. "She's one of the world's great cheerleaders. I just love her because she never has a bad day. Just like [late Calgary Flames coach] Bob Johnson. She never has a bad day in her life it seems."

What impressed Coates more directly was the desire of the people in Saint John to have top-flight hockey in their new rink. Almost immediately 3,400 season ticket packages were sold, a total unheard of in the other Atlantic franchises. The hunger for professional hockey was obvious and that meant a stable future for the NHL team's talent pool.

Shrewd hockey man that he is, Coates also knew the players would become instant celebrities in Saint John and would respond positively to the intense scrutiny of the adoring community. "There's absolutely no place you can hide in that city if you're playing for the Saint John Flames. Everybody knows who you are and there's pressure for you to succeed as a person exactly as there is in Calgary."

Along with Elsie Wayne and Gord Thorne, Al Coates dropped the first puck at Harbour Station when it opened its doors on October 19, 1993, and the home-town Flames battled to a 1–1 overtime tie with the Adirondack Red Wings. In the time that has passed since, he has seen Saint John develop into Atlantic Canada's most successful AHL franchise. The team averages better than five thousand fans per game and is consistently competitive; the rink has hosted the first AHL All Star game played in Canada. All in all, it looks like Coates and the Calgary organization made the right choice for their future development.

Professional hockey is a precarious proposition in Canada these days and Al Coates knows that better than most. The NHL Flames are constantly upgrading the Saddledome to meet the increasing needs for revenue in a burgeoning NHL that requires cash flow. Calgary struggles to keep its expanding payroll manageable in order to survive in one of the league's smaller markets. Coates knows that the Alberta city went without big-league hockey for many years and it is worth protecting. He understands the same to be true on a smaller scale in Saint John and doesn't hesitate to remind the people there how important the new rink and the Flames are to the community's economic viability.

"They should never take that franchise and the American Hockey League for granted and what the people have gone through to make that happen. It's not unlike how we as Canadian fans should appreciate the six remaining teams in this country. We've already seen two cities lose their teams. When it happens, when it's gone, it's too late and people need to wake up and have an appreciation of what they have when they have it, rather than feel sorry about it after it's gone," he said.

Elsie Wayne has a reverence for hockey players. Although she says she never played herself, she acts out the game's twists and turns in a constant gyration from her perch less than fifteen feet from the ice surface. They are the movements of someone who knows and loves hockey. Elsie talks all the time but never allows her glance to stray from the action. Her boys are ahead of Binghamton in the second period, and an obvious pride glows from her naturally exuberant face.

Motioning to the ice as if to prove a point, Wayne starts to sound like a general manager defending Saint John's record as a producer of talent. "You look at our hockey history and you'll find a lot of our players move up the ladder right to the top. Gordie Drillon and the rest of them," she says confidently.

The attachment to Saint John is a stretch. The late Gordie Drillon, the only player born in one of the three Maritime provinces to be inducted into the Hockey Hall of Fame, is actually a native of Moncton. Saint John allows itself to claim the former Toronto Maple Leaf and Montreal

Elsie Wayne, the dynamic former mayor of Saint John, now sits as a member of Parliament. She is a Flames season-ticket holder

Canadien, however, because he played a season of senior hockey there in the 1930s. Drillon also retired to Saint John after his playing career ended following the 1942–43 season.

New York Islander head coach Rick Bowness remembered Drillon as a jubilant man. "He was one of my dad's best friends," said Bowness. "He'd come and spend every summer with us. He never had any kids so we became his kids too."

As a high-scoring right-winger, Drillon played seven seasons in the NHL, the majority with the Leafs, where he helped Toronto win a Stanley Cup in 1942. His prolific touch around the net became his legacy, and he captured the Art Ross trophy as the NHL's leading scorer in the 1937–38 season with twenty-six goals and a total of fifty-two points. What has guaranteed Gordie Drillon's longevity in National Hockey League folklore is the fact that he was the last Toronto Maple Leaf to win the league's scoring championship. Half a century's worth of legend seems a worthwhile achievement for Saint John to stake a claim to.

New Brunswickers who have made a huge impression at the highest level of hockey are few and far between. Aside from Drillon's, the name that stands out most clearly is that of Danny Grant. In the 1974–75 season, when playing with the Detroit Red Wings, Grant distinguished himself as a fifty-goal scorer, a feat that was still considered rare at the NHL level. Grant played thirteen years in the league with four teams and won a Stanley Cup with Montreal while accumulating an eye-catching 536 career points. But Saint Johners cannot make him their own—he is a proud native of the provincial capital of Fredericton.

The number of players who have had modest NHL success and who list Saint John as their home is legion. Reg Sinclair spent three seasons with Detroit and the New York Rangers, scoring ninety-two points in the 208 big-league games he played. Jackie Keating, who later coached the senior Saint John Beavers, had two seasons of play with the New York Americans. In the post-expansion era, Neil Nicholson caught on for parts of four campaigns with the Oakland Seals and New York Islanders.

Yvan Vautour's career turned out to be more extensive. Born in Saint John, Vautour played his minor hockey at the Lord Beaverbrook Rink before leaving to make a name for himself in major junior hockey in Laval, Quebec. There, he was a linemate of Mike Bossy, the Hall of Famer who went on to score fifty goals in nine consecutive seasons with the New York Islanders. Vautour was drafted by the Isles along with Bossy and over the course of six years in the league posted fifty-nine points. After toiling in the AHL for some time, he returned to Saint John to play and coach with two senior teams, the Schooners and Vitos.

Just down the road from Saint John is the town of Sussex, and its most admired hero is Mike Eagles, who continues to distinguish himself as one of the NHL's hardest-working defensive specialists. There is also Andrew McKim, a finalist as the Canadian major junior player of the year in 1990, who may still get his chance in the big leagues. Aside from these skaters and a few others, the game's faithful in Saint John tend to recall the achievements of individuals who played in local and regional leagues when boasting of their hockey history.

At Harbour Station, the current players who eagerly jump over the boards for the Flames are a reflection of the five thousand or so patrons in the cushy seats above. For both groups, the dream of professional hockey is just beginning to bloom and hopes are extremely high. The AHL is a minor league, but it is the major development ground for young talent on its way to the top. The warriors are young and each has an abiding wish to move on, away from Saint John and to the greater promise of the National Hockey League.

Paul Baxter of Charleswood, Manitoba, coached the Flames in the 1995–96 season

Coach Paul Baxter knows that this characteristic of his charges makes the hockey exciting and guarantees enthusiastic crowds at the rink. "The players have an opportunity to thrive and develop and to understand what it takes to win. When that happens they'll be ready for the National Hockey League," he says.

A young red-haired defenceman named Marc Hussey from Chatham, New Brunswick, patrols the Saint John blueline with considerable poise, denying most of the Binghamton Ranger attackers before they organize. Standing six foot four and weighing 210 pounds, Hussey has all the right attributes to become a solid, stay-at-home defender in professional hockey. He is short on flash and dash but he hits hard, skates well and is serious about his job. He is hungry to make an impression and there is no better time than the present. The big team in Calgary has lost some of its regular rearguards. Zarley Zalapski, James Patrick and Steve Chiasson are out due to injury. The organization's head scout, Nick Polano, sits in the Harbour Station press box and surveys the action with a view to finding NHL reinforcements. Hussey can barely keep his focus.

Earlier in the day, at historic Fort Howe, which overlooks the harbour city, Hussey talked of his ambitions. "It would mean the world to me," he said, when asked about the personal significance of playing in the National Hockey League. "I've been working at this for twenty-two years of my life and I'm only twenty-two years old."

There was a desperation in his voice as he spoke the words and it is detectable now in his movements as I watch him on the ice. With his team leading, Hussey is playing it safe, taking care of business but somehow too afraid of messing up to really stand out. Perhaps he thinks his room for error here is too slight to risk flamboyant play. Maybe he has already deduced that his teammate, a young Finnish player named Sami Helenius, is the one Polano has his eye on for immediate promotion to Calgary.

Hussey has played two full seasons past junior hockey. In 1994–95, he had eleven games with the St. John's Maple Leafs of the American League before he decided to get himself some international experience and joined Canada's national team. The Flames spotted him at the Olympic squad's training facility in Calgary and signed him as a free agent to play the next season in Saint John. Part of Hussey's attractiveness to the organization was his place of birth. Being a New Brunswick native, he had fan appeal, something the developing AHL franchise could use to sell tickets.

That first season with the minor league Flames went well. Hussey provided leadership, maturity and thirty-one points from the blueline. In addition, there were 120 penalty minutes in the sixty-eight games he played, proving that the Flames' number 5 was not to be messed with. The fans at Harbour Station warmed to Hussey because he was the closest thing they had to a native son. He continues to return the affection, all the while wishing he were playing much farther west. "If you're going to play in the Maritimes, Saint John is the place to be because this is a good old blue-collar hockey town," he says.

Like all the young players in the American Hockey League, Marc Hussey must continue to have faith in his ability to find a way out of here. Harbour Station is a beautiful rink, the stands are full most nights and he is one of the crowd's favourites. The problem is that time is marching on, and at twenty-two years of age, Hussey should have made it to the big team by now. Watching his sturdy strides and piercing eyes, I remember the last thing he told me as we looked down on the rink from the historic citadel. "I've been thinking about this since I was really young," he said. "It's gonna be a dream come true and I'm sure it'll happen someday soon."

For some players, someday has already happened and may come again. It could be the case for Scott Fraser of Moncton, New Brunswick. He's a twenty-four-year-old forward with a nice scoring touch. Earlier in the season, Fraser was traded to the Flames from the Fredericton Canadiens, Saint John's fiercest AHL rival. Going the other way was David Ling, a diminutive forward and proud Prince Edward Islander who was once named Canada's top junior player. Again, the Flames considered the advantages of having another native of the home province on their roster, even though Fraser is three years older than Ling.

In Fraser's second season as a pro, the Montreal Canadiens took a liking to his aggressive style, and he was promoted to the NHL line-up with a chance to catch the eye of its fiery coach, Mario Tremblay. He stuck for fifteen games but the bruising forward could not produce at a rate anywhere near his Fredericton totals from the year before. Nor could he duplicate the free-wheeling ease he once knew as a college sensation at Dartmouth.

Fraser did score in his first trip to the National Hockey League. That initial goal, that breakthrough that all hockey players visualize even as they first handle a stick, happened, strangely enough, against the Calgary Flames. More importantly, it happened at hockey's acknowledged shrine, the Montreal Forum, and in front of a national television audience. "It seems so far away," Fraser said wistfully on the morning of game day. Recalling what he once thought was the watershed is not an easy thing for him to do. Not knowing whether the opportunity will come again is even harder.

Against the Rangers, with a team he has played only a few games for, Scott Fraser is igniting the Harbour Station crowd. The game is not nearly through and already he has a hat trick to his credit. The trade for David Ling looks awfully good to the partisan crowd at the festive rink. Finally, an exciting home-grown talent they can hang their hats on. Someone the kids can look up to and model themselves after. Little do they know that Scott Fraser is excelling on the ice as part of his desperate plot to escape Saint John.

"Every once in a while I think about scoring my first goal on 'Hockey Night in Canada,'" Fraser admitted earlier. "It just drives me to work that much harder to get back up there." While he enjoys playing close to his home, Scott Fraser has ambition beyond these parochial borders. His greatest achievement will be for Calgary to take him away from all this adulation, as appreciated as it is. I wish I could tell him what I already know. The Flames' general manager, Al Coates, had confided in me that he intended to give Fraser another NHL chance after the All Star break.

In the American Hockey League, the promise of the game motivates the players more than the money does. Some understand this completely and willingly live within those limitations. Jarrod Skalde's visions of million-dollar contracts and lasting immortality in the Hockey Hall of Fame are fading rapidly. He is almost twenty-six years old now and, in six full seasons since being drafted in the second round, twenty-sixth overall by the New Jersey Devils, Skalde has bounced around. He has played for three different NHL teams, toiled in another three American League cities and spent time in the nether regions of the International Hockey League with Cincinnati, San Diego and Las Vegas.

Being the captain of the Saint John Flames is an honour for Skalde but it is also a curse. It means he is revered for his ability to lead and counsel younger players. It further suggests that his development time is nearing its end and that he will remain a minor-leaguer for a large portion of his career.

Born in Niagara Falls, Ontario, Skalde began to play in the late seventies at the Stanford Arena in that city and returns there every summer. "It looks like a barn with a loop on it," he says. "I go back to skate and I walk up the little ramp to the ice thinking nothing at all has changed from the time I was nine years old."

There have been many changes, as well as many victories, on the way to Harbour Station for this swift-skating forward. The most important was likely a Memorial Cup championship won with the Oshawa Generals in 1990. With current Philadelphia Flyer superstar Eric Lindros as a teammate, Skalde helped the Generals defeat the Kitchener Rangers in a dramatic double overtime at Hamilton's Copps Coliseum. Even in the midst of the great celebration that day, he sensed a fork in the road. "It's a bit of a confusing feeling after you win," Skalde says. "You go so far and you don't know which way to turn."

Full of hope following that Canadian Junior championship and on the heels of a promising draft selection, he went to the Devils camp in the fall of 1990. New Jersey liked his hustle and his skating style but he lasted only a single game in the NHL although he recorded an assist in that first outing. Skalde was sent to Jersey's AHL farm club in Utica and three games later was back with the OHL Generals to mature as a player. From there a trade to the Belleville Bulls was followed by twenty-seven more games with the Devils and moves to organizations in Anaheim and subsequently Calgary. Jarrod Skalde has forty-eight games and seven NHL goals to his credit to go along with a foggy understanding of why he has not graduated to the big leagues. He still possesses a wonder for the game in spite of all that has and has not unfolded for him. "The intangibles that happen," he says. "You can't describe them or predict them."

Skalde is a fan of his new home rink in Saint John and the feeling is mutual. They love him here because he scores, on average, a point per game and finds time for the community when he has a chance. He talks enthusiastically of the arena's openness, the excitement and the noise level. When he scores against the Rangers, the crowd erupts and confirms his place as an adopted idol in what was once a place starved for this brand of hockey. Skalde knows the importance of his role and refuses to let his ambition minimize the impact of the team he plays for in this setting. "People are very proud of this club. Everyone feels that they've contributed in some way and deserve this rink and this organization."

As he leads the Flames to the ice for the third period of play, Skalde marches briskly by and pumps his fist at the applauding people who stand above the ramp to the ice. With short, strong bursts from his skates, he picks up speed on the freshly flooded playing surface and circles the end Saint John will defend for twenty more minutes. His NHL hopes may be fading but he understands he can help with those of the younger players. "That's their dream and no one is going to deny them," Skalde says. "I think that rubs off on the older guys. It's why it's such a great league to be playing in because you can keep your enthusiasm about the game."

Harbour Station comes alive again with the drop of the puck. The Flames are leading by a single goal with one period to play. The night has delivered excitement in abundance in this hard-hitting, fast-paced affair. Skalde is in the thick of the action and skates

Flames captain Jarrod Skalde is running out of time to make it to the NHL

tirelessly as coach Paul Baxter double shifts him in an effort to maintain an edge for the home team. The carnival-like atmosphere reveals that this arena means a great deal to these people. Watching Jarrod Skalde, I am reminded of what he told me about the rink's impact on players like him: "It's the place where dreams start and sometimes end."

The voice at the other end of the line was hesitant at first. Gordie Clark is used to the New York press hounding him at his Long Island residence. The new director of player personnel for the Islanders spends much of his time explaining why his young team is slow turning potential into points in the standings. Caution gave way to exuberance when he learned that someone was asking about his home town of Saint John. Clark, flattered that he was being contacted, obviously values the connection to New Brunswick. His origins were given away when a Maritime accent began to creep across the long-distance line. "The Saint John paper, the *Telegraph Journal*, still calls," he said. "As each move in my career happens they keep in touch. The folks back home have stuck with me quite a bit."

Clark's picture hangs in the lobby of Harbour Station as one of the honoured members of Saint John's Sports Hall of Fame. There it is, a pen-and-pencil sketch in a simple black frame, which somehow is reflective of his career as a professional hockey player. Gordie Clark played eight games in the NHL with the Boston Bruins and entered the official league records with a single assist in 1975. In his case, being an Atlantic Canadian and making it to the revered Bruins line-up was an accomplishment in itself.

Clark was born in Scotland in the early 1950s and did not begin playing hockey until he was eleven or twelve years old. He remembers being a house-leaguer and skating outdoors in the old city at a place called Rockwood Park and indoors briefly at the Saint John Forum. The brand-new Lord Beaverbrook Rink had tremendous demands on its ice time and as Clark was not an élite player or member of a "travelling" team, he did not get much time in that arena as a kid. He does remember one of the LBR's quirks and it amazes him even today. The penalty box gates, as well as the doors to the players' benches, open onto the ice surface instead of inward towards the bleachers. One can imagine a visiting team player steaming down the ice only to have the local squad throw the gate in his way. Talk about home-ice advantage. "The only other rink that I've ever seen which had gates that opened onto the ice was the old barn in Providence, Rhode Island," Clark said. "When you have that situation, there are a lot of near misses, let me tell you!"

Growing up as a hockey player in industrial Saint John in the 1960s meant following the senior teams that dominated the local sporting landscape. As a spectator in the frigid stands on countless Saturday nights, Clark developed a respect for the game played in the LBR, a rink he came to regard as a temple. "Even though it wasn't pro hockey it was where the senior league Mooseheads played," he recalled. "Guys like Earl Rice and 'Crow' Hewey were my heroes. What I remember was they all seemed to be such talented hockey players. So skilled."

In time, Clark developed a substantial measure of his own skill and turned into a speedy forward who could put the puck in the net. He graduated to the Tier II Saint John Schooners and soon caught the eye of collegiate scouts from the United States. His choice was the University of New Hampshire, and while there he became a two-time All American competing in the East Coast Athletic Conference.

At New Hampshire Clark discovered a trait he believes is common among young hockey players who come from Canada's Maritime provinces. "When I was in New Hampshire, I couldn't wait to go home for the summer," he said. His yearning to be close to Saint John would not allow him to stray too far afield in his hockey career. In fact, Clark has always stayed in the east. After New Hampshire, he played in Boston and Providence and then coached in Portland, Maine, and then Boston again before being hired by the Islanders.

"I was told by an old coach in university that Maritime players might only last a semester away from home. [They were] good hockey players that for some reason just got homesick. The same thing, I think, happens when Maritime boys go to the major juniors. They miss home. They get homesick and don't do as well as they should."

On the heels of being chosen in the seventh round in the 1972 draft by the Bruins, Clark made a connection with another easterner that had a profound effect on his professional career. In the first training camp scrimmage, he lined up against a rugged young American-born defenceman named Mike Milbury. While at New Hampshire, Clark had scrapped with Milbury, who played for Colgate University at the time. In one particular playoff game, there was a scene at centre ice. "Someone in the crowd had given me a shot and I thought it was him so I sort of flung my stick at him through the melee," he recalled. "The next year at Bruins camp we were lining up for the scrimmage and there I was on the wing. Milbury was the left defenceman and I thought... *oh my God*."

The two quickly overcame their rivalry and turned into fast friends, even rooming together for a time while both played in the Bruins organization. Milbury stuck more permanently with the big club while Clark toiled in the American Hockey League, content to stay close to home and in the game he loved. The highlight of his professional playing days came as the Maine Mariners won the 1979 Calder Cup with Clark as the marquee forward. He scored fifty goals that year and was the toast of Portland, a major star in the minor leagues.

The hockey rink has been the home base of Gordie Clark's life. In the wake of his satisfying days as a player, he took a job managing the new Portland Ice Arena in the city's downtown core. As a sideline, he originated the University of Southern Maine's varsity hockey team and became its first coach and manager. While running the rink in Portland, an old connection advanced Clark's career and eventually led him back to the NHL. Mike

Milbury had been hired to coach Boston's AHL farm team in Maine and, learning that Clark was running the arena, wondered if there was a chance his old pal might agree to be his assistant coach. The catch was there was no money to pay Clark on a full-time basis. "I told him, I don't want to go into this if all I'm gonna do is move pucks around," he said. "Milbury told me that wouldn't be the case and he stuck to his word. He's been straight with me ever since."

With a loyalty so strongly identified with hockey, Mike Milbury has since taken Gordie Clark with him most places. After he became head coach of the Bruins in 1989, Milbury elevated Clark to be his assistant. In that first year together, the pair guided their team to the Stanley Cup final against Edmonton. The Oilers, led by Mark Messier, prevailed in five games to claim their fifth championship in seven seasons, but the scrappy Bruins served notice that their hard-working tradition was still intact.

Milbury's tenure lasted only two seasons in Boston, and he left the Bruins for the relative security of coaching collegiate hockey in his native Massachusetts. Clark remained as an assistant to the incoming coach, who happened to be Rick Bowness—another Maritimer. In their only year shaping Boston's NHL strategy, Bowness and Clark led the Bruins to another winning season and knocked off Montreal in the first round of the playoffs. Although Bowness was let go after the post-season and went on to become the expansion Ottawa Senators' first coach, Gordie Clark remained in the Bruins organization as a scout.

Clark remembered walking into Harbour Station for the first time and feeling an immense pride in his city and its finally realized dream of professional hockey. "I knew it would be a good marriage if people understood what it was like to be a minor league city," he said. "In all the years of them waiting for pro hockey, I thought, as a native of the city, they should be given the chance to prove they could back it."

They did, and it came as no surprise to Clark, who had served most of his professional career in the shadows of the major league game. He reckons that Saint John, unlike some Maritime cities where minor pro hockey has come and gone, is firmly in tune with its place in the world of sport. Clark, for instance, refers to Halifax as a "Tweener" city. The Nova Scotia capital had the original American Hockey League franchise based in Canada, then lost the Voyageurs and subsequently the Citadels because of its indifferent support. "[Halifax] didn't know whether [it was] a minor league town that felt [it] should support the juniors or [a town that] wanted pro hockey.

They couldn't decide what to do because they were somewhere in between," Clark rationalized. "Saint John is the place. If the American Hockey League could stay in the Maritimes it could stay here."

As director of player personnel for the Islanders, Gordie Clark spends a great deal of time on the road. He was hired by his old pal Mike Milbury, who has also shown a devotion to Rick Bowness. Bowness is New York's new head coach, having been promoted so that Milbury can concentrate on his duties as general manager. Roots run deep for Gordie Clark, and he anxiously attempted to draw parallels between his professional experiences and those of his home town as he watched the folks congregate at Harbour Station for the first time. "I can remember walking in to the rink and as the game started, the fun that people were having was obvious. I was just so glad the people of Saint John were able to experience that excitement," he said.

It is almost as if Clark sees his own image in the glittering new arena in Saint John's downtown. Both he and the city were at one time fringe players in hockey's larger scheme of things. Both have since found a meaningful place in the game at a level that is perfectly suitable. In his first glimpse of Harbour Station, Gordie Clark's recollection is not of the game or the score but of the people, many of whom were his neighbours. "When I was there and saw people from the top down like Elsie Wayne in the stands, I understood that it was the whole city working together and saying it's time," he said with great deliberation. "It's the minor leagues but it's the major leagues to them."

Elsie Wayne's smile is growing by the minute. Her Flames are well ahead of the invaders from Binghamton and the crowd is into the game. It is a perfect opportunity for the silver-haired bundle of energy to preach with an almost religious zeal on the value of this place of hockey worship. "There are people of all ages here. It's a beautiful night out," she exclaims. "The people just love it, let me tell you!"

There is a tendency to brag about Harbour Station among those most intimately involved with the arena. Ewen Cameron is the building engineer from Campbellton, New Brunswick, and runs this rink as if it were Buckingham Palace. Fastidious by nature, Cameron's crowning achievement as a stationary engineer will be the smooth operation of Harbour Station. It is immaculate and well lit. Early on game day, the yellow Zambonis—with Irving Oil decals prominently displayed—roared to life and cruised effortlessly over the mid-morning ice. Cameron stood at the gaping end zone beyond the sparkling glass and declared this region has never seen the likes of the beautiful rink. "The people of Halifax are jealous and the people of Fredericton are jealous. It's quite a spot, and there's no doubt a heckuva reputation has developed."

Cameron and his crew learned the ins and outs of the rink's most important feature from the late Doug Moore, the originator of Jet Ice. Jet Ice is a chemical process involving water purification that ensures a harder and faster playing surface. Moore's reputation in the field led him to travel the world and become a sort of ice guru called in to solve the problems of slushy rinks in heavily used buildings such as New York's Madison Square Garden and Montreal's aging Forum. He instituted referees' ice reports to gauge the success of his work as he constantly sought to provide what could be called a level playing field for the game.

"When we built this building, we took three guys who were green and we taught them the Doug Moore way so there could be no bad attitudes," Cameron said. "They say even our practice ice is better than game ice in almost any other rink." Looking down to the milk-white surface from the other side of the glass, I could not see a rut or a hole where the edge of a skate might catch and cause a player injury. The ice was like a sheet of marble with veins of red and blue, and Cameron could not take his eyes away from it.

The statistical capabilities of the rink spilled from his lips as we sat in the corner of the empty stands and took in the otherwise silent expanse. "We've melted games out of here in two hours in order to get a trade show in at four in the morning," he said. "We can take three thousand lower bowl seats out as well as glass and ice in six hours." Cameron emphasized that 350,000 patrons came here in the building's first year, that the Flames have the AHL attendance record for Canadian teams and that in 1994 this building led the league in sell-outs. There are stories of Rita MacNeil's performance here, the Rankin Family, Don Messer's Jubilee and many others. But the most important feature for him is that the place is accessible to all because, in many ways, Harbour Station defeats the things that make other hockey rinks forbidding places. "The bathrooms are clean and therefore the older generation just loves to come here," he said.

With little time to spare for idle chit-chat, Cameron was eager to get on with preparing his palace for hockey in just a few hours. Before he marched off to his office just behind the Zamboni entrance, he got out what he really wanted to say about the place. "This building is the show," he deadpanned.

"You might as well say it's longshoreman's night here most of the time, it's such a festive atmosphere." Imagining the arena full is not difficult. There are two tiers of seats and they seem very close to the ice surface. Cameron added that some Saint Johners have a small-town attitude and are not fully aware of what a prize this facility is. "They still think the upper bowl is the boonies," he claimed. Then he gave the most impressive statistic about the arena from a hockey perspective. "There's no seat here that's more than a hundred feet from centre ice." As I visualized the far reaches of the Molson Centre in Montreal and Vancouver's G.M. Place, Harbour Station suddenly became a near perfect theatre for hockey.

The Saint John Flames. Ambitious young players at home in Harbour Station

She is doing the macarena not more than ten feet from the Flames' bench, and coach Paul Baxter takes the time to cast his glance her way. He allows himself a little grin as he thinks of his club's biggest fan. Then he turns his attention to the approaching players and tries to figure out what to say to them during the time-out. Elsie Wayne is in the spotlight again as the music blares from Harbour Station's giant speakers attached to the scoreboard at centre ice. A break in the action means time for the member of Parliament from Saint John to make a little hay. Hockey, you see, has only one rival in this region of the country and that's good old-fashioned politics. Wayne is on the hustings every time she takes her seat in the rink.

In America, political rallies and meetings are traditionally held in large hotels. Future presidents accept nominations to stand for office at giant convention centres in Chicago or Los Angeles or other such venues. In this country, the largest place of gathering has commonly been the hockey rink. Maple Leaf Gardens, the Forum in Montreal, Ottawa's Civic Centre—all have been the stage for politicians and promises, the launching pad of careers that have eventually had dramatic consequences for the country.

With every break in the play, Elsie is shaking hands, slapping backs and joking with kids and pensioners alike. "For me it's a night out to get away from all that political stuff," she says, but it is hard to believe as she works the crowd with the expertise of a daytime talk-show host. Most of her constituents in the federal riding of Saint John will pass through this building to take in a Flames game at one time or another this season, and Wayne is at as many of those matches as she can possibly be. On a shuttle from Parliament Hill to Harbour Station, Elsie Wayne is keeping in touch with her electorate. The hockey game is the ideal backdrop.

She, like the community, goes against the grain in New Brunswick and the country when it comes to matters of politics. Only Jean Charest shares her partisan shade of blue in Ottawa at this time. These two are the surviving remnants of the once powerful Progressive Conservative Party. Saint John is a Tory enclave in what has been an overwhelmingly Liberal province for the last decade or so. Wayne, defiant in her difference, relishes the role and plays to loyal supporters surrounding her perch in the arena as she refers to the multitudes wearing Flames T-shirts and sweaters. "When I came here tonight and saw all the red, I thought, God! Chrétien knows I'm coming to the game!" The folks beside her titter and clap their hands as Elsie's eyes search for their approval.

He is the captain of a hockey team called the Big Red Machine, a shifty centreman who has been known to go into the corners and come out with the puck. "We only get a few outings a year but yes, we still have a team," Frank McKenna acknowledged as he rolled down the Trans-Canada Highway from the provincial capital of Fredericton to Sussex, just outside Saint John. The forty-nine-year-old premier of New Brunswick was on his way to speak to local businessmen when he called from his cell phone. He was going to fill them in on his recent trip to Asia as part of the Team Canada trade mission organized by Prime Minister Jean Chrétien. During the trip, McKenna had been accused of being less than a team player by other premiers as he tried to drum up as much business for his native province as possible. For a moment, the premier seemed thankful to talk about another game, one perhaps even closer to his heart.

McKenna was instrumental in getting Harbour Station built. A hockey fan and season-ticket holder of the AHL Fredericton Canadiens, he gets to as many games as his onerous schedule allows. His family is hockey crazy, with his oldest son still playing long after post-secondary graduation. His youngest son and daughter both play at the university level, and their father

New Brunswick's Big Red Machine. A centre and the captain is Premier Frank McKenna, front row, fourth from right

is their devoted and loyal supporter. McKenna believes that the game has an importance beyond the competition on the ice, that hockey has a cultural significance that exceeds most people's expectations. "I believe in the sport. I think it's a big part of what makes us Canadian," he said. "I think the socialization and discipline of being in a team sport is excellent. It's something that we're good at and something that really binds us together. I don't think we're ever prouder as Canadians than when we end up on the world stage in a hockey game."

A native of the small village of Apohaqui, not far from Sussex and Saint John, Frank McKenna is old enough to have begun his hockey career on a frozen sheet of outdoor ice. He is also young enough to remember the excitement of making it beyond the confines of his hamlet to the greater world of the game in Saint John as a high school player. "The river ran by our house, so sometimes when we were really daring we'd get out there and skate all the way to Apohaqui where we had an outdoor rink. That was a thrill!" he recalled. "I also played hockey in Rothesay and Saint John, not in the rinks but on the ponds. When we got to the rink in Saint John, it was a big deal for us because it was such a hockey-mad city. They always had a big crowd out and you always had the chance to meet some pretty nice people."

When he was competing as a high school player, McKenna encountered the Lord Beaverbrook Rink with its penalty box gates that opened onto the ice instead of in. He laughed, thinking of the hazards presented by the arena's quirks, but insisted, for a kid from a small village, it was really something to play there. "The LBR to me was really a big, world-class facility. It was quite a treat to go there and play hockey—it was pretty spectacular." Even as a teenager, though, he recognized the rink's limitations. "It was very constrained. The ice surface was small and the seating capacity was quite small," he said.

Like most hockey fans in the area, McKenna longed for the game at its highest level and remembers going to see the Russians play in Saint John, as well as becoming a devoted follower of the Senior Mooseheads. Sometimes the crowd was jammed so tightly into the smoke-filled LBR that they could hardly move. As a young player, McKenna was startled by the arena's grandeur, but he now reflects on the inadequacies of the Lord Beaverbrook Rink he knew back then and the part it played in limiting the growth of the province's largest community as a hockey centre. "It did prohibit professional hockey and that was always a major constraint. What was probably the best hockey city in Atlantic Canada couldn't have the pro game," he commented.

As premier, McKenna could help make Saint John into a professional hockey city. Not an easy task, given the retreat of the American Hockey League from Atlantic Canada during the late eighties and early nineties. Although the trend has seen the Prince Edward Island Senators, the Cape Breton Oilers and the Moncton Hawks become extinct, Saint John's potential was never in doubt as far as McKenna was concerned. "I think we have to challenge the notion that the American Hockey League doesn't do well in Atlantic Canada," he said. "Our problem is that the league just keeps getting richer and getting into bigger American rinks and bigger American cities that have lots of people and lots of corporate sponsorship."

In fact, Saint John was fertile ground for the AHL. It was a city that had never known the professional game but that had an active business and corporate community, as well as a population base of more than a hundred thousand people. The challenge was to create the right kind of facility to house a team in a league that was growing in wealth. The rink needed to be the right size for the community in which it operated. To that end, McKenna established a tripartite committee to examine the building of cultural institutions in the province's most populated urban centre. An almost unopposed Liberal premier in the provincial legislature, McKenna ended up making strange bedfellows with the feisty mayor, Elsie Wayne, and the Tory federal government. "It was complicated but not tough," McKenna reflected. "At the end of the day, we were working on everybody's priorities simultaneously and it seemed to work out." The finding of the committee: Saint John was ripe for a new rink as well as pro hockey.

Frank McKenna is not easy to get hold of. One of the most active and aggressive political leaders in the country, he is a tireless worker and keeps an almost inhuman schedule. He does, however, welcome the chance to talk about hockey and its intrinsic value to his beloved New Brunswick. "We always felt that hockey would catch on at the professional level in Saint John," he declared. "But I think all of us have been surprised at how wildly successful it has been."

McKenna is an avid supporter of his province and is clearly impressed by Harbour Station's impact on the community and the AHL. It has become the model franchise for the storied league in the space of four seasons of operation, a fact not lost on the American Hockey League's president, David Andrews, himself a Nova Scotian. "The first Canadian-based team to host the all-star game in the sixty-one-year history of the league is Saint John," said Andrews. "It is a community that doesn't have to be a big city or a big market."

The shipyard in Saint John has seen better days, and the economy still struggles along. There's not a lot of cash in this city no matter which way you choose to look at it. Still, there is enough money for fans to flock to Harbour Station in increasing numbers as each season unfolds for the Flames. Frank McKenna revelled in the knowledge that this is one hockey arena that was built in the right place and with exactly the right motivation. "In Saint John, [the arena] is truly at the centre of what is happening in the city. It is where people go to meet people," he emphasized. "It is where business is transacted, and it is where entertainment is provided. It's where meals are eaten and where beer is drunk." In short, Harbour Station, to the premier's way of thinking, is where the city lives.

The drive to Saint John from Fredericton and the duties of office is not much more than a couple of hours for Frank McKenna. He claimed that he and his wife will make the trip frequently in the winter just to be a part of the gathering at the hockey rink. The openness attracts him, the chance to mingle with neighbours and acquaintances that he may have known as a child growing up in Apohaqui. "It's so open that you are always part of a moving crowd it seems," he said with evident enthusiasm. "In most rinks you just don't see that. You don't have a chance to say hello to your neighbour the same way you do at Harbour Station."

It is, after all, only a hockey rink. Just concrete and glass with a bright blue roof that appears like a circus tent might as you gaze down on it from the old garrison at Fort Howe. It is a nice building, stylish, yet in keeping with the architecture of the Maritime port city, but McKenna sees more than that. As a mega-project for his government, it has been a gigantic success. Not too much money lost—in fact, as his old rival Elsie Wayne has mentioned, the rink may break even soon and begin paying for itself. McKenna is a hockey man dressed up in a politician's suit and sees the rink for what it is: a place to play the game and a great hall for the people to gather in its celebration. "I have a chance to meet with medical doctors and shipyard workers, big businessmen and local cab drivers," he said. "It's where all the people meet and it's where everybody is equal."

As he approached Sussex, Frank McKenna ran out of the luxury of time to talk hockey. There was one thing left to discuss—an urban myth, of sorts, which says that he was once asked to let his name stand as the new commissioner of the National Hockey League before Gary Bettman was eventually hired. McKenna balked noticeably at the mention of such a rumour. Then, in considered tones, he admitted its veracity. "Only informally," he stressed. "It was raised with me and I made it pretty clear that while I was flattered, I was not interested in leaving the job that I was in. And that was all there was to it."

The rest of our conversation was marked by the typical jocularity of hockey's devout followers. McKenna, I am sure, is a guardian of the game, and Harbour Station is partly an expression of his faith in the strength of hockey in New Brunswick. He is now relegated to being a fan but clings to the thrill of active play in the friendly enclosures of skating rinks. "Every time Ronald Corey, the president of the Montreal Canadiens, calls about some issue or another, I always start off by saying, 'I'm ready coach! Anytime you want to call me I'm ready to go up,'" he laughed. "Hockey is something that every young Canadian has experienced first-hand. It's still a big part of my life—'Hockey Night in Canada' is still a big part of my life."

As New Brunswick's premier hung up the car phone and slipped back into his life as a guarded and wise political strategist, I imagined him making two quick calls before he reached his destination. One was to book a couple of tickets for that night's Flames game against the Portland Pirates. The other was to his old cronies in an attempt to reunite the Big Red Machine as soon as humanly possible.

With the game well in hand and the seconds clicking rapidly from the million-dollar clock suspended above the ice surface, a fight erupts in the Flames' end of the rink. An enormous Binghamton defenceman named Eric Cairns from

Oakville, Ontario, has taken a run at Ian Gordon, the Saint John goalie. Gordon hails from Yorkton, Saskatchewan, and his teammate Clarke Wilm is quick to replace him in fisticuffs with the six-foot-six, 230-pound Cairns. Wilm, a native of Central Butte, Saskatchewan, knows his efforts will please not only the fans but Nick Polano, the scout watching with critical attention from the press-box loft. Polano comes from Hamilton, Ontario, and spent his entire fifteen-year playing career in the minor leagues, the only exception being a brief stint with Philadelphia of the old World Hockey Association. Having never made it to the National Hockey League as a player, he now judges desire and talent in youngsters and determines their professional fate. In this and every other AHL rink, Polano's responsibility is a heavy one.

Elsie Wayne cheers the battle on, standing and almost growling at the Binghamton player. She might have left the arena half an hour ago, as the game was all but decided in her team's favour. She hangs in, however, demonstrating that the luxury of this team and this rink is worth every moment it affords her. Almost all the nearly six thousand who saw the opening face-off three hours ago have taken Elsie's lead and remain in the building, loudly supporting the Flames to the final buzzer. It is as if they are making a statement about their steadfast commitment to this hallowed ground in their city.

Harbour Station is a strange but alluring name for a hockey arena. Most are called "the Centre," "the Forum," "the Gardens" or, on a more trendy note, such and such "Place." Harbour is a shelter to come to anchor in. Station is a stopping place en route to some other destination. It is either a strange coincidence that Saint John's new palace of hockey was named so perfectly, or part of the master plan that has led to such great success in the city's first foray into professional hockey.

To observe the congregation of devoted local fans in the stands and the young, ambitious players on the ice is to understand the amazing capacity of this hockey rink. It has, in a short period of time, made amends for the past. It also allows tremendous promise for the future.

Elsie Wayne knows that Saint John is stemming the tide when it comes to professional hockey in this part of the country. The Flames are becoming an institution while many of their Atlantic rivals are bound for extinction. This city has been patient too long to allow the pledge of Harbour Station to become tainted. "Oh, it's gonna stay here," she says with fire in her voice. "They're never gonna take it away from me. They're never gonna take the AHL from us. Not on your life!" I believe her completely.

5 Viking Carena
Viking, Alberta

Chris Cuthbert

It is perhaps fitting that this fastest of all games has become almost as much of a national symbol as the maple leaf or the beaver. Most young Canadians, in fact, are born with skates on their feet rather than with silver spoons in their mouths.

—Lester B. Pearson

IT WAS THE MORNING OF THE seventh game of the 1996 Eastern Conference Championship series. The upstart Florida Panthers were preparing to face the Pittsburgh Penguins in a one-game showdown for the right to meet Colorado in the Stanley Cup final. A lifetime of dreams was hanging like an icy fog over the "Igloo" in Pittsburgh as the two teams conducted their pre-game skates. In the stands, the media entourage had assembled in pursuit of a quote or a clue to what might unfold that evening. I approached Panthers assistant coach Duane Sutter, who had been a source of insight throughout this roller-coaster affair; he was a veteran of these wars, having won four Stanley Cups with the Islanders dynasty of the early eighties. Even the usually open Sutter had a more focused demeanour on this morning. As an ice-breaker I resorted to the most elementary media query concerning a seventh game: Would home ice carry any advantage for Pittsburgh? Indulging me, Duane looked beyond the ice full of Penguins, and said, "You could play game seven at the Viking Carena and it wouldn't make any difference." On the eve of the biggest game of his coaching career, his home-town rink was a comforting frame of reference. His smile revealed he had played countless seventh games and Stanley Cup finals in his imagination in that wonderfully named rink in rural Alberta.

Six months after the Panthers' seventh-game victory over Pittsburgh, after their improbable run to the Stanley Cup final, I made a pilgrimage to a farming community 128 kilometres southeast of Edmonton—Viking, which had made its mark long before the Sutters became the most remark-

Viking Carena able family story in NHL history. With a population of only 1,268, it is a town that displayed a creative and enterprising spirit to fund a rink that became the envy of every town its size in western Canada; a community that boasts not one, but two native sons to coach the Chicago Blackhawks; a place where Glen Sather, one of the NHL's most successful hockey men, skated indoors for the first time; a place where the most distinct landmark is the arched metal roof of the building at the corner of 51st Street and 53rd Avenue with the bright red letters that spell Carena.

Viking wasn't always a hockey town. In fact, the dominant winter pastime of the first half century was curling. In 1911, a year after the Village of Viking was founded, a makeshift roof was built over the first local sheet of curling ice. Five years later, a new curling rink equipped with gas lamps was erected, only to be replaced by a $4,000 facility in 1919. The local cattlemen and mixed farmers were smitten with a game on ice that didn't require skates. In a local publication, *Viking in Progress*, published in 1937, only eleven lines were devoted to the local hockey scene. Two and a half pages chronicled the fortunes of Vikings' curlers: "No game has ever equaled curling for engaging so many men and women in active sport." By 1941, one of their own, John Slavik, represented Alberta in the Brier, Canada's national curling championship.

This was not to suggest that the Viking sports scene was strictly a sedate haven for the curling set. By the mid-thirties, local farm boy Eddie Wenstob, who trained in the family barn punching a bag of grain hung from the rafters, battled his way to the number-three ranking in boxing's heavyweight division. On a barnstorming European tour, Wenstob defeated Irish champion Pat Marrinan in Belfast, igniting a riot that required 150 policemen to quell.

Later he fought South African Ben Foord to a draw in front of more than 65,000 fans at Wembley Stadium in London, England. His grit and determination overcame a thirty-pound weight disadvantage and a broken right hand he had suffered in the fight. Later, a controversial home-town decision against Tommy Farr cost Wenstob a shot at the title against legendary Joe Louis. Like the Sutters to follow, Wenstob had put Viking on the international sporting map with a game and unyielding reputation.

These were characteristics imperative just to endure the unforgiving environment of early day Viking. The local newspaper's first editorial, on April 28, 1910, spelled out the philosophy for survival and success in this burgeoning community. It's a credo that the Sutters probably have never read but have unwittingly followed in their ascent to the NHL.

The *Viking Gazette* wants you to understand that this is not the land for the indolent, the dreamer or the lazy. It is not the land where wealth can be accumulated without effort. But it is the land for the man in whose veins there flows the red rich blood, the man of action, the man of ambition and the man who wishes to work and seek an honest living, and by effort in this way he will succeed.

Laurie Rasmussen was a local sports success story, an athlete, builder and visionary who fired the hockey passions of Viking. He arrived in town as an eighteen-year-old in 1925, working as the telegraph operator and night agent for the CNR, but Rasmussen's life was sports. If it was played in Viking, Laurie was involved—as a player, coach or official in local basketball, soccer, tennis, volleyball, swimming, gymnastics, boxing and curling programs. A women's softball team known as Laurie's Lovelies gained provincial notoriety. He was also manager and goaltender for the Viking senior hockey team, a position he occupied for twenty-seven years, leading to the nickname "Father Time" in his later playing days. For most of his goaltending career, the Viking senior team played on an open-air rink. Gas lights hung over the ice surface and fans were more apt to stand on snowbanks outside the rink to watch than pay ten cents admission to stand along the boards. A few hundred would brave the frigid conditions to support the home side and crowd around the pot-bellied gas stove for relief during intermissions.

Without an indoor rink like those that were sprouting up in larger centres, the long-term survival of competitive hockey in Viking was endangered. By 1950, it was time for Rasmussen to take action with an open letter to the citizens of the area, to make the case for the construction of a new indoor rink. "Without proper facilities and accommodation for the different winter sports we are more or less being ostracized and left out of the hockey promotions around us," he wrote. "Therefore I feel with this added fixture the town will eventually bring more and better players from the country and set a higher standard of hockey in the small towns. Therefore let's go out and make the new arena another shining example of community spirit and grand cooperation among all of us in town and country combined."

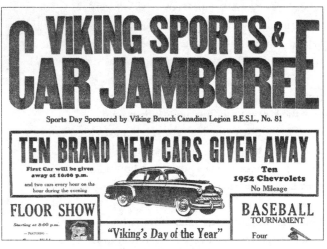

From Laurie Rasmussen's advertising poster for the grand opening of the Carena in 1952

Viking had already balked at a plebiscite for water and sewers, so the rink proposal would be a tough sell. But Laurie Rasmussen was a master salesman and promoter who had a scheme that would capture the imagination of not only Viking and district but much of western Canada. He called it the "Car of the Month Club"—a grandiose lottery, with tickets at five dollars apiece, for a one-in-a-thousand chance of winning one of twelve new Plymouth Deluxe sedans. "Put a five spot in the arena, folks!" blared the posters put up throughout the district, while CFRN radio in Edmonton spread the news of the car lottery to the rest of western Canada. So widespread was word of the lottery that the first winner hailed from Hay River, Northwest Territories. The first Car of the Month series netted more than $53,000 in ticket sales. The cost of the cars was $26,650. One thousand dollars was donated to the ACT Crippled Children's fund, an act of goodwill, perhaps to help legitimize what might have been interpreted as an illegal gaming operation. After the first year, the Car of the Month Club netted more than $20,000 for the Viking Arena Fund. In three years, thirty-two Plymouths, Meteors and Chevrolets were raffled off, raising more than $60,000 dollars for the fund.

"Laurie had a thousand ideas a day and 999 were absolutely silly," says Don Place, who along with Rasmussen sat on Viking council. "He'd work all night long and then would go running all day selling these tickets up and down Main Street, talking to everybody, trying to convince them. It was a tough job. I would have quit. Only Rasmussen had enough gumption to stay with it."

Rasmussen wasn't finished yet. His *pièce de resistance* was the grand opening of the new arena on July 9, 1952, the greatest day in Viking's history. Although the population was just over seven hundred at the time, more than five thousand people jammed the village to admire the new Carena, suitably named in honour of the funding drive that had made it possible. The town streets looked like a massive parking lot, which was appropriate, since much of the fuss revolved around another ten cars to be raffled off that evening. Ticket-holders from across western Canada and American visitors from as far away as Wisconsin and California were party to the Car of the Month frenzy. It was an evening of celebration and dancing, and every hour on the hour, from ten o'clock until two in the morning, a pair of new cars was given away. Enhancing the prestige of this showcase event was the presence of Foster Hewitt, who for decades had brought the excitement of NHL rinks into the living rooms of rural Albertans with his radio descriptions of the Toronto Maple Leafs. Hewitt, perhaps more popular than any of the NHL players of the day, played to the captive audience by starting his address in trademark style. "Max Bentley cuts in and takes a pass from Howie Meeker—he shoots—he scores!" Hewitt thrilled the throng, as he made the first play-by-play call from Viking's new rink.

Caught up in the jubilation of the evening was one of the area's keenest hockey fans, Louis Sutter. He still cherishes his recollections of that first night in the Carena, even if the still-single farmer had no idea how the new rink would affect his life. "I remember Foster Hewitt saying that someday there might be an Ole Olson in the NHL," recalls Sutter. Olson, a local prospect, never made good on Hewitt's prediction, but the star of "Hockey Night in Canada" was indeed prophetic, as was *Edmonton Journal* reporter Gord Williamson, who wrote, "It's not beyond the realm of possibility that the village of Viking, hoping to receive recognition as a town in the near future, could also in the future have young men playing a prominent part under the big top of hockey."

In recognition of his exemplary community spirit and tireless work to make the Carena a reality, Laurie Rasmussen was dismissed from his job with the CNR. The endless hours of hawking tickets during the day left him weary and unproductive on the night shift and, as far as the railroad was concerned, dispensable. That wasn't how the people of Viking saw it. In appreciation for creating the vision of the Carena and seeing it through,

Rasmussen was presented with a new car, an extravagance he was unable to afford on a night operator's wage, as well as a new job. Rasmussen became the mayor of Viking. The lure of the rink, however, was too difficult to ignore. Within two years, Laurie left Viking to become the manager of the Edmonton Gardens, one of the biggest and busiest arenas in western Canada. At the same time, he consulted on other fund-raising projects for rinks across the west and could have made that a full-time venture if he had desired. Doing so, however, would have left little time for his other sporting pursuits. Surprisingly, it was for his work in softball, not hockey, that Laurie Rasmussen was honoured with induction into the Alberta Sports Hall of Fame. He will be remembered, however, as the most influential hockey builder in one of Canada's most passionate hockey towns.

Clem Loughlin didn't have Laurie Rasmussen's boundless energy for community sports but he did have an imposing stature in Viking. The owner of the Viking Hotel had made a name for himself in the NHL as a player with

Clem Loughlin Chicago and Detroit and as the coach of the Blackhawks for three seasons from 1934–37, over a half century before another Viking product, Darryl Sutter, assumed the Hawks' coaching mantle. Loughlin, who won the Allan Cup with the Winnipeg Monarchs in 1915, also put his name on the Stanley Cup as a member of Lester Patrick's Victoria Cougars in 1925–26, the final year of the early east-west battles for the Cup. Following Victoria's Stanley Cup triumph over the Montreal Canadiens, the Western Canada Hockey League disbanded and its players were sold to Chicago, Detroit and the New York Rangers. Loughlin, a rugged defenceman, became the property of Detroit, playing for two seasons with the Red Wings and one final year with the Blackhawks.

At the conclusion of his NHL career, Loughlin, a native of Carroll, Manitoba, settled in Viking. He farmed, raising pure-bred shorthorn cattle and Yorkshire hogs, and later built the local hotel, which he managed. He was not influential on the local hockey scene in a hands-on manner until his later years, when he adopted another role as hockey godfather.

Like the Sutters, Loughlin was from a family of seven boys. His brother Wilf had been a member of the Toronto St. Pats, playing fourteen games during the 1923–24 campaign. Clem took a shine to the rough-and-tumble Sutter boys he spotted playing at the Carena. In 1974, his final year of minor hockey in Viking, Darryl Sutter, a future Blackhawks coach, was guided by the experienced hand of the former Blackhawks mentor. "Clem coached me in midget. I think he was eighty-one or eighty-two then," Darryl recalled. "We'd known Clem since we were little boys. He was like an idol to us kids. He'd come in his old topcoat and fedora and he'd wear that out on the ice for practice. He still wore the old skates that he'd finished his NHL career with. Old steel-blade skates with soft leather toes. I turned them over once and it said Chicago Blackhawks, 1930–something on them. It was amazing. When we were growing up, we got a duffle bag full of equipment from Clem. It had all his old equipment, like black leather gloves and an old wool jersey, from that Victoria team he'd play on in the NHL. Now if you still had that sweater…" Darryl paused to ponder its value. "But we wore it right out, all that equipment. Now everybody is into collecting that stuff."

What the Sutters collected instead was insight and inspiration. Loughlin had the most profound impact on Brian Sutter, the first of the brothers to play in the NHL. "He was somebody I really looked up to," said the former Blues winger who went on to coach St. Louis and the Boston Bruins. "From the time I was ten, he'd bring me to Viking in the summer and put me up in the hotel for a few weeks. It was like a summer holiday and I would do chores for him in the field or shovel grain. At lunch he would bring me a hamburger and a chocolate bar. We'd sit on the tractor and talk hockey. He'd talk about things to teach you a lesson but never about himself. He'd always have stories that would leave you thinking, even when I was ten or eleven. I knew he spent time with me that he didn't spend with anybody else."

Brian Sutter learned his lessons well from Clem Loughlin, who gave the stamp of approval to his prodigy on a night that fuelled the NHL aspirations of a younger brother. "I remember going with Clem to see Brian play a junior game in Spruce Grove," Darryl reminisced. "We had a busload of people from Viking, and I sat at the back with Clem because I wanted to listen to him. He'd talk about the old days but he'd want to talk more about the game. He'd ask us what we would do in this situation or that. We were good listeners and maybe that's why we learned a little about the game. On the way back, he put his arm around me and said, 'Your brother is going to play in the NHL.' I can remember being so happy. All it did was reaffirm what we had dreamed of doing since we were little kids. I guess for Clem to say that gave us another tank of gas to go on."

Perhaps Clem Loughlin had seen a little of himself in the Sutter boys. That might explain why they received his old equipment and his undivided attention. Their enthusiasm had brought Clem back to the rink on a more frequent basis. His declaration that Brian was bound for the NHL was, of course, correct. Sadly, however, Clem didn't get a chance to witness the Sutters' NHL breakthrough. On the eve of Brian's first game with the St. Louis Blues, the night he was summoned from the minors in 1976, Clem Loughlin, at the age of eighty-four, died in his sleep. His last coaching assignment had been completed.

Glen Sather has vague recollections of Clem Loughlin, more distinct memories of climbing trees on the Loughlin farm. "We used to build tree houses on his farm when I was a kid," recalled the Edmonton Oilers' president and general manager, who lived in Viking from age ten through twelve. "He was probably the first hockey person I ever met." From Loughlin's trees to the Carena, Sather started his hockey climb in the first indoor rink of his hockey career. "I played there before the Sutters," he boasted playfully. "We used to scale the rafters going from one side of the building to the other right over centre ice. It was as exciting as hell. Our next trick was to bring up a two-by-ten and suspend it between the rafters and then shimmy across."

As a twelve-year-old who played street hockey when he wasn't on or above the Carena ice, Glen Sather's dreams of an NHL career were not yet clearly developed. There were a few nights at the Carena that helped bring the dream into sharper focus. "Viking had a great senior team that played the Edmonton Oil Kings in exhibition games," Sather recalled. "That was the first exposure I had to anything beyond pick-up hockey. I remember watching Johnny Bucyk and Len Lunde and guys of that era at the Carena. That was big-time hockey."

A dozen years later, Sather himself was in the big time, a teammate of Bucyk's with the Boston Bruins. Sather had followed Bucyk's path through the Edmonton Oil Kings' junior program, where he was taken under wing by a familiar figure, the rink manager, Laurie Rasmussen. "The first year of junior hockey I boarded with Laurie. I'd known him from Viking. He was a real character, always coaching us, making sure we didn't miss curfews, didn't get into trouble."

Decades later Sather laments being unable to orchestrate another Viking reunion with the acquisition of one of the Sutters for the Oilers. "I wish out of all those years I'd got one of those Sutters but it never worked out. They were good players and you just couldn't get to them. I tried but I couldn't move a guy like Mark Messier to do it. It would have been nice to have one of those guys on your team."

Like most expert climbers, Glen Sather rarely looks down from the dizzying heights he's reached as the architect of the Oilers dynasty in the eighties. When he does look back the view is endless. "The first time I ever was in an arena was in Viking, then the Edmonton Gardens. I didn't think anything was as big as the Edmonton Gardens. After I moved from there, I went to Detroit training camp, and saw Maple Leaf Gardens and all the other great arenas across the continent. It's really something, from that little arena in Viking to seeing all the great arenas in North America."

Beyond the front doors, along the side wall of the Carena lobby, is a glass display case dedicated to Viking's favourite sons. NHL jerseys and pictures of the Sutter brothers are proudly displayed for visitors but are just part of the furnishings for Carena regulars. Other local stars who have enjoyed a measure of hockey success, NHL draft picks Scott Brower, Dallas Gaume and Dean Antos, are also acknowledged. Above the door to the dressing rooms, over the "No Spitting" sign, is a large Cash Draw board divided into two hundred squares. Each square has been purchased for $100, giving the holder of that square twelve chances at winning a monthly draw of $1,000. On another wall there are 393 engraved plates acknowledging donors to the roof fund. The snack bar, which is open only on the weekends, is run by minor hockey parent volunteers who have the option of paying an annual fee of $100 to support the concession stand or volunteer for behind-the-counter work. The fund-raising spirit of Laurie Rasmussen is alive and well.

The Carena has a silver lining. A glimmering tarp is draped across the ceiling to reflect light and to prevent run-off from the defrosting beams in the spring. Before the canopy was installed, the spring melt-down rained onto the playing surface. Soon after, the ice assumed the complexion of a cavern floor studded with stalagmites. At the far end of the rink are the chutes used for the summer rodeo. Down one side are five rows of grey wooden stands. Along the other flank, the boards merge with the outer wall, indented only by two players' benches and the penalty box. Above the "sin bin," the

flags of Canada and Alberta are un-
furled, as well as championship pennants from Viking's minor hockey
booty.

Wednesday is the busiest hockey
day of the work week for Darryl
Sutter's family. Shortly after rink
manager Ned Kearns unlocks the
Carena doors at the end of school,
the Viking Novices, including nine-
year-old Brett Sutter, hit the ice
under the watchful eye of Coach
Sutter. A couple of hours later, after
she has done her homework in
the Carena lobby, eleven-year-old
Jessica Sutter dons her goaltending

Darryl Sutter's team between coaching assignments in Chicago and San Jose gear for practice. Later, if he has enough energy in reserve after a day of farm chores and minor hockey workouts, Darryl will suit up for Viking's senior team, the Chicken Hawks.

There is, however, some concern about the whereabouts of Darryl Sutter on this Wednesday. His team is poised to hit the ice for practice but the coach has yet to arrive. If he were still with the Blackhawks, being late would be punishable by a team fine. Then again, Sutter didn't have farm chores and a temperamental truck to repair when he was in Chicago. Before any fines are imposed, Darryl arrives, appearing more at ease than he ever did before conducting a Blackhawks workout. Of course, the only controversy about coaching at this level Sutter has faced is the issue of his qualifications to guide a team of eight- and nine-year-olds. "The Viking minor hockey board was informed that all coaches would have to have a coaching certificate," he recounts sheepishly. "Somebody called back to ask if I needed one. They said most definitely. I never did get it. I'll be reprimanded this year and I'll have to get it. Actually, it's not a bad idea because a lot of these certifications include first aid and that could help if a kid gets hurt. It was just funny at the time. Everyone was kidding me about it. I didn't think anybody knew, but everybody knew."

After putting a dozen of his charges through the most efficient minor hockey practice ever conducted by a non-certified coach, we sit down in the Carena lobby to discuss the roots of a career that blossomed into the captaincy and coaching reigns of one of hockey's most storied franchises, and why he returned to Viking in the prime of his hockey career.

As youngsters whirl around the Carena ice on the other side of the lobby glass, Sutter reflects on his childhood days at the rink that helped shape his character. "I can remember when it was twenty below outside, it was forty below inside and you'd be freezing your ass in here. The floors were all plywood and you'd walk around in your old wool socks full of slivers," says Darryl, while admiring the improvements of today's Carena. "There were benches all around the lobby where you'd put your skates on because it was warmer. I remember one day, when we were little guys, Brian was bawling in here because his feet were frozen. Dad said if he ever caught us crying in the Carena again, we'd never come back to the rink. Even more than hockey moments, that sticks in my mind."

The Sutter boys would come back to the Carena every Saturday during the winter after their parents, Louis and Grace, had taken them to Marshall Wells Hardware Store to outfit the family with skates for the season. "Mom and Dad couldn't afford to buy us all new skates. We'd wait for all the other kids to trade their skates for new ones, then we'd all go in to be outfitted for another year with the old skates. I remember one year being jealous of Gary and Brian. They got brand-new skates for Christmas with Bobby Hull's autograph on them." With six other brothers and few luxuries, Darryl understood that petty jealousy would not be tolerated, but those skates would have felt so good on his feet. After all, Chicago was his team, Hull his idol, and playing for the Blackhawks was his dream. However, realizing his fantasy seemed as distant as a trip from Viking to the Windy City for a youngster whose minor hockey career was progressing without much fanfare. "We were never the best players on our team, not even close, other than Brent," Darryl concedes.

By his early teens, though, the benefits of slinging hay bales on the farm, the guidance of his parents and Clem Loughlin, the inspiration of his trail-blazing brother Brian and most importantly his own passion for the game gave Darryl a fighting chance. His affinity for hockey crystallized on a lonely spring night at the Carena. "I was fourteen or fifteen and we'd just come back from the provincials in Westlock. I got dropped off at a friend's house and had to walk through town to catch a ride home. I was walking by the Carena and the big back doors were open and the ice had all melted. I walked in and stood in the middle of the rink and thought, oh God, I won't see this place again for another two or three months. It was so sad."

Even now Sutter speaks of that moment as if recounting the moving break-up of a teenage romance. He bridges the years with the memory of a more emotional rink farewell while coaching in Chicago in 1994. "That year we had training camp in the Chicago Stadium before they opened the United Center for the regular season. After the last practice, the ice plant was shut down. I remember going back in and there wasn't a soul there. I walked through the old building and it was so sad. It's even hard to talk about it now," he says in a voice cracking with emotion. "Later I remember driving out of the United Center after a game at about three in the morning and across the street at the stadium the goddamn wrecking ball was pounding away. I just sat there and watched."

Sutter couldn't just drive away as the iron ball began to wreak havoc on his rink of dreams. The glorious roar of the stadium, known as "the Mad-house on Madison Avenue," was being silenced forever. They were razing the roof and bringing the house down once and for all. It was more than maddening. It was tragic, and it could not have affected Darryl more deeply had they been tearing down the Carena in Viking. "The goddamn wreck-ing ball!" In the aftermath, bricks from the rubble were peddled as souvenirs but what Sutter salvaged that night were priceless memories that cannot be destroyed.

"I have two favourite Blackhawk moments, and they have nothing to do with playing or coaching. When I talk about them, I get shivers," Sutter says, his voice quaking with emotion. "The nights they retired Bobby Hull's and Stan Mikita's numbers. I was on the bench and it was a great thrill. The other was being in the All Star game at the Stadium when they played the U.S. national anthem. It was during the Gulf War. Mr. Wirtz [Blackhawk owner William Wirtz] was so proud because General Schwarzkopf sent a telegram saying that instead of addressing the troops he showed them a videotape of the playing of the anthem in the stadium. It was great, people were waving flags, it was unbelievable."

Darryl Sutter is too modest to catalogue personal moments of achieve-ment, although there are many. He proved the Blackhawks wrong when they drafted him as an afterthought with a throwaway eleventh-round pick in 1978. Instead of relishing the fulfilment of a childhood dream, Sutter bris-tled at the lack of genuine interest Chicago had demonstrated in him. Darryl spurned the Blackhawks to play his first professional season as far away from Chicago as he could get, in the Japanese professional league. The Black-hawks would have to wait a year for his help. He's too modest to gloat about the forty goals he scored in his first full season when he finally joined the Hawks, underscoring how badly he had been underestimated in the draft, too humble to reveal the pride of wearing the "C" as captain of the Black-hawks by his third year. He overlooks the single-season Chicago playoff goal scoring record of twelve in the 1984–85 post-season, which broke the previous mark held by his idol, Bobby Hull. Nor does he dwell on the litany of injuries that sidelined his career prematurely at age twenty-nine. There is, however, a fierce sense of accomplishment and pride about competing against his brothers at the highest level.

"When I first played Brian, it was a bit of a distraction because he was kind of my hero growing up. I got called up to the Hawks for the first time during the playoffs and Chicago was playing St. Louis. Eddie Johnston was our coach and he thought if I played against Brian all the time I could get him off his game. If you stopped Brian and Bernie Federko, you'd beat St. Louis. It might have affected his game a little because we beat them three straight."

Brian has conceded that it may have been the only time he was distracted by sibling rivalry at the NHL level. It was never again a factor as the two Sutters butted heads regularly, embroiled in one of hockey's most bitter rivalries, Darryl, captain of the Blackhawks, Brian, captain of the Blues. A few years later they were matching wits as rival coaches. "When we coached against each other, it never entered my mind," Darryl says. "At the same time I really followed how his team was doing. When they got in trouble and he was replaced, it really hurt."

After two seasons as the Blackhawks' associate coach under Mike Keenan, Sutter assumed the responsibilities of head coach in Chicago, the position once held by Clem Loughlin. He was as successful behind the bench as he was on the ice, guiding the Blackhawks to first place in the Norris division in his initial season, advancing to the 1995 Conference Championship series in his third and, for now, final year. After bowing out to the Detroit Red Wings in five hard-fought games, which included three overtime losses, Sutter stunned the hockey world by announcing his resignation. He cited personal and family reasons for his decision to leave the NHL spotlight to return to the rural tranquillity of Viking. Of particular concern was his desire to spend more time with his infant son Christopher who was born with Down's syndrome.

In this modern era of big money and bigger egos in professional sports, Sutter's decision went dramatically against the current. Few sports personalities have departed in their prime citing family considerations. It was difficult for some to take his decision at face value. In Chicago, speculation was rampant that Sutter had instead had his fill of pampered athletes, specifically Jeremy Roenick, who didn't bring the same work ethic to the rink that was a Sutter trademark. "It's still a misunderstood thing with Jeremy," Darryl says, wincing at the mention of a subject he's not anxious to discuss. "We didn't have any more problems than I did with any other player. It got to be a money thing. He considered me management, he was a player. When I was with the owners, I would say that's your call [on how much he should be paid] but I would tell them that Jeremy is going to lay it on the line when he goes on the ice, and he always did." Feeding the media speculation of a severe rift between coach and player was a controversial post-season interview in which the star forward intimated he didn't want to play for Sutter any longer. "That's not what he said," Darryl says firmly. "Jeremy told a reporter he couldn't care less if I came back. At that point it didn't matter because I had already told the Hawks that I was leaving. Jeremy was the first one to call when I visited Chicago the next fall and said we've got to get together. He said he was just so wound up after the playoffs, that we'd lost out and he'd been hurt and frustrated." Hoping he's set the record straight, Sutter adds, "You've got to understand that coaches have a lot of those battles."

The battle Darryl Sutter continues to wage is within. He thrives in the rural lifestyle in which he was raised, but he has been alienated from the competitive hockey fires that still burn inside. For now, Darryl Sutter the farmer is winning the inner battle. "Next to hockey, I love being out with the cattle and horses. Even people around here said to me that coming back was a mistake, to stay with hockey as long as you can, don't quit on it yet. I just tell them they live a better quality of life than I do. I envied their lifestyle."

Al Arbour, the Hall of Fame coach of the New York Islanders, once said, "I can't see any of the Sutters returning to the serenity of the farm. They're just too damned competitive for that." Darryl is putting that theory to the test. He manages twelve sections of land, which can be more grinding than ploughing through an NHL season. Yet his hockey side, the competitiveness Arbour admires, gnaws away. "I fight it too," he volunteers. "Sometimes I would be watching a game and I'd be watching as a coach. I'd end up turning it off and going outside. I have a hard time watching hockey on TV with other people. I don't know why. I'll watch alone or with Brett. Otherwise I won't watch it. Friends are always asking me to come over to watch a game. I'll find a reason not to."

Darryl's inner turmoil was brought to the boil when the Winnipeg Jets, on the move to Phoenix, offered him their head coaching position during the summer of 1996. For three weeks, he weighed the pros and cons of a return to the NHL. He considered the offer, which exceeded his highest salary as a player. His family took a vote so he could gauge their willingness to leave Viking. Only nine-year-old son Brett rejected the possible move outright. During the three-week period in which he weighed the opportunity, Sutter was stricken with persistent headaches. From the moment he declined the Phoenix offer, the headaches went away. It was another triumph for the side of Darryl Sutter that wants to be a farmer and family man. But he is aware that the hockey fires have not all been extinguished yet. "You never get it out of you. I still think right now it would be hard to coach anybody but Chicago. It's like I'm still tied there."

A two-hour drive from Viking, in the refurbished old Red Deer rink, the Optimist Chiefs AAA midgets were arriving for practice. As each player strode by the coach's door, he was welcomed with a high-energy greeting. "Hey Swanee! How you doin', Bretsky?" the coach barked with a jocular cadence, already trying to rev his team up for the work ahead. It's the attitude Brian Sutter has brought to the rink since his childhood days at the Carena.

There's no disputing the credentials this Sutter brings to the rink either. He wears them for every player to see. Skates and gloves from St. Louis, where he was honoured with the retirement of his number 11 jersey; the equipment bag and grease board from the Boston Bruins, where his winning percentage was over .600 as a coach in three seasons; a Team Canada track suit he earned as an assistant coach with the '91 Canada Cup champions.

The Red Deer Optimist Chiefs have a storied past among minor hockey organizations. In the rink's trophy case, the Chiefs' Shield of Honour boasts the names of former stars such as Bill Ranford, Mark Tinordi and the Moller brothers, Randy and Mike. Red Deer had one of the premier midget clubs in Canada for the previous four seasons, advancing each year to the national midget championships but each year falling short of the title. Brian Sutter was intent on putting the Chiefs over the top and was encouraged with his club's early progress. "We're starting to improve. We have persevered. We can look shit in the eye now," said the coach approvingly of the team he wants playing in his image.

Inside the dressing room, before the on-ice session, Coach Sutter spelled out the day's battle plan to his troops, which included sixteen-year-old son

Shaun. "Today is work day, boys. We've had a good weekend. What do we take from last weekend? We take what we did well and get better at it. We know what we got to get better at. Consistency and preparing every day, so you start today. Okay, boys? How we start practising today is how we're gonna play this weekend. Let's do everything full speed, boys. Don't be afraid to make mistakes, guys. Hard work, lots of enthusiasm, lots of life out there. Any questions? Okay, boys, let's have a good one!"

His coaching philosophy is simple. An overdose of hard work and an allegiance to each other and the fundamentals of the game. "What do coaches do when their teams are struggling?" he asked and then, without hesitation, answered himself. "They go back to fundamentals. Why wait until you're losing to do it?"

As Sutter led the Chiefs onto the ice, his old Red Deer Rustlers' junior coach, Cec Swanson, sharpened skates in a small shop at the front of the rink. Swanson coached or managed all six Sutter brothers who played in the NHL, beginning with Brian's arrival as a fifteen-year-old in 1971. Brian was also the first and only Sutter cut by Swanson. "It all started with a salesman from Coca-Cola who used to go to Viking and heard about the Sutter brothers. He recommended them to me," Cec explained, while thumbing the edge of a skate blade. "The year Brian came to camp we started with roughly 120 kids and by the third day I would take the boys that weren't going to make it into a room, tell them they were cut and why. I remember Brian coming in, a farm boy, tall and thin."

Brian Sutter remembers the day too—the moment his hockey career nearly ended before it was getting started. "I was scared to call Dad," Brian recalled. I walked around all day before calling Mom and Dad that night. Dad asked me if I wanted to be a hockey player or whether I wanted to come home. He told me if I wanted to play I better get my ass back in there and talk to somebody. So I went back in. I guess they weren't used to a kid saying I'm not leaving so they sent me to the Junior Bs. I stayed with them for two or three weeks and then I was back with the Rustlers to stay." If Brian had accepted Swanson's initial decision, had Louis Sutter not been so forthright with his fatherly guidance, the Sutters' amazing story may never have materialized. For it was Brian who blazed the trail for his brothers to follow from Viking all the way to the NHL. He possessed all the admirable qualities that his younger brothers emulated. If Brian couldn't make it, it's quite possible the spirit of the others would have been broken as well. "I would say that as far as overall hockey players, they were all about the same, but

Brian had something a little different," Cec Swanson acknowledged. "His hustle and determination. He just made up his mind he was going to make it. They followed his footsteps."

Cec hasn't forgotten how Brian despised losing, becoming more despondent over a playoff loss in the western Canadian final against Kelowna than the coach did. He still recalls Brian potting four goals and an assist when the Rustlers knocked off a powerful touring Finnish squad that featured Jari Kurri. "Brian was all hockey. He never broke curfew. I never caught a Sutter breaking curfew," Swanson added. Brian Sutter has never overlooked Cec's impact on his career. In Swanson's living room is the plaque Sutter received from St. Louis in recognition of his forty-six-goal season in the 1982–83 campaign, a franchise record for left-wingers. Sutter presented it to Cec as a token of his appreciation. "And he still calls me Mr. Swanson when he sees me."

There was a special reward for the Chiefs' labour on this night. The team jackets had arrived. Ryan Melbourne, "Melby" to his coach, was one of the first to claim his parka. Sutter encouraged Ryan to try it on. "Stand there," ordered the coach as he sized Melbourne up. "You look sharp, partner." After all the players donned their jackets, Sutter claimed his own. His face lit up like a youngster who had just received his first pair of skates. "I'm proud of this," he said emphatically.

Brian Sutter has always worn that pride on his sleeve, never boastfully, but more as a positive reinforcement for the benefits of dedication and loyalty. "I played twelve years in the NHL. I was hurt for over a year and a half. I played for ten years and scored over three hundred goals. People were always telling me I couldn't skate well enough, yet I was always in the top four or five of All Star voting and the Selke award as a defensive player. As I get older, I do take more pride in it."

His attitude hasn't deviated since his early days on the farm when he'd travel into Viking to prove his mettle. "When I went into Viking, the town kids weren't going to beat me," he said firmly. "When our Viking teams went to another town, they weren't going to beat us." It's a philosophy he took from the farm into Viking, from Viking into Wainwright, from St. Louis into Chicago.

"To me the Carena was almost a shrine," Brian said, turning the clock back. "My friend Jim Laskosky and I used to skip school and go skate there for hours. The school was right across the street from the Carena. You'd just crawl out a bathroom window and it wasn't too far to go. We'd take a screwdriver to the lock, go in and skate in the dark whenever we felt like it. We did it so much that we hid our skates in the rink. They put artificial ice in after I left. All I remember is this excellent natural ice. They would flood it with five-gallon barrels with pipes out the back and a gunnysack. It was a real honour to be one of the scrapers."

After leaving the practice ice, Brian, his son Shaun and I reconvened at the Sutter Club in the heart of Red Deer. It's a sprawling sports establishment encompassing nearly ten thousand square feet, which makes it feel as vast as the Carena. Not surprisingly, the Sutter Club caters to families and sports teams. On the walls are mementoes of the brothers' hockey accomplishments, particularly in Red Deer, where Brent and the twins, Rich and Ron, were members of the Centennial Cup champion Rustlers in 1980. Under this familiar backdrop, Brian retraced his steps to the NHL. He was not only the first of the Sutters to play for the Rustlers, he also led their advance to Lethbridge of the Western Junior Hockey League, where he blossomed on a line with Bryan Trottier. In 1976, the St. Louis Blues used a second-round selection, twentieth pick overall, to claim the first of six brothers and Carena graduates to play in the NHL.

From the time Sutter donned his Blues jersey until it was retired to the rafters, Brian Sutter was the organization's most faithful employee. It was a loyalty frequently tested throughout his twelve-year playing career by the instability of Blues' ownership. "I was always considered one of the top left-wingers in the game, and I know I didn't earn the money everyone else did," he said without a trace of bitterness. "I was owed thousands of dollars lots of times, tens of thousands, but I stayed in St. Louis and loved it there. I knew a couple of times teams offered a million dollars for me. I would not dream of wanting to go anyplace else no matter how drastic the situation. I guess I'm an extremely loyal person.

"There was a ten-year period when I was in St. Louis when there was no team in hockey that had a better record than the Blues except for the teams that won the Stanley Cup. St. Louis was probably the first team which money tore apart. We lost Mike Liut, Joe Mullen, Doug Gilmour and Rob Ramage, on and on."

Sutter still dwells on the elusiveness of hockey's most coveted reward, which neither fierce allegiance nor an owner's money can buy. In the 1986 Stanley Cup playoffs, the Blues flirted with a trip to the Cup final, losing a heartbreaking seven-game series to the Calgary Flames. It's a defeat that still haunts him. "It was 2–1 in the seventh game with about thirty seconds to go. I tripped one of their defencemen. Dougie [Gilmour] went into the corner for the puck, and I went to the front of the net. Dougie threw it out and it hit Al MacInnis on the toe of his skate blade and stopped dead. I was standing wide open in front, and if I got the puck there I was going to score. I had one of the top shooting percentages every year but the puck never reached me."

The cruel irony is that Brian forged the Sutters' path to the NHL but was sidetracked on the Stanley Cup trail. Yet his brothers Duane and Brent captured Stanley Cup titles in each of their rookie seasons with the New York Islanders. Brian celebrated their good fortune but it was a bittersweet cup of cheer. "I was happy for Duane, but I also thought, you sonofabitch. I go and work my balls off. I fought every guy in the league, I'm one of the top goal-scorers and supposed to be one of the top defensive players. Then Brent goes and does it too. I'm happy for those guys and disappointed. Those guys still don't know how lucky they are."

After 779 games of distinguished service to the Blues in which he amassed 303 goals, 636 points and 1,786 penalty minutes, Sutter retired from the ice to move to coaching, continuing his dedicated service to the organization. In four years, he became the most successful coach in Blues' history, surpassing the records of Scotty Bowman. Just as in his playing career, Sutter overachieved in an environment that was not conducive to winning. The Blues continued to deal players they could not afford to retain in exchange for compensation below market value. Sutter's frustration reached its zenith when Blues management unloaded Doug Gilmour to Calgary in 1988, spurning more lucrative offers from other clubs. "I was so mad in the Minnesota airport when I heard the news I ripped the whole pay phone right out of the wall. Not just the receiver, the whole phone," he described, a hint of anger lingering in his voice.

Sutter and the Blues were permanently disconnected following the 1991–92 season when the Blues won eleven fewer games than the season before when Brian had been the NHL's Coach of the Year. A few weeks after the Blues dismissed Sutter, the Boston Bruins, a franchise noted for the grinding style that was also Brian's trademark, named him their coach. He repaid their confidence by leading Boston to its best season in a decade: 51 wins, 109 points and second place overall. "We took them from three years when they were very average to three excellent years," Sutter declared. "There were only a couple of teams in hockey that won more games than we did in those three years in Boston."

Unfortunately, his playoff frustration continued there. Although Sutter isn't openly critical of the Bruins' ownership, Boston, like St. Louis, was unwilling to provide the resources to produce a champion. "One year against New Jersey [in the 1993–94 eastern conference semifinal], we lost in six games," he lamented. "They scored four even-strength goals, we scored three. Oates, Bourque, Smolinski and Don Sweeney played their hearts out. The Devils had a bigger, tougher, stronger team. They had a team to beat you in the playoffs. I was proud of our guys. People questioned the players and the coach. But do you know what we did in three years there? There were only two teams in the regular season and playoffs that won more than we did. I'm proud of those things. Al Arbour once told me that they aren't going to know how good a coach you are until you leave. When I left St. Louis the Blues went down. It also happened in Boston."

After the Bruins fired Sutter, he was hesitant to return to the hot seat. He retreated to his farm near Sylvan Lake, Alberta, with five quarter sections and 150 head of pure-bred Angus cattle. Following the 1995–96 campaign, there were coaching offers to consider, the most enticing from San Jose. Sutter declined. "People wonder why you turn down $700,000 when on the farm you might make $70,000 or lose it all in a hailstorm or a crazy fall like we had. Even when we lived down in the States, I considered myself a farmer. We've really looked forward to doing this. It's been great for us. I've been able to watch Shaun, to do things with my daughter Abby I'd never done before. My wife, Judy, and I have had more time."

Yet like brother Darryl, the competitive embers are still glowing. Over the Christmas holidays of the 1996–97 hockey season, Brian confided to family that it was time to get back to work in the NHL. That feeling may be reciprocal within the NHL. Glen Sather revealed that he had recently received a call from a fellow general manager inquiring about Sutter. "I don't think he's been forgotten," said Sather.

For now, though, Brian Sutter is the coach of the Red Deer Optimist Chiefs and proud of it. It's an assignment that has brought his career full circle. After having a dramatic impact on his brothers' careers, Sutter is in a position to make the difference again. "I look in their eyes and I see them dreaming," he said, fully aware of the beauty of that vision. "Some of them have a real good chance of playing somewhere in the future. All I want to be able to do is give them a little insight on how to get there."

From her cash register at the IGA in Viking, Grace Sutter has a bird's-eye view of the Carena across the street. "I work here to be independent," she said proudly. Grace was approaching her sixteenth anniversary with the store, the same length of time she carted her seven boys to the Carena on a weekly basis. When the store is quiet, she still passes time in quiet contemplation, gazing across the road, drifting back to those wondrous years of minor hockey's cheers and tears. Grace fondly relives those delightfully chaotic Saturdays when she would pack lunches for her roster and spend the entire day at the Carena rooting for her boys. "You had to get your kids involved," said the matriarch of the Sutter clan. "It was my thinking that as long as you kept them busy they wouldn't get into trouble." Typically, the only problems Grace had to deal with erupted during the return trip to the farm following a game in which the Sutter boys had faced off against each other. "Brent did play one year against the twins," she explained. "They'd get into the car and start arguing. I'd say, listen you guys, that game ended out there. No more!"

Those Saturdays were a welcome diversion from the spartan life of the Sutters' early years on the farm. In the 1968 publication *Let Us Not Forget: The History of Viking and District*, Grace documented the simplicity and hardships of the time. "We lived like our neighbours with no modern conveniences, no phones, no running water or power, with wood and coal stoves for heating and cooking; in September of 1964, the fall after the twins arrived, we had electricity. My what a great convenience!" Three years later, the Sutters had another luxury, running water. "Some days the boys had five baths each," she wrote.

She is known as "Grandma Grace" at the IGA and throughout Viking, a beloved figure, not because six of her boys made it to the NHL, but because she is a respected, caring figure in a close-knit town. However, during the Islanders–Oilers Stanley Cup battles, Grandma Grace was a target for a hostile minority in the local community. "It was a tough time even at work," she said. "It was bad. There was a woman who intentionally came to my till during the final between the Oilers and Islanders and started talking really nasty about the Islanders. I said, I wish you wouldn't talk like that. I have two sons on that team. She said, I know that but why can't they play for the Oilers? She was really badmouthing the boys individually. I never saw that woman again.

"We had things happen to our car, a hood ornament ripped off. Another time it looked like somebody had taken two nails and gouged the car from the trunk all the way along the side, right up to the roof. We'd left the car by the rink at night. A lot of people were jealous."

The malicious acts and venomous words of a small fringe in Viking were triggered, in part, by a story in the *Edmonton Sun* during the 1983 final. It's a subject that, more than a decade later, Duane Sutter is hesitant to broach. "Terry Jones [*Sun* columnist] asked me who the people in Viking would cheer for during the series," Duane recounted. "I told him it didn't matter as long as when we returned home for the summer, if they had cheered for the Oilers, that they didn't pretend to be Islanders fans. That would be two-faced. We fly into Edmonton the next day and there's a story which says I called Viking fans two-faced. I never said that but it got Mom, Dad and Gary into a couple of binds in town."

The bond between the Sutter family and the people of Viking is as resilient as the Sutter boys are rugged. Any fence-mending required by the community in the aftermath of those spiteful incidents has long been completed. It was just part of the growing pains of a small-town success story. "I think even the coaches of their minor hockey teams needed to learn how to deal with their success," said Grace. "With Darryl and Gary working with the hockey teams at the Carena again, people can see that they are bringing a little bit back to the town."

There was a night of appreciation in honour of the Sutters in Viking. They are also acknowledged on the highway signpost greeting visitors into town: "Welcome to Viking—Home of the Sutters." Beyond that they are on equal footing with other families in the district, which is how both the Sutters and the townsfolk prefer it. "They don't want people to think that they're celebrities," said Angela Hanson, editor of the Viking newspaper, whose son is a member of Darryl's novice hockey team. "It's not that the community doesn't appreciate them. It's funny, we get weak-kneed seeing one of the Oilers in Edmonton, but not when we're around one of our guys. That's the way they want to be treated."

The Sutter farm, fourteen kilometres from Viking, sits on a plateau that is the highest point of elevation between the Rockies and Winnipeg on the western plain. Their property is adjacent to a sacred native rock formation called the Rib Stones. A century ago, the Plains Indians carved the images of buffalo ribs into the rocks as they hunted the roaming herd of prairie bison. The Indians left sacrificial gifts on the site to ensure a successful buffalo hunt. As the neighbouring Sutters' success in the NHL has grown to mythic proportions, one wonders if the magical powers of the Rib Stones seeped into the family's farmland.

Like any farmhouse, the kitchen is the focal point of the Sutter home, at its heart a table and chairs that can still accommodate all seven boys at one sitting. The living room is highlighted by a painting of the Sutters' original homestead, the work of Brian's wife, Judy. A satellite guide and an NHL schedule are at the ready. Hockey is the television fare every night whether one of the boys is in action or not. Hanging over the stairwell leading to the lower level is a painting, commissioned by Duane, depicting the seven brothers after a game of shinny on the farmyard slough. In the family room below is Grace's motherlode of hockey memories and memorabilia.

Encompassing the early

days of the Carena to the Stanley Cup, the room allowed Grace to keep in touch with her boys even when they were scattered far afield, sometimes waging battle against each other. In one corner is a striking portrait of Darryl in a Blackhawks uniform, which emits an ethereal glow. "Sometimes when I'm really down, I come here for inspiration," Grace said of her prized keepsake. "That picture says, smarten up, Mom! You are a much better person than that to let things get you down."

There are trophies and photos from her eldest son Gary's hockey past. Gary was a promising teenage offensive defenceman, the only Sutter to play the position. "He was the only one of us who could skate backwards," Duane quipped. Gary was slated to accompany Brian to Red Deer for that

The Sutter boys pose on Louis's new tractor in 1980. Clockwise from top left, Rich, Darryl, Brent, Ron, Gary, Duane and Brian

first junior training camp with Cec Swanson. Instead he chose his girlfriend over hockey, forgoing any chance of a pro career in favour of matrimony. His love of the game, however, outlasted the marriage. The two parted ways a few years later but Gary's window of opportunity to play in the NHL had closed. "People tell me that it still affects me today," he said of the decision that annulled his chance of a pro hockey career. "I suppose it does, in a way."

He returned to his sports passion as a star in local senior hockey, coached the Calgary Canucks of the Alberta Junior loop and scouted for Tacoma of the Western Hockey League. As an assistant coach with the Red Deer Rustlers, Gary shared the thrill of capturing the Centennial Cup with brothers Brent, Rich and Ron. He has followed his brothers' NHL careers every step of the way.

Now Gary has returned to the Carena to coach the Viking midget team, the same age group as brother Brian's Red Deer squad. Fittingly, these two midget coaches have been cast in roles tailored to their life experiences; Brian guides AAA prospects with NHL aspirations, and Gary advises youngsters with more limited hockey opportunities. "The message I'm trying to get through is basically what Brian is telling his kids, concentrate on the fundamentals; with those come a good attitude and desire," he said, reciting the Sutter principles of hockey and life. As he continued, Gary put his personal stamp on the message. "I tell them in three years you're in the real world, when you'll be expected to work hard. Why not start now? If you play hard enough, you might be able to play hockey in college, university or learn a trade. Keep your options open through hockey."

Amid the myriad of hockey spoils is Brent's award as the MVP of the Centennial Cup, but Grace was concerned that a nagging groin injury was threatening her fifth son's career. Brent, a centre in Chicago, in his sixteenth pro season, is the most decorated Sutter. He has won two Stanley Cups with the Islanders, was a member of two Canada Cup winners and is the leading NHL scorer among the Sutters, surpassing 350 goals and 800 points, impressive totals for the shy, introspective son who earned the distasteful nickname "Puke" by throwing up daily as a child on the bus ride to school. However, at the Carena he would clean up, the Sutter closest to superstar status. "Everybody talks about how many goals Wayne Gretzky scored as a kid," Darryl Sutter recounted. "Brett did that every year. He plays a different style now, but that's how good he was."

Back in the Sutters' trophy room, there was paraphernalia from the Flyers days when the twins, whom Grace still refers to as "Ronald and Richard," played together in Philadelphia. They were inseparable throughout their hockey careers from the Carena, where they won peewee, bantam and midget provincial titles. The banners from those minor hockey championships are displayed prominently inside the Carena. The twins rode tandem through the junior ranks into the NHL, except for a brief period when Rich began his career in Pittsburgh. "I remember them playing together and how they would drive teams crazy," said brother Duane. "Their coach, John Chapman, labelled them 'hack and slash' in junior. It started way back in minor hockey. The way they went after teams with their forechecking and tenacity—it was awfully impressive to see them, even as eight- and nine-year-olds." Darryl Sutter had a different perspective on their tag-team routine when he faced them for the first time in Chicago. "I hadn't seen the twins much because I left home when they were little. When I saw them with Philly, I couldn't believe it. I said to myself, look at those little peckerheads yapping. I still thought of them as little boys but they were out there spearing and creating havoc."

After four seasons in Philadelphia, the twins were separated by Mike Keenan, who dealt Rich to Vancouver. Then "Iron Mike" had to deal with an outraged mother. "He still says it's one of the worst talking-tos he ever had," said Grace, with a hint of a smile beneath the dismay. "I said to him, Who is your best plus-minus player? He stuttered and stammered and finally said it was Rich. Then why is he going to be a Canuck? I asked. He couldn't answer that."

The twins were reunited for a day at the Edmonton Coliseum near the midway point of the 1996–97 NHL season. Ron is now a member of the San Jose Sharks, his sixth NHL team. Rich, living in Lethbridge, is enrolled in computer courses as he adapts to life after hockey. He made the trip to Edmonton to cheer on his kindred spirit. I spoke with them individually, but the twins provided a similar theme of Carena memories. "I used to love scraping the ice between periods," said Ron, following a morning skate with the Sharks. "They'd let a few of us kids push the shovels before they would flood the ice. It reminded me of clearing the snow off the sloughs where we played. It made it feel special, like it was your ice." For Rich that ice-cleaning ritual became a source of motivation. "We never had a Zamboni until the last year," he said. "Instead we pulled a five-gallon drum around to flood the ice. People with the city teams we played would sit up in the stands and laugh at us. I'd say to myself, let them make fun. It gave us more incentive to beat them and we always did."

In the Sutters' basement gallery there is a picture of Grace and Louis posing with the Stanley Cup in Vancouver, after the Islanders' third of four championship seasons in 1982. It is the only time the proud Sutter parents ever witnessed a Cup victory first hand. Three other times they watched in disappointment as their boys lost Stanley Cup series in Edmonton in '84, '85 and '87. Beneath the picture are Stanley Cup replicas from Duane's four championship seasons with the Islanders. His first, in 1980, will always be most treasured for ensuring the Sutter name would be inscribed on hockey's most coveted silverware, and for the telephone call he made from the delirious dressing room afterwards. "It was like phoning our parents about a new child in the family," Duane said of the call to Sylvan Lake where the family had gathered to celebrate. "I feel for Brian, Darryl and the twins for not winning the Cup. There's only one thing in life that has given me the excitement that's even close to winning the Cup. That's being with my wife when our children were born."

In that clinching game, Duane scored one of the most controversial goals in Stanley Cup history on a play that television replays revealed was clearly offside. "I hear about it all the time," Duane said with a laugh. "Every time I see Leon Stickle [the linesman who missed the call], we chuckle about it. Usually when you're offside, you just instinctively let up. To this day I don't know why I didn't stop on that play. I could have easily held up and been checked from behind. I guess it was meant to be. I'm glad I didn't stop because it was one of the biggest goals I ever scored."

After Grace and I rekindled countless memories from the Sutter "Hall of Fame," Louis volunteered to escort me to the red barn that doubles as the family arena. Along the way, I tried to confirm a rumour that he once boxed on a fight card at the Carena. "No," he replied modestly. "Foster Hewitt and Webb Pierce [a country singer] played the Carena. Not me." Nevertheless, the sinewy Sutter did enjoy a modest boxing career in the Viking district before his seven sons were born. "I've seen him bounce a few guys around so he must have been all right," Darryl had informed me earlier. Like the boys, Louis inherited the muscular frame of his father, Charles, who had been the city wrestling champion of Edmonton. In his sixties, Louis still looked as though he could pin a snorting bull.

We ascended a set of well-worn steps to the loft, where bales of hay long ago gave way to hockey. The sloping wooden roof creates the appearance of a typical prairie rink. In the mind of a hockey-crazed Sutter boy it would have been easy to imagine that barn being the Chicago Stadium or Montreal

Forum. Its dimensions are ideally suited for three-on-three hockey. "It's thirty feet by fifty," Louis said, directing my attention to a spot near the staircase. "That's where Duane would stand to be Foster Hewitt." Along one wall twenty sticks are lined up, like players during the national anthem, at the ready for the next game. A sheet of plywood with holes cut out at the four corners was used for shooting drills. "Darryl still comes up and shoots occasionally," Louis said. "He can really fire a puck." Then he opened the doors at either end, allowing sunlight to flood the entire loft. Chicken wire has been strung across the openings to prevent flying rubber from hitting the unsuspecting livestock that graze below.

It was time for me to leave so Louis could resume his chores. There is never an off-season for a farmer. As he trudged through the snow into the fields, I was reminded of a conversation I had with Duane about his parents. "When you have your own kids, you start to realize how important your parents are," he said. "They worked very hard to make sure we had clothes on our backs and food on the table. Dad put in long hours, getting up with the sun and going to bed at sundown. That's the life of a small-town farmer. Hours and hours of total dedication to provide for your family."

The 1996–97 hockey season marked the twentieth anniversary of the Sutter family's participation in the NHL. "It's a long time for a bunch of farmers to be around," joked Brian. By the All Star break, these farmers were easily the most prolific brother act in NHL history, approaching 4,700 games of service, with 1,300 goals, 2,900 points and more than 7,660 penalty minutes, the equivalent of more than 127 games—over a season and a half of time served in the penalty box.

As Brent idles through his sixteenth NHL season handicapped by injury, and Ron backchecks in the twilight of his career, the Sutters' golden era is slowly drawing to a close. With luck, and the usual measure of Sutter determination, there may be one, perhaps two more years of NHL action for this current generation of Sutter players. Like a bumper crop, their remarkable exploits are cause for thanksgiving. There is, however, a tinge of melancholy that this magnificent story is ending. "I'm missing it already," said Grace, torn between the joy of welcoming her boys home and the sadness of their hockey careers concluding. "Hopefully the grandchildren will carry on."

As the Montreal Canadiens' tradition is sustained by the symbolic passing of the torch, there is, within the Sutter family, that expectation of continuity from this generation to the next as well. It is not regarded as a false hope or a burden but a challenge for the next line of Sutters.

Sixteen-year-old Shaun Sutter is a forward on the Red Deer Optimist Chiefs. His stride and tenacious demeanour remind regulars at the Red Deer Arena of his uncle Rich. Shaun's junior rights belong to the Lethbridge Hurricanes, the same program that channelled the previous six Sutters to the NHL. He is regarded as a blue-chip prospect and will toil full-time in the Western Hockey League next year. Until then, he's under the watchful eye of his coach and father, Brian. "He expects more out of me," acknowledged Shaun after being chewed out at practice by the coach. "I am probably harder on him than the rest of the boys," admitted Brian. "But he's lucky too because I can see lots of things that make him good, and a lot of little things that can make him better."

With the Sutter name on his jersey, it's not only the coach who is more demanding. "I get extra attention because of the name," Shaun said without complaint. Nevertheless, he is intent on making a name for himself, patterning the style of a current NHL player he is not related to. "I'm like Esa Tikkanen. I can score but I'm not a guy that can be a sniper. But I can be a pretty good aggravator." Brian understands the delicate balance of pros and cons inherent with a famous name. "He's got it tough in some ways because he has our name. He has people, wherever he goes, that feel he has something to live up to, but it's better to have something to live up to than nothing at all."

There is another Sutter anxious to blaze a new hockey trail. Duane's eldest daughter, Darby, a twelve-year-old hockey phenomenon in Florida, happily accepts the challenge passed to the next generation of Sutters. Her sights are set on becoming the first member of her family to play for the U.S. Olympic women's hockey team. Meanwhile, her father continues his hockey career as a Panthers assistant coach. Duane is still learning the coaching craft. Should he follow his brothers Brian and Darryl into the head coaching ranks, the Sutters would become the first family in league history to have three brothers hold NHL coaching positions.

Back at the Carena, the brightest prospect on the horizon is nine-year-old Brett Sutter. Recently Brett shot his age, scoring nine goals in an exhibition game against his sister Jessica, who was tending goal for the opposition. The grooming of another Sutter in the NHL is underway. "Yes, I think about it and talk to Brett about it," says his father, Darryl. "I think if you talk about it, you reinforce what you expect of him. I say that in the sense that it's not the be-all and end-all to play in the NHL. If he thinks it's going to be a free ride because of his last name, if he thinks it's an easy road, then it's not going to happen. I tell him that I don't care how good he is, but he better be the hardest worker out there every time he's on the ice. You don't have to be the best kid but if you're the hardest worker then you have a better chance."

Everyone accepts that four-year-old Christopher is one Sutter who won't play in the NHL. He was born with Down's syndrome, in March 1993. His condition was unsettling not only for the tight-knit Sutter clan but, by extension, for Darryl's Blackhawks team. Privately, Chicago players have confided to the family that they lost focus following Christopher's birth. They were more concerned with how their beloved coach was coping than with their own game. In the 1993 Stanley Cup playoffs, the Blackhawks were swept by St. Louis in the opening round.

Two seasons later the NHL was shut down by a lock-out. One of the few benefits of that exercise was the time it gave Darryl to devote to his family, paving the way for their return to Viking. "We had three or four months when I could take Chris to the rink when Brett played and he really enjoyed it," Darryl says, with one eye trained on his wandering youngster. "We had talked about it a lot when Chris was born. It looked like he was going to need a lot of help. Everyone we talked to, all the specialists say it's better if both parents are involved, not just one. It makes sense. We said that if hockey ever got in the way of him, we were coming home. It wasn't a tough decision to make. It was tough the day we had to make the announcement in Chicago, but it wasn't something that just happened. We had known all along."

In Viking, Christopher goes to school three times a week and attends a day-long speech therapy session every Tuesday in Camrose. Most importantly, Christopher and his parents are surrounded by a much larger support group. "God gave us that child for a special reason," Grandma Grace had said proudly. "It's really great to be able to help them raise their family, especially Christopher. Uncle Gary and him are just like this." She crossed her fingers and beamed.

At the Carena, Christopher is just as at home as the other Sutter youngsters. He watches transfixed through the lobby glass while his brother Brett stickhandles expertly around his novice teammates. Occasionally he'll bolt for the rink door before he's reeled in. I intervene once after he's body-checked a garbage can that appears ready to tip back in his direction. Then he's on the move again like a Sutter on the forecheck. Briefly, I'm in pursuit but his mother, Wanda, discourages me. "He'll be here all winter. We might

as well let him get used to the place," she says. Soon, he's back at the window wishing it was his turn to be on the ice.

Darryl has told me that Down's children are unable to skate. Sizing up Christopher's mobility and his apparent desire, I suggest it could be another obstacle that a Sutter will overcome. "I know he'll try, that's for sure," Darryl says, nodding in agreement. "He tries to emulate Brett so much. He practises at home now with his skates on. He gets in front of the television when somebody scores. It's fun, a different kind of fun."

Lacing up with Darryl and Christopher

The most fun, though, is yet to come. Brett's practice has finally concluded. As the Viking novices file off, Darryl opens the lobby door and beckons Christopher. It's the moment he's been waiting for. Finally, it's his turn to have Dad and the Carena ice to himself. They fit into each other's arms as only a parent and infant child can. As Darryl starts to circle the ice, the perpetual game face he brings to the rink disappears. Christopher's expression illuminates the entire Carena.

In one lap, these two Sutters have answered all the questions of Darryl's departure from Chicago. An icy mist rises, making it appear as if they are skating in the clouds. Different images flicker through my mind. There is a flash of Darryl cradling the Stanley Cup in Chicago. A delirious mob at the stadium explodes as the captain of the Blackhawks lifts the Cup to the ceiling. It is the defining moment that Darryl Sutter so desperately sought, but which eluded him, as a player and coach. In the next instant, I am back at the Carena. It's Christopher that Darryl is holding overhead. There isn't a sound in the rink, except for the laughter of a father and a son.

6 Cominco Arena
Trail, British Columbia

Scott Russell

Give me but one firm spot on which to stand, and I will move the earth.
—Archimedes

"THERE'S A 50–50 CHANCE WE'LL BE landing in Castlegar because there's not much visibility," the pilot is saying as the Dash-8 climbs out of Penticton. "If we can't make it, then we're going on to Calgary. Stay tuned!" It is a sinking feeling knowing that the journey to Trail in the dead of winter is such a tenuous proposition. Waiting at the Cominco Arena, just twenty minutes down Highway 22 from the airport in Castlegar, are three members of the 1961 Smoke Eaters. Cal Hockley, Norm Lenardon and Addy Tambellini are anxious to watch the Grey Cup game between the Edmonton Eskimos and the Toronto Argonauts later in the afternoon but have willingly obliged a request to reflect on a world championship they won three and a half decades ago. The only problems are the thick cover of cloud and the advancing blanket of snow, both of which are being draped over British Columbia's interior on this late November morning.

For years this part of the country has been a bastion of hockey's mythology. Out of the mountain passes, world champions have emerged with startling frequency to find a place in the folklore of the game. Back in 1937, the Kimberley Dynamiters became the first club from British Columbia to capture the global amateur title with their success in London, England. Two years later in Basel, Switzerland, the Trail Smoke Eaters turned the trick by recording an amazing seven shut-outs in the eight-game tournament. One of their better players, Joe Benoit, went on to star with the Montreal Canadiens in the era of Toe Blake and Elmer Lach.

In 1955, the Penticton Vees burst out of the Okanagan to reclaim world supremacy for Canada by avenging the USSR's defeat of the Toronto York Lyndhursts the year before. Led by the Warwick brothers, Grant, Dick and Billy, the Vees whipped the Russians 5–0 in the final game at Krefeld, Germany, and took the trophy home, as it turned out, for good. "I still have it tucked away at my place here in Edmonton," said a mischevious Billy Warwick. His eyes lit up forty-two years later while watching a Flyers–Oilers game at the Coliseum. "You didn't think we'd go all that way and come home empty-handed, did you?" After the final, Warwick had snatched the original world championship trophy, which had fallen into disrepair, deciding then and there it was never to end up in the hands of the despised Soviets again. The battle-scarred Warwick cleaned it up and polished its silver to a sparkling brilliance it had seldom seen. He guards the old trophy to this day as if it were the Holy Grail.

Ray Ferraro, a Trail native and member of the Los Angeles Kings, had warned that the flight into Castlegar would be the air traveller's adventure of a lifetime. Suddenly, the twin engines groan and the nose of the plane dips into the milkiness of the surrounding clouds. For several moments, not a soul on board utters a word. It appears the captain is avoiding the detour to Calgary after all, as he pushes downward to the ground, which we all hope is advancing at the right rate. Without warning, there is a pronounced bank to the left, followed by an immediate levelling and the appearance of the undercarriage. The passengers are still blind as the windows reveal only a blank and colourless wall. Then a few dark dots pop through the white and become trees. Just seconds later, the wheels scorch the tarmac, the engines roar before feathering and we coast towards the tiny terminal building.

The sobering effect of looking up, once outside the fuselage of the plane, is astounding. The mountain on the far side of the runway and the one in front of it mean that a narrow laneway is the only approach to the airport at Castlegar. "Don't count on getting out of here tomorrow," the agent at the gate warns. "There's more snow on the way and we'll likely be socked right in!" From this unlikely, almost forbidding point of departure, the last Canadian club team to conquer hockey's world had launched its assault on a place in history.

The short drive along the highway south into Trail traces the western bank of the Columbia River. Like everything else in the landscape, the water exudes a strength of character. It flows a steel grey as stark contrast to the brilliant white of the snow-covered shore. The clue that Trail is close appears in the form of two enormous smoke-stacks that belch clouds of vapour into the sky. The giant Cominco refinery under that pair of chimneys is every bit like a fortress that guards the entrance to the town. Cominco (Consolidated Mining and Smelting Company Limited) is the dominant industry in the West Kootenay region of British Columbia. Once the largest lead and zinc refinery of its kind in the world, Cominco is a benevolent corporate citizen that has allowed aspiring hockey players in Trail to excel in astonishing numbers. Down the hill and to the left, the community unfolds in the shadow of the imposing factory.

Smoke Eaters was the nickname bestowed on Trail's senior hockey club in the late twenties. Although the jerseys bear a picture of the Cominco stacks on the crest, the origin of the name is based on something quite different. In the winter of 1929, Trail faced a tough team from Vancouver in a crucial playoff game on the road. The host team took a bad penalty late in the contest, and the fans littered the ice with everything they had in their possession. One of the objects was a pipe still billowing with tobacco smoke. Trail's star centre at the time, Carroll Kendall, picked up the pipe and skated around the arena, puffing on it luxuriously to the fans' delight. The next day, a cartoon in the *Vancouver Province* newspaper depicted the episode as a token of good luck to the victorious squad from Trail. That was when sportswriter A.R.

The Trail Memorial Centre, which houses Cominco Arena, was completed in 1949. Cominco Ltd., once the largest lead and zinc smelter in the world, overlooks the arena

Dingman dubbed the team the "Smoke Eaters from Trail."

The "Smokies," as some choose to call the hockey club, have been housed since 1949 in the Trail Memorial Centre, strategically located at the base of fortress Cominco. It is a landmark facility that defines the town's

Western Interior
Hockey League
action between
the Smoke
Eaters and the
Nelson Maple
Leafs. The
helmeted Billy
Warwick, a
member of the
1955 World
Champion
Penticton Vees,
scores for Trail
on goalie Gus
Adams. Adams
is the father of
current Dallas
Stars forward
Greg Adams

centre at the confluence of business and residential neighbourhoods. On a Sunday afternoon, the parking lot is full and families stream almost constantly through the doors under the red neon marquee. For a city of fewer than eight thousand people, the arena complex is massive and dominates the modest skyline while dwarfing surrounding structures.

"This is your arena. Please help us keep it clean. No gum, no sunflower seeds," says the simple sign just over the stairs through the entrance doors. In the outer lobby, three men rise in unison from the wooden bench they have been resting on and welcome me to their immaculate hockey temple. They are like three wise men of hockey as they stand unified in the foyer of their rink. Adolph—"Addy"—Tambellini is the first one to put out his hand. "So you made it, eh? Thought nothing was getting through for sure," he says. Tambellini is the youngest of the Smoke Eaters who captured the world championship in 1961. A speedy centreman turned left-winger, Addy has just turned sixty and is the current recreation director for his native city of Trail.

"Saw you doing the Canucks game last night," exclaims Norm Lenardon. Removing his glasses, he reveals the sharp features and easy smile that I saw

in the Smoke Eaters team picture at the Hockey Hall of Fame. Lenardon is three years older than Tambellini and was employed as a bricklayer while playing right wing for the Smokies in the fifties and sixties. It was his goal in a 5–1 final-game victory that ensured victory for Canada over the Russians at the world championship. Now retired, Lenardon is a soft-spoken but fiercely proud individual, and unofficial president of the 1961 Smoke Eaters alumni, known affectionately around town as the "61ers."

The leader is the most imposing figure and, strangely, the only member of the trio who was not born in Trail. "I'm from Fernie, B.C., and I came here in 1956," says Cal Hockley. "I used to play for the Kimberley Dyna-miters before that and I thought I was coming here to play one season. Cripes! I've been here ever since!" Hockley is the senior Smoke Eater and he remains the team captain thirty-five years after the victory in Europe. Now sixty-five years old, he is still a bull of a man who relishes his hockey legacy in these parts. His reputation is built on an unrelenting determina-tion to succeed. "I was a right-winger too, except I always thought I owned the whole rink," Hockley says. "I didn't play any particular position. I just told the other guys to get the hell out of my way!"

As a unit, they lead the way up the stairs to the main floor of the complex. Tambellini does most of the talking and acts as the tour guide because he is most directly involved with the Memorial Centre on a day-to-day basis. To the left, he indicates the city library and, beyond that, a gymnasium complete with a shimmering hardwood floor and old-fashioned permanent bleach-ers. Walking past the impressive Trail Sports Hall of Memories, Tambellini pauses and points to a couple of artifacts in the glass display cases that flank the hallway. The collection is the legacy of the late Allan Tognatti, the museum's curator, who is heralded on a memorial plaque as "A native son and city booster." The threesome surveys the precious skates, sticks, photographs and jerseys while Lenardon surmises that Tognatti may have been the Smoke Eaters' biggest fan.

In addition, the Memorial Centre has squash and racquetball courts, banquet halls, dance studios, arts and crafts rooms, a fitness centre, a curl-ing rink and a children's skating rink. It is an all-purpose gathering place for the people of Trail and it is easy to estimate its value on that basis alone. Then Tambellini leads to the right and swings open the orange door to Cominco Arena, the anchor to the facility and what many believe is the hockey showcase of the entire region.

Simplicity and symmetry are the best words to describe this hockey rink. It has an NHL-sized ice surface two hundred feet by eighty-five feet. In a perfect, uninterrupted bowl there are places for 2,538 people to sit on glossy orange bleacher seats. The walls are ivory coloured and the ceiling looks like it might be made of the cedar taken from a thousand saunas. On this lazy afternoon, the old-timers are struggling up and down the ice, which bears none of the gaudy advertising that clutters so many modern arenas. Painted inside a huge centre circle are the sinister twin smoke-stacks from the Cominco refinery that have become the enduring symbol of the home-town teams. At one end are four banners. Two, in orange, proclaim the senior

Smoke Eaters as Allan Cup champions in 1938 and 1962. The other pair, a contrasting white, are more precious still. They honour the young men from Trail who captured world championships in 1939 and 1961. In the centre of the pennants, bordered by two Canadian flags, is the portrait of a young Queen Eliza-

The championship banners won by Trail over the last sixty years hang from the rafters in Cominco Arena

beth II. The three wise men all claim the rink looks much the same as the day it was completed nearly half a century ago.

Cominco Arena bears the name of its founder and builder. Although the most important industry in the West Kootenay region of British Columbia did not pay taxes to the city of Trail until 1971, long before then, Cominco pumped money into facilities that would improve the community it overlooked. The refinery's management formed a "projects society" that saw the company match every dollar donated by its employees towards the building of a new recreational facility slated for completion in 1949. It was in this way that Cominco put up $1.2 million for the hockey rink and then gave it to the people of Trail. The residents of the city also had a great sense of pride in their new ice palace because of their own financial contributions, but their industrious nature also played a significant part. "People would come down from the plant and wheel dirt, and the bricklayers would bricklay for nothing," says Lenardon. "Almost everything was done on a volunteer basis."

When it was finished, Cominco Arena immediately became the toast of not only the town, but a large section of the province. "When Cominco built the arena, it was second to none," Hockley explains. "The first five years they averaged 2,750 people a game here. Everybody felt they built it too damn small but the rink was two and a half times bigger than anything else in the interior of B.C.!"

In 1953, a separate and smaller hockey surface was attached to the Memorial Centre and was reserved for the younger players of the city. Like Cominco Arena, it was funded by the Trail District Recreational Projects

The Rink

Society and has come to reflect the self-reliant nature of the population. The tiny rink looks alarmingly like an oversized handball court, with a tremendously high ceiling painted with the same whitewash as its supporting walls. There are no bleachers. The ice is all that counts. It has always been known as the Kids' Rink, and the raw materials processed here over the years have aspired to the lofty ideals its builders had in mind. "Dedicated to Canada's greatest resource . . . our children," is the message engraved on a bronze plaque by the entrance.

The senior hockey team that played out of Cominco Arena had a reputation to live up to throughout the 1950s and '60s. The old 1938 Smoke Eaters had won the Allan Cup to become Canadian champions and then had gone on to claim the world title a year later. It was the last officially recognized championship of its kind until 1947 because of the outbreak of World War II. With a new rink, Trail went about rebuilding its competitive fire, with the city's main industry helping to forge the resulting product. "Cominco actually recruited athletes. They preferred to hire someone who could play baseball or hockey," explains Hockley. "The players got preferential treatment, in fact, and a very large portion of those guys never left."

So it was that Hockley became a well-paid metallurgical research technician who was rock steady on the right side of the Smoke Eater's on-ice attack. Addy Tambellini held several staff jobs in the Cominco office, including his work in the shipping department. It was his blazing speed on skates, however, that stood out most prominently on his résumé. Norm Lenardon worked laying bricks and repairing roasters "up the hill," as the players often referred to the refinery. Roasters are large ovens made of brick where much of the smelting process takes place.

Once, in January of 1960, the Moscow Selects came to play an exhibition game in Trail. They had not lost a single match on their cross-Canada tour. "The time we played the Russians, I worked laying bricks all night in the oven," Lenardon recalls. "I got off just before one in the afternoon and went down to the rink." That evening, Cominco Arena was packed to the bursting point, well beyond its capacity of 2,538 souls. "We don't tell the fire marshal about this, but there were 5,900-plus in the rink for that one," claims Tambellini. With an exhausted Norm Lenardon in the line-up and others like goaltender Seth Martin, who had finished his shift as a fireman at the plant a few hours earlier, the Smokies became the only Canadian team to defeat that edition of the Russians.

In an extraordinary twist, it was an outsider who determined that the team from Trail should concentrate on developing local talent if it was to challenge for the Allan Cup in a serious way. Bobby Kromm, a native of Calgary, Alberta, had played senior hockey in Cape Breton and Kimberley, British Columbia, with the Dynamiters before catching on with the Smoke Eaters in 1950–51. He was a fierce competitor and uncompromising in his desire to win. In the spring of 1959, Kromm captained the Smokies but was forced out of the line-up with a broken arm. As compensation, he assumed the coaching responsibilities and became firmly convinced the infusion of big-name players from other places was getting the team nowhere. It was decided that the best way for Trail to succeed was to rely on the boys from home. By 1960, they had advanced to the Allan Cup final against the Chatham Maroons.

"There were ten people who played on that team who went right through the minor hockey program in Trail," boasts Tambellini. "Right from peewee," chips in Lenardon. "Right from peewee and I don't think that's happened anywhere else, let alone a town of seven thousand people," Tambellini adds.

In the Allan Cup final, Trail looked respectable but ended up losing to the high-scoring Maroons, the Ontario-based team from Chatham. Ironically, the Maroons were fortified by a goaltender who was the property of the Toronto Maple Leafs and a native of Trail. Cesare Maniago found it strange playing for the Canadian senior championship as a visitor in Cominco Arena, the rink where he had grown up. "I had so many friends in the area and one was the goal judge," Maniago reflected. "In those days, you had just the screen behind you. There was no glass. He'd be giving me shit for letting one in and at the same time he was cheering for the Trail Smoke Eaters!"

In those days, it was customary for the reigning Allan Cup champions to represent Canada at the following year's world hockey championships. By the time the next summit in Switzerland rolled around, Cesare Maniago had turned pro and the Chatham Maroons opted not to attend because they could not afford the trip to Europe. The Canadian Amateur Hockey Association, therefore, offered the opportunity to the Smoke Eaters, the runners-up. Trail could no more handle the prohibitive cost of the journey than the Maroons could—but they accepted the challenge. Bobby Kromm was not the sort of coach who could resist a test of his team's mettle. "When Bobby started coaching the hockey club here, he had twelve or fourteen athletes who would have walked through a wall to go on a trip to represent Canada," says Tambellini. "He was a fierce competitor when he was playing hockey. He had a tough job to try and mould everything together."

Cominco came to the rescue in one respect. Each player from the Smoke Eaters' line-up who worked for the company was granted a seven-week, fully paid leave of absence in order to compete in the exhibition schedule leading up to the tournament, as well as to attend the world championship itself. The rest of the money was to be raised by private sponsors and fund-raising events—not a problem in the hockey-mad community that realized its beloved Smokies were about to embark on a once-in-a-lifetime adventure. For its part, the CAHA pledged some of the proceeds from the five-week, eighteen-game exhibition tour as well as providing transportation, accommodations and meals. As it turned out, the Smoke Eaters got a lot more than they bargained for from the governing body of Canadian amateur hockey. Most of it was unwelcome interference for a team on the move.

The representative team was allowed to bolster its line-up for the world championships with players who were not on the original roster. The CAHA hoped to take advantage of this rule by dramatically altering the look of the Smoke Eaters. "They wanted to make wholesale changes," says Norm Lenardon, shaking his head with anger. "We're talking about eight or ten guys they wanted to get rid of and bring in outsiders from the east to take their places." The CAHA was worried, for instance, that goaltender Seth Martin, a native of Rossland, British Columbia, was not up to snuff. They wanted a more experienced netminder to take his place. Bobby Kromm had already relented in other areas of the team's composition and had taken on defenceman Darryl Sly from the Kitchener-Waterloo Dutchmen as well as former New York Ranger Jackie McLeod, who was playing in Moose Jaw. He had also scoured Trail's surrounding area and found three valuable players in George Ferguson, Hal Jones and Hugh "Pinoke" McIntyre, all of whom had toiled for the Rossland Warriors a scant seven miles away. In addition, there was Dave Rusnell, a slick centre from the Yorkton Terriers in Saskatchewan. Rusnell was given a job at Cominco and remains in the community to this day. Left-winger Walt Peacosh came over from the rival Penticton Vees for the same enticement. Seth Martin's place on the team was never in doubt. Norm Lenardon had his differences with Bobby Kromm, but he knew the coach would stand by his netminder. "In the end, Bobby told the CAHA to go to hell," Lenardon sneers.

When all was said and done, the CAHA was able to force only two players on the Smoke Eaters. They were a couple of Quebeckers—centre Mike Legace and substitute goaltender Claude Cyr. In order to accommodate Legace, a proud Addy Tambellini shifted over to left wing. "I was a faster skater anyway, so it made more sense," allows Tambellini. Cal Hockley is not as generous. "We actually left guys here who would have been just as good to us as Legace was," he claims.

More than thirty years of hindsight have softened the three Smoke Eaters' estimation of the interlopers who joined their team in advance of the world championship marathon. To a man, they concede that Legace and Cyr were "good guys," after all. Still, there was a price to be paid by the outsiders as a sort of initiation. "Claude Cyr joined us on the prairies in Moose Jaw," says a playful Hockley. "We decided we'd test him out so we gave him to the team from Yorkton for an exhibition game the next night. We scored fourteen goals on him and after that he had a little more respect for us." Norm Lenardon chuckles at the thought of the hell they put Cyr through. "Claude told Kromm that Jacques Plante didn't skate in the practices. Kromm growled right back, 'You ain't Jacques Plante!'"

The first order of business for the Smoke Eaters was an eighteen-game exhibition swing through Europe that began in Oslo, Norway, on January 29, 1961. Visits to the far reaches of hockey's world followed, with

The Trail Smoke stops on the tour including Czechoslovakia, East Germany, Italy and the
Eaters, Soviet Union. The world championship would not be decided until mid-
1961 World March, and the Smokies had much to prove to hostile crowds overseas as
Hockey well as a sceptical following back home. "Jim Proudfoot, the writer from the
Champions *Toronto Star*, was the one guy from Canada who gave us a snowball's chance in hell of winning," says Lenardon. Hockley nods his head in agreement. He confirms that Trail's team was not well regarded by most of the press corps that followed them to Europe. The captain knew that the true believers were the players, who had traded the orange and black jerseys with smokestacks on the crest for red uniforms adorned by the maple leaf. "We left here

and knew we had a good hockey team. I don't think we had many doubts about what we could do," says Hockley. "We knew damn well we were going to win the cup because we went through hell to get there."

Jim Proudfoot was twenty-eight years old at the time and was caught up in the excitement of his first European assignment. As he followed the Smoke Eaters, the native of Parry Sound, Ontario, was already on his way to becoming one of the most widely read sports columnists in Canada. "It was the classic motivation of a hockey team," remembered Proudfoot. "That siege mentality of us against everybody else. For them, it was the best possible approach."

During the exhibition tour, which was designed to defray some of the team's costs as well as showcase the awesome Canadian talent, the Smoke Eaters struggled. There had been a humiliating 4–0 loss at the hands of Sweden's national squad in Stockholm. Rated as the top team in Europe heading into the world championships, the Swedes had peppered fifty-six shots at netminder Seth Martin. The Canadians managed only twenty-seven against the Swedish goalie, Kjell Svensson, who stopped them all. What was worse, the local press had depicted the Smoke Eaters as "angels on ice" and declared Trail to be one of the weakest and most polite teams Canada had ever sent to Europe. Proudfoot recalls the ridicule and its foundation. "Their reputation as a scrappy team was greatly exaggerated," he says. "If anything, they reversed the stereotype by playing a non-physical, non-violent game throughout."

It was not beyond the Smoke Eaters to play an aggressive game. They followed up the shut-out loss with a 4–1 physical pounding of Sweden the next night. Trail swept the final two exhibition contests in Stockholm partly because the Swedes suddenly refused to dress some of the players on their world championship roster for games that meant nothing. Addy Tambellini prefers to credit a rebirth in the Canadian team's sense of purpose following the shut-out humiliation. "You realized suddenly, as you were going through the whole ordeal, that you weren't just representing Trail any more," he declares proudly. "You were representing Canada."

Several difficulties away from the rink during the course of the exhibition tour drained the team's spirit as the championship approached. In the five weeks of barnstorming, the Smoke Eaters travelled across the continent in buses and, less frequently, by rail. They stayed in hotels of questionable comfort and ate food they were not used to. Moreover, the president of the

CAHA, Jack Roxborough, and his wife chaperoned the team most of the way. The proud men from Trail were not amused at the continuing lack of respect they were being afforded by Canada's hockey officials. Tambellini, it is said, told off Roxborough's wife to her face, and at the Brandenburg Gate in Germany, everyone cheered when she lost her passport. Cal Hockley reflects with venom on the interference. "That's indicative of what the CAHA thought of our hockey team," he snarls. "I mean—can you imagine? We're all twenty-five- to thirty-year-old guys and we've got a sixty-two-year-old woman travelling with us all over Europe!"

On paper, the record at the conclusion of the exhibition showcase was favourable to the Canadians. They had won fifteen games, lost two, and tied another. Disturbing to observers back home was a three-game sojourn to the Soviet Union that had yielded only one victory. The European pundits, meanwhile, claimed that the Smoke Eaters were not inspirational by any means. This was a team, they said, that was vulnerable.

Further evidence that they were on their own became apparent to the Smokies as they wound up the exhibition tour in Cortina, Italy, and prepared to travel to Switzerland for the games that really counted. The CAHA had abandoned them a couple of days earlier, having flown to Lausanne to get established in the cushy hotel that would be their world championship headquarters. "At the end of the game there were only three of us left on the ice because the rest of the guys were changing so we didn't miss the bus," says Hockley. "We drove half the night to Austria. Then we got on a damn train and they didn't even put the heat on in the coach."

"It was a cattle car," adds Tambellini. "We were all wrapped up in our Hudson Bay coats to try to keep warm going to the world tournament in Switzerland, and the CAHA is sitting there in a fancy hotel waiting for us." Cal Hockley is getting wound up now. "We were going to win that thing in spite of the CAHA!"

The final impediment to Trail's success in Switzerland was removed when their bench boss decided to withdraw from the active roster of the team. Bobby Kromm had spent a decade with the Smoke Eaters as a feisty and popular right-winger. His tenure as a player-coach, on the other hand, was fraught with acrimony. During the European tour, Kromm drove his team to the point of exhaustion because of his obsession with winning combined with a preoccupation to prove the Smokies' critics wrong. "We'd pull into a town at five o'clock in the afternoon when dinner was being served, but we'd have to go to the rink and practise for two hours," recalls Hockley.

"There was one time in Finland when we said, piss on you, Kromm! You practise and we're going out for dinner. He stood at the door and screamed at us, but we went out for dinner."

What the three Smoke Eaters realize thirty-five years later is that Kromm had whipped the team into excellent physical condition as a direct result of his dictatorial ways. Norm Lenardon had battled with the coach openly in Europe, but understands him better after the fact. "He didn't make you do any more than he would do himself," Lenardon says, in somewhat reserved tones. "He was the first one on the ice and the last one off. You had to respect that."

Kromm had become isolated and almost

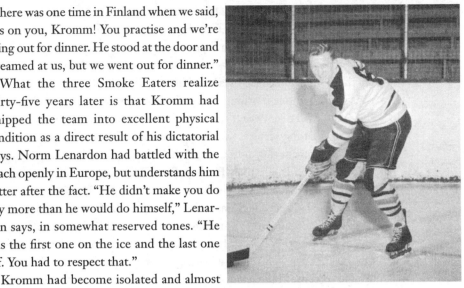

Bobby Kromm was a feisty winger and the player-coach of the 1961 Smoke Eaters. He went on to coach professionally with Winnipeg and Detroit

paranoid in his relationships with most of the players in his line-up during the time right before the world championship. One fable, which has been embellished over the years, has a Norwegian player breaking Kromm's nose with a nasty bit of stickwork in the first period of a game in Oslo. The story goes that members of the Canadian team, feeling their coach got his due, stood and applauded as Kromm was taken from the ice to a local hospital for repairs. Cal Hockley denies this but acknowledges that Kromm had made more than a few enemies among his players. "At times we got so annoyed with him that it would have been easy to push him off the bus."

Jim Proudfoot could see that Kromm's demeanour had alienated a substantial portion of the Smokies' roster but grudgingly gives the coach credit for turning this to his advantage on the eve of the championship tournament. "He was such a belligerent, irritating guy I can't imagine he had all this figured out," surmised Proudfoot. "Still, when he said, I'm going to be the bench coach for this tournament, the players were not only pleased, they were relieved." As the captain, Cal Hockley assumed more of an on-ice leadership role with Kromm's retreat to the safety of the bench. In retrospect, Hockley feels it may have calmed the team down substantially. "He was nuts when it came to competition," he says. "I think it helped, to a certain extent, that he wasn't going to be active as a player at the world championships."

When they finally got to Switzerland, the players from Trail had unwittingly survived the greatest ordeals Europe had to offer. They checked into

Lausanne's luxurious Royal Hotel and looked forward to a well-deserved twenty-four hours of rest before they met Sweden in the opening game. "Suddenly all the things that had pissed them off so much were over," Proudfoot emphasized. "Their days now consisted of one delightful thing after another. Suddenly a nice meal. Suddenly all fifteen of them were cured of constipation in one morning. They washed their uniforms and cleaned up their stuff." All that was left was for the Smoke Eaters to win a world championship that the sceptics said they could not. They had been underdogs from the moment they bused out of their tiny and remote company town, more than five weeks earlier. The boys from Trail would revel in their unique and challenging identity to the bitter end.

The Swedes were a legitimate threat to upset the Canadians in the tournament's opening game, which was to be played in the main venue at Geneva, a bus trip of about forty miles from the team's base in Lausanne. On this first trip, centreman Mike Legace forgot his sweater. They turned around to retrieve the jersey but when they finally got to the ice rink, the players were forced to unload their own equipment. Once all the bags were completely off the bus, they were told by arena officials that they would have to reload and use another entrance door on the opposite side of the building. Although they were infuriated, the Smoke Eaters complied and were barely able to get themselves ready for the opening face-off. Hockley believes the further inconvenience served to motivate the Canadian representatives. "When that gate opened, we came out of there like a stick of dynamite," he roars. "We intimidated the Swedes, I think," adds a more diplomatic Addy Tambellini.

Jackie McLeod led the way with two goals for Trail as they completely dominated Sweden and took their first victory in the seven-game tournament by a score of 6–1. McLeod went on to lead the Canadian attack throughout, eventually finishing second in the overall scoring championship. That first game's success, on the other hand, may have hinged on the exploits of the assistant captain, a defenceman named Don Fletcher.

"Fletcher faked that he was grievously hurt, and trainer Joe Garay went running onto the ice," said Jim Proudfoot, as he recounted the incident that broke open a one-goal game in Canada's favour. "Poor Fletcher was lying there as if unconscious. Garay leans over and asks, 'What's wrong here?' The first thing Fletcher asks when he opens one eye is, 'Did the Swede get a penalty?' Garay says, 'Yes, he got a major.' 'Good!' Fletcher said, jumping up and skating to the bench as if nothing had happened."

It was a classic case of role reversal. A Canadian player taking a dive and forcing the Swedish player to assume the role of villain was just another example of how resourceful the Smoke Eaters had become. "The game turned for them by doing exactly what the f—ing Swedes had done to them so often," chuckles Proudfoot. "Drawing that penalty meant that everything started to flow."

The team was now brimming with confidence, and perhaps more importantly, they felt a togetherness that came from their shared place of origin. The vast majority of the players in the Smoke Eaters' dressing room had known one another since early childhood. "We all grew up together," says Norm Lenardon. "We couldn't get mad at each other and we thought, Boy! a little town and we are going to do this!" It was a familial atmosphere. Canada's national team that year resembled a fraternity as much as it did a collection of hockey stars.

Bobby Kromm was quite clearly in control of the team, but he was an outsider. As a coach, he could only observe the resolve that developed among the natives of Trail as the tournament wore on. Lenardon describes the emotion that swept over the Smokies with immense pride. "We were all together and to hell with the big city," he says. "We could have played the New York Rangers and beaten them. It's true! I've never had a fight with my brothers."

Following the triumph over Sweden, it was back on the bus for the forty-mile trek back to Lausanne for a game against the West Germans. The main arena in Geneva had been state of the art, but the secondary rink in Lausanne was an open-air facility. The ice was poor, as a result of the skating surface being constructed on top of a swimming pool. It made little difference to the Smoke Eaters, as they demolished their opponents 9–1. Dave Rusnell was the star of that game, posting a hat trick, while Addy Tambellini and Jackie McLeod scored two goals apiece.

Two more victories were added in Geneva, against the United States and East Germany, by scores of 7–4 and 5–2 respectively. Seth Martin and Claude Cyr had shared the goaltending duties and first-place Trail had not been seriously challenged on their way to a record of four wins and no losses. While his team started to swagger, Bobby Kromm was wary of the next three games, which involved serious competition from Czechoslovakia, Finland and, of course, the Soviet Union.

The pivotal figure in the most crucial matches for Canada at the 1961 world championship turned out to be the player the CAHA was most concerned about. Seth Martin was a twenty-seven-year-old fireman at the Cominco plant and had been the Trail Smoke Eaters' regular goaltender for eight seasons. Although he had been a steady player for a long time in British Columbia's interior, he did not have the confidence of most of those in Canadian hockey circles. In addition, Martin wore a mask, something rare in hockey and unheard of in the international arena.

Although officials flinched at Martin's protective face gear—which he fashioned in the plastics shop "up the hill" at Cominco—his teammates thought nothing of it. "I watched that guy get hit in the face with a puck more than a few times because I played junior with him, too," says Cal Hockley. "I don't think any of us had any qualms about him wearing a mask." Montreal Canadiens great Jacques Plante had introduced the mask to the hockey world in November 1959 while playing against the New York Rangers. Seth Martin became an international innovator when he donned it against the Swedes in Game 1, stopping eighteen shots.

"Seth Martin established his reputation as a miraculous goalie," Jim Proudfoot said firmly. "The Europeans were scared shitless of him. They always were. He had them figured out." This became clear in a hard-fought game with the Czechs. It was a struggle that produced few shots on goal, and Trail was forechecked to death by their aggressive and hard-working opponents. There was no score deep into the first period, and Martin had been solid in the Smoke Eaters' net. "I was on the ice when a puck hit Seth on both skates and then hit a goal post and crossed the damned line," says Hockley, shaking his head. The Czechs managed to take the lead on that shot with a mere ten seconds left in the period.

"They scored that first goal and then they played Kitty Bar the Door," recalls Norm Lenardon. "We had a hell of a time!" There was no scoring in the second period until the sixteen-minute mark when "Pinoke" McIntyre, who was nicknamed for his impish looks, converted with the help of Jackie McLeod. After that, Seth Martin shut the Czechs down the rest of the way and the game ended in a 1–1 draw. Although the goaltending and defence had been superb, the Smokies had put themselves in a precarious position because the team from Czechoslovakia was also undefeated after its first five games of the tournament. Should both teams win their final two matches and wind up tied, goal differentials would be taken involving games played among the top five finishers of the round-robin format.

With little time to think about eventualities, Trail lived up to its name and "smoked" the team from Finland 12–1 in their next-to-last outing. Seth

Martin stopped thirteen of fourteen shots while the Canadians fired forty-eight at the Finnish goaltender, Lahtinen. In the end, the blow-out was of little advantage as the Finns failed to make the top five. The eleven-goal bulge would not count in Canada's favour in the event of a deadlock with Czechoslovakia.

The Czechs completed their task with a 5–2 victory over Sweden in their seventh and final game. Trail now had to face the Russian nationals as the climax to the tournament. In the exhibition tour, the Smokies had played three weaker Russian club teams and emerged with a single victory, giving many observers cause for concern. The team's next challenge was obviously going to be its greatest since leaving Canada.

In hard numbers, Trail's task was clear prior to playing the Russians. In games among the top five—Canada, Russia, Czechoslovakia, East Germany and Sweden—the Canadian goals-for-and-against record was 12–4, for a difference of eight. Czechoslovakia had a mark of 17–8, for a margin of nine. To be world champions, the Smoke Eaters would have to beat Russia by at least two goals. If they lost, the Russians would be the champions, but a one-goal victory in favour of Trail or a tie meant that Czechoslovakia would drink from the cup. "We knew we were gonna beat them," recalls Hockley. "We had some doubt about two goals, but we knew we were gonna beat them."

Seth Martin was outstanding, as his chums from Trail knew he would be. The Smoke Eaters' penalty-killers did their part as well, and the Russian attack was thwarted time after time. In all, there were only twelve shots delivered on the Canadian net over the course of the exciting match. The Smokies built a 4–0 lead on two goals by Jackie McLeod and singles by Harold Jones and Harry Smith. Still, it was the play of the Cominco fireman, Seth Martin, that won the day. "Seth was unbelievable over there," Addy Tambellini says, with wonder in his voice. "He knew what Jacques Plante knew ten years or more later," claimed Jim Proudfoot. "The Russians based their offensive patterns on soccer. Instead of banging away, they wanted to have an open shot. Knowing that, Seth always knew where the shot was coming from. By the time they got the pass to the open guy, Seth was already in front of them."

After the Russians managed one goal in the third, Norm Lenardon sealed the fate of the anxious Czechs, who were sitting helplessly in the stands. With two minutes left, Lenardon stole the puck in the Russian end and, after a struggle, fired it into the net while falling to the ice. The score was 5–1 and the Trail Smoke Eaters had their improbable world championship.

All these years later, a retired bricklayer with half-glasses perched on his nose glances at a picture of the hockey club from his home town. It is very much like Norm Lenardon's countless schoolboy photographs. He is surrounded by his childhood friends and his workmates from Cominco. As long as they stuck together, he knew they could conquer the world. "I scored a goal in that final game but it was the teamwork that counted most," he says.

Lenardon's captain, Cal Hockley, reaches over and touches his arm while adding to his pal's sentiment. "Nobody was a superstar. There was nobody that was bitching or moaning more than anyone else," declares Hockley. "We had a group that would walk through fire for any one of the other guys. I still think we have the best hockey team that's ever been put together."

A capacity crowd at an exhibition game between Canada and Sweden in the early 1970s. Many of the players on Canada's roster had played for the 1961 World Champion Smokies

The aura of the 1961 Trail Smoke Eaters has grown over time, in spite of the fact that very few players on that roster went on to star at higher levels of the game. Seth Martin did see action for the St. Louis Blues, winning eight of the thirty games he played in. Bobby Kromm coached in the World Hockey Association with Winnipeg and also with the Detroit Red Wings of the NHL. Most went back home for good when the world championship was over. The three wise men estimate there are still nine or ten of the Smokies living in the immediate vicinity. All agree that they won the title first for Trail and second for Canada. Their reasoning is simple—it was Cominco and the local fans who believed in them from the outset. "Trail had a lot to do with it," says Hockley. "Even when we walk around town today, we're remembered as the Trail Smoke Eaters, not as Canada's championship team."

Addy Tambellini has lived in the territory beneath Cominco's overwhelming smoke-stacks all his life. He continues to work in the arena that he starred in as a player. Tambellini will always feel that Trail and the "61ers" have a distinct place in the memories of devout hockey followers. In light of that, he hastens to relive the moment of victory that took him far beyond the limits of his birthplace. "After we won the championship, everyone was on the blueline singing 'O Canada,'" he recalls. "I could see a few air force guys who had come from the Canadian base in Germany. They were cheering us and it was great!"

For his part, Jim Proudfoot hopes the Smoke Eaters are always remembered for their resilience and their unswerving belief in their right to be at the world championship. Proudfoot has seen a lot of hockey since he witnessed the players from Trail with gold medals around their necks, yet he says he cannot recall a team that went through more in order to find itself on the victory podium. Proudfoot related a vignette which he believes tells the story of the Trail experience.

"On the flagpole, the Canadian flag starts to go up and 'O Canada' begins to play. The players looked at themselves and all at once they realized that nobody in the crowd was going to sing. So they sang. It was like a recital. They were the only people in the joint singing and I'll always remember what it was like. Twenty men singing—the players, the coaches, the manager, the club president and the training staff. I don't think I've ever heard it done as well."

A native of Trail, Cesare Maniago was known as the "Milestone Goalie." He gave up "Boom Boom" Geoffrion's fiftieth goal, Bobby Hull's fifty-first goal, and Jean Béliveau's four-hundredth assist

Cesare Maniago has a mystical-sounding name that some have called the most appealing in the annals of goaltending. Maniago chuckles at the thought of such fame, but one of Trail's favourite sons will never take his notoriety for granted. In Cominco Arena's Hall of Memories, the message Maniago once scrawled on the blade of his professional goal stick says it all: "To my friends in Trail. Thanks for helping me make it!!"

A tall, skinny kid, Cesare grew up in the shadow of the Cominco refinery where his father was part of the general work-force. It was with a certain

trepidation then, one day in 1956, that the senior Maniago reported as requested to the office of Pete McIntyre, the assistant general manager of the plant. "He was just crapping his pants and he didn't know what he might have done wrong," said Maniago of his father. "It turns out McIntyre was a personal friend of Conn Smythe, and that helped. I guess they were in the war together. The big thing is, he took a liking to my play in Trail."

The lanky goaltender was on his way. It was agreed, on McIntyre's recommendation to Smythe, that Cesare would leave his home town and head to St. Michael's College in Toronto. While there, he starred as a junior and eventually became the property of the Maple Leafs. It was the fast track to success in the big leagues that most kids from the company town craved. "Trail in those years was the hockey hotbed in British Columbia. We dreamt it. We lived it. We ate it. It was seven days a week in the wintertime," recalled Maniago. "There was minimal time in the rink but we had a pond up in the Cominco area which was basically a slough. It was really just some run-off from the generating plant. We'd have great games there on the weekends."

He was disappointed with his first year of pro play with the Leafs. George "Punch" Imlach, Toronto's coach, wanted Cesare to be the full-time practice goalie. The youngster from Trail had other plans. Following his junior career, Maniago had thought about continuing his education at Michigan Tech but was convinced by the legendary St. Michael's coach, Father David Bauer, to give professional hockey a "two-year shot." Keeping that in mind, he agreed to be loaned to a series of Ontario senior teams during the 1960 season. There were stops in Kitchener, Whitby and Windsor, then Maniago caught on with the Chatham Maroons and helped them win the Allan Cup final against the Trail Smoke Eaters.

By the time Chatham declined the opportunity to go to the world championships, Cesare Maniago had turned pro and watched his friends become world champions from his position as a National Hockey League goaltender in Toronto. "I was tickled pink for them," he said with pride. "Hey, half those guys I grew up with and played with. So that's telling me we came from a strong hockey background in Trail. Something was done right."

In fifteen NHL seasons, Cesare played with five different teams—Toronto, Montreal, the New York Rangers, Minnesota and Vancouver. His thirty shut-outs are a testament to Maniago's ability. He is remembered most often, however, as the "milestone netminder" who gave up significant goals in more than one superstar's career.

"They had a roast for me down in Chinatown when I turned thirty-nine.

The master of ceremonies started with the "who" questions: Who is this fella that let in Boom Boom Geoffrion's fiftieth? Who is the guy who couldn't stop Bobby Hull's fifty-first? Who is this goalie that gave up Jean Béliveau's four-hundredth assist?" Reflecting on his adventures in the NHL, Maniago takes delight in documenting the origins of the good-natured teasing. He also jumps at every opportunity to maintain his special place in hockey history. "I've made sure the joking continues when the old-timers go on tour," he explained. "I rig the whole thing up at the banquet and start asking the who questions. When I'm done, all of the guys on the team jump up and they point the finger at me!"

Prior to Cesare Maniago, no Trail native had performed at the NHL level for such a long period of time and with such consistency. While the Smoke Eaters are revered for their world championship, Maniago is the first individual from Trail to achieve a measure of star status at the highest level of hockey. He was discovered and nurtured by Cominco and played his formative years in the rink the company built. Maniago can still vividly describe in great detail the spotless rink he grew up in. "I still go back there and to me it's a shrine," he said firmly. "Just for a few minutes, I sit there by myself and reminisce and let the memories come back."

As much as Maniago reflects on the physical structure of the rink, he pays homage to the people of the town who were his neighbours and greatest supporters. There are clear memories of his first coach, a man named Ernie Gare, whose son Danny went on to a noteworthy NHL career. Through recollections of his years playing peewee, midget, juvenile and Junior B hockey in Trail, he drifts most often to tales of the important people in his development, the coaches and the volunteers who made him, by his own admission, everything he is and has been.

Cesare, now retired, still makes two or three trips a year to Trail to play in a golf tournament, make a speech or just see old friends. "I can't give enough back to them," he said. The gratitude is genuine and obvious in his voice. The little things have meant the most to Maniago: a friendly word from his dad's boss that got him started; the goal judge who spurred him on while he played for the Smoke Eaters' rivals; the back-yard neighbour named Pete Lauriente.

"He had a wooden picket fence and no kids. During the winter I'd have a puck and try to break the top part of each picket off. I'm telling you, I just demolished his fence! In the spring, he'd come out and replace all the pickets and repaint the fence. This went on year after year after year. You don't realize, as a kid, that you're damaging anybody's property unless he really gives you hell. Years later, they had a night for me in Trail after my first year pro. There he was in the front row. Pete Lauriente, my neighbour and the man whose fence I ruined. All of a sudden it hit me that this guy has been an important part of my success. I pointed him out to the crowd during my speech that night and we both ended up crying."

Mid-morning, sitting in the lobby of a downtown Toronto hotel, Ray Ferraro's eyes brightened at the mention of his boyhood hero. "Cesare is a legend," Ferraro said with conviction. "I think he's the most popular athlete to ever come out of Trail." It is high praise from a man who could, quite rightly, stake a claim to that title himself.

Ferraro is languishing in the NHL's version of purgatory these days. He is still performing with the vigour that has made him a twenty-goal scorer eleven times in a thirteen-year career. The fire of competition still burns within him—nothing could dampen the emptiness of never having won the Stanley Cup. He was close once, when he played with the upstart New York Islanders of 1993. Now, with the post-Gretzky Los Angeles Kings, the prospect of capturing hockey's ultimate prize is withering.

"I'd be lying if I said I don't still have the dream," Ferraro said, as he stared somewhere into the distance. It had been a year since the New York Rangers traded him to the Kings. At the time, New York was taking a run at a second Stanley Cup in three years. In order to get the services of the legendary Finnish sniper Jari Kurri and tough guy Marty McSorley, they sacrificed Ferraro to a rebuilding situation in sunny California. Looking back, he was almost ashamed at his initial reaction to the trade. "The rest of the year I skated around and occupied time on the ice," he confessed. "I didn't play, I just occupied time."

It was an uncharacteristic period of crisis for Ferraro. Through his years with the Hartford Whalers and the New York Islanders, he had been a pesky threat each time he skated into the fray. Not a dominant player but a supremely qualified competitor who, at times, could beat the other team with good old-fashioned heart. As he waited for his team's noon meal in preparation for that night's game with the Toronto Maple Leafs, Ferraro attempted to define his concept of hockey's most valuable intangible. The heart he spoke of had only gradually returned to him in Los Angeles. "I would be so disrespectful to the way I was raised if I didn't come out and give a full effort," he explained. "It means that you come to work, you go out and do the best that you're supposed to do. That comes from where I live and how I was brought up."

At thirty-two years of age, he is nearing a milestone for longevity. The nasty gash on the bridge of his prominent nose is a reminder that Ferraro is one of hockey's honest labourers who will have punched in for a thousand games before his career is over. Ferraro comes from a family that helped build the arena in which he played during his formative years. His father left Cominco in 1947 to start up a concrete business called Korpack, which is now the third-largest employer in the city and is operated by Ferraro's brothers, Tony and Eddie. If all goes according to plan, Ray will assume a share of Korpack's day-to-day operation when he retires. He steadfastly maintains it has always been his ambition to live in his home town when his playing days are through. "I'm really lucky to come from there and I just love living there," he declared.

From the age of five until he left to play major junior hockey in Penticton as a seventeen-year-old, Ferraro competed in the Trail Memorial Centre. As a child, it was mostly in the Kids' Rink, but as a bantam and subsequently as a member of the Junior B Smoke Eaters, Ray skated on the big ice surface of Cominco Arena. He wore the same style sweater as the fabled "61ers" and even then was aware of the great tradition of which he had become a part. "To wear the same sweater they wore was a big thing," Ferraro said. "You always had a connection. Someone you played with as a kid had an uncle or a cousin that was one of the '61ers.' As a matter of fact, whenever my dad was buying me skates or sticks, we bought them at Seth Martin's Sport Shop. I don't remember buying decent equipment anywhere else except Seth's until he closed his shop."

Through his developing hockey years, Ferraro admired the exploits of the world champion Smoke Eaters as he glanced at the banners during warm-ups in Cominco Arena. He was also in the stands to watch a speedy young star develop named Steve Tambellini—the son of Addy Tambellini, who had performed so brilliantly for the "61ers." There were trips to senior games on Friday nights, with his father, to marvel at one-time Blackhawks great Eric Nesterenko, who played for Trail after retiring from the NHL. Ray soaked up the battles between the Smoke Eaters and their fierce rivals from Cranbrook, Kimberley and Spokane. "There were fathers and sons everywhere," he said of the capacity crowds. "That's what you did on Friday nights."

As a prospect, Ferraro went to Bobby Kromm's hockey school in Trail. It took over the whole building, making use of the arena, as well as the meeting rooms, gymnasium and library. Ray heard tall tales from the Smoke Eaters' long-time equipment man and trainer, "Mushy" Encelmo. "Wherever you saw the Smokies go, there was Mushy," he recalled. "He was a volunteer. If he got paid by the hour, you would say he's got the worst job in the world because I don't think he ever got a cent. He was what a Trailite volunteer meant to the community."

John DeMarci was the rink attendant, and Ray checked for him each time he ventured onto the ice. Ferraro constantly reminds himself of how comfortable he was in that place and he has turned familiar objects from the rink into touchstones. He has a special affection for the old, analogue clock he remembers from his earliest days there. "It used to go in a complete sixty-minute circle," he demonstrated. "You needed a degree to figure out how to read it. I mean if there was a penalty, God help you!" The clock is gone and so is John DeMarci, but the importance of the arena lingers with Ferraro.

It was before the last game of his career playing for Trail that he sensed what might lie ahead. The seventh and deciding match of the playoffs confirmed his career path. "I remember skating around in warm-up and thinking that this is what the NHL is like," he said, still wide-eyed at the recollection. "The building was packed. There were 3,200 people in there and we won in double overtime. That's the first game I can really remember lots about, as a player, that made a real impact on me."

To say that Ray Ferraro has had an impact on hockey since leaving Trail would be a gross understatement. As a member of the Brandon Wheat Kings, he scored 108 goals in the 1983–84 season, a mark that still stands as a Western Hockey League record. Ferraro was also chosen as western Canada's most valuable junior player that season. He lost the national honours to a rising young star from Laval of the Quebec league—Mario Lemieux.

Drafted in 1982 by Hartford in the fifth round and eighty-eighth overall, Ray got to the NHL as a twenty-year-old. In his first full season with the Whalers, he scored thirty goals and helped take the franchise to its first significant post-season appearance, losing the divisional final to the eventual Stanley Cup champions, the Montreal Canadiens. Since then he has produced NHL totals of nearly 350 goals and 700 points with the Whalers, Islanders, Rangers and Kings.

Although there has been no Stanley Cup victory yet, Ferraro takes special pride in two silver medals won at the international level playing for Canada. His first appearance at the world championship came in 1989, as a collection of pros from teams who had missed or been eliminated from the playoffs finished second. "No Canadian team had won the gold since the Smokies had done it in '61," he said. "Do you not think that I wanted to be on the next team that won? I would have loved that so I could bring my gold medal back to Trail and put it with theirs."

He got a second chance at the end of the 1996 season. Canada advanced to the gold medal game, this time against the Czech Republic. "I'm thinking how cool this would be to bring back the big medal to Trail," said Ferraro. "There would have been myself and Travis Green from Castlegar. Two more gold medals coming back to the Kootenays." As it turned out, Ray's dream of repeating the Smoke Eaters' victory of thirty-five years earlier fell just short. The Czech Republic won and Canada, with a fiercely proud Ferraro in the line-up, had silver medals around their necks.

In the lavish expanse of the ritzy hotel, he looked like a regular guy as much as the million-dollar player that he is. Ferraro's dress shirt was open-necked and slightly untucked on one side. He got emotional when talking about Trail and there was a longing in his voice as he resigned himself to a hockey life in Hollywood. There was no question as to the place he would rather be. "When you drive down the street and you hear a horn honking in Trail, it's a horn of recognition. They're saying hello to me," he said. "It's not like where I've lived the last twelve years. When you hear a horn there, it means get off your ass and move farther down the road!"

While describing Cominco Arena, Ferraro relied less heavily on the physical detail of the structure and more on what has been accomplished there. The names of the 1961 Smoke Eaters rolled off his tongue as if they were his contemporaries. Cesare Maniago became the goalie he emulated as a little kid on endless evenings of road hockey. He talked of the thirty-seven blue and gold banners that hang from Cominco's rafters. They are simple reminders of the many B.C. champions that have come from that rink. Ray Ferraro has left a lasting impression on the great arenas of the National Hockey League but he is most influenced by the rink that gave his career unlimited promise. "Trail's tradition is so strong with all of the sportsmen who have come from there, that you can't help but be touched by it," he declared. "It's impossible not to notice the history and the heritage of the place."

Ferraro seldom mentioned his own accomplishments. Even as he reluctantly rose to guide his teammates to the meal, he hurried in a few more words about Trail. There was a quick story about Addy Tambellini, a description of his Cesare Maniago hockey card, a reminder that Adam Deadmarsh of the Stanely Cup champion Colorado Avalanche is from Fruitvale, British Columbia, just down the road, a mention of Steven McCarthy, a fifteen-year-old playing for the Junior Smoke Eaters and the first draft choice of the WHL Edmonton Ice.

There was one final thought from Trail's most accomplished athlete as he boarded the escalator on the way to a feast of pre-game pasta. Ray Ferraro offered an articulate estimation of the modest place he has always celebrated. "The continuity of the small town is astounding," he said with a knowing smile.

Tom Renney has an appreciation for the value of lineage and the connections that allow the traditions of hockey to grow. The forty-three-year-old freshman head coach of the Vancouver Canucks is another example of Trail's legacy to the game.

His hair is generously speckled with grey, but Renney looks and sounds younger than he is. He eagerly gathered one of the National Hockey League's most talented teams to the side boards of palatial General Motors Place and began to instruct. The lesson of the day was about strategy in the neutral zone. "Listen, let's get ourselves ready to play tonight," Renney barked. "Let's get some jump!" It was a hackneyed morsel of the pep talk that litters the standard lexicon of coaching. Much of what he preaches, Tom Renney first learned at the Cominco Arena.

"I went to Trail to run a clothing store for a group of people from Cranbrook," said Renney, who was bent on something quite different from a career as a haberdasher. The store was simply a means to an end. "I guess it's the place where I first stepped on the banana peel," he concluded. "Working for myself allowed me to do what I should have been doing in the first place, and that was to coach."

While the clothing store struggled, Renney blossomed in Trail's intense hockey environment. His Junior B Smoke Eaters won the B.C. championship and Renney was selected as the league's best coach for four consecutive years. From his vantage point behind the bench at Cominco Arena, the Cranbrook native became fascinated with the story of the Smoke Eaters who had conquered the international hockey world in 1961. "I'm sort of a hockey traditionalist and certainly very patriotic when it comes to Canadian hockey," Renney explained. "I felt like I was in a hockey hotbed in a traditional way and had become a part of where the game was really rooted."

Walking back to his office, Renney skirted a piece of the rubberized carpet directly in front of the Canucks' locker room. There is a message boldly inscribed on a huge tile that cannot be avoided. "Master technique but let the spirit prevail," it dictated. It is a strange philosophy in the midst of highly paid professional hockey players and some might even say it is a questionable motivational tool. Renney makes no apologies and confirmed that he asked to have the inscription placed there. "I'd like to claim credit for the words, too," he offered. Instead, he readily acknowledged the author. "Father David Bauer. One of my mentors," Renney said, with pride.

Like Bauer, Renney spent time coaching Canada's national hockey team, but not before he enjoyed great success at the major junior level in the Western Hockey League. In two years guiding the Kamloops Blazers, he was victorious in 101 games and still holds the record for the highest winning percentage in Canadian junior hockey. The Blazers also captured the Memorial Cup in 1992 under Renney's tutelage. He claims that the trademarks of his subsequent teams were learned from his days coaching in Trail. "It was a bigger rink. Basically an NHL-sized ice surface, two hundred by eighty-five feet," he pointed out. "When I was coaching there, I saw an obligation to play a certain style. A real hot forecheck. Real physical and get the emotions of the fans behind you."

Lessons learned and a string of dramatic successes led Tom Renney to the Canadian Olympic program to start the 1993–94 season. As had been the case throughout his meteoric rise through the ranks of hockey, Renney continued to win. The 1994 Olympics in Lillehammer, Norway, were a resounding success as Canada came within a whisker of capturing the gold medal for the first time since 1952.

After the Olympics that year, the Canadian team was again bolstered by professional players for the world championship, to be held in Milan, Italy. Netminder Bill Ranford of the Edmonton Oilers and scoring ace Luc Robitaille of the Los Angeles Kings were two of the high-profile talents to join Renney's roster. Before leaving Canada for the journey overseas, the coaching staff invoked the spirit of the last team from this country to win the title. Bobby Kromm came to speak to the players in Toronto at Renney's request. "He told them all about the '61ers' from Trail and related the things that we hoped would inspire the players of the day. It was important and we thought it was very effective."

As the Canadians progressed through the world championship tournament in 1994, Renney used Kromm's Smoke Eater jersey from 1961 as a sort of inspirational prop. He would suspend it in the dressing room before each game and, with each successive victory, would unfurl the sweater, revealing larger portions of the team crest. When Canada captured the final match and its first gold medal in thirty-three years, the symbol of the Smoke Eaters was resplendent in the championship locker-room and became a centrepiece of the celebration. It was a link to the storied past, which Renney believes his players not only understood, but came to revere. "Damn right I'm proud to be the coach of a team that won the world championship," he declared. "The '61 Smoke Eaters are symbolic of a connection that we should all maintain with all of our world champions."

Two more years navigating the national team yielded more success for Renney. There was a bronze medal at the world tournament in 1995 and then, with Trail native Ray Ferraro as a key component of the team, a close silver in 1996. That summer Renney's services were coveted by two high-profile NHL clubs, the Toronto Maple Leafs and the Vancouver Canucks. He accepted the offer in Vancouver partly because it was close to his Cranbrook roots. Renney also saw great opportunity with the Canucks because the franchise was loaded with talent that included Pavel Bure, Alexander Mogilny, Trevor Linden and his one-time Olympic goalie, Corey Hirsch. Although he is one of the most qualified coaching prospects in all of hockey, signing with Vancouver made Tom Renney the lowest-paid coach in the National Hockey League.

Money has never been Renney's motive to excel in the game. In fact, the professional level has been the only place where his dramatic career has sputtered. By Christmas 1996, Tom Renney's Canucks were mediocre at best, and his capacity to reach some of his more talented players was in question. They went on to miss the playoffs for the first time in six seasons. Perhaps he had failed to grasp the various driving forces of the modern professional player, which have nothing to do with sacrifice and pride. Maybe his first year of struggle in the National Hockey League was a result of his stubbornly romantic attachment to the purity of the game.

His connection to the spirit of Trail has seemingly left him out of step with the advancing complexity of pro hockey, at least for the time being. It is a confusion he never bargained for when he was coaching in Trail. "Just the ambience of a rink like that. The smell. The visceral feeling you get when you walk in there," he said. "The appreciation not just of hockey tradition but also the reflection of family values and community. Just the sense of being together and enjoying something which is Canadiana. I don't believe there's enough of that happening any more. I've experienced many rinks over the years. That one is one of the few that I just want to sit in."

Graduates of Cominco Arena have also managed to leave a permanent impression on the most storied trophy in North American sport. The Stanley Cup bears the names of two Trail area natives who helped win championships with the New York Islanders and, more recently, the Colorado Avalanche.

Steve Tambellini is currently a vice-president of the Vancouver Canucks, responsible for many of the hockey club's administrative affairs such as team travel, community relations and public affairs. In his playing days, as a rookie, he was part of the New York Islanders' blossoming dynasty—a team that defeated Pat Quinn's Philadelphia Flyers in seven games to capture the Stanley Cup in the spring of 1980. Quinn is now Tambellini's boss in Vancouver, and the Canucks' president and general manager still lacks the glittering ring that all Cup champions possess.

"Hockey is life… right?" Tambellini asked the question rhetorically while diverting his attention from the action between the Canucks and Penguins on the ice below. He turned his thoughts to his home city of Trail. "In that town, nothing aside from winning the championship or maybe your own division was acceptable. There was a constant demand to be the best at all times."

In his ten-year career, with five different teams, Tambellini accumulated 310 NHL points. Drafted fifteenth overall by the Islanders in 1978, he had graduated from Lethbridge of the Western Hockey League; his defining skill was his superb skating. Heralded as one of the fastest and most fluid players to come along in years, Steve was similar in style to his father, Addy, who had starred for the 1961 world champions. "They were so respected within the community," Tambellini said of his dad and the rest of the Smokies. "They were looked upon as our stars, as the people of Vancouver look upon the guys that play for the Canucks."

Tambellini beamed with pride as he turned into a one-man public relations firm, lauding the virtues of his home town, tucked away in the interior. He claimed that more provincial champions have come from Trail than any other town in British Columbia. He acknowledged, correctly, that the Trail Minor Hockey Association was the founding body for Minor Hockey Week in Canada, now a national institution. Tambellini also holds a special reverence for the moments he first enjoyed in the invigorating atmosphere at Cominco. "I remember as a young kid being able to walk into that Trail Smoke Eaters dressing room," he recalled. "That was my time of the winter. I had a chance to go on the ice maybe ten minutes a day with Dad. I knew they were champions, but I couldn't tell or didn't realize how good they were."

It was the focal point of the community, Tambellini said of the Trail Memorial Centre complex. The arena meant everything to Steve Tambellini. He worked out in the gym beside the ice and studied in the library across the hall. But there was one more important connection made there. While on skates, he met his future wife, Denise. "It was public skating one Friday night. I saw her and said... Yeah!"

Steven McCarthy was the WHL's top draft pick in 1996 and a defenceman with the Trail Junior Smoke Eaters

Steven McCarthy has just finished a stretch that has seen him play eight games in ten days. Throughout, he has attended high school and tried, with varying degrees of success, to keep up his studies. It is a tough task for a fifteen-year-old but not without its rewards. McCarthy is six feet tall and growing. He has light brown hair and dark brown eyes. He already cuts an imposing figure at 185 pounds, but his reputation is growing more weighty

with each passing day. "Hockey is just within him," says McCarthy's father, Dan. "He loves playing the game!"

Trail's next hockey legend is honing his craft at Cominco Arena as a highly skilled defenceman with the Tier II Junior Smoke Eaters. Steven McCarthy is acknowledged as the brightest prospect of his age in the entire country. The numbers reflect his amazing prowess. He is a bantam competing with and against much older players. McCarthy has recorded twenty-one goals and forty-six assists in a scant forty-nine games and has recently been drafted number one overall by the major junior Edmonton Ice of the Western Hockey League. He is, in the minds of most learned hockey observers, a "can't miss" NHL prospect who will someday have a dramatic effect on the professional game.

"He is a big-time player," exclaims Jeff

Chynoweth, the vice-president of the Ice. Chynoweth can hardly contain himself on the subject of McCarthy's prospects. He is almost drooling at the thought of having him in the Alberta capital next season. "There just aren't that many superstars in junior hockey, but he's one of them. No question!"

It is safe to say that McCarthy comes from rock-solid hockey stock. His father played in the WHL for the Saskatoon Blades and the Swift Current Broncos in the early 1970s. The elder McCarthy also works as a fireman at Cominco and was, at one time, the colleague of legendary Smoke Eaters goalie Seth Martin. While Steven acknowledges his admiration for great NHLers like Trevor Linden of the Canucks and Theoren Fleury of the Flames, he repeats a sentiment often expressed by aspiring Canadian hockey players. "Probably my dad is the guy I look up to the most," says Steven, without hesitation. "He's helped me so much and he played in the WHL, which is where I want to get to next. He's been just a huge inspiration to me."

Dan McCarthy must wince at times when he hears his son confuse the year of the last Smoke Eaters world championship. "Actually I have heard some stories of the 1969 world champions. Seth Martin was the goalie... right?" inquires Steven. He says he has never met Adam Deadmarsh and although he has encountered Ray Ferraro on occasion, he is sure the Los Angeles Kings star from Trail does not know who he is. It is true, Dan McCarthy sometimes wonders at the diminishing connection that seems to exist between his son and the community's glorious history in the game. "Trail is such a great hockey town," says the father, wistfully. "I know he doesn't set goals for himself. I do, but I try not to let him know about them."

The goals have everything to do with living up to an impeccable folklore in the sport. While Dan McCarthy can articulate them, Steven can make them come to life even though he is not fully aware of their foundations. "There seems to be so much tradition there," he says of Cominco. Apart from this, there are no further reflections on the old Smoke Eaters. No wide-eyed recitation of historical trivia that countless other devout fans might provide. Steven McCarthy is far too busy concentrating on being the best and playing with a single-mindedness common to players from this place.

At his tender age, Steven has already played two games at the next level with Edmonton. "He has the ability to play a regular shift in the WHL right now," states Jeff Chynoweth. There was a goal and an assist in the

B.C. Junior League All Star game. McCarthy also won the hardest-shot competition. His appointment with professional greatness would appear to be inevitable.

Cominco sponsors the team McCarthy plays for and is, in many ways, making his dream of playing in the NHL a possibility. It is the same company that sent the "61ers" abroad in order to make them world champions and, more importantly, a genuine article of Canadian hockey lore. It is a process that involves Trail refining, and then exporting, its wealth of hockey talent. The similarities over time are striking. "Once I asked him to list the pros and cons of playing hockey at a higher level because I knew he was going to have to leave home to do it," recounts Dan McCarthy. "He came back with a single sheet of paper that said: I love it . . . I love it . . . I love it!"

Steven McCarthy is confident but still very modest about his awesome talent. He hesitates to isolate a particular skill or ability that allows him to be that much better than the rest. When prodded, he expresses an intangible quality that astute judges of hockey potential agree is common to the greatest champions. "I think I'm able to excite the crowd," he admits. "I'm able to do things that no one expects. I think I surprise a lot of people and they never know what I'm about to do." It is exactly the same power the world champion Smoke Eaters demonstrated in Switzerland all those years ago.

For a moment, as the old-timers retreat to the locker room and the figure skaters gather in the wings, the Cominco Arena is empty on this Sunday evening. The ice has been freshly resurfaced and the Zamboni's roar has subsided while every article of litter has been swept, bagged and removed. All that exists is the rink and a low, droning noise that fills the hallowed space with a reassuring sound. The caretaker pops her head through the doorway and, when asked, says the noise is from the electrical plant in the basement of the building. It seems so much bigger than that, so powerful and constant, as if to remind someone that the arena could never be completely silent.

Outside, the relentless snow has been tamed and turned into a few flakes drifting lazily to earth. The black sky is cluttered now by countless stars and the billowing white clouds from the smoke-stacks just "up the hill." The noise that first revealed itself inside the arena is amplified several times as I turn to look at the factory. It is the sound of a giant locomotive.

A passerby in the parking lot tells me that the shift has just changed at Cominco. It becomes apparent now that production at the refinery is not only prolific, but endless as well. In the town below, a similar future is in store for this cherished rink. Trail's hockey icons will continue to be produced without interruption.

7 Whitney Forum
Flin Flon, Manitoba

Chris Cuthbert

The arena was a place where working men and working-class masculinity were honoured, where miners and machinists and men who worked in Loblaws could establish their own sense of community.
—Richard Gruneau and David Whitson, *Hockey Night in Canada: Sport, Identities and Cultural Politics*

"YOU'RE NOT GOING TO FLY THERE, are you?" Barry Melrose asked incredulously. "That's cheating, man." For Melrose, a former defenceman of the Kamloops Chiefs, and other Western Hockey League players of the late sixties and early seventies, there weren't any shortcuts to Flin Flon, Manitoba, the most remote outpost and dreaded destination in hockey. Nor were there any shortcuts on the ice at the Whitney Forum, in the Western League's truest test of courage, a weekend double-header against the feared home-town Bombers.

Melrose, who coached the Los Angeles Kings to the '93 Stanley Cup final, made me think twice about taking the easy way to Flin Flon. Nonetheless, I resolved that the nine and a half hours it would take from Saskatoon or the eleven hours to travel northwest from Winnipeg would be time better spent in the hard-rock mining town situated above the fifty-fourth parallel. I thought that I deserved credit just for showing up. That was more than could be said for a few teams frozen with fear by the prospects of a road trip to Bobby Clarke's home town. "The Brandon Wheat Kings got as far as The Pas, which was about a hundred miles south of Flin Flon," said former Bomber defenceman Jack McIlhargey derisively. "They phoned up and said the whole team was sick so they turned around and went back. That was the Flin Flon flu for sure."

A million miles away in San Jose, California, a newly staked territory in hockey's current gold rush, the Heroes of Hockey were lacing up for a return to glory as part of the 1997 NHL All Star weekend. Among them were John Ferguson, Lanny McDonald and Bernie Federko, who exchanged stories about the good old days. Strangely, those forbidding treks to Flin Flon had evolved with time into fond recollections of adventure travel. "When you went up there you had to take your own puck," chortled John Ferguson as he lumbered back to the Heroes' dressing room after a morning skate. "We could beat them in Melville but we couldn't beat them in Flin Flon. The three years I played junior hockey in Melville we never won a game in Flin Flon."

Indeed, it's a wonder any visiting team ever triumphed there considering the transportation nightmares that haunted road trips to Flin Flon in the dead of winter. "We would get the train up there from Canora [Saskatchewan]," Ferguson continued. "One year the train went off the tracks. We lost all power and the train was frozen. We ended up with four players sleeping together in each bed to stay warm rather than freezing to death."

Bernie Federko's bus trips to Flin Flon with the Saskatoon Blades were equally restless. "It took twelve hours on the Hanson Lake Road, a logging road with no pavement," recalled Federko, a fourteen-year veteran of one thousand NHL games. "By the time you got there you were so shaken up from hitting the bumps the entire way, they used to drop us off about two blocks from the Whitney Forum to let us get the bus out of our legs. We'd walk to the rink in the freezing cold thinking maybe we should just get lost."

By train or bus, the seemingly endless trip gave each player plenty of time for contemplation. For most, their thoughts had one prevailing theme. "You just hated going there in the first place. The fans would throw coal at us," bristled Lanny McDonald through his trademark moustache. "The Bombers played like the Flyers in their heyday. In the NHL it was, 'Oh God, do we have to go to Philly?' In junior it was, 'Oh God, do we have to go to Flin Flon?'"

Once the opposition arrived, the Bombers made them wish they had never come. "I remember Ken Arndt playing for us," said Federko. "He followed through on a shot and his stick caught Cam Connor of the Bombers right between the eyes. It cut him badly. Poor Kenny hadn't done it on purpose, but this was Flin Flon. He went to the penalty box and Connor followed him. Cam just glared at him while the blood was pouring. He said he was going to kill Kenny when he got out of the penalty box. After the five-minute major, Kenny came back to the bench and said he wasn't going out again. He wouldn't play the rest of the game.

"Another time our goaltender, Randy Ireland, came out of his net and trapped the puck along the boards. A fan reached over the boards and grabbed him inside the eye holes of his mask. Randy got up, swinging his stick, and we all left the bench, skated across the ice and went into the stands. There were sparks flying from the skate blades on concrete, people being whacked with sticks, fans punching us. They had to delay the game while we all went to get our skates resharpened."

Vancouver Canucks assistant coaches Glen Hanlon and Stan Smyl are both Western Hockey League graduates of the Flin Flon battles. Like Federko, they discovered that in Flin Flon you didn't take on just the Bombers but the entire town. "We had our typical weekend series," recounted Hanlon, who played for a Brandon team not afflicted by the Flin Flon flu. "The first game was physical, to say the least. In the second game, we had a brawl in the pre-game warm-up. Some of the big miners thought they could help their team, so the fans started streaming onto the ice. The RCMP, wearing their big fur hats, had to break it up. It was a night you were not going to forget."

Equally unforgettable were the post-game festivities that Smyl was exposed to. "We had a hotel room right over the main drag," said the former captain of the New Westminster Bruins. "We saw one of the best brawls ever. The fights just spilled out of the bar below our window. There were a number of fights in the street. A car ran over someone who went flying through the air. We had front-row seats."

Entrance to Whitney Forum with the HBM & S north mine shaft in the background

It was all in a typical weekend trip to Flin Flon. The circumstances altered slightly with each visit, but for Bombers opponents there was one overriding sentiment. "Everything about Flin Flon intimidated you," summed up Bernie Federko. "The size of the Whitney Forum, the way the fans hollered and screamed. You were there for the weekend and just to come out of it alive was the best part of it."

The sign at the Flin Flon airport greets visitors to their "Friendly City." When I arrive, there isn't a snarling welcoming committee, fisticuffs in the terminal or an angry mob rocking my cab outside. It certainly doesn't appear on first inspection to be a "seething pit of hostility," words that have been used to describe its glory days in the Western Hockey League. Then again, visiting teams didn't arrive via the airport.

Stew Lloyd, who runs the Bombers' Historical Society, is waiting for me at the Whitney Forum. When I tell him I have been collecting stories about the rink from opposing players, he knows what to expect. "I bet they had a lot of nice things to say," he responds sarcastically. We meet in front of Stew's pride and joy, the Bombers' Hall of Fame. Displayed behind him are pictures of sixty-nine of eighty Bombers who graduated to the NHL or WHA. "If we included everybody who ever played pro, it would extend down there," says Stew, pointing to the opposite end of the rink. On the wall is a dazzling array of stars from many eras: Sid Abel, who played in the thirties prior to his Hall of Fame career in Detroit; Ted Hampson, captain of the Memorial Cup champions of 1957; Bobby Clarke and Reggie Leach of the glory days in the sixties; current NHLers Ken Baumgartner and Reid Simpson. The latter pair, like so many recognized on the wall, are Flin Flon natives as well.

Stew Lloyd was a typical local kid, raised on hockey and the dream of one day becoming a Bomber. As a child, he'd watch the Bombers' games from a chicken-wire cage called "The Bullpen," situated at one end of the old Main Arena. "They locked you in for the whole period so you weren't running around the rink," he recalls. "You couldn't go to the bathroom until the end of the period. Then you had to be back in The Bullpen before the start of the next period or they'd kick you out. You'd have a hundred kids in there. We had some good times."

When he played bantam hockey, his dressing-room stall was the same one used by his boyhood hero Cliff Pennington, who went on to an NHL career in Boston. Lloyd didn't realize his talent would fall shy of the junior level until his midget year, when another local youngster began toying with Stew and his teammates. "I thought, who the heck is this guy?" says Lloyd with wide-eyed admiration. "He just whizzed right through us. They started to slaughter teams 15–1. He was the kingpin. He'd scored five goals a night. It was Bobby Clarke."

That season defined the hockey fates of both Lloyd and Clarke. Bobby was destined for stardom as the greatest Flin Flon product ever. Stew would contribute in other ways. "We used to go to the local pool hall to see the visiting team," Stew says. "We'd tell them they were going to get their asses kicked that night and we'd threaten to kick their asses right in the pool hall. It was intimidation from the time they came to town."

When it came to the Bombers, however, Stew Lloyd made them feel right at home. In later years, he and his wife, Normajean, boarded seventy local players over an eight-year period. It was his way of being a part of the team, experiencing the camaraderie and spirit of junior hockey. "One of the kids we boarded was Brad Spicer, a tough kid and a real prankster," recalls Stew, who at one time housed seven Bombers. "One night the boys were going out for a game. Coach Ginnell had a dress code of suits and ties. Everybody is all dressed in their suits but two guys can't find their shoes. I know Spicer has done something with those damn shoes. It's got to be forty below out. All of a sudden they discover the shoes are on the roof of our house. There are guys crawling out the windows, climbing on the roof in forty-below weather to get their shoes."

Lloyd laughed with the players, cheered them on from the stands and, when necessary, fought for them. It almost came to that one night when the Bombers' mystique of toughness was crumbling in the late seventies. "One of my boarders, Terry Ballingall, got into a fight with a guy from Swift Current," Lloyd recounts. "Terry was the captain and he'd do anything to fire up his team. That night he was overmatched. Another guy from the Broncos jumped him. It was one of the worst nights because no one came off our bench to help. I came down out of the crowd. I was going to jump on the ice myself, I was so upset. They weren't the same Bombers at the end."

It wasn't long after that Flin Flon lost its major junior franchise. The Western Hockey League had outgrown the tiny mining community on the Saskatchewan–Manitoba border that once hosted its flagship franchise. Flin Flon went from being the home of the world junior champions of 1957 and arguably the best major junior team in Canada a decade later to a hockey town without a league to play in. "It was like losing a member of the family," Lloyd says of Flin Flon's darkest winter. "Hockey was like a religion here and suddenly you didn't have it. You pretty near had to play bingo because there was nothing else. I found it very difficult to live here that year."

Near the main entrance of the Whitney Forum is a glass display case that holds the priceless relics of a proud franchise. Stew Lloyd canvassed the mining town for mementoes and discovered a gold mine of hockey treasures. There is Cy Gilmore's woollen sweater from the thirties with the same exploding "B" logo worn today. Reg Leach's red jersey is displayed from the 1966–67 team. It was the only year the Bombers departed from their traditional maroon jerseys. The Detroit Red Wings, sponsors of the Bombers at the time, donated an old set of uniforms when the local club was in need of assistance. The Wings' logo was removed from the front and replaced with the Bombers' crest. There are programs marking visits of Gordie Howe and the Red Wings in 1962, and the Moscow Selects in 1968. And there is a hoard of artifacts from the year Flin Flon reigned as Memorial Cup champions.

There aren't many rinks across the country that can match the hockey spoils of this northern mining town, not many towns in Canada where the love of the game runs so deep. "It's sacred," says Lloyd as he locks up the Hall of Fame display case. "Hockey is a religion in Flin Flon, always has been, always will be. At one time every kid that ever put on a pair of skates wanted to wear that Bomber uniform. If you could wear that jersey for one day, life was worth living. I'm wearing it now by running the Historical Society. That's the only way I could wear it. There are Leafs' fans and Canadiens fans but we're Bombers fans first."

Down at the far end of the Whitney Forum, trainer Steve Hildebrand is preparing to close up the Bombers' dressing room for the night but is delighted to oblige with a quick tour. "A lot of character has been through here," he says, revealing the inner sanctum of the home-town heroes who now compete in the Saskatchewan Junior Hockey League. The room sports the team colours of maroon and white, the team logo emblazoned in the middle of the floor. Hanging from the roof is a chain to which the players add a link for each victory. The chain is not as long as it would have been in past years, but not for lack of motivation. Inspirational signs occupy much of the wall space. "Be the best you can be at all times." "Play for the name on the front of the sweater not the name on the back." "Offence may win some games, defence wins championships." It's a room that reeks of tradition and has the pungent aroma of a storied past.

Hildebrand is a twenty-year-old native of Morden, Manitoba, cut from the same cloth as his NHL colleagues. In hockey there is often no one more passionate about the game, more loyal to his team and more approachable than the trainer. "I'd rather be here than in the WHL because of this history," Hildebrand admits. He leads me to a cubicle tucked in the corner of the dressing room that he shares with the coach. Scrawled on its low cement ceiling is the ultimate Bombers autograph collection. It has become a team ritual for graduating players to leave their mark not only on the ice but overhead. Instantly, I spot the signatures of Ken Baumgartner and Reid

Simpson. Hildebrand points to the place where the greatest Bomber ever wrote only his last name and number: Clarke, 11. "For back-to-back games, I'll sleep in here on an air mattress," says Steve. It's a trainer's version of sleeping under the stars, with a hockey constellation of names, from snipers like Leach and Blaine Stoughton to hard-nosed enforcers like Dennis Polonich and Garry Howatt, above.

There is a tangible quality to the tradition confined in the room. The ghosts of the past can still influence Flin Flon's current stars. "It came up one day in the dressing room," Hildebrand confirms. "The guys figured out that Bobby Clarke's stall was where Graham Borne was sitting. Borney thought about sitting in Clarke's spot and then went out and played a great game. The coach had used it as motivation—Borney had been down in the dumps until then. When guys come here, they feel a lot of tradition and are honoured to wear the jersey."

That jersey has undergone a slight alteration this year. Hildebrand proudly exhibits the back of the sweater like a haberdasher peddling a rich fabric. "We wanted a more modern look so we added a little black on the back of the jerseys. From the front, it still looks like an old-time jersey, on the back it looks more like the Colorado Avalanche–style with the black numbers. I wouldn't change the logo in a million years, though. They'd run me out of town."

We exit through the rink door with the sign that reads "Time to Work, Check your Egos at the Door." It's eleven o'clock and Steve Hildebrand's work day is finally completed. He takes one last admiring glance over his shoulder before locking up. "It's a dream come true to look after a room with this much character," he confesses.

The next morning I discovered an historic link between the changehouse at the Trout Lake mine site and the Flin Flon Bombers' dressing room. Until the late seventies, every Bomber player would store his equipment in a basket hooked to a chain. With a yank of the chain connected to a pulley, the gear would be raised to the ceiling, suspended in mid-air under the heating ducts to dry. It was a routine unique in junior hockey but not to Flin Flon. The Bombers had recycled the idea from the miners who hung their work clothes and equipment in the same fashion, and it is one small example of the pervasive influence the mine has had on almost every facet of Flin Flon life, including hockey. For a majority of Bombers, the work day began at the mine. On this day, I found myself looking upward at the night crew's floating equipment as I suited up in coveralls, boots, work belt, helmet and head-lamp to begin my first shift ever underground.

Pat Jones is a foreman at the Trout Lake mine site. He's a strapping miner with a handlebar moustache who once worked for Bobby Clarke's father, Cliff. Now, Jones has assumed the retired Clarke's position. At first glance, you could imagine Pat as a former Bomber. He seemed destined to patrol the Flin Flon blueline as a rugged six-foot, 180-pound fourteen-year-old prospect. He embodied the robust style that was the trademark of Flin Flon hockey. There was only one problem. A series of injuries sidelined him from the game. Not injuries he suffered, but those he inflicted on opponents who had the misfortune of trespassing on his frozen turf. "I broke one guy's jaw catching him with his head down coming over the blueline, a second player dislocated his shoulder," he said remorsefully. "A third tried to duck by me along the boards. I caught him with my hip and split his head wide open."

It was the brand of hockey his coaches encouraged in the Flin Flon tradition. Pat, however, could not reconcile their approval with the guilt he felt. "The coaches taught you there were no friendships on the ice. When you stepped off the ice, you could become friends again. I never was comfortable with that," Pat said. Eventually, Jones concluded that the game had become too rough for his liking, just as it was for three of his unfortunate opponents.

For twenty-two years, Pat Jones has worked underground in the one-hundred-mile labyrinth of subterranean roadways beneath his home town. We descended into the darkness, headed towards the deepest recesses of the mine at the 1,070-metre level, over a kilometre below the surface. Winding our way down the corkscrew tunnel, which is eighteen feet wide and fourteen feet high, I was reminded of the fictional character who is the inspiration for the town's name.

In 1905, British author J.R. Preston Muddock wrote a forgettable piece of science fiction entitled *The Sunless City*. The book's main character was a New York grocer and amateur scientist with an unlikely name, Josiah Flintabbatey Flonatin. The eccentric Flonatin built a submarine to investigate a bottomless lake in the Rockies. His journey took him to the centre of the earth and a discovery that was the wildest fantasy of any prospector or miner: the earth's core was laden with solid gold.

"As he surveyed this stupendous tract, assuming that the gold was only two inches in depth—though he later proved by the crevasses and fissures that it was many feet thick—he made a rough calculation that there was sufficient gold there to pave the streets and roads of every large city and every town and village in the United States."

Muddock was never mistaken for H.G. Wells and *The Sunless City* did not pave the author's way with gold. Curiously, however, a copy of the book was found and read by prospector Tom Creighton in northern Manitoba in 1915. Shortly thereafter, while hunting for moose, Creighton fell through the ice into one of the area's countless lakes. Beneath the surface, the rock bed of the lake shimmered with what the prospector recognized as an untapped mineral treasure. Creighton staked his claim and proposed the lake be named Flin Flon after the fictional character who had stirred his imagination.

As we plunged further underground, I asked Pat if Tom Creighton's story wasn't fiction as well. Was it really possible for the rocks to glisten so noticeably underwater? Moments later, Jones pulled our Toyota Man Carrier into a dead end. In an old stope, water and copper ore exposed to the air had oxidized, creating a brilliant turquoise gleam. "The higher the grade, the nicer the blues," he said. "I always said I'd like to have a car painted that colour."

The next stop was a powder magazine where 25,000 pounds of explosives are stored. The men of the Hudson Bay Mining and Smelting Company have been blasting for over six decades, burrowing deeper beneath the surface. Frequently, a drift round consisting of six hundred pounds of explosives is detonated. When a full production blast of more than thirty thousand pounds is charged, the changehouse on the surface is rocked.

Canadian Industries Limited, which supplied the first explosives to the mine in 1936, also provided the design for Flin Flon's trademark hockey crest—the word Bombers with the middle B bursting in an explosion. A few of the Bombers who wore that logo were also involved with explosives underground. To qualify for a blast certificate, a miner is required to take a six-month course and pass a written examination. Rarely did players reach that level during their on-ice careers, but a few Flin Flon Bombers lived up to the tradition of the team name by hauling explosives from the powder magazines to the blasting sites.

At the 870-metre depth, we inspected a freshly blasted stope, an underground canyon 150 feet wide, 90 feet deep. From areas like this 2,600 tons of ore are removed each day to extract the ore's contents, which are three per cent copper and six per cent zinc. The rich mineralized veins visible along the rock walls create a pattern that fuels a miner's eternal optimism. "Ore bodies are like fingers on a hand," Pat explained. "We keep digging deeper to find the palm. If we do find it, the mine will be here a hundred years from now."

Ascending the serpentine passage, the subject again returned to hockey. Pat replayed the provincial final in which his Flin Flon bantam team lost 6–4 to Brandon. It's a game they should have won after unleashing an eighty-four-shot barrage at future NHL netminder Glen Hanlon. Jones still plays industrial-league hockey and in an annual tournament involving Flin Flon-ners who have relocated throughout western Canada. There are enough hockey-loving alumni to form eight teams.

Currently, Pat derives most of his hockey pleasure from watching his sons, fourteen-year-old Michael and Gary, who is twelve. "Both boys have the dream," he said. While Gary aspires to be a goaltender, Michael has already established himself as a "Bobby Clarke–like" scorer at the minor level. "In his first year of atom, he scored 127 goals," Jones reported proudly. "He was the most valuable player and top scorer in the peewee league and now he's in his first year of bantam. They're looking for really big numbers from him next year."

Cliff Clarke often said that he didn't wish for his son Bobby to work in the mine. Pat Jones, who still thrives on the challenges of his job, concurs. "You always want something better for your kids," he said. He understands a Hall of Fame NHL career is a long shot for his youngsters. There are no guarantees the boys will even become Bombers. All Jones knows for certain is that the hours they spend at the Whitney Forum are meaningful. "It's Bomber pride, Flin Flon pride. The rink means a lot to me. I've spent two-thirds of my life there. I often say, give me the kids from the north and I'll take on city kids in a championship game. I'll guarantee the kids from the north will win on heart alone."

Flin Flon is stuck between the rocks and hard places surrounding Ross Lake in northern Manitoba. It is perched on the outer fringe of the Canadian Shield, the nation's Precambrian breastplate that stretches across Canada's heart from Quebec to the prairies. The landscape of Flin Flon is as rugged as its citizenry of eight thousand, and in the numbing minus-thirty-five-degree chill of this dreary noon hour, Flin Flon seems a long way from anywhere. Colourful Winnipeg junior coach Eddie Dorohoy once quipped, "Flin Flon should be in the proposed International League with the Russians. They're only an hour away."

The drive uptown was my first view of Flin Flon in the light of day, having arrived after dusk and with my morning spent underground. A statue of Josiah Flintabbatey Flonatin welcomes visitors at the city limits. It was donated by the creator of L'il Abner, Al Capp, who was charmed by the city's love affair with the fictional character.

A few moments later, the cab driver pointed out another distinct Flin Flon landmark. "This has got to be the only town I know of with sewer pipes above ground," he said. The pipes snake their way over the craggy topography, in many places encased by wooden planks that double as sidewalks. A tourist brochure lists the wooden sewer boxes as a local attraction.

Beyond Third Avenue and Sipple Hills, the skyline is dominated by two structures of the Hudson Bay Mining and Smelting Company: the massive red head frame of the north mine shaft, and the towering smelter smokestack that stretches 825 feet into the northern sky. The south mine shaft is less than a mile away in a section of Flin Flon that lies on the other side of the provincial boundary—the town straddles the border.

The Hudson Bay Mining and Smelting Company—HBM & S for short—has been the life-blood of the community since 1927. Currently it employs more than two thousand local residents. If the mine ever closed, Flin Flon would shut down. The company's headquarters are located on a large tract of land to the west of Main Street. The mine, smelter, mill and a neighbourhood of company cottages that house mining families are here, as well as the Whitney Forum.

Hockey was first played for recreation in Flin Flon on the frozen lakes and later at an open-air rink. Early local teams sported names like Kopper Kings and Gold-Diggers. It wasn't long before the mining brass of this remote centre recognized the benefits of the game as a source of entertainment for its employees and a means of recruiting labour. "As soon as the mine started regular operations many unemployed hockey players headed north," Vince Leah wrote in *One Hundred Years of Manitoba Hockey: A History*. The town was also beginning to earn its reputation as honest and hard-nosed. Local reporter George Mainwaring chronicled the atmosphere of the early days with an account that could have applied to a fractious hockey game: "Flin Flon was not altogether a mining camp in the wild way usually associated with such places. There were hardy men but none of them were tough in the sense that crime could be considered a problem. Petty theft was almost unknown. There were fights aplenty but never any really vicious men. Occasionally someone would get carved up but the general idea was to get patched up and back to the job."

The Flin Flon Bombers were also becoming a robust force on the ice, winning their first of three consecutive Northern Senior League titles in 1928–29. As the mine flourished in the mid-thirties, so did hockey. The HBM & S built an indoor rink, the Main Arena, in 1935 and scoured Manitoba for the best available talent to toil in its new hockey facility and mine. Two years later, Fred Bowman, a nineteen-year-old junior from Portage La Prairie, was recruited. He played seven years with the Bombers and worked forty-four years with the mine. "Odie Lowe was the coach of the Bombers. He'd been scouting us in the playoffs," said Bowman, now a spry eighty-year-old. "He offered me a job. I started at fifty cents an hour and that was pretty good money back then. It was during the Depression and you couldn't get a job. If you did, it wasn't for more than twenty-five cents an hour."

Bowman joined an impressive line-up that boasted Sid Abel and Jimmy Skinner. Both would later serve as coach and general manager of the Detroit Red Wings. Also on the twelve-man roster was Marcel Tremblay, who later joined the Montreal Canadiens. In the 1937–38 season, the Senior Bombers played eighty-eight games, losing only fourteen prior to their elimination by the Trail Smoke Eaters in the Allan Cup semifinals. The next season, Flin Flon defeated Trail twice in a weekend series before the Smoke Eaters reeled off fifty-one consecutive wins en route to the world amateur championship.

In 1940, Bowman was transferred to the mine's power plant at Island Falls, more than seventy miles away. After the move, even home games became astonishing road trips for Bowman. "In the winter of 1941–42, I came out by dog team. It was a two-day trip. I met the coach on the street and he said, 'Be at the rink, we're playing tonight.' I think I had two goals and an assist that night. The following year, we skated from Island Falls across the lakes and walked across the portages."

During Fred Bowman's playing career, Flin Flon became a hockey boom town. "It was the big thing because there wasn't a road in here and there wasn't television," he said. "When we played, the rink was always packed. We had a population of eight thousand and there were usually two thousand at the rink for each game. It was that big."

The mining and hockey operations of the HBM & S were so tightly intertwined that the company still retains records of its hockey involvement—purchase orders for uniforms, equipment and gold watches that rewarded championship teams. The files include payroll deductions for employees' season tickets, personnel transfers to other mine sites to adjust the competitive balance of mining leagues and memoranda of financial support as recent as the mid-seventies, when money was tight for both team and company. The general manager of HBM & S sent the following correspondence to the Bombers' board of directors, dated April 27, 1976: "The long tradition of Bomber teams and their special relationship to their fans and the city is so unique that it sets it apart from any other franchise I am familiar with. I am authorizing a $10,000 grant and a forgivable loan of $15,000. For every dollar the Board raises by fund-raising schemes in the community we would forgive a dollar."

By 1982, however, the mine, like the Bombers, had fallen on hard times. Precious metal prices plunged, and the HBM & S was forced to shut down underground operations for two months. The company also terminated its tradition, more than forty years old, of supplying employment to Bomber players. From Fred Bowman in the thirties to Jack McIlhargey in the seventies, mining jobs enhanced Flin Flon's reputation as a hockey haven. That fringe benefit laid the foundation for the Bombers' winning heritage and was the envy of its opponents. "They seemed to be able to recruit players better because they would put them in the mine. They were making $300 a month and we were playing for $125 in Melville," said John Ferguson.

Whether the mine received compensatory value from its hockey labourers is debatable. McIlhargey, who later patrolled the blueline for Philadelphia, Vancouver and Hartford, candidly admits he wasn't as productive underground as he was on the ice. "You'd learn the tricks pretty fast," confessed McIlhargey, currently the coach of the AHL's Syracuse Crunch. "You'd get down in an old tunnel, turn the light off your helmet, find a nice sand pile in a warm area and go to sleep." A memo, written by a shift foreman, indicates that McIlhargey was the rule rather than the exception: "The shift bosses and myself resent hockey players in general since they consume a high proportion of our time because of their childish pranks and avoidance of work. Some examples are letting the air out of wheel barrow tires in an attempt to have an excuse to avoid pushing the wheel barrow, unscrewing all the light bulbs between the leaching plant and the zinc plant changehouse on their way off work, hiding the personal property of their supervisor after taking it away from his locker chain in the changehouse, and wandering away from their place of work and hiding from the bullgang boss. A lot of these pranks etc. are done on the last few minutes at work before a road trip since they realize they will not see the shift boss for quite awhile because after they return from a road trip they will be on a different shift."

Another memo indicates the players were just as troublesome off shift. "At one time when we provided dormitory accommodations for hockey players, it was a watchman's nightmare to try and maintain discipline and order with an unruley [*sic*] bunch of hockey players."

In particular, the shift bosses were galled by the task of completing time cards for incompetent workers while the Bombers were away on road trips. When the team was in town, the players worked four-hour morning shifts and practised in the afternoon. But they were paid for eight hours a day, six days a week, even when the Bombers weren't within five hundred miles of the job site. Mine superintendent Brian Murphy acknowledges the rancour this created among foremen. "One guy said, 'I've had enough of those "bleeping" Bombers. I'd like to fire the whole lot of them.' The mine manager, his superior, was on the Bombers' board of directors. He said, 'The only guy firing the Bombers is [coach] Paddy Ginnell.'"

While musing over the mine's hockey file, I was joined by Ted Baumgartner, who has contributed significantly to both the company and the team. He has been an exploration geologist for the HBM & S since moving to Flin Flon in 1964. "I arrived on May 26 and it was snowing," he laughed, removing his furskin hat. "I wondered how long winter lasted here."

During the long winters, Ted watched his three sons, Kevin, Mark and Ken, progress through the local minor hockey system to fulfil their dreams of playing for the Bombers. Ken kept advancing and is currently with the NHL's Mighty Ducks of Anaheim. "I think I lived in the Whitney Forum for fourteen years chasing three boys and three hockey teams," Ted said. "Then they built the Sportex over in Creighton. I was at one rink or the other. Sometimes it was both places at the same time."

Ted Baumgartner has never played the game himself. The Montreal native had been discouraged by his father, who didn't value sports participation. That didn't prevent Ted from becoming an intercollegiate football player at St. Francis Xavier University. He possessed athletic ability, but the Baumgartners' hockey success is less a product of genetic inheritance than the Flin Flon environment, which puts a distinct stamp on its graduates. "They're all hard workers," said Ted. "They may not have the greatest talent but they made it on determination. They come to play. Reid Simpson is like that. A good hockey player but not a superstar. There's a certain determination a lot of kids have had out of here that goes beyond Clarke and Leach."

Two weeks later, Ken Baumgartner was in Edmonton as the Mighty Ducks tangled with the Oilers. In his tenth NHL season, Baumgartner is a veteran of more than five hundred games as a part-time forward, sometime defence-man and full-time enforcer. A protracted scar on his right cheek-bone and penalty minutes rapidly approaching two thousand are testament to his style. "My roots are who I am," he said in a quiet, thoughtful manner, belying the image he projects on the ice. "I wouldn't be in the NHL without the upbring-ing I had. There was only one mould of hockey player to come out of Flin Flon, hard-working guys who weren't afraid to get involved. It wasn't a finesse game I was taught. When your role models were Bobby Clarke and the Philadelphia Flyers in the mid-seventies, that's who you watched, that's who you idolized. There was a connection."

For most of his childhood, Baumgartner was raised in a company cottage just four houses from the Whitney Forum. He could almost roll out of bed and onto the ice. Each day spent at the rink further stoked his hockey aspi-rations. "You saw the pictures of championship teams. You saw players who thrived in the past, made the junior ranks and then graduated to the NHL. That was a great incentive," he said. But the early impetus of a Flin Flon youngster was not primarily to play in the NHL for Toronto, Philadelphia, or even a Disney-owned team in southern California. "Toronto and Vancou-ver seemed a long ways away, as did the NHL," said "the Bomber." "In Flin Flon every young child who put on skates wanted to play junior hockey for the Bombers. It was the promised land."

In Baumgartner's eyes, playing for the Bombers was Utopia, but beyond that a future in Flin Flon held little promise. Prior to the construction of the mammoth smelter smoke-stack, his home town was frequently engulfed by a thick haze more suffocating than southern Californian smog. As a teenager he toiled at the smelter. The money was good and the labour built character. It also forged a resolve that the mine wasn't a career alternative. "One summer I was a swamper, the next I was a crane chaser," he said. "It was hard work and very dangerous. It provided the incentive for me to continue my education and work hard at my hockey."

Baumgartner's career break came at the Whitney Forum in a Bombers game that showcased his best qualities. "I had a goal, a couple of good hits and a fight," he recalled. "There was a scout there from the Prince Albert Raiders. I had been told by Medicine Hat and Winnipeg that I'd never play in the Western League. A three-day try-out in P.A. turned into three years of junior hockey."

In sharp contrast to the early Bombers, who came to Flin Flon in pursuit of mining jobs, Baumgartner is representative of the new generation of players who used hockey as a vehicle to escape the mining town. "I had friends that went to work there when they were eighteen. It provided them with a good life. I chose the path less travelled."

A slapshot away from the main offices of the HBM & S Company is its greatest legacy to this hockey-crazed community, the Whitney Forum. It is a large, ashen-coloured structure that looks like a bunker melded into a hillside. In 1960, company president C.V. Whitney approved a grant of $250,000 to repair and enlarge the old Main Arena, which the mine had built twenty-five years earlier. A plaque on the rink door acknowledges Mr. Whitney's largesse.

"Today, the arena is named Whitney Forum by the Flin Flon Community Club in appreciation of the donation of the building by the Hudson Bay Mining and Smelting Company Limited on October 15, 1960."

Building the Whitney Forum, 1960

In the mid-afternoon calm, prior to the evening's scheduled tilt between the Bombers and the North Battleford North Stars, the Whitney Forum is a community recreation centre. A dozen women exercise on the walking track that surrounds the rink. At one end of the ice, a trio of teenagers has skipped classes for remedial shooting practice. At the other end, a pair of pre-schoolers are experiencing their first joyful steps on skates. One wears a Montreal Canadiens jersey, the other is clad in beloved Bomber maroon.

Dodging the oncoming pedestrian traffic on the track, I peruse the photo gallery of Bombers' hockey teams along the Forum's east wall. It's a historic walk, leading from the seven-man squads of the late twenties to the Bombers' most recent title-holders in 1992–93. The display's centrepiece is the 1956–57

Memorial Cup championship team. Ted Hampson, Mel Pearson, Pat Ginnell, Orland Kurtenbach and the rest of the Bombers pose proudly after conquering a star-laden junior affiliate of the Montreal Canadiens led by Sam Pollock and Scotty Bowman. It was a titanic seven-game classic steeped in dramatic, emotional and comedic sidebars worthy of a Stanley Cup final, a series Flin Flon will never forget.

The Bombers had been expected to win the Memorial Cup a year earlier, but Regina had other ideas and upset the northern rivals in the league final. Flin Flon management had no intention of finishing second again. With the mine's assistance, Bombers recruitment shifted into overdrive. Even after a torrid start, the Bombers bolstered their roster with two highly regarded players, Pat Ginnell and Barry Beatty. Charges ensued that Flin Flon was attempting to buy the Memorial Cup. The *Hockey News* commented, "Around Regina there is a feeling that the northerners are trying to do just that. Coach Bobby Kirk's Bombers burst out with 9 wins in their first 10 starts in the Saskatchewan Junior Hockey League. But apparently they weren't satisfied with that fine record for they announced the acquisition of two outstanding players. Employment in the mines is one of the best attractions that brings boys like Ginnell and Beatty to Flin Flon."

Ironically, negative press from Flin Flon also spurred the Bombers' auspicious start. "When our two local papers rated us third and fourth in our own league, we felt we had something to prove," recalled team captain Ted Hampson, now the head scout of the St. Louis Blues.

The "alien" team, as the only Manitoba entry in the SJHL was dubbed, answered the critics by amassing a 64–9–2 record, making a shambles of the league. Flin Flon crushed Humboldt, Prince Albert, Edmonton and Fort William in the playoffs to qualify for a berth in the national final against the vaunted Ottawa-Hull Canadiens. At the time, the Memorial Cup was also considered the unofficial world junior championship.

A western entry hadn't captured the Memorial Cup in a decade. Despite their imposing record, the odds of a Flin Flon victory were considered as remote as the northern community's locale. The Winnipeg papers made the Bombers 80–1 underdogs, listing 3–1 odds in favour of an Ottawa-Hull sweep. However, history and the bookmakers weren't Flin Flon's greatest adversary.

The junior Canadiens' roster boasted prospective NHL stars Ralph Backstrom, Bobby Rousseau, Gilles Tremblay and Murray Balfour. Also in the line-up was a younger brother of the famed Richards. In the tradition of Maurice, "The Rocket," and Henri, "The Pocket Rocket," Claude Richard was known as "The Vest-Pocket Rocket." Sam Pollock and Scotty Bowman, the masterminds of an impending Montreal dynasty, were behind the bench. A future Canadiens coach was their prized defenceman. "The surprise of the club is little Claude Ruel, who his coach believes, is the finest junior rearguard in the game on a pound for pound basis," wrote the *Hockey News*.

Ottawa-Hull not only had proven its superiority over all junior challengers in eastern Canada but were remarkably competitive in a pair of NHL exhibition games, defeated 5–4 by Detroit and 2–1 against Chicago. It appeared the only way the Canadiens could lose the Memorial Cup was by not showing up.

Incredibly, that is what almost happened. Sam Pollock stubbornly detained his team in Winnipeg for three days hoping to avoid the daunting trek 550 miles north. The date of the series opener arrived with Ottawa-Hull inexplicably absent from the Memorial Cup site. Publicly, Pollock offered alibis of cancelled flights, inclement weather and an inadequate train schedule for his team's absence. Forty years later, Pollock's assistant Scotty Bowman confirms that it was an orchestrated power play to change the venue. "Originally we were going to play the series in Winnipeg," admitted Bowman, the NHL's all-time leader in coaching victories. "We held out to try to have it there. We made it a tougher situation for our team because we didn't go initially. The whole town was wrapped up with their team. They gave us a tough time and the media was on us pretty good."

By the time Pollock brought his Canadiens north by train, under harsh orders from the CAHA, he had become public enemy number one. Flin Flon was in a frenzy as the series began. The venerable Main Arena was refurbished to accommodate ticket demand. An end wall, plastered with advertising during the regular season, was demolished to make room for two hundred bleacher seats. The band shell was also dismantled, creating space for sixty additional spots. Tickets priced at seventy-five cents during the regular season sold for three dollars to meet the CAHA's minimum gate requirement of $4,500. Every seat was sold, and fans lined up overnight for tickets to Games 2 and 3 also slated for Flin Flon. Those without what was truly the hottest ticket in town could listen to one of four radio broadcasts providing live coverage.

Pollock's antics had ignited a rivalry before the teams ever faced off. His actions magnified the east-west tensions and small town–big city conflict that made the match-up so compelling. But if there was a mystique about the late-arriving Ottawa-Hull squad, it vanished once the Bombers saw them hit the ice. "We made a point of watching them practise when they finally got there," Ted Hampson recalled. "After their practice, we thought, we can skate with these guys. We didn't know if we were going to win, but we knew we weren't going to be embarrassed."

The circus-like atmosphere that preceded the Memorial Cup continued into Game 1. It was a night that Orland Kurtenbach, a post-season addition to the Bombers from Prince Albert, will never forget. "There were so many people packed in the rink that night. They were jammed in right along the boards. Suddenly, the boards collapsed on one side. The whole thing went down," laughed Kurtenbach, a thirteen-year NHL veteran of New York, Boston, Toronto and Vancouver. "It was a shocker. Fortunately, nobody was hurt."

The Bombers brought the house down as well on opening night, completing a 3–1 victory, which seemed to mock the 3 to 1 odds of an Ottawa-Hull sweep. In the late stages of Game 2, some Flin Flon fans might have been anticipating a Bomber sweep as the locals protected another 3–1 lead. Unlike the opener, the boards didn't collapse, but the home team did. The Bombers surrendered three goals in the final four minutes as the Canadiens evened the series at one game apiece.

Game 3 would be the season finale at the Main Arena. The remaining four games, if necessary, were scheduled for Regina, home town of Ottawa-Hull forward Murray Balfour. Balfour, however, might have preferred to remain in Flin Flon where he always shone. A year earlier, playing for Regina, he had single-handedly defeated the Bombers in the league final. In this Memorial Cup, Balfour, who later played for Montreal, Chicago and Boston in the NHL, was at it again. He fired a hat trick to lead Ottawa-Hull to a 5–2 victory and a 2–1 series advantage. The loss triggered concern, suspicion and an uproarious accusation from the Flin Flon camp.

"When we left Flin Flon, people had written us off," Ted Hampson remembered. "People said, they've won their one game. That will be it."

In the glum aftermath of Game 3, the local press was already proposing excuses for what many believed was impending defeat. They accused Sam Pollock of hockey espionage. "They know all our little weaknesses. Certainly a lot more than anyone could pick up in two or three games," charged local sportswriter Tom Dobson.

Flin Flon was just beginning to understand Pollock's hockey genius, why he was destined to become the architect of a Montreal Canadiens dynasty and earn induction into the Hockey Hall of Fame. His stalling tactics in Winnipeg had backfired. However, once in Flin Flon, his thorough preparation and attention to detail were evident. As Ottawa-Hull fled town in a convoy of taxis to Regina, a scene from the Keystone Kops presented Pollock with an opportunity to showcase his rapier wit as well.

Coinciding with Ottawa-Hull's hasty getaway was the disappearance of a Bombers team picture from the local taxi stand. The Flin Flon constabulary was called in. The Canadiens were prime suspects. A few hours later, an RCMP roadblock collared Pollock's convoy north of Swan River, Manitoba. Pollock's whimsical response to the ludicrous charge made great copy in advance of Game 4 as he compared the heist to the "swiping of the Mona Lisa."

"They don't steal horses in the west any more. Now it's pictures. A framed picture of the Bombers! At first I thought I'd laugh. But when I started thinking about the framed picture the police described, I wondered who was getting framed. Officer, I yelled, nobody with this team in his right mind would lift a picture of the Flin Flon Bombers. We don't need a picture to be reminded of the Bombers. We're playing them every other night. The Bombers may be heroes in Flin Flon but they're not heroes to us. They're pains in the neck! That's the picture as far as we're concerned. I'll tell you, though. If the Canadiens win, I'll send a framed picture of the team up to Flin Flon. If they can't find the one that was swiped they might use ours just to keep the nail occupied."

In the 1957 playoffs, Flin Flon had won each of its four previous playoff series on the road. The Bombers wouldn't surrender just because the series had shifted to Regina. In fact, they continued to enjoy home-ice advantage at the Queen City Gardens. "When we played in Regina during the regular season, they hated us," said Bombers sniper Mel Pearson. "But in the Memorial Cup they just loved us there." Riding that support, Flin Flon rebounded to win Games 4 and 5, assuming a 3–2 series lead.

In the fifth game, the legendary men behind the Ottawa-Hull bench lost their composure in a 3–2 defeat. Pollock was ejected after forty minutes for protesting a call too vigorously. At the final buzzer, Scotty Bowman charged onto the ice to confront the Edmonton-based officials. "I hope I did," kidded Bowman, with a hint of bitterness still remaining forty years later. "Those two referees from western Canada were something. They gave us as tough a time as they could."

Undeterred by the officials, Ottawa-Hull exacted a measure of revenge in Game 6, employing a physical style to pound out a 4–2 victory. From Flin Flon's viewpoint, the loss had more to do with the ice. "The weather was warm, which made the ice extremely slow," recalled Bomber captain Ted

Hampson. "When the weather turned cold again, we were pretty happy. With fast ice we felt we could win Game 7."

The posturing and tension mounted prior to the decisive game. Bombers coach Bobby Kirk countered Pollock's hockey savvy with a master stroke of psychological warfare. Kirk vowed that his team would not succumb to Ottawa-Hull's rough-house tactics. "If the Canadiens try roughing it up tonight, my club will not back down an inch," he declared to the press. "Our kids have been taught to play hockey and not this professional style that only calls for stopping the man. It's very simple to teach a kid to elbow, high-stick and hold. Teaching him to play the game properly is the difficult task." Kirk's volley was a direct shot at Pollock and a thinly veiled signal to the officials to crack down on the rough stuff. Kirk believed if the physical play were constrained by the officials, his fleet Bombers would benefit.

On the eve of Game 7, Kirk, a former New York Ranger, was confronted with his own critical judgment call after many Bombers were caught breaking curfew. "The night before, we were very nervous," recalled Mel Pearson. "A few of us went out around midnight for Chinese food because we couldn't sleep. We didn't get back until two or so. Somebody saw us coming in late. The next day the coach wanted to know if it was true that we'd been out having a good time." Discipline had not been a problem on this team, which had made a commitment following the playoff disappointment of the previous year. "We made a pledge during the season not to party throughout the year," said captain Ted Hampson. "We had one party at Christmas because we had a ten-day break. Then we repledged ourselves and said every time we win a series we'll have a little party in the playoffs." Kirk accepted the players' explanation for their soirée and no disciplinary action was meted out before the historic showdown.

The referees, however, did crack down as Coach Kirk had urged. Early in Game 7, Ottawa-Hull was assessed back-to-back penalties, presenting Flin Flon with a two-man advantage. That set the tone for the entire game. On the power play, Pat Ginnell scored his twenty-fifth goal in twenty-two playoff games for a 1–0 Bombers lead. Mel Pearson, a fifty-nine-goal scorer during the regular season, calmed his jittery nerves by making it 2–0. In the third period, after the Canadiens had drawn within a goal, Ted Hampson, the club's leading point-getter throughout the year, restored the Bombers' two-goal advantage. The Canadiens' final reply came with one tick remaining on the clock. Their second goal was scored into an empty Flin Flon net vacated by goaltender George Wood, who had already begun to celebrate. When the final horn sounded, the Bombers had triumphed 3–2, becoming Dominion of Canada champions!

A wild celebration ensued in the Queen City Gardens as Bomber supporters flooded the ice. In Flin Flon, jubilant fans rejoiced in the streets. The *Flin Flon Daily Miner* described the celebration: "Pedestrians formed a congo line snaking up and down Main Street. Oldtimers standing aside, making room for their young counterparts to celebrate, claim it was the wildest and most carefree demonstration since VE Day and more than one expressed the opinion that even the end of the Second World War did not match the hockey celebration."

1957 Memorial Cup champion Flin Flon Bombers

In the champagne-drenched Bombers dressing room, coach Bobby Kirk paid tribute to the minor hockey coaches of Flin Flon for their role in grooming the national champions. "It is the fellows in the minor setup back in Flin Flon who have worked night after night and given so freely of their time, that had just as much to do with winning the Memorial Cup as we here tonight."

Montreal Canadiens coach Toe Blake, whose team had won the Stanley Cup three weeks earlier, conveyed his organization's congratulations to the victors. Meanwhile, Sam Pollock, whose career would be marked by few setbacks, was bitter in defeat. "The referees beat us," he moaned. "We got twenty of the twenty-nine minutes in penalties handed out."

New York Rangers general manager Muzz Patrick attended the finale. Impressed by the Bombers' performance, Patrick invited seven Flin Flon players to the Rangers' training camp the following September. One of the invitees was Ted Hampson, who proceeded to a twelve-year NHL career and four seasons in the WHA. Although Hampson was awarded the Masterton Trophy for sportsmanship, perseverance and dedication to hockey in 1969, the Memorial Cup victory is unmatched in his hockey memories. "Playing in the NHL and my first NHL goal were great but the Memorial Cup

Bobby Clarke

is my hockey highlight. The whole town of Flin Flon celebrated with us. It went on for several weeks. We still celebrate sometimes even today."

Among the elated Flin Flonners on that glorious spring night in '57 was an eight-year-old miner's son clinging to every word of the radio broadcast. Sprawled on his living-room floor, Bobby Clarke visualized the day he would become the Bombers' captain. "For most of my youth, I wanted to be Teddy Hampson," confirmed Clarke. "When you played on the outdoor rinks, you'd pretend to be Howe or Béliveau but I couldn't imagine how good they were because we never saw them play. We only heard their names on the radio."

That changed in 1962 when the NHL arrived on Clarke's doorstep. The Detroit Red Wings staged a pre-season game against the Edmonton Senior Flyers at the Whitney Forum. Former Bomber Sid Abel delivered a star-studded line-up that included future Hall of Famers Gordie Howe, Terry Sawchuk, Norm Ullman, Bill Gadsby and Alex Delvecchio. This rare spectacle gave Clarke a tangible hook on which to hang his dreams. "Obviously, Gordie was the guy. It was like God coming to town," said Clarke. "It was the first time I'd seen anybody try to get an autograph. For me, just to see them play was special." Ironically, Vic Stasiuk, Clarke's first NHL coach in Philadelphia, was also on the Red Wing roster.

Within five years, Bobby Clarke was the marquee attraction, the hottest discovery in Flin Flon since prospector Tom Creighton crashed through the ice. Clarke ascended from rink rat and stick boy to saviour of the Bombers franchise. In the spring of 1966, he emerged as a midget prodigy leading his team to the provincial title. Two weeks later, he was recruited by the juvenile Bombers for another Manitoba championship series. Flin Flon routed the Winnipeg Orioles, and future NHL referee Andy van Hellemond, 22–9 in the two-game total-goal final. Bobby, playing against opponents in some cases three years older, notched a hat trick in the clinching game. "The only thing important to me was the next game," he remembered. "In those days, if you were good at fourteen, you played against sixteen- and seventeen-year-olds. They moved you up and down. We could go to the city and beat the city kids all the time."

The emergence of Clarke's hockey genius coincided with the looming collapse of the Junior Bombers. The 1957 Memorial Cup champions had been a tough act to follow. Subsequent teams failed to perpetuate Flin Flon's winning tradition. By the 1965–66 season, the Bombers limped to an embarrassing 8–49–1 record, while being outscored 480–197. Local hockey historian Cyril Hume wrote a prophetic indictment of the Bombers in disarray: "This would have to be the poorest and most indifferent effort ever made by our Juniors. A drastic change is a must."

The Bombers were also teetering on the brink of insolvency. A one-night radio campaign, which raised $3,000, was needed to bail out the franchise. It bought enough time until the arrival of Bobby Clarke.

Clarke was a critical component of the Bombers' rebuilding plan, but there were other elements as well. Paddy Ginnell, a playoff hero for the Memorial Cup champs, relinquished his job as a brewery rep in northern Manitoba to coach. Reggie Leach, a promising sixteen-year-old from Riverton, Manitoba, was given a bus ticket to Flin Flon by Detroit Red Wings scout Danny Simmons. A year earlier, Leach had been unstoppable, playing defence in a men's intermediate league, scoring sixty-five goals in thirty-three games.

From their debut in the Manitoba Junior Hockey League, Clarke and Leach were as explosive as the dynamite charges in the Flin Flon mines. The Bombers won their first two games by scores of 13–3 and 11–2 and never looked back. In one weekend double-header, Clarke amassed an astounding twenty-five points in two games! By January, the Whitney Forum was bursting with more than 2,000 fans a game. It was 1957 revisited as the Bombers rolled to a twenty-one-game winning streak, a franchise high since the Memorial Cup. Clarke finished the season with a league-leading 71 goals and 183 points; Leach had 67 goals, 113 points.

More importantly, Clarke and Leach forged a bond that would catapult them to NHL stardom. "Right from the first time we met, we were friends," said Clarke. "We worked together, roomed together, looked out for each other. Reggie was easy-going. I was driven. He needed my commitment to the sport to push him. I needed his ability. There was no better player than Reggie. He could skate, shoot and in

Reg Leach (number 9, identified with arrow) scores a WCJHL record eighty-seventh goal, with Bobby Clarke celebrating in front of the net at the Whitney Forum in 1968

junior he could fight too. As a pro he didn't fight much because he didn't have to."

The following year, Flin Flon returned to the Western Canada Hockey League. The Bombers were projected to finish no better than fifth against the stiffer competition. Paddy Ginnell had loftier goals. He implemented a punishing style that made Flin Flon the WCHL's most feared destination. It also led to his new moniker, "Hamburger" Paddy. "Every team that ever came in there was scared," said Clarke, who could just as easily be referring to the Broad Street Bullies at the Spectrum. "Ginnell used to say, 'Shoot the puck in and hit everything that moves.'" Games at the Whitney Forum became so raucous that WCHL commissioner Frank Boucher paid an early visit to Flin Flon to investigate, and his findings prompted a league-wide ultimatum: "All clubs are hereby warned that in future games at Flin Flon, if players are not controlled properly by the clubs, the referee is instructed to terminate the game and both will forfeit two points."

Ginnell's Bombers would not be intimidated by their opponents or the commissioner. Flin Flon reeled off twenty-six consecutive victories at the Whitney Forum. The highlight of the regular season was a record-smashing eighty-seventh goal by Leach, breaking Fran Huck's old standard. Bobby Clarke set up the historic tally with nineteen seconds remaining in the season finale. "I wanted it [the record] as much as he did, probably more," Clarke recalled. "Reggie didn't have a selfish bone in his body. It wasn't like he wanted the record for himself. He wanted to do it because it was there. And the rest of us wanted him to do it." Clarke's assist was his 168th point of the season, eclipsing Huck's WCHL points record by fifteen.

One of the few setbacks of the 1967–68 campaign was an exhibition loss to the Moscow Selects. The touring Russian squad included Boris Mikhailov, Victor Kuzkin and Vladimir Shadrin, who would face Clarke in a more significant hockey showdown four years later. Every corner of the Whitney Forum was crammed beyond capacity as the Selects emerged with a 5–3 triumph. "They led 3–0 in the first period," recalled Clarke's former linemate Ron Burwash. "We ended up outscoring them over the last two periods. We were used to them by then. They passed the puck so much and we stood around watching at first. If we had another period, we would have beaten them."

"Those were the days when we had to beat those 'goddamn Russians,'" said Clarke of the prevailing Canadian sentiment. "But we weren't playing for our country, we were playing for the Bombers. We didn't lose too often in those days and we didn't want to lose to the Russians."

In 1972, Clarke got another shot against the Soviets. This time national pride was at stake. He had learned the lessons of '68 well. In the "Summit Series," Phil Esposito was Team Canada's leader, Paul Henderson scored the pivotal goals, but the Russians regarded Bobby Clarke as Team Canada's premier player. Their admiration for Clarke was grudging. He eliminated Valery Kharlamov, the Soviets' most dangerous forward, from the series with a vicious slash across the ankle in Game 6. Unlike Pat Jones, Clarke had accepted the Flin Flon hockey philosophy of doing whatever it took to win without remorse.

The 1967–68 Bombers season ended on a sour note. Their combative style over the lengthy campaign had taken its toll. Flin Flon limped into the championship series without six regulars and were upset by the Estevan Bruins. It would cost Bobby Clarke his only opportunity to claim the Memorial Cup.

The following year a rift between the WCHL and the CAHA over the use of twenty-one-year-olds provoked the factions to sever ties. The western alliance became an "outlaw" league ineligible for Memorial Cup competition. But it was business as usual in Flin Flon as the Bombers skated roughshod over league rivals. They posted a 47–13 record, accumulating 1,747 penalty minutes, nearly seven hundred more than their nearest opponents. Clarke led the scoring derby again with 137 points. In two WCHL seasons he amassed 305 points in 117 games. He also polished his leadership skills off the ice. "Bobby tried to look after everybody on the team," said former Bombers goaltender Cal Hammond, now a Flin Flon assistant coach. "If there was somebody having a problem, whether it was rookie or veteran, he'd take you uptown for a coffee or a beer to talk it out."

Both Bombers netminders, Hammond and Ray Martyniuk, were drafted by the Montreal Canadiens in the 1970 amateur draft. Martyniuk was the fifth player selected overall. A goaltender has never been selected higher in the history of the NHL entry draft. However, neither was able to crack the Canadiens' line-up. "They kept Ken Dryden instead of me," joked Hammond. "I guess that was Sam Pollock's revenge for 1957."

The Bombers were crowned WCHL champions following a six-game triumph over the Edmonton Oil Kings. Flin Flon advanced to a newly created national final, designed to rival the Memorial Cup, against the St. Thomas

(Ontario) Barons. The series, like a seedy boxing mismatch, failed to go the distance. By Game 4, the Barons were being outclassed physically and on the scoreboard. Flin Flon led 4–0 in the second period when St. Thomas threw in the towel. Charging the Bombers with violent play, the Barons deserted the ice, forfeiting the series. "They didn't quit because it was rough. They quit because we were a lot better than them," recalled Clarke. "It was not a matter of whether we were going to beat them, but how badly. So they just went home."

Seven years later, Clarke experienced déjà vu when Central Red Army surrendered, albeit temporarily, in an emotionally charged showdown at the Spectrum in Philadelphia. A punishing check by Ed Van Impe against Valery Kharlamov triggered a Russian exodus. "When the Russians walked off, they were taking the easy way out," said Clarke. "It wasn't because of the check Van Impe threw, or that we were playing dirty. They just knew they were going to get beat. The difference in that game was that the Russians had competed against everybody else and done well. So had they wanted to compete against us, they could have. I don't think management has the right to quit on a team. It was the Russian coaches and managers that quit that day, not the players."

After the St. Thomas débâcle, the Bombers challenged the Memorial Cup champion Montreal Junior Canadiens to an unofficial national showdown in Winnipeg. It would have been a riveting rematch of the same proud organizations that had clashed in 1957. "Jimmy Skinner was the chief scout of Detroit at the time," recalled Ron Burwash. "Skinner said we would have beaten Montreal in six games. Paddy Ginnell told us to stay in shape and be ready." It was all in vain. Sam Pollock had had his fill of Flin Flon a dozen years earlier. The Canadiens declined the Bombers' challenge.

Clarke was ranked one of the top five juniors eligible for the NHL's 1969 entry draft. He would not be selected until the second round, seventeenth overall. Every NHL team, including the Flyers, bypassed the future Hall of Famer at least once. With its first choice, Philadelphia opted for centre Bob Currier of Cornwall instead of Clarke. Currier would not play a single game in the NHL. Hockey's most astute minds were unwilling to risk a blue-chip selection on a player with diabetes, even though Clarke had received medical clearance from the Mayo Clinic prior to the draft.

He had already proved local sceptics wrong four years earlier when the initial diagnosis was made. At the time, doctors urged Clarke to quit hockey unless he was prepared to consider playing goal. (The suggestion conjures up the image of a stick-wielding netminder in the mould of Billy Smith or Ron Hextall.) His concerned mother offered a similar second opinion. But Clarke would not allow the medical profession, his mother or his own body to sideline him. Instead, Bobby gave himself an injection of insulin daily, drank Coke with extra sugar before games and orange juice between periods and worked harder than ever. Periodically he showed signs of fatigue. But it was from the cumulative effect of forty minutes of ice time a night, not diabetes.

Early in his NHL career, he shunned interviews because of the media's preoccupation with the diabetes angle. Even now, he is reluctant to dwell on the disease that was affixed to his career like the "C" on his jersey. "I was lucky to have a guy like Paddy Ginnell, who at a young age made you work hard, made you understand that hockey was hard work," he said, broaching the issue indirectly. "Whether I had diabetes or not, I still had to work hard. I bought that theory. It works for everybody, actually. Only some players don't buy it."

In Clarke's eyes, the most imposing obstacle to the NHL was the culture shock of uprooting from his remote home town for the urban chaos of Philadelphia. His first visit to the Spectrum provoked chills of stage fright as he realized there weren't enough people in Flin Flon to fill the vast building. "I was scared as hell," he said of his initial trip to Philly. "I had never seen anything like Philadelphia—the people, the cars. Then to try and sign a contract that I didn't know anything about. All I wanted to do was go home."

Clarke, however, adapted quickly. He scored his first goal against Ed Giacomin and the New York Rangers in his eighth NHL game. With boyish enthusiasm, he plunged into the net to recover the historic memento. From that goal until his 1,144th NHL game, his ebullience never waned. Clarke led by example as he did in Flin Flon, and his teammates and fans responded in turn. In many ways, the Flyers' upswing closely mirrored the Bombers' earlier revival. Philadelphia finished eighteen games below .500 in Clarke's rookie season but under his leadership by the fifth year they had posted a record of 50–16–12. Crowds at the Spectrum that had averaged less than 12,000 before Clarke's arrival were transformed into nightly sell-outs of 17,077. The Spectrum became as daunting a place to visit as the Whitney Forum was at the junior level. "We had some pretty good players on those two teams. But it never hurt to have that atmosphere," understated Clarke.

In 1972, he won the Masterton Trophy, like his boyhood hero Ted Hampson. The following season, Clarke collected his first of three Hart Trophies as the NHL's Most Valuable Player. In Flin Flon, his legend grew, and with it swelled civic pride. Blue Monday, a local rock group, recorded a ballad in their hockey hero's honour.

The transition in his early Philadelphia years was eased by the presence of junior teammate Lew Morrison. Ron Burwash also received an invitation to the Flyers' training camp on Clarke's recommendation. Later, Flyers general manager Keith Allen consulted his captain about the merits of acquiring another familiar face, Reg Leach. "He asked me if I thought Reggie would be a good player for us," Clarke recalled. "Reggie was having off-ice problems at the time. I felt Reggie would score forty goals for us in a bad year."

Clarke's scouting report was as precise as Leach's blazing shot. With Clarke and Leach reunited, the Flyers reached hockey's pinnacle, winning consecutive Stanley Cups in 1975 and '76. Leach scored 106 goals alongside his junior centre in the Flyers' Cup-winning seasons. In the 1976 Stanley Cup playoffs, Leach fired nineteen goals in sixteen games to set a post-season record. "When Reggie came to Philadelphia it was the same thing [as Flin Flon]," Clarke said. "We always roomed together, drove to the rink together. We really trusted each other. Eventually I think Reggie got tired of me driving him all the time to be a better player. The relationship is never going to sour but we just kind of drifted apart. Reggie was twenty-eight or twenty-nine by then. We'd played together for a lot of years. He got tired of me pushing him."

Another common element linking the Bombers and Flyers was the coaching direction of Paddy Ginnell and Fred Shero. "Ginnell was a terrific coach," Clarke assessed. "He kept the team really close. It was our team against everybody else, our small town against bigger cities. The refs were going to screw us, the fans hated us. Ginnell used all those things to unite the Bombers, and it worked. Paddy was much more emotional, but with Fred it was the same philosophy. It was us against the world. It was a tremendous way of unifying your club. With Shero, if the plane was late it was because they wanted to screw the Flyers. In hindsight, their philosophies were similar."

So too was the coaches' esteem for their on-ice general. Upon the retirement of Clarke's Bomber jersey 11 in 1969, Paddy Ginnell offered this tribute. "I cannot think of a player past, present or future who could wear that sweater with the same determination as Bob did over the past three years."

In 1984, the Flyers also recognized Clarke's legacy—fifteen years of passionate leadership and the franchise's all-time leading scorer—with the retirement of his legendary number 16. Fred Shero echoed Ginnell's reverence for his captain. "I've never seen a man contribute more to a hockey club on and off the ice than Bobby Clarke," Shero said. "I've never seen a captain with the respect of the players he has."

On that unforgettable night, Bob Clarke addressed the Flyers faithful at centre ice. "I got all I could out of this body for fifteen years," he said in a voice cracking with emotion. "I'll cherish this evening forever and if I had my choice, I'd love to do it all over again."

So much of Bob Clarke's hockey career has been like a recurring plot line, his success as a Bomber repeated on a grander scale as a Flyer. And given the opportunity, he'd repeat his Flin Flon career too. "The Bombers played a huge role in my life," he said with pride. "The success I had is directly related to having played for the Bombers and having played in Flin Flon. I have a great fondness for them."

Currently, Bob Clarke is the president and general manager of the team that awards the Bobby Clarke trophy to its most valuable player. As the Flyers boss, he has guided his beloved franchise to four Stanley Cup finals, but was fired by the Flyers after Philadelphia failed to qualify for the 1990 Stanley Cup playoffs. The following year, he took the Minnesota North Stars to the NHL's championship series. Later, he became the first general manager of the Florida Panthers, building the firm foundation that resulted in the Panthers' surprising berth in the 1996 final. Although he's been fired by the Flyers, Clarke's devotion to the franchise is so resolute he agreed to manage them "all over again."

In 1998, he's taking on the added duties of general manager for Canada's Olympic team. Clarke is as uneasy selling himself as he is discussing his diabetic condition, and therein lies one reason his Olympic appointment received lukewarm approval across Canada. But considering his Stanley Cup and international track record as a player and manager, who better to lead Canada's pursuit of Olympic gold than a miner's son from Flin Flon?

The pulse of the Whitney Forum quickens in the late afternoon. Early-arriving Bombers congregate by the stick rack outside the Flin Flon dressing room. They gossip, exchange insults and tinker with their sticks, expending nervous energy before the evening's clash with North Battleford. A brawl erupted in their last battle against the North Stars. A Bomber was injured in the melee and suspensions were levied against both teams. There's a tangible feeling that "things are going to happen tonight!"

Warren Ayers is the Bombers' captain, another Flin Flon kid who has fulfilled his hockey dream. "There's no junior team in Canada I'd rather play for," the red-headed centre declares. "Even though we haven't been that successful here in the last three years I have no regrets. It's just an honour to play for this team. People say the hockey gods at the top of the rink are watching down on you. From the first time I walked into the rink, there was an overwhelming presence."

Hanging from the rafters are three banners of honour. The numbers of Bobby Clarke and Reggie Leach flank a pennant raised in tribute to Dale Fox, a fellow Bomber who wore the Flin Flon jersey with equal pride. "He was no superstar but his heart was in the game," says his mother, Maureen. "He worked hard, coached a girls' team and loved his hockey. He bucksawed wood instead of using a power saw to improve the strength in his arms."

Fox was a true Bomber, a consummate team player. "When kids came to play for Flin Flon from out of town, Dale was the one who made them feel welcome," Maureen says. Fox also stood up for his teammates. In his midget year, Dale, an assistant captain, and many of his mates were repeatedly benched without explanation by an erratic coach. "Dale felt every kid should be given a chance to play," says his mother. "He handed in his 'A' and walked off the team. It took guts to do that."

In the autumn of 1982, Dale Fox volunteered to be the designated driver for the team after a pre-season gathering. A few days later, before his second Bombers training camp, Dale was killed in a car crash, the victim of a drunk driver. He was eighteen years old. Commemorative plaques honour "Foxy" at both the Whitney Forum and the Sportex in Creighton.

Beneath Dale Fox's banner, rink manager Guy Rideout, known locally as "Beastie," admires the fresh sheet of ice he has prepared. "It's 186 feet by 85, almost the same as the old Boston and Buffalo rinks," he says. Rideout resembles a biker with his shaved head and goatee, but Beastie's machine is an old, cherry-red Massey-Ferguson tractor parked beside the Bombers' dressing room. The garage, with only a seven-foot clearance, couldn't house a modern Zamboni even if it could be afforded.

I ask Rideout about an infamous speed bump on the ice near the visitors' bench. "From years of frost and run-off, the floor would heave, crack and burst open," he explains. "Throughout the winter we'd just keep flooding over it. Opposing players would comment on that 'shitty piece of ice.' I'd just say that's the only way they could raise the puck with their slapshots."

Ninety minutes before the opening face-off, the visiting North Stars finally make an undignified entrance at the Whitney Forum. The Stars straggle in, one by one, wearing their travel fatigue. Although the Bombers are no longer the formidable opponents their predecessors were, the trip to Flin Flon is as arduous as ever. En route to the visitors' dressing room, the players linger over the photos in the Bombers' Hall of Fame. "You're glad you don't have to play those Bombers now," says goaltender Josh Esler, in reference to the imposing line-up on the wall. Esler confirms that North Battleford's sojourn has been fraught with the difficulties that typify most Flin Flon excursions.

Facing the Queen before a playoff game at the Whitney Forum in 1969

"The roads were horrible, as usual," he says. "A couple times we even contemplated not coming. Halfway here we almost turned around because the snow was blowing so badly we couldn't see." From experience, Esler knows that a visit to the Whitney Forum won't be a respite from the day's journey. "You show up with dead legs and the fans are different here than other fans. They're pretty wild. We've had our hair pulled on the bench. It can get out of hand."

I meet Bombers coach Larry Wintoniak below a regal portrait of Queen Elizabeth at the north end of the Forum. "I like the Queen," he says, referring to the painting displayed here since the fifties. George Garner, the mine's paint shop foreman, rendered the work shortly after her coronation. For many years at the Whitney Forum, "O Canada" was sung prior to games, "God Save the Queen" at game's end. "How many rinks still have pictures of the Queen?" Larry asks. "This is a character rink."

Wintoniak, a Thunder Bay native, assumed the coaching reins at mid-season. He understands his obligation to Flin Flon's hearty fans. "These people work six hundred metres below the ground for twelve-hour shifts," he says. "When they come out, they want to see good tough hockey." That has been Flin Flon's calling card for decades, but Wintoniak has inherited a team with a dearth of toughness. He's also hamstrung by league rules that water down the fringe benefits of home ice that Flin Flon once enjoyed. In their glory days, the Bombers would pound out victories in the opening period while travel-weary opponents searched for their skating legs. "The way the league works now, referees clamp down on everything in the first ten minutes," he explains. "That takes away the advantage the home teams used to have. It's not like it used to be when you could put your heavyweights on that first shift to throw their weight around. It benefits teams coming in now."

But Wintoniak understands that he was hired to produce results, not excuses. That is a coach's plight anywhere. In Flin Flon, however, the scrutiny is intense. "Everybody is under a microscope here," he acknowledges. "There's a coffee shop named Johnny's. If we don't have a good practice in the morning, people at the rink will tell the people at Johnny's. The next thing you know it's all over town. When I first came here a couple of people said, 'You've passed the test.' I said, 'What do you mean by that?' 'They say at Johnny's the practices have been pretty good the last couple of days.'"

Tonight's game is a critical test. The Bombers are desperate for a victory to maintain their slim playoff prospects. "Welcome to the famed Whitney Forum," greets the public-address announcer. A sparse gathering of about five hundred regulars has assembled on this bitterly cold February night. The dip in attendance reflects the team's current record, the shrinking Flin Flon population and a night shift at the mine that divides the Bombers' potential audience in half. During the glory days, there was only a day shift at the mine. Flin Flon's evening shift was at the Whitney Forum.

Thirty-nine seconds after the opening face-off, Josh Esler misplays a long-range Bomber shot for a 1–0 Bombers lead. The goaltender's reflexes appear dulled by the day's travel. For the home-town fans, it is a blast from the past, reminiscent of when Flin Flon always got the early jump on its rivals. However, unlike the glory days, the lead will be short-lived. North Battleford responds quickly, tying the score and dictating the tempo.

In the second period, locked in a 3–3 tie, North Battleford storms the Flin Flon net unabated. After a wild goal-mouth scramble, the North Stars finally notch the go-ahead tally. It's more than a Bombers legend can bear. "How can they stand around and let them whack away at the goaltender like that?" demands Mel Pearson, from his perch in the north end. "I can't understand it. We'd have put them on their ass in our day."

"Let's put another link in the chain," is the Bombers' rallying cry as they take the ice for the third period. Team captain Warren Ayers, who wears Bobby Clarke's famed number 16, plays with "Clarke-like" tenacity in the third. Ayers's persistence is promptly rewarded with the tying goal. It triggers the loudest roar of the evening at the Whitney Forum. Nevertheless, the occasion is not momentous enough to be marked by a hockey custom unique to Flin Flon. In Detroit, Red Wings fans throw octopus onto the ice; in Miami they toss rats. Bombers fans have gone bigger, if not better, by heaving moose legs from the stands in celebration. Thankfully, the moose have been spared tonight.

The heckling from behind the North Battleford bench intensifies. A pack of local teens has been antagonizing the North Stars with a barrage of lewd gestures and crude remarks throughout the game. They play their agitating roles as Stew Lloyd once did. The visitors, though, respond with an effective silencer. The North Stars fire the winning goal in the dying moments of regulation time.

Now the only unfinished business for the Bombers is to settle the score from their last encounter. Newly acquired Flin Flon bruiser Steve Zinger accepts the assignment. Zinger, who models the brightly bleached hair of a snowboarder, crashes over defenceless Josh Esler in the North Stars' net. Bart Redden, whose younger brother Wade is a promising blueliner for the Ottawa Senators, rushes to Esler's defence. The pair grapple in a spirited round of fisticuffs, while the Whitney Forum throng howls with delight. They cheer Zinger for restoring the Bombers' honour. And even in hostile territory, Redden is applauded for his noble retaliation.

As the sticks and gloves of the combatants are retrieved, I feel a tap on my shoulder. Fourteen-year-old Michael Jones, whose father guided me through the mine, introduces himself. He is fair and lean, exuding an air of self-assurance much like his idol Wayne Gretzky at the same age. "So you're going to be a Bomber?" I ask. Michael gazes towards centre ice in wide-eyed wonder, nodding affirmatively. "That's been my dream since I was three years old," he replies.

8

Le Colisée
Quebec City, Quebec

Scott Russell

The winters of my childhood were long, long seasons. We lived in three places—
the school, the church and the skating rink—but our real life was on the skat-
ing rink. Real battles were won on the skating rink. Real strength appeared on
the skating rink. The real leaders showed themselves on the skating rink.
                                        —Roch Carrier, *The Hockey Sweater*

TO WATCH THEM THAT SEASON was to ache all over. The Quebec
Nordiques of 1988–89 were tragically inept. The young franchise was, after
all, the pride of a French-speaking province, and through the years it had
been mightily successful. Their brilliant white costumes adorned with the
royal blue fleur-de-lis seemed as much the battle garb of virtuous crusaders
as the utilitarian uniforms they were. The Nords had missed the playoffs
only twice in their nine-year history, and the people of la Vieille Capitale
loved them without fail. Like a withering rose, this team had won just ten
of its first thirty-two games, and the boastful Canadiens were about to pay
their pre-Christmas visit.

The contest on December 15, 1988, was, by any estimation, a foregone conclusion, another episode in the NHL's "Battle of Quebec," won
by the powerful *bleu, blanc, rouge* at the expense of a team in transition.
It was corporate Montreal versus provincial Quebec City—and the story
line should never have been in doubt. Then again, le Colisée was the
venue that night. The players, particularly those born nearby, were known
to be driven by a heightened sense of urgency there. Throughout its
history, this rink had been a stage where hockey was acted out as a passion
play to an adoring audience. What's more, on a strange and memorable

evening an unfolding tragedy involving the Nordiques was about to transform sport into real-life theatre.

Ron Lapointe of Verdun was living a lifelong dream. Since early the previous season, the coach of the Nordiques had always wanted to be behind the bench at the NHL level. He had toiled as an assistant with the Washington Capitals and in the minors as the head man at Quebec's American League affiliate in Fredericton. Before the 1987–88 season was completed, Lapointe had replaced one-time Nordiques star André Savard as the coach of the big-league club. For Lapointe, a boy from la Belle Province, the chance to direct the show at le Colisée was to be the triumphant climax of a career. The bright lights and festive aura of this insanely devoted hockey city hid the truth from Ron Lapointe. His time in the limelight would be short and painful.

"He had inherited a team that was really struggling. Bad drafting, bad trades," recalled Randy Moller, one of the Nordiques' veteran defencemen. The 1987–88 campaign had yielded a mere sixty-nine points and, for the first time in eight seasons, a playoff miss. Lapointe's once cherished responsibility had turned into a salvage job. His players knew that restoring the lustre to a club that, not so long ago, had seriously challenged the Montreal Canadiens' monopoly on the affections of Quebecois hockey fans was a herculean task. "He jumped into the middle of a fire there," Moller said. "He thought he could turn it around in three or four weeks, and it completely backfired on him."

The team got worse. Early in the 1988–89 season, losing streaks became prolonged and even the powers of superstar players like Peter Stastny and Michel Goulet seemed diminished. The Nordiques languished in last place in their division and became doormats to the despised Canadiens, who were experiencing a renaissance in Montreal under rookie head coach Pat Burns. The pressure-cooker of Quebec was working overtime and le Colisée, once joyous and welcoming, became increasingly hostile for the struggling Nordiques and their beleaguered coach. "It was a very emotional building," remembered Mike Hough, a forward who had also played for Lapointe in Fredericton. "Ron was a very emotional coach. He would often get more emotional than the players would and he showed it."

The fans at le Colisée turned on Ron Lapointe in mid-December during the waning moments of an embarrassing loss to the Capitals. In a taunting melody, they sang the name of Jean Perron from the stands in the final minutes of the game. "PERRON... PERRON... PERRON," they intoned as a demand for Lapointe's firing and his replacement with the former Montreal coach who had won the Stanley Cup in 1986. To make matters worse, the vociferous hockey media in Quebec City openly questioned Lapointe's handling of the team. They asked questions for which he had few, if any, answers. In the dressing room, the players had lost faith in their ability to win. "There was a lot of dissension on the hockey club," said Randy Moller. "It was a very stressful time."

It was life at le Colisée, the showcase of a city that had but one great love, and that was ice hockey. In the provincial capital there were no other professional teams to divert attention from the Nordiques. Rock concerts often skipped Quebec City because promoters knew potential ticket buyers preferred to save their money in order to see the stars of the NHL. In this market there was a focus on hockey that made huge demands on the players, but it was also an invigorating place to perform. "The most fun I ever had in my life was playing for the Quebec Nordiques," said Moller, now a radio commentator with the Florida Panthers. "The games. You couldn't wait to play the games, and you knew there was more to each game than what took place on the ice."

On the morning of December 15, Ron Lapointe was told by the Nordiques' physician, Pierre Beauchemin, that he had kidney cancer and that surgery was required immediately. There was no way he could continue to pursue his coaching career in Quebec, no possible hope that he could redeem the team's sorrowful performance. Lapointe was finished with the Nordiques, but not before he'd made a simple request. He asked for one last game and a chance to direct the club that night against the Montreal Canadiens. On the surface, it seemed a futile effort, but the team's management agreed to the request. Lapointe would coach his final game, then say goodbye, regardless of the result.

"We found out the day of the game after the morning skate," remembered Mike Hough. "Our general manager, Martin Madden, came in and told us that Ron Lapointe had cancer and that he was being relieved of his coaching duties. He said that this would be Lapointe's last game."

"It was like, what else could happen to us?" Moller asked rhetorically. "It was very emotional in the dressing room. Very quiet."

Everyone in the building knew of Ron Lapointe's illness by game time. Le Colisée holds 15,399 hockey fans, but that night there were many more because of those standing in the crammed aisles and ramps of the historic arena. As always, when the two teams met, the atmosphere seemed electrically charged. Even in the depths of the Nordiques' despair, here was an occasion to pull together, a chance to cheer for something bigger than the game. When Quebec's team burst onto the ice that night, the fans erupted in a prolonged ovation of welcome. As soon as the puck was dropped, the home team barely resembled the flawed heroes they had been.

"He wanted this game," Hough said of Lapointe. "We went into it very emotionally, very excited." From the start, goaltender Mario Gosselin was brilliant as he repelled the powerful Canadiens attackers time and again, while the Quebec skaters drew on an offensive impetus that had been missing too often during the course of the season. As Lapointe paced behind the bench, his face grew flushed and glistened with a gathering sweat. The crowd roared at each rush by the Nordiques and collectively gasped whenever the bright-red Canadiens threatened their zone. The failings of the recent past were forgotten with so much at stake. "The fans in Quebec were unbelievable," said Moller, shaking his head in wonder. "There hasn't been a rivalry that comes close since the Quebec Nordiques and the Montreal Canadiens were split apart."

Ron Lapointe's last game as coach of the Quebec Nordiques on December 15, 1988

After two periods, the Canadiens led Lapointe's Nordiques by a slim margin. There were twenty minutes left in the job that he had aspired to for so long. In the third period, the place lit up and the faithful at le Colisée took over. In the stands, they started singing, and this time, the friendly chorus served to inspire the rushing Nordiques. Gosselin continued to stand on his head in defence of the goal, and the Quebec snipers scored three times to come from behind and claim the lead with the final moments racing by.

Albert Ladoucer writes about hockey for *Le Journal de Québec* and remembers an outpouring of emotion in the dying seconds of the game with the Nordiques ahead 6–4. "Everyone was crying," said Ladoucer. "Even in the press box there were many tears." Down below, the Nordiques' president and part owner, Marcel Aubut, had ventured behind the bench, and in full view of a cheering throng at le Colisée, held a weeping Ron Lapointe in his arms. The victory was secure and the coach's wish was lovingly granted.

Peter Stastny retrieved the puck as the final siren went and presented it to Lapointe by the players' bench. In a rare and tender moment, Canadiens coach Pat Burns came to hug his long-time rival, whom he had battled against in the National Hockey League and in the AHL when both were working in the minors. As the fans stood and applauded, Lapointe left the rinkside and followed his team to the locker room for the last time.

"He came in after the game and thanked us all for the effort we put forward and then he just turned around and walked out," said Randy Moller. "For a lot of players that was the last they ever saw of him."

Mike Hough has recently been to the Stanley Cup final as a member of the Florida Panthers. The emotion of Ron Lapointe's last game at le Colisée is etched permanently in his thoughts. "It was just meant to be," he claimed. "We were able to rise to the occasion and win a game for him. He wanted to leave as a winner and I think he did that."

On December 16, 1988, Jean Perron became the coach of the Quebec Nordiques, and the team improved but still failed to make the playoffs for the second year in a row. Ron Lapointe had cancer surgery a week after the victory over Montreal, and the only Nordiques player to visit him in hospital, by his own account, was Randy Moller. Following his convalescence, Lapointe joined the Vancouver Canucks organization to resume coaching at the minor-league level and eventually finished his career as a scout.

His final days in hockey were spent in the bitter cold of countless junior rinks all over the province of Quebec as he evaluated talent for a pro team on the Pacific coast. Huddled in the bleachers with the other scouts, grasping a Styrofoam coffee cup indistinguishable from the preceding thousand, he watched the game unfold as a part of the supporting cast. Not long before, he had played the lead on Quebec City's hockey stage. In the early spring of 1992, Ron Lapointe died of cancer having performed his part in the great drama that is le Colisée.

Le Colisée on a frozen winter's day. It was completed in 1949 and renovated in the early 1980s

It is like anticipating a trip to an amusement park where the only theme—the only attraction—is hockey. On a bright blue Sunday in early February, one rushes to the door at the northwest corner of le Colisée, the cold biting more deeply with each advancing step. Inside, a multilingual chatter in the foyer breezes from youngsters in a rainbow of team jackets. Men in toques, like street buskers, trade gold and silver pins on the crumbling and unpainted concrete floor. In an alcove, where the windows to the outside magnify the warmth of the sun, teenagers wearing snowmobile boots shuffle up and down while chasing a tennis ball in a primitive game of shinny. From the centre of the buzzing action the sound of a jubilant organ rises to a crescendo.

The Quebec International Pee-Wee Tournament is in its thirty-eighth year. On the opening weekend 2,300 players from 108 teams representing clubs from fourteen countries have great expectations swirling in their heads. It is the most prestigious gathering for thirteen- and fourteen-year-old hockey players anywhere on the face of the earth, hence its billing as the World Pee-Wee Championship. Over the years, 521 players have graduated from this tournament and played at the highest level of the professional game. The alumni includes Wayne Gretzky, Mario Lemieux, Guy Lafleur and even Eric Lindros. The fans flock to le Colisée to catch a glimpse of a child who may be the next great phenomenon. On average, 200,000 spectators pass through the turnstiles over the course of the eleven days of competition.

"Get your bodies stretched out, boys!" Mark McConnell, one of the coaches of the South Shore Kings from suburban Boston, is winding up his team for its opening game against Guelph. The young men look larger than their years should allow, as they stand on their skates and wave padded arms and shoulders in pre-game callisthenics. A bulldog of a man named Buddy Yandle slips to the doorway and is eager to chatter away the nervousness of the coaching staff. "It's such a thrill for kids to see an old venue like this. An old building where professionals have played," he exclaims, in a thick Boston accent. Yandle grew up half a mile away from the ancient Boston Garden and coached high school games there. He has an appreciation for tradition that is not lost on the kids who are now under his guidance. "They are really thrilled about it when they look up and see the banners of Stastny, Guy Lafleur and Jean Béliveau. There are great hockey experiences here," he says. "This is the experience of a lifetime for these boys."

The team from Austria has just completed a 6–0 whitewash of the squad from Grenoble, France. To the cadence of the ever-present organ music, the Zamboni cleans the ice in advance of Quebec's winter mascot, Bonhomme Carnaval, while the South Shore Kings and Guelph wait in the hallway by the Nordiques' old locker-room. As they dart onto le Colisée's playing surface, they are welcomed by the largest gathering that each team has played in front of. Perhaps five or six thousand clap and whistle to the players' arrival, with the Bostonian loyalists being the most vocal. Beginning their first loop in the warm-up, the Kings skate directly beneath a banner bearing the number 9, as well as the name of the greatest star ever to play with the Aces of the old Quebec Senior Hockey League. Le Colisée, legend has it, is the rink that was built for a hockey player called Jean Arthur Béliveau.

"It makes you feel good! The house that Béliveau built and that Lafleur paid for," Jean Béliveau admitted. Sitting, posture perfect, on a stool in the television studio at Montreal's Molson Centre, he is the closest thing there is to hockey's royal family. Béliveau is sixty-six years old now and as majestic in the crisp, blue business suit he wears today as he was when he was adorned with the tri-colours of the Montreal Canadiens uniform a quarter of a century ago. He is a Hall of Famer who defines the term with grace and substance, and a man who has the good sense to recall his beginnings. "They treated me like a king," he said of the provincial capital. "They decided right after the fire at the old Coliseum to start construction, hoping that I'd be coming to Quebec."

The old Colisée burned early in 1949 while Jean Béliveau was playing for the Victoriaville Tigers of the Quebec Junior League. He was marked from an early age as a great prospect by the Montreal Canadiens, who had long understood the value of knowing and developing hockey talent in their own back yard. Even as a fourteen-year-old, playing for Sacred Heart College in his home town of Victoriaville, Jean was developing a reputation. "It was an intermediate league and I was known because we played outside in certain of the smaller towns," Béliveau reminisced. "I was known as the big, skinny, tall guy with the blue toque!"

When it was announced that Victoriaville was going to cease its junior operation after the 1948–49 season, Béliveau and his teammates were declared to be free to play with any team they wished. The Quebec Citadels were anxious to acquire his services because, being from Victoriaville, he was considered, territorially at least, their property. "They really wanted him in Quebec," said former Victoriaville Tiger goaltender Denis Brodeur. "He has always been a franchise player." Brodeur, unlike Béliveau, went to Montreal to play for the Nationals and later for Canada's bronze-medal-winning team at the 1956 Olympics in Cortina, Italy. His youngest son, Martin, also plays goal and helped lead the New Jersey Devils to the Stanley Cup in 1995.

Now a sports photographer, the elder Brodeur recalls meeting Béliveau's Citadels in the playoffs at the newly opened Colisée. The Nationals were without their star offensive threat, Bernard "Boom Boom" Geoffrion, which meant their defensive specialist, "Skippy" Burchell, was forced into a new role. "When we got to the playoffs Boomer had to have his appendix out so we had to let Burchell try and score," said Brodeur. "It ended up that Béliveau filled the net and beat us by himself."

The story of those first playoffs at le Colisée was the building itself, and the response of the people in Quebec to their newly acquired hockey star. Jean Béliveau packed them in at an astounding rate. "We still have the attendance record set in the playoffs in the spring of 1950," Béliveau said with glee. "The last section of the stands was wide open with no seats. People were standing up. The record is still 16,800 for one of those games." Denis Brodeur added that le Colisée was hardly a palace of hockey in its first season. "I remember one game had to be stopped in the third period," he said. "There was a leak in the roof and water was pouring down in front of me and flooding my crease. It was not completely finished!"

The calm confidence of the regal Béliveau is refreshing in hockey's modern era. His fame suits him well as he draws on the recollections of youth. His accomplishments are beyond remarkable; they reflect a life of superstardom that extends well beyond the playing surface. Jean Béliveau played an even twenty years in the National Hockey League, all with Montreal, and drank from the Stanley Cup an astounding ten times. He has more than five hundred goals to his credit, as well as 1,219 total points. More often than not, he dominated the playoffs, and he was named the recipient of the inaugural Conn Smythe Trophy as the post-season's most valuable player in 1965. Béliveau is also a two-time winner of the Hart Trophy, as the player judged to be most valuable in the league. He led the NHL in scoring once and was regarded as the quintessential on-ice leader in Montreal during his tenure as the Canadiens' captain. For two decades Béliveau was known as "le Gros Bill" or "The Gentle Giant" in Montreal. His induction to the Hall of Fame was never in question and took place in 1972, a scant year following his retirement from active play with the Canadiens.

After his illustrious on-ice career came to an end, Béliveau ascended to Montreal's management office. For two decades and more, he was the Canadiens' senior vice-president of corporate affairs and became synonymous with the sparkling reputation of professional hockey's most successful and distinguished organization. It is a further testament to Jean Béliveau's stature across Canada that he was once asked by Prime Minister Jean Chrétien to consider assuming the post of governor general. It was an offer Béliveau declined because of an overwhelming commitment to family during his retirement years.

The ease of notoriety was not always second nature to Béliveau. In two years with the Citadels, playing in front of the constant frenzy and adoration of the fans at le Colisée, he had to come to grips with his role as the virtuoso performer. "You leave home at eighteen. You're the oldest of the family and all of a sudden you find yourself in the limelight like that," he reflected. "This was a completely new life to me. I had to adjust."

His performance on the ice met all expectations and the Citadels were contenders because of Béliveau's presence. Still, there was a struggle going on for his services and, more importantly, for his loyalty. The Montreal Canadiens constantly sent their emissaries east, along the highway, to court and cajole the young star. The general manager, Frank Selke, would make visits to pay homage to him as would Emile "Butch" Bouchard, the Canadiens' captain. Their aim was to bring Béliveau closer to what would be his eventual hockey home, and the possessive fans of Quebec were naturally worried. "Every September I would come to the Montreal Canadiens' train-

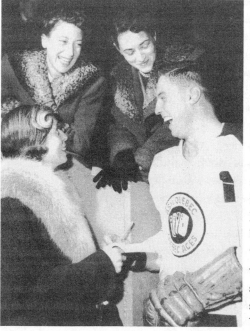

Jean Béliveau was treated like a king while playing at le Colisée for the senior league Quebec Aces from 1951 to '53

ing camp because they were starting earlier than the Quebec teams," Béliveau explained. "Whenever I left Quebec like that, they were afraid I wouldn't come back. They used to tell me whatever the offer was in Montreal, it will be the same thing here."

He was, as he freely admits, paid very well, and he fell in love with his status as the centrepiece of le Colisée. There was a comfortable understanding that he would be allowed to grow into superstardom in this friendly environment, but Denis Brodeur knew the legendary Béliveau had vulnerabilities off the ice in those formative years. "Jean Béliveau at that age was very quiet, very reserved and very shy," he said. "In the summer we used to play baseball together, sit in front of his house on the porch and talk. We'd eat a few hot dogs and have fun. He was so shy that he didn't talk to those he didn't know. He was always a leader but very soft spoken."

At le Colisée, Béliveau could do no wrong. The new building was alive because of his efforts. The fans showered him with gifts and recognition and devoted themselves to watching him play on their behalf. It was a mutual admiration because at the end of two years of junior play, Béliveau resisted the lure of Montreal and the National Hockey League. While having dinner with his future wife, Elise, and Roland Mercier, the general manager of the Citadels, Jean considered the loyalty of the fans in Quebec City. "I asked what I could do to thank the people for the way they had treated me those first two years," Béliveau recalled. "Somebody during the course of the conversation, I think maybe it was Elise, suggested, and I listened, that I should decide to play another year in Quebec to thank them."

Hockey fans in Montreal were frustrated at management's inability to sign Béliveau to a contract with the Canadiens. Commentators were equally miffed with the young star, saying that his fragile psyche was allowing him to hide from the pressures of the NHL in Quebec. In 1951, Jean Béliveau signed to play with the Quebec Aces of the semi-professional Quebec Senior Hockey League and was paid extremely well, even by major-league standards. The team was owned by a large company called Anglo-Canadian Pulp and Paper, Aces being an acronym for Anglo-Canadian Employees Society. The company could afford to attract good players who had spent time in the big leagues, as well as keep a marquee talent like Béliveau in town to fill le Colisée to capacity. It was an arrangement that suited everyone extremely well, with the exception of the Montreal Canadiens.

"It could have been bad for me," says Béliveau of his time with the Aces. "The fact was, we had good experienced players on what turned out to be a strong team. It meant that I was still learning." Gaye Stewart, a former rookie of the year in the NHL with Toronto, was also in the Aces line-up and the coach was the irascible George "Punch" Imlach, himself on the way to greatness at a higher level of hockey. "I know Punch had a lot of enemies," Béliveau conceded. "To me personally he was a great help. A very smart man." Imlach would point out the flaws in Jean's skating style and send players chasing after him for hours on the ice at le Colisée so that he would improve the first three or four steps of his start.

Already accomplished at his chosen craft, Béliveau claims to have improved dramatically because of the two years with the Aces in the senior league. He says he learned about rivalries. There were the personal ones, such as those with Les Douglas and André Corriveau, his combatants in the race to see who would be the league's leading scorer. There were also rivalries that were timeless and consuming, battle lines that would shape hockey in the province for years to come. "I remember coming to the Montreal Forum on Sunday afternoon to play the Royals and half the building would be cheering for us," Béliveau said. "The Nordiques and the Canadiens were nothing new because when I was with the Aces, half the building in Montreal was wearing our uniform!"

There were struggles against Valleyfield and Chicoutimi and tales of playoff series that started out as the best of seven, only to wind up as much longer affairs in order to avoid too much leisure time for the finishing teams. "All of a sudden we woke up and were involved in the best of eleven. You had to win six games to move on," Béliveau said, with a chuckle. Le Colisée was always full, and the Aces won the 1953 Alexander Cup, emblematic of eastern Canadian senior hockey supremacy, by defeating the Saint John Beavers in the final. Jean won the scoring championship of the Quebec league in each of the two years he played and became the undisputed hero in the provincial capital.

Lessons Béliveau learned during the years from 1951 to 1953 were the most important rewards for the developing star. Le Colisée became like a preparatory school for him as he readied himself for a life in hockey in Montreal, the most demanding market of all. "There's a fellow who is still alive today—Jo-Jo Graboski, what a skater!" Béliveau's eyebrows lifted as he recited the teachings of an early mentor. "He used to play for the Quebec Aces before me and would come to our practices at le Colisée. Jo-Jo told me to practise my skating because the game of hockey was about speeding up. He had in mind that I would make it to the NHL. He was right!"

While Jean Béliveau's career with the Montreal Canadiens is legendary and held in high esteem by devout followers of the game, le Colisée is also his enduring legacy. It was as if his personality shaped the building's future and the unique atmosphere contained within its walls. With an endearing humility, Béliveau understands the role he played in developing a lasting hockey institution. "I think you have to look at it from the fans' point of view. They now had a great place to go to a game," he said. "I see people today of my generation and older and they remind me all the time of how great it was when I was with the Quebec Citadels as a junior and the Aces after that. I have a feeling that those first four years for Quebecers at le Colisée must have been a good start for them."

His role in the rink's construction is essential, although Béliveau is hesitant to take all the credit for le Colisée's existence. "The house that Béliveau built" is not a phrase that he coined or encourages but he does acknowledge that it has some foundation. "I never thought about it. I've heard it," he admitted. "It makes me feel nice, especially now, that maybe I was indirectly responsible."

Unlike the Molson Centre or the Forum before it, le Colisée is not owned and managed by a major, private business concern. The Quebec Exhibition Authority is an organization owned by the city and therefore the rink is a public shrine in the hockey-mad community. Denis Brodeur captured the relationship that existed between the patrons and the performers during the Béliveau years. "It's a government city and not that big. They always helped their team and believed in their team," he said. "I think people felt when they went into that arena it was like going home."

Le Colisée from the south

Briefcase in hand and on his way to another appointment, "le Gros Bill" had a final offering as he navigated his way out of the Molson Centre's challenging complexity. "I think le Colisée in Quebec was looked at as a great dream in 1949," Béliveau said, with some consideration. "There's no doubt, not only in Quebec but wherever you are, if you want to build a new arena, attendance is the key and it is a big help to have a big star." There is little doubt, even nearly half a century later, that le Colisée was constructed as a rostrum for a player who continues to distinguish himself as one of hockey's greatest ambassadors.

The South Shore Kings have overcome their opening-game jitters and lead the team from Guelph 5–2 in a match they have dominated from start to finish. The third period has become increasingly one-sided and it calls for some crowd motivation on the part of Marcel Lajeunesse. From his loft, high in the south end of le Colisée, the heavy-set man in a formal black jacket allows his fingers to dance freely over the ivory keys of his Roland E-86 electric organ.

"You can't play fancy music, it gets lost," Lajeunesse says, with conviction. "You have to play with punch. Keep it simple." As a perfect illustration, he foreshadows an impending face-off by punching the keys in staccato fashion, and the fans respond with short bursts of clapping in order to keep pace. He turns around once the puck is dropped and flashes a knowing look, as if to say, "I told you so!"

Lajeunesse has played the organ at le Colisée since 1983 when, as a twenty-two-year-old, he charged up the fans for the Quebec Nordiques. With originality, he tailored his repertoire to reflect the personalities of the star performers on the hockey club. So it was that le Colisée rocked to "Eye of the Tiger" when pugnacious coach Michel Bergeron berated the referee. The prolific Michel Goulet had his goals celebrated to the melody of "You're Sixteen, You're Beautiful and You're Mine," because of the number he wore on his jersey. Meanwhile, the popular sniper Peter Stastny's exploits were generally followed by a rendition of "The Theme from Peter Gunn." Lajeunesse was rewarded for his ingenuity by being chosen as The Hockey News Best Organist in the NHL for 1986–87. It is an honour of which he is fiercely proud.

Since the Nordiques' migration to Colorado in 1995, Lajeunesse has relied on work as an organist in a shopping-mall night club to make a living. That, combined with his eleven-day engagement each season as the music man for the peewee tournament, makes ends meet. The tournament, and the chance to play at a hockey game, is something he always looks forward to. Like this type of rink, which is devoid of private boxes and cavernous concourses, organ players are rapidly becoming extinct in the modern National Hockey League. House music tends to come from compact discs spun by space-age disc jockeys tucked away behind the smoked glass of entertainment control centres, well back from the ice surface.

Marcel Lajeunesse has trouble understanding why live music-makers are becoming obsolete in hockey rinks. It is, he believes, part of the arena's charm, making it a more lively and theatrical place. "You have to cheer up the fans," Lajeunesse stresses while pounding on the keys. "Remember, this is not an action crowd. It is a reaction crowd." With that, the final buzzer goes and the opportunistic organist spins out an old favourite: "NA ... NA ... NA ... NAH ... HEY ... HEY ... HEY ... GOO-OODBYE ..."

Scrambling down to ice level via the backstages of le Colisée is like charting a course through the catacombs. Narrow hallways lead to thinner stairwells and eventually into a network of dusty tunnels, which become the rink's

arterial system. In the tributaries, aging tournament organizers in blue blazers and grey flannel pants scurry around with clipboards, taking notes and
answering a thousand questions. Lit by fluorescent bulbs, Mario Talbot's
Pro Shop is tucked away in a corner of the basement level. He is working
furiously to keep up with the equipment demands of the ambitious players
and their parents. Talbot will fine-tune more than one hundred pairs of
skates a day and peddle enough white and black tape to choke an elephant.
Countless varieties of sticks and jock straps line his shelves, alongside plain
and waxed laces of every size. Some folks walk into his shop just to talk
hockey over a cup of coffee that Mario rarely has time to drink.

Gaston Filion is a director of the tournament in charge of making sure
the players' equipment is safely stored. Rising from his little desk, he swings
open a chain link fence that allows entry to the place the hockey bags are
kept. There are mountains of the stuff. The orange and blue of the powerhouse Detroit Little Caesars stand out in front of the five-foot stack of
duffle bags that bear the name of Fort McMurray Syncrude. "Seventy-five

Gaston Filion is in charge of the basement at le Colisée where thousands of equipment bags are stored for the tournament

to eighty teams' worth," Gaston announces
proudly. "I know exactly where everybody's
gear is." He makes a check mark on his list
and then ushers in the guys from South
Shore who are arriving with their well-
stowed pads.

Buddy Yandle is chirping jovially about
the ambience of le Colisée following his
team's first-round victory. "The old Boston
Garden had personality just like this place,"
he declares. "Back there you knew the rats
by name!"

Tiny Jack Greeley totes a bag that seems
to dwarf him. He is a centreman competing for the first time in Quebec, although
his brother Steve played here two years ago.
Flashing a grin and revealing a gap between
his two front teeth that you could drive a
Zamboni through, Greeley descibes his first
reaction to the arena as he stepped onto the
ice. "I was scared to death," he admits. "The
crowd was a bit intimidating. It's such a big

The first Swiss team to play at the Quebec Pee-Wee Tournament drew more than fifteen thousand fans to le Colisée for their game against Brantford

rink and all these people. We've never played in front of people like this."

Greeley is wearing a baseball cap, and when he lifts the bill, he reveals a ton of freckles that make him look younger than his thirteen years. He had glanced into the rafters during his first couple of tours of le Colisée but failed to recognize many of the names on the banners that hang over the ice. Jack wasn't even born when Jean Béliveau, Marc Tardif and J.C. Tremblay were in their playing days. He has not got the foggiest clue who the Aces or the Quebec Bulldogs are. Still, he is from Boston and can make one connection with the building's glorious tradition. Greeley saw the pennant tattooed with the symbol of the Quebec Remparts. "I've heard of Guy Lafleur," he says confidently. "I know he was a great player!"

Guy Lafleur was almost apologetic when he called back on a Saturday afternoon prior to the Canadiens' last game of the regular season. "Sorry I wasn't there for your call this morning," he explained. "But I had to take my kid Marc to the rink and his game. Some things you just don't want to miss." With a little laugh, Lafleur revealed his boyish attachment to the rhythm of the weekend in Quebec. Mornings are for hockey and for legendary fathers to witness the rites of passage in the game they have made their life's work. Evenings are spent worshipping *"les glorieux"* and hoping that they have enough left to chase the Stanley Cup for a twenty-fifth time.

Lafleur has been gone from the active NHL for six full seasons now, the second retirement he has had to endure. Once known as "le Démon Blond" and "the Flower," he acts these days as a goodwill ambassador for the Montreal Canadiens and appears several times a year, in all parts of the country, on their behalf. A Hall of Famer and two-time winner of the Hart Trophy as the most valuable player, Lafleur has not authored a huge portion of the National Hockey League's record book. His career was very productive but, more importantly, it was marked by an incredible flair. Guy Lafleur came

The Rink

to be a great French-Canadian icon, a sensitive and complex character who played hockey as an artist would stroke a brush over canvas. Lafleur became the people's ambition, and in him, they hoped for a more favourable reflection of themselves.

His first trip to le Colisée was in 1962 as a member of the peewee team from Rockland, Ontario. Guy was actually from Thurso, Quebec, but played for the club right across the river from his home. "We had always played in small rinks," he recalled. "We travelled by train to Quebec City and they took us on a tour of the rink where we would play the next day. We just couldn't believe how big it was!"

The overpowering size of the structure impressed Lafleur but so did the arena's aura. It was, after all, a place where his favourite, Jean Béliveau, had played much of his early hockey. Guy wore the same number 4 as Béliveau had assumed since joining the Montreal Canadiens for good in the fall of 1953. At his first tournament, Lafleur scored seven goals in a single game and his team went on to win the International Cup in the B group. They had captured the Jean Béliveau Trophy, which was presented by "le Gros Bill" himself, as he was nursing an injury which kept him out of Montreal's line-up. "It was very big because Jean was my idol at the time," said a genuinely impressed Lafleur. "It was something very special for a kid like me to play in that tournament."

In two succeeding years, Lafleur came back to Quebec City and the peewee tournament as a member of the team from Thurso. Twice more he helped win the Jean Béliveau Trophy. In light of the fact that the tourney was still in its formative years, Lafleur's impact on the people of the provincial capital was immense. Here was a young French-Canadian skater who sparkled in his own back yard and delighted the fans like few others before him. Lafleur was marked from the age of ten as one of the next great Quebecois superstars, someone who, in a very short time, could succeed Jean Béliveau as the leading light at le Colisée. "They wanted me to go there and play right away at twelve years old," Lafleur said. "My dad told me I was too young but I was crying to go! He told me to wait two years and see if I was still interested."

Quebec City was more than interested in getting Guy Lafleur to come east and play his junior hockey there. Paul Dumont, the director of the Junior As, was responsible for recruiting talent and immediately understood Lafleur's ultimate value to the community. Since Béliveau had left to play for the Canadiens in 1953, the intense love affair with hockey had

subsided in Quebec, and le Colisée had witnessed a steady decline in attendance. The Memorial Cup, symbolizing supremacy in Canadian junior
hockey, had not been won by a Quebec-based team in nine years, and even
then, the Ottawa-Hull Canadiens were closely affiliated with cosmopoli-
tan Montreal. Le Colisée needed a new star to bolster the city's diminishing self-image as well as to put people in the stands. "Paul Dumont was
phoning all the time to see if I would change my mind and come to Quebec,"
Lafleur remembered. "I felt very much at home there. The first year it was
very tough to have left the family. I cried to come home every night. My
dad told me that I had cried before to come to Quebec and now that I was
there, I was going to stay!"

Arriving just before his fifteenth birthday, Guy Lafleur had an immediate impact on the quality of hockey in the Quebec Junior League and on
the level of expectation at le Colisée. Once again, people began coming to
the games in large numbers to see the bright young prospect from Thurso.
Although he was lonely at first, Lafleur gradually warmed to the feeling of
the environment and the ease of the city that had so readily adopted him.
He boarded with a widow named Madame Baribeau, not far from le Colisée.
She had three grown boys who had all married and moved on, and in a short
period of time, Lafleur became like her closest kin as she doted on his every
concern. "When I came to Quebec, she treated me as if I were her son,"
Lafleur said fondly. The atmosphere at the rink where he played was intense
but comfortable. The fans were demanding, but of his own kind, and Lafleur
blossomed in their warm light. "It was a big family," he said. "There may
have been ten thousand people in that building many times, but it was
a family."

The seats at le Colisée rise steeply from the ice. Rows of red, blue and
white lead to the black arc of the roof where the banners dangle in the brilliant light above the ice surface. It is a place made exclusively for hockey
and, although attractions of other kinds have succeeded within these four
walls, it is never more alive than when the great spectacle of the game reaches
a fever pitch. As Guy Lafleur's prowess grew, the renaissance of the rink
gathered momentum. In his last two years of junior hockey, Lafleur chose
to stay in Quebec and play for the Remparts while resisting the lure of the
Montreal Junior Canadiens and the Ottawa 67s, who played their games in
the Ontario League. While Lafleur stayed put, another French-Canadian
prospect named Marcel Dionne had decided to escape the overwhelming
pressures of Drummondville and moved to St. Catharines, Ontario, to play

for the Blackhawks. Even today, Lafleur celebrates the decision he made. "It was a great atmosphere to play in," he stressed. "People were dancing during the games. I had never seen or heard anyplace like that before. People would sleep overnight outdoors to get tickets for junior games. They were just crazy about the Remparts at the time."

In a short period, Guy Lafleur took Quebec's junior circuit to respectability and his team to the Memorial Cup final against the St. Catharines Blackhawks and Marcel Dionne in the spring of 1971. "It was like, live or die," Lafleur said, with a little tension in his voice. "People were so close to our team that they followed us wherever we went. When we went to St. Catharines they had over twenty buses go from Quebec City." Part of the attraction was the rivalry between Quebec-born players Guy Lafleur and Marcel Dionne. It was something that had smouldered for a number of years and was now about to be ignited in the crucible of the Memorial Cup championship series. It turned out to be one of the most inflamed episodes in le Colisée's history and it demonstrated the jealous attachment that the fans in Quebec City have to their beloved stars of hockey.

When the series returned to Quebec from St. Catharines, the Remparts and Blackhawks entered an emotionally charged situation. It became, in the press and in the stands, Lafleur—the patriotic francophone—against Dionne—the traitor. At le Colisée, the young sniper from Drummondville had purchased forty tickets for friends and family to see the game. Marcel Dionne was taunted on the ice while his relatives in the seats were verbally abused by the Remparts' supporters. Dionne remembers standing at the face-off circle and seeing his parents bombarded by garbage that rained down from the upper reaches of the arena. Years later, Guy Lafleur was hesitant to chastise the over-zealous fans. "They worked very hard in the stands to help us on the ice," he justified. "Maybe it got nasty at one point at le Colisée but I'm sure our fans got the same treatment in St. Catharines."

After the fervent Quebec fans attacked and rocked the bus that Dionne was reported to be on, the Blackhawks refused to complete the championship series and the Remparts won the Memorial Cup by default as much as anything else. The Edmonton Oil Kings agreed to play two final games but they were easily disposed of by Lafleur's superior squad. In winning the championship, the Remparts had made history for the Quebec Junior League, and the ugly incident at le Colisée sticks with "the Flower" to this day. He somehow understands why Marcel Dionne was made to suffer their wrath and feels it has a logical foundation. "I think the people of Quebec believe that if you stick with them they will respect you for life. They will do anything for you," he explained. "If a guy leaves because he thinks it's better on the other side, the people will be upset. They are very, very close to the team—but don't hurt them!"

In the June draft, following the Memorial Cup, Guy Lafleur was taken by the Montreal Canadiens and anointed the greatest prospect of the day. The Habs' crafty general manager, Sam Pollock, had engineered the process by making a trade with the California Golden Seals to ensure Montreal's ability to claim Lafleur. The Detroit Red Wings had the second choice in 1971 and selected Marcel Dionne. While the first years of his career in Montreal were uneasy because of his adjustment to a larger and more complex city, as well as struggles with learning a new language, Lafleur achieved legendary status with the Canadiens. There were five Stanley Cups, three scoring championships and countless exciting moments as "le Démon Blond" became the most talked-about player of a generation. He was loved in Montreal and spent fourteen glorious years there, calling it quits at the age of thirty-three when he felt the team no longer craved his talents, as they once had.

Life away from the rink was strange for Lafleur, his time out of the limelight more oppressive than he had envisioned. There were no crowds cheering any more, no breathless moments as he forged a ferocious path to the other team's net. His first off-ice role as a public-relations personality for the Canadiens was uncomfortable as Lafleur struggled to cope with diminishing demands and expectations. Over a period of four years, he wandered through a stage of self-doubt, feeling unfulfilled and unappreciated by the team to which he had given his professional life.

In 1988, he ended his self-imposed exile from the NHL and returned to active play with the New York Rangers. After Lafleur's respectable comeback season, the Rangers changed management and the Hall of Famer was not offered an extension to his contract. He went searching for other teams and ended up in the arms of the Quebec Nordiques, who had rehired Michel Bergeron to coach the struggling franchise. It had been at Bergeron's urging that the Rangers became convinced that Lafleur still had something to give, even after such a long time away.

"It was a wonderful feeling to go back there because it was a reminder of my years there as a junior," Lafleur said, with obvious feelings for Quebec City. "They were so happy and glad to have me back." It was true. The Quebec Nordiques had endured two seasons of missing the playoffs, and the first year that Lafleur donned the fleur-de-lis, the team was an unmitigated disaster. They won only twelve hockey games and accumulated a meagre total of thirty-one points, yet the arena was sold out every night. It was during this lean season that Guy Lafleur became fully aware of the unique affection that the people of le Colisée have for hockey. "The fans were very fanatic and very close to the players," he said. "There is a difference between Montreal and Quebec when it comes to hockey. In Montreal they say, 'The Canadiens lost tonight.' In Quebec City they say, 'We lost tonight.' It was the whole town. All fifteen thousand fans in the building. That's the way they think."

When he retired again in 1991, Guy Lafleur hung up his professional skates for good. He was satisfied that he had achieved a measure of stardom with the Montreal Canadiens and perhaps, just as importantly, returned to his roots in Quebec City. At le Colisée they had come to see him play even when others felt he was no longer of much use. They had demonstrated in the place where he first rose to stardom that a brilliant thespian will always play to a packed house. "They gave me the opportunity of retiring in peace," he said. "I have always believed that they gave something back to me after what I had done for them. I really appreciated that."

Le Colisée may be the best known of any of the Canadian hockey rinks, without exception. It has an international reputation that challenges that of fabled shrines like the Montreal Forum or Maple Leaf Gardens in Toronto. While it is true that these buildings have served as the showcases for inspiring confrontations between the best players in Canada, Russia and hockey's handful of world powers, le Colisée has a wider constituency. Children from the four corners of the world aspire to play in Quebec City, and from the moment they conceive of Canada as hockey's heartland, they struggle to get to this rink.

"I think they're learning traditions as a whole," Marc Melanson is saying of his team from Mexico City as they march to the ice. Melanson is the director of hockey schools at La Pista, a five-rink complex in the heart of Mexico's capital city. He is originally from New Brunswick but lived in Dorval, a suburb of Montreal, and played at the peewee tournament years ago. Glancing at his team, which is clad in the black, red and gold of the Vancouver Canucks, Melanson is fairly sure they will put up a fight against the squad from Hachinohe, Japan. Although he is an entrepreneur who profits from the game's blossoming popularity in Mexico, Marc stresses the value of history and what it can mean to youngsters who are learning a new sport.

"There was a [Mexican] team that came here in 1966," Melanson points out. He indicates one of the parents, Alejandro Saenz, who played for the Mexico Selects and lost 8–3 to the Quebec Lions that year. The first ice rink in Mexico opened in 1960, and it is estimated there are now three thousand minor hockey players in the country, with the numbers growing substantially every year. "When I got to Mexico City, I was like a missionary." Melanson is waving his arms. Standing by the boards he warms to the ambience of le Colisée. "I told everyone, you gotta get to Quebec—you gotta get there!"

As they circle during the warm-up period, it is obvious the Mexicans have a long way to go in their skill development. The sense of occasion is striking as they haltingly do the crossovers that make for mechanical cornering. "OLE... OLE... OLE... OLE," they chant with bright smiles underneath their plexiglass face shields. They, too, have heard all about this temple of hockey and are feeling inspired by the ice, so hard and fast.

"They might remember Guy Lafleur but they're more into the Yzermans and all the rest of the stars of today," Melanson concedes, his eyes always on the Mexicans. He is a Canadian spreading hockey's word in a place where the game is an acquired obsession. At le Colisée it has always been accepted that this sport is not the exclusive property of the initiated. It is instead an event to be shared and appreciated by a wide variety of people. "They know what's going on," Melanson says of his Mexican peewees. "They probably know a lot more than we think they do."

In the early 1970s, Quebec City found itself fertile ground for professional hockey's rapidly expanding territory. The World Hockey Association was formed and began play as a twelve-team operation in 1972–73. There was now a rival to the NHL and along with it came opportunities for hundreds of hockey players, as well as a few good hockey cities in Canada like Edmonton, Winnipeg and Quebec. Already a proven hotbed, Quebec City had an ideal facility in the ten-thousand-seat Colisée, and a tradition that would deliver the new league instant credibility. Marc Tardif, a high-flying forward who had broken in with the Montreal Canadiens, was the star attraction along with stalwart defenceman J.C. Tremblay, who had also played for the Habs with great distinction. The Nordiques, as Quebec's team was called, tried Maurice "Rocket" Richard as coach for a while and won the Avco Cup as league champions in 1976–77. As had perennially been the case, le Colisée was sold out every night the city's number-one team played. Although the league was short-lived, the Nordiques were one of the WHA's glittering success stories and the faithful fans made a case to get to the next level, which was of course, the National Hockey League.

Kevin Lowe of Lachute, Quebec, played for the junior Remparts during the last years the WHA Nordiques were in existence. After six Stanley Cups, five with Edmonton and another as part of the 1994 New York Rangers, Lowe is still amazed at the game's importance in his native province. "People love hockey in Quebec," he said, while sipping a coffee at Edmonton Coliseum. "I've been a little out of touch for the last eighteen years living in big cities like Edmonton and New York. But the way I grew up in Quebec, the rink was the focal point of the community, the gathering place. A lot went on there."

Lowe anchored the Rempart defence in 1977–78, taking the team to the Quebec League final. The next year he was a second-team all-star and caught the eye of the Edmonton Oilers, who were about to embark on their first NHL season as one of four WHA teams absorbed by the surviving league. Drafted twenty-first overall, he has played in the All Star game seven times and has also won the King Clancy Memorial Trophy for leadership on and off the ice. It is an award given to a player who has made a humanitarian contribution to his community. The importance of hockey's patrons is something that Lowe has never lost sight of throughout his lucrative career. "I had played in Quebec and felt determined to speak highly about it," said the bilingual Lowe. "Quebec is a very small town, unlike Montreal. There was so much pride in their hockey team. I think it was their way of putting a handle on themselves that they were a big city."

On many occasions, Lowe's Remparts filled le Colisée when the Nordiques had played at home the night before. Attendance was never a problem, and as a member of the city's junior team, Kevin was made to feel special. The church was close to the rink and the players attended Sunday mass as celebrities, well recognized and almost fawned over. "The junior team was like a pro team back then," he recalled. "They had the WHA there but the juniors were pretty close to pro hockey. They still are I guess."

To Lowe, le Colisée was at the centre of life. The huge white mecca that the townsfolk drifted towards during the long winter months is in an area of the city north of the St. Lawrence River and far below the Citadel. It is the tallest building in the vicinity, with the exception of the Catholic cathedral. The harness racing track, in the nearby exhibition grounds, is dwarfed by its presence. If you played junior hockey in Quebec and came from out of town, it was tradition as well as the only accepted practice to board next door to le Colisée. "All the junior players lived in the area of the rink. Within walking distance," said Lowe. Although he has properties in Edmonton and Whistler, British Columbia, and has resided in an exclusive bedroom community of Manhattan while playing for the Rangers, Kevin Lowe still holds a special fondness for his digs in le Colisée's shadow. "When going back as a pro I could see the area I lived in," he said, "the hole in the fence I used to cut through when we got back at four in the morning after a road trip. It was freezing cold the last time I played there. I could still see that hole in the fence."

Alex Légaré has been president of the Quebec Pee-Wee Tournament for twenty-three years

Gingerly tiptoeing his way down the steps, Alex Légaré moves to an open seat near the glass in the northwest corner of le Colisée. The sixty-nine-year-old chairman of the peewee tournament eases himself into the red chair after a quick dusting of the folding seat. While *chien chaud* vendors swirl around him and cotton candy floats by in the clutches of much younger fans, Légaré is already lost in the game at hand. Through his slightly tinted spectacles, his eyes become wider and keenly focused on the furious action of the rink.

"I liked to organize better than being organized," Légaré admits. He has been running this Canadian hockey institution for twenty-three years now, having succeeded the founder, Gerard Bolduc, in 1975. Under Légaré's stewardship the peewee tournament has enjoyed astronomical success. While 108 teams are taking part in this thirty-eighth edition, at least that many have been politely refused entry in order to keep the whole thing manageable. Even at that, the numbers Légaré modestly reveals are astounding, to say the least. "We have reached a great summit now," he boasts rather shyly. "Two hundred thousand spectators every year. It is something that we have aspired to."

Le Colisée is the epicentre of Quebec's Winter Carnival for ten days in February. The rink is the warmth that draws hockey fans into a friendly and colourful fantasy where the aspirations of youth are on display. The easy mix of young and old is an obvious theme, grandparents and grandchildren sharing Pepsi and chocolate bars, intent on the hockey stars of tomorrow. There are no obvious barriers in this building, nothing that distinguishes one team-jacketed, hot-dog-eating fan from another. "There are no problems in Quebec's le Colisée," Alex Légaré is proud to report. "The language and the colour don't count. It's hockey that counts here."

In all, there are about fifteen hundred Quebecers directly involved on a volunteer basis with the peewee tournament's continued success. It takes five hundred families to billet fifty-one teams from far-away places. The huge transportation committee will log 35,000 kilometres, as its drivers shuttle players and equipment to and from le Colisée and all over the celebrating city. At the cafeteria down the street, the kitchen staff will dish out twelve thousand meals over the course of the tournament. Local companies have donated $30,000 worth of food to keep the ravenous players from Switzerland, Saskatchewan and everywhere else well fed. Every player who celebrates a birthday during the tournament will get a cake and be "fêted" in proper Quebecois fashion. It is a well-oiled machine that makes hockey's youthful dreams a comfortable reality. Everything for the players is taken care of, and their only responsibility is to perform. In the first thirty-seven years of this captivating spectacle, almost six million have come to le Colisée to watch. Attendance at this welcoming palace of hockey has never been a problem—not once.

Alex Légaré relishes the chance to just sit for a while and watch the game unfold, free from the countless responsibilities that go along with his position. "For the first fifteen years of the tournament, I was a spectator," he says. "Now that I'm the president, I don't get to see as many games. It's too bad for me because I like hockey!" In spite of that, Légaré is a keen judge of the talent on display as well as the evolving style of the hockey that is played. Over the years he has seen the greatest players on earth blossom in the hothouse of le Colisée. Players like the tournament's first accomplished graduate, Brad Park of the 1960 Scarborough Lions, who went on to a Hall of Fame career as a defenceman with New York, Boston and Detroit of the NHL. The great Guy Lafleur made three consecutive appearances between 1962 and 1964, setting single-game scoring records and capturing three Jean Béliveau trophies with teams from Rockland, Ontario, and Thurso, Quebec. Wayne Gretzky played for Brantford in 1974 and filled the nets to the delight of the awestruck fans at le Colisée. "Walter Gretzky told me once that the career of Wayne started in Quebec as a peewee," Légaré recalls. There are too many other graduates who went on to stellar NHL careers to list them.

In recent years, Légaré has noticed a change in the style of play on le Colisée's ice, a fundamental shift that has lessened some of the game's mystique at this level. "There were a lot of great individual players," he says. "It's not as individual as it was at one time. There is improved team play now and the coaches are much better than they were before." Nevertheless, Légaré's voice betrays a hint of sadness as he defers to the well-trained youngsters who play their postions so efficiently in the high-speed game that rages at present. He tends to talk about the attractiveness of a slower brand of hockey that affords stickhandling and beautiful playmaking on the part of gifted and skilled performers.

There is also, in Alex Légaré's evaluation of le Colisée, the need for a local star to ignite the passions of the crowd. Most of the fans in the seats are from Quebec City and, although they understand and appreciate great play from all the teams, the exploits of a talented boy from home are valued above everything else. "In the last twenty-three years the best one I saw that could fill up le Colisée was Sylvain Côté when he played for Quebec D.S.N.C.O.," Légaré remembers, with great fondness. "Sylvain was at that time as tall as the players from Toronto it seemed. He was so much better than the other players."

Sylvain Côté was a late addition to Team Canada's roster in the fall of 1996. The thirty-year-old Washington Capitals defenceman was summoned by general manager Glen Sather because of injuries to key players in the early stages of the inaugural World Cup of Hockey, and he did not hesitate to answer the call. For a dozen seasons, he has toiled in relative anonymity for professional hockey's hinterland teams based in Hartford, Connecticut, and Landover, Maryland. Côté comes from a Canadian place where the game is a part of the soul. He was born and raised in Quebec City. At le Colisée he has basked in the glow of the fabled arena's footlights and delivered a string of memorable performances.

"In Quebec it didn't matter if you were good or bad. If you were a peewee, you were going in that tournament," he brightly suggested, surveying the sticks in the rack outside the visitors' locker-room at Maple Leaf Gardens. Côté was dressed in a sports jacket and slacks that only professional athletes and pop singers would be able to afford. His tightly cropped hair was still wet from the post-practice shower and, clean as a whistle, he grabbed a roll of gooey black tape and began to wrap the blade of the weapon he would use that night against Toronto. "It was a great experience for a young kid to play in the same building as the Quebec Nordiques back then. There were more than my parents there. Wow! There was my uncle and my grandpa. It was a very exciting moment."

As a professional, Côté has turned into what the intitiated call "a steady stay-at-home defenceman." He has accumulated more than three hundred points in his consistent career, but fewer than one hundred goals in his first dozen campaigns suggest that he is not a sniper, by any stretch of the imagination. In the 1979 peewee tournament, Sylvain took his defending team from Quebec, which represented the communities of Duverger les Sources, Neufchatel and Charlesbourg Ouest, into the final against a solid outfit from Toronto. Le Colisée was still not renovated and the seating capacity was just slightly over ten thousand. The presence of a "boy from home" meant that the place was bursting beyond its limits. "There were at least fifteen thousand people in there and we couldn't see the stairs in the aisle way," Côté said, in disbelief. "There was a lot of pressure for a kid but the whole thing was so much fun!"

Alex Légaré cherishes the memory of a local talent shining so brightly at le Colisée. "They won 6–3 against Toronto and he was marvellous," says the elder statesman. "He scored three goals and looked something like Mario Lemieux, I would say. But he was a defenceman at the time." It was Côté's finest hour as an aspiring hockey player, the moment the spotlight focused only on him, when he excelled in front of an ecstatic throng of loyal and friendly fans. "With the crowd supporting us like that, I don't think the other team had a chance," Sylvain said, his jaw thrust proudly forward. "If we scored, the whole building would shake."

Côté went on to play for the Quebec Remparts of the Quebec Major Junior Hockey League and was drafted in the first round, eleventh overall, by the Hartford Whalers in 1984. Throughout his travels, he has always remained impressed by the celebratory nature of le Colisée and its fans. To him, the place has always risen above its purpose as a facility where hockey games are contested. Along with his father, Sylvain would return to watch other peewees play, and his family billeted players from Ontario, the United States and Europe for ten years. He once witnessed Wayne Gretzky playing at the tournament and, to this day, remains awestruck at the thought of "The Great One" on the same ice where he also started. Côté even went to le Colisée with things other than hockey on his mind. "I used to go to the tournament after I played there with my pals," he grinned mischievously. "It was a great place to meet chicks, you know!"

Côté never had the chance to play professionally with Quebec because first Hartford, and then Washington, considered him too valuable to be traded to a jealous rival. There is little question that the struggling Nordiques of the late 1980s anxiously coveted the services of their local hero. For his part, Côté does not deeply regret spending his entire career playing for teams so far away from Quebec City's vibrant atmosphere. However, a trace of nostalgia gripped him as he pondered the extinction of the NHL Nordiques. "Maybe it would have been nice down the road to play for Quebec for a couple of years," he decided. "To see first-hand all that Canadian tradition of hockey and all the hoopla that goes around it like we see in Toronto or Montreal all the time."

The source of Sylvain Côté's fascination with Quebec City as a hockey town is this venue around which the community orbits. He revels in le Colisée and seems pleasingly puzzled at the antics of the fans who inhabit its upper reaches. When asked about his greatest moment in the building, Côté did not recount a particular goal he scored or trophy he paraded around the ice. Instead, he thought of a time he visited as a member of the Hartford Whalers. With the Nordiques trailing badly, the fans directed their ire at the referee, who they thought was clearly conspiring against them. With wonderment, Côté watched the tide turn in a matter of moments. The potentially ugly mob was transformed into something like a street party. "People started throwing toilet paper rolls. Flying from high in the stands they would come down like giant streamers. There were thousands of them. They had to stop the game for ten minutes or more. It was, all of a sudden, euphoria in there. At first they were mad, but after a while it was like a great big carnival!"

Another native of Quebec City has gone on to brilliance at the NHL level that has rarely, if ever, been rivalled. Patrick Roy, in return, has lukewarm feelings about le Colisée as a place to shine. "I never played my best there." The three-time Stanley Cup champion sighed at the thought of it. "I just always tried my best. For some reason, it never happened that my really good games were there."

Roy, many would argue, is the best playoff goaltender that hockey has ever seen. Twice he backstopped dark-horse Montreal Canadiens teams to league supremacy, in 1986 and again in 1993. On neither occasion was Montreal expected to win the title and, experts agree, the exploits of Roy became the determining factor. Both times he was selected to be the Conn Smythe Trophy winner as the post-season's pre-eminent figure while the

Habs collected their twenty-third and twenty-fourth Stanley Cup conquests. He won again with Colorado after being traded there by Montreal in late 1995. Ironically, the Cup win for Roy with the Avalanche came the year after the franchise had left Quebec City, a place where Saint Patrick had painful playoff memories.

The last time the Canadiens faced the Nordiques in a best-of-seven series was in the opening round of the 1993 post-season. Quebec City had finished the year with 104 points, two more than Montreal, and had advanced to the Cup playdowns for the first time in six years. There were great expectations at le Colisée as the showdown got underway, and the long-suffering fans pinned their hopes on young stars like Joe Sakic of Burnaby, British Columbia, Sweden's Mats Sundin and former Philadelphia Flyers goalie Ron Hextall of Brandon, Manitoba. In Canada's francophone hockey shrine, a strange script was about to be acted out with the local star, Patrick Roy, cast in the role of the villain.

The youthful Nordiques won the first two games to build a huge advantage heading back to Montreal, and Roy looked decidedly off his game. He mishandled pucks and seemed unable to rise to the occasion as the revered "Battle of Quebec" rolled to a fever pitch after years of relative calm. The media questioned Roy's capabilities openly and wondered aloud if his career had reached its peak and was already in a state of decline. On the bus trip back to the Forum, Roy looked forlornly out the window and refused to speak for three hours. His failure at le Colisée had become a personal watershed. "Those two games were a good lesson for me," he said in retrospect. "That's what I love about hockey. You learn from the games that you play. I knew that I had hit the bottom of the bag, or the barrel, or whatever it is. For me, it was time to do something about it."

Patrick Roy treated the two defeats in his home town as an embarrassment, but Montreal's coach, Jacques Demers, says he never seriously considered replacing him in the Canadiens' net as the series entered a critical stage for the trailing team. The remaining story of the 1993 playoff year belongs almost entirely to Roy as he, nearly single-handedly, refused to allow other teams to beat him. The Canadiens came back to win four straight against the Nordiques to eliminate them and then rolled over Buffalo, the Islanders and Wayne Gretzky's Los Angeles Kings en route to the Stanley Cup. In their final eighteen games of the playoffs, Montreal was beaten only twice and won an incredible ten consecutive overtime victories. It was proof that Patrick Roy had overcome the humiliation of the first two games at le Colisée.

He said the rink never had the same charm as the Chicago Stadium or the Boston Garden. Roy granted that the ice was to his liking at le Colisée but the fans weren't on top of him and he could not really feel the crowd as he could in those other great buildings. There is, however, a special reverence on the great goalie's part for the demands that a place of tradition places on a worshipped figure in the game. Le Colisée, and two bitter losses within its confines, taught Patrick Roy that, in that place, a native son could not be second best. "They made me a better player after they were over," he concluded. "The only thing I had left to do was to get back on top. That's what I did."

With the exception of the banner that commemorates Peter Stastny's number 26, there are few indications in le Colisée acknowledging the contributions of players other than those of francophone origin. Stastny played with the Nordiques for a decade—1980 to 1990—and established a club record for career points that still stands. He was a beloved celebrity in Quebec City and learned to speak fluent French at the same time that he mastered English. A native of Slovakia, Stastny may soon enter the Hockey Hall of Fame and will likely be remembered primarily for his exploits as one of the best two-way forwards in NHL history, as well as pioneering the advancement of European players in North American pro hockey.

During the tenure of the Nordiques in the National Hockey League, it was accepted that their home arena was a francophone house first and foremost. All the public-address announcements were made in French and the ravenous press demanded that players and coaches make an attempt to deal with the public in that language. It was only natural, given the demographics of the community in which the team played. Most of the coaching was done in English to accommodate the majority of players on the team, but once they were off the ice, everyone became immersed in a Quebecois environment. "Everything was in French," said Martin Gelinas, a native of Shawinigan who played for Quebec briefly in 1993. "A French-speaking star was a big thing for them. There was a lot more pressure on me because I always had to deal with the press."

Gelinas felt suffocated by the extra demands and was soon on his way to Vancouver, where he has excelled for three seasons. Others flourished because of the special status they were afforded at le Colisée. Flashy winger Michel Goulet scored fifty goals, five straight years in the 1980s, and was the team's darling. "You had to have a star at le Colisée and he had to be French Canadian," said John Garrett, a former goaltender and teammate of Goulet's. Between 1981 and 1983, Garrett shared goaltending duties in Quebec with Daniel Bouchard. While the native of Trenton, Ontario, played in a fair number of games with the Nordiques, most of them were on the road, and rarely was he given a chance to participate in the exhilarating matches against the Montreal Canadiens. "I remember Michel Bergeron, the coach, dealing

with it when Dan Bouchard wasn't going very well," Garrett recounted. "I had played a couple of good games, and he said Dan would play against the Canadiens anyway. I asked him why. He told me that the Nordiques and Canadiens was a French-Canadian thing."

John Garrett played goal for the Nordiques from 1981 to '83. He always felt like a visitor in what he called the "French shrine"

Another goaltender who played for the Nordiques under Bergeron is Greg Millen, originally from Toronto. His time was also markedly short in Quebec City. "Quite frankly, going in there was very difficult because the focus was not on anybody who was an English player," Millen said. He had participated in the Quebec peewee tournament three times, and Millen was enthralled by the atmosphere of le Colisée, although he found it foreign in many ways. He now understands that this had a great deal to do with the culture of the fans and the emotion they brought through the turnstiles and into the rink. "It was a very unique building because of it," Millen emphasized. "Every play was special, it seemed. If they missed the net there was an OOOH! ringing in your mask. Or a rush with some speed involved meant that the whole place just lit up. That was the passion that they identified with more than anything."

Both Millen and Garrett marvelled at the devotion of the hockey fans they encountered during their time with the Nordiques. Both agreed that they have never played in a place where the media attention was as great, or where fans talked as obsessively about the team as they did in Quebec City. Pages and pages of newspaper coverage throughout the year meant that the public knew everything there was to know about its only professional sports team.

"They were so knowledgeable about the game." Garrett shook his head. "And no matter where you went, the game was all they talked about."

One anglophone player in the early eighties by the name of Dale Hoganson was befriended by an older Quebecois couple who held season's tickets at le Colisée. Jean-Pierre Gaudreau and his wife would invite Hoganson to their modest flat in a working-class district of the city for dinner several times during the season. He enjoyed their honest devotion to the sport and welcomed their interest in him as a player. When John Garrett joined the team after being traded from the Hartford Whalers, he tagged along with Hoganson to the Gaudreaus for the occasional meal. "A very meagre household and yet, they were season's ticket holders," Garrett said, almost in disbelief. "Their social thing was the Nordiques. You could forget about them going to a show or downtown to eat. Hockey was it for them!"

The next season Garrett brought his young family to Quebec and when they were settled in, he asked Hoganson about their old mutual friend Jean-Pierre Gaudreau. "He had passed away that summer," Garrett recalled. "Dale had gone to the funeral and told me that Jean-Pierre had asked to be buried in his Nordiques sweater. He was laid to rest in Dale Hoganson's game sweater."

The anglophone Nordiques enjoyed the unique and patriotic milieu of the old city's arena although it was strangely new to them. English-speaking players like Millen and Garrett have rarely been celebrated at le Colisée, but they can appreciate the building for what it delivers to the fabric of the game. "It was the town hall. The focal point of the community without question," Millen exclaimed. "Everything that happened in that town happened around the Nordiques and the building. That's just the way it was."

Always the wise guy, Garrett remembered hoarding hot dogs from the vendor behind the visitors' locker-room when he was a back-up netminder. He would send the trainers to buy them and then stuff them into his pads so as to sneak his contraband onto the bench. "The *chien chauds* were the best in the league, hands down," he claimed. Millen concurred with his former teammate's assessment. It seems that both of them spent a great deal of time backing up other goalies as well as consuming hot dogs at le Colisée.

One night, while contemplating the latest save he had made in defence of the Nordiques' goal, John Garrett cast his glance to the rafters of the aging building and was struck by the tradition of the place. "It was sort of like playing at the Forum," Garrett reckoned. "There was so much tradition and yet, it was a different kind of tradition. Béliveau, Lafleur, even Marc Tardif. When you went in there you knew that this was the French-Canadian shrine. We were just visiting."

A one-time coach known as *"le Petit Tigre"* is less ferocious now than he was when he prowled the Nordiques' bench in the early 1980s. Michel Bergeron orchestrated Quebec's greatest success in the National Hockey League, twice guiding the team to the playoff semi-finals and, for a brief moment, supplanting the Canadiens as the darlings of *la belle province*. A Montrealer who coached junior in Trois-Rivières, Bergeron is small in stature but blessed with an enormous amount of character, hence his nickname, "the little tiger." At first he balked at the title, which was given to him by a Montreal sportswriter, Marc Lachapelle. However, it grew on him very quickly as the coach in the province of Quebec's second city. "You know, the tiger is a nice animal," he said, smiling. "Very aggressive!"

Bergeron's style was to pace behind the bench and act as the defender of his team's rights. He was blatantly partisan and cast the Nordiques in the role of the underdogs who were constantly overachieving. On an average evening at the rink, *le Tigre* would rail against the referees and especially against the Montreal Canadiens whenever the two fierce rivals met. His greatest satisfaction was turning the hockey game into an unfolding drama and bringing the enraptured customers at le Colisée along for the ride. "It was a personal thing and the fans knew the players very well," Bergeron contended. "They were involved with the team. It's not like Toronto or Montreal. There were not too many corporations who bought season tickets. It was the average guy."

The coach played it to the hilt and fired up his troops with increasing success early in his career. In 1982, the Nordiques were able to eliminate the Canadiens in a five-game playoff series as Dale Hunter of Petrolia, Ontario, scored in overtime at the Forum. It was the first time the upstarts from Quebec City had proven their ability to challenge the lofty heights the Habs had for so long occupied. When they arrived home, there were ten thousand screaming fans waiting for them at the airport, safe in the knowledge that their beloved team would be even better in the next round at le Colisée. History repeated itself three years later in 1985, as Peter Stastny scored in the seventh game to beat the Canadiens, again at the fabled Forum. The reaction was similar, as the conquering heroes were welcomed back to the capital city. "Beating Montreal twice made quite a difference," Bergeron said. "The province of Quebec didn't look at us the same way any more. We were not the new team in the league now. We had some respect."

Never did it cross Bergeron's mind that a player would not want to play in Quebec City and in front of such loyal fans as le Colisée could boast. It was simply incomprehensible to him that the white-hot hockey environment in which the Nordiques toiled was unattractive to any self-respecting and ambitious big-leaguer. He only knew one language and it had everything to do with hockey. "The players who didn't want to play in Quebec always had an excuse," he said, grinding the words out. "I remember one guy who claimed his wife couldn't order a pizza because she didn't speak French. I told him that he'd better retire or divorce because he was going to stay on my team!"

The arena was Bergeron's personal playhouse for seven years and he called most of the shots. The Nordiques never missed the playoffs under his tutelage, and he became as celebrated as most of the superstar players on his roster. So great was his impact in Quebec City that he was lured away in the spring of 1987 by the New York Rangers, who desperately needed his emotion to revive them. Once in Manhattan, he found out how different things could be outside the protective walls of le Colisée. "The fans owned the team at the time," he said of his battling Nordiques. "They loved the players, the players knew it and in turn, they were good to the people."

Michel Bergeron's favourite player was Dale Hunter, a hard-nosed checking forward who had one ambition, and that was to play in the National Hockey League as long as he could. He was chosen by Quebec in the second round, forty-first overall, of the 1979 entry draft and suited up for the team the following season after finishing his junior career in Sudbury. "I didn't care about the language." Hunter bristled at the thought of it. "When I first went there I just wanted to stay in the NHL. They took to me right away. They kinda liked the rough style of play and my intensity. Me and Quebec— we got along great!"

Part of the attraction was the way Bergeron handled his new player. In Hunter he had a soul mate—not the most imposing figure on the ice but willing to beat you with every weapon in his arsenal. "Dale Hunter was the heart of the team," Bergeron said. "He used to play so hard for us." In his career, Hunter has scored more than three hundred goals and will soon reach a thousand points, but he has at least an equal amount of satisfaction tied up in his awesome accumulation of penalty minutes. There are more than 3,500 in the books, second on the NHL's all-time list to Dave "Tiger"

Williams. Hunter credits his old coach with allowing him to play with unrestrained emotion. "Bergie was great to me," Hunter said firmly. "He had such great intensity behind the bench. He would wind me up like a top, send me out onto the ice and then let me spin!"

Hunter was suited to the traditon of the old arena. In his first year playing in Quebec, there were still only ten thousand seats in le Colisée, which was slated to be renovated by the city in early 1980 with the financial help of all three levels of government. Making his way through the tunnels for the first time, he took note of the lay of the land. "It was a very old building and when you walked through to the dressing rooms there, it was like walking through a dungeon. It had a lot of great character there." Once the renovation was done, the nearly six thousand additional seats did not ruin the rink's feel in Hunter's mind. It was still close and cosy—perfect for a player of his type. "You could spot anyone in the stands and see the expression on their face. That's how bright it was," he said. "Everybody that ever played there loved playing in that building."

He played at le Colisée as a sentimental favourite for seven seasons and missed a total of three games before breaking his leg in his final campaign as a Nordique. Following his return and Quebec's second-round exit in the 1987 playoffs, Hunter was dealt to the Washington Capitals along with goaltender Clint Malarchuk for two players and a first-round draft choice, which turned out to be future Conn Smythe Trophy winner Joe Sakic. He has since become the Capitals' captain, and his coach Jim Schoenfeld recently said of him in the *Montreal Gazette*, "He's what I think an ideal player should be—skilled, courageous, tough and determined." They are all the qualities that drew Hunter to le Colisée as if it were his natural habitat. In describing the physical attributes of the rink, he pretended to hold his stick and act out a compelling scene while talking to an old adversary, Greg Millen. "It was quick. It was like playing in a pinball machine," Millen contended.

"You know what it was? The puck never stayed in the corners," Hunter countered. "As soon as it was shot in—BANG—it was out again. You never had to play the game in the corners for long. You were out wheeling in the open ice."

The people of the place attracted him the most. Dale Hunter couldn't speak their language but, the son of a cattle farmer in southwestern Ontario, he understood a vast majority of the patrons better than most of the players did. He saw very few corporate suits and ties in the stands. Instead, he recognized folks in le Colisée's seats who were just like him. "It was the little people that all went to the games. No big companies were buying blocks of seats," he explained. "In Quebec it was little people, off the streets, buying tickets and going to games. I think that's why you get a different atmosphere." Removed by ten full seasons from the rink where he began his extraordinary professional career, Dale Hunter is still slightly haunted by the fans who loved him better than most. "There was so much tension. People walking down the street. You could see that they were worried if you were behind."

All things fall into place for the final game of the thirty-eighth Quebec Pee-Wee Hockey Tournament. Le Colisée is jammed with people there to witness a battle between the South Shore Kings and the Richmond Hill Stars. The game is being covered by network television and sent to countries around the world. There are images of pom-pom-waving partisans from both sides, of singing mothers in team jackets who sway side to side between the action and the face-offs. On the ice, the players stride furiously in an effort to cover the immense playing surface with their adolescent legs pushed to the limit. A kid in the South Shore net who has French-Canadian ancestry is the developing story of the struggle. Michael Boudreau flings his body across the goal crease to block the bullets fired his way by the Stars. On the bench, a nervous Buddy Yandle is pacing a mile a minute and chomping on a wad of gum the size of a hockey puck. Brian McConnell, the son of the Kings' other coach, Mark, has scored in the first period to give South Shore a 1–0 lead, but Richmond Hill is relentless as the seconds click away.

The Pee-Wees' president and director of the spectacle, Alex Légaré, is standing near the runway that leads from the locker-rooms to take it all in. "You have to live it," he had remarked at the tournament's outset. "You have to come and see the games. In the last three days here, it's a circus!"

The television announcer has lost himself in the revelry and, listening to him, one gets the impression he has deluded himself into believing he is calling the Stanley Cup final. "You have to love that Jack Greeley," the announcer sings out. "He's a little guy who plays with a lot of heart!" Meantime, the Stars' pressing attack is working the puck dangerously close to the Kings' net. With one minute and forty-five seconds left, Jonathan Kerr guides the puck into a vacated space and ties the game 1–1. The Richmond Hill players fly off the bench and engage in a glorious team hug as the fans at le Colisée stand and cheer. An extra period of play is assured and they anxiously anticipate one of hockey's highs, the impending drama of sudden-death overtime.

It does not take very long. As the horns subside with the dropping of the puck, Marcel Lajeunesse takes his fingers from the organ keys and le Colisée is enveloped by the sounds of hockey—the slicing of skate blades and the slapping sound that pucks make when they find the right stick after a well-placed pass. The OOOH that goalie Greg Millen talked about can be heard as the Kings advance into the Stars' zone, then the eruption of the thousands assembled as a boy named Michael Morris tucks the little disc into Richmond Hill's net behind the goalie. The final score is 2–1, and the South Shore Kings have conquered Quebec for the first time ever.

The celebrating players have names like Flynn, Johnson and Grover. Little Jack Greeley is hugging a teammate twice his size and flashing the gap-toothed smile that identifies him so readily. There are tears of joy from the South Shore players and others of anguish from the Stars, who are slumped in defeat somewhere inside their blueline. Up above, other teams from far-away countries are applauding the efforts of both sides. "They lose a game but after a few days they won't cry any more," Alex Légaré had gently observed. "People send their kids to this tournament knowing that living with the Quebec family is something they'll never forget. Independent of the language, you see. It's not a problem for us. English or French or Russian or Japanese. All they have to know is where the Frigidaire is and how to get to the rink."

Le Colisée has always been a showcase of hockey. In reality, it's a monument to the game that the people of Quebec hold so close to their souls. Rendezvous '87 brought the Soviet Red Army to the rink, as the NHL dispensed with the often meaningless All Star game and replaced it with a two-game challenge series between the league's best and the visitors. The two sides each won a game but the real victor was Quebec City. It demonstrated an ability to glorify and celebrate the sport that far exceeded the subsequent attempts of Hollywood. Many observers would later say that Rendezvous '87 was like having hockey at home for a while.

The same was true at the last great congregation of professional players in le Colisée. The best juniors in the world were to be selected in the entry draft of 1993, and Quebec City had been chosen as the host community. The NHL Nordiques, until recently, had struggled on the ice for the better part of six years. Beyond that, Marcel Aubut, the team's president and part owner, had warned that failure to build a new facility meant the team was likely to leave Quebec for a more lucrative market south of the border. It was against this ominous backdrop that the people of le Colisée witnessed an act of faith on a sweltering day in June.

In a parade from the Citadel to le Colisée, the brightest prospects in hockey rode in open carriages with the legends of the game. It was a regal procession, with the lead being taken by Jean Béliveau and his travelling partner, Alexandre Daigle of the Victoriaville Tigers. The lineage was remarkable—the history not lost on the fans who lined Le Grand Allée to watch the past and future wind through their city, and eventually funnel through the doors of their temple of hockey. Sitting beside Maurice "Rocket" Richard was a diminutive youngster from Montreal named Jocelyn Thibault, a goalie coveted by the home-town Nordiques. "I knew I was sitting with a legend," Thibault gushed. "Gretzky and Mario Lemieux are going to be legends but for me, Maurice Richard, at that time, was the biggest legend in hockey who was still alive."

The Nordiques' general manager was Pierre Page, a native of St. Hermas, Quebec. He had vowed not to repeat the mistakes of his predecessors by choosing a francophone player just to appease the fans. "You can't afford to take a local kid in the first round if he's not the best player that's available to you," Page maintained. The Nordiques had learned this in the 1988 draft as they passed up American-born sniper Jeremy Roenick for Drummondville forward Daniel Dore. Roenick has gone on to a couple of fifty-goal seasons and is still a force with the Phoenix Coyotes. Daniel Dore played a total of seventeen games and is now retired from the game.

The air-conditioning in le Colisée is suspect at best. On a hot and humid day in June, the rising temperature in the building was almost unbearable. Still, the fans crammed in to watch the next great French-Canadian player take his place at the highest level of the game. Alexandre Daigle was chosen first by the Ottawa Senators, and the throng was delighted. The Nordiques would choose tenth, and well before that, a chant went up from the crowd. "Before Pierre Page actually got up at le Colisée to announce my selection, all the fans in the stands cheered me by name," Jocelyn Thibault recalled. "It was THIBAULT… THIBAULT… I had such a great feeling and I couldn't believe what I was hearing at that time."

Page made the choice because he believed it was warranted. The Nordiques desired the services of the young netminder, who had been the Canadian Major Junior Goaltender of the Year playing with Sherbrooke, the previous season. "That was the guy we wanted anyway," Page stressed.

Then he broke into a knowing smile. "He's a very good goalie and a good person. The crowd erupted. It was one of those things that doesn't happen too often when you have the draft in your town and the first pick for your team turns out to be a local."

Since then Thibault has participated in the playoffs for the Nordiques and witnessed their saddening migration to Colorado. In 1995, he was traded to the Canadiens as part of a package deal that saw his idol, Patrick Roy, exchange his Montreal tricolours for the maroon of the Avalanche. A modest and thoughtful young man, Thibault will always remember the lasting significance of his draft day at le Colisée. "Fans were very happy to see young French players get there," he said carefully. "Everywhere we went, the people could talk to us. I think it helps people to identify with local guys. They think maybe it could happen to them too."

Following their elimination from the 1995 playoffs, the Quebec Nordiques were sold to interests from Denver, Colorado, and the team went south with little outcry. There were few public demonstrations, as there were in Winnipeg when the Jets escaped to Phoenix. No last-minute fundraising campaigns as a desperate people attempted to cling to the NHL. No eleventh-hour season-ticket drives to prove to the league's commissioner that this was, indeed, a good hockey town. Quebecers had always filled le Colisée even through the Nordiques' lean years when the team won very few games. Attendance was not the problem. The old building was. It had no corporate suites, not enough pricey seats, and no one in Quebec was willing to build a replacement. The awful truth is—le Colisée was not good enough for the modern National Hockey League, and so its loyal fans were forsaken.

The one thing the Avalanche could not pack up and take to Denver was tradition and a special understanding of the game that exists in a unique fashion at le Colisée. The banners of Béliveau, Lafleur, Goulet and Stastny remain in the rafters and the building is still alive with hockey. The International League Quebec Rafales are among the attendance leaders in minor pro hockey and the peewee tournament still crams them in. The game survives in le Colisée and grows in spite of the Nordiques' exit.

In Quebec there is often a comparison made between hockey and religion. On the surface, it is a hackneyed metaphor that commentators fall back on when describing the importance of the Montreal Canadiens to the people of the province. Guy Lafleur confirmed the truth of it, nonetheless, especially as it relates to le Colisée. "You spent more time in the hockey rink than the church," he said. "Priests envied a big building like le Colisée where they had a lot of success and they filled up the place every night the team played. Buildings like that never change. If there were no team, then it would be a different story. As long as they have a team with some hope of success, the people will go to le Colisée instead of going to church."

Lafleur chuckled at his explanation. Many years ago, he recognized where the people of this city say their prayers. "The priests should think about having their mass at le Colisée."

9

Sault Memorial Gardens
Sault Ste. Marie, Ontario

Chris Cuthbert

We were the only ones in the arena, the crowd's noise simply the casing in which we would move, the other players simply the setting to force the crowd's focus on us.

—Roy MacGregor, *The Last Season*

THE ICE OF MIKE ZUKE'S back-yard rink is receding faster than hairlines in the Oldtimers' hockey leagues. It is early March, and the longest season is loosening its stranglehold on Sault Ste. Marie, Ontario, a hockey haven cradled between Lakes Huron and Superior. Zuke, an effervescent sixty-eight-year-old, has entertained runny-nosed neighbourhood kids at his rink for the past forty-four years. A few, like his son Mike Jr., Ron Francis and Paul DiPietro, skated all the way from this back yard into the NHL. Recently, the Soo Greyhounds, a Canadian junior powerhouse, abandoned their Memorial Gardens ice for the sheer joy of playing shinny here.

It has been another winning season for Sault Ste. Marie's second most celebrated rink after an uncertain beginning. "At the end of November, we decided it was too much to do again this winter," Zuke says. "Then my wife goes to the grocery store and meets one of the boys who was a rink rat at our place. Now he has a son who is six or seven. The boy comes up to June and says, 'Mrs. Zuke, I'm going to play on your rink this year.' My wife had tears in her eyes so I said, 'We'll make a small one.'"

"The small one" is sixty feet by thirty, fully equipped with boards, screens behind each net and utility poles suspending heavy-duty lights. In years past, it has sprawled over ninety-two feet long and sixty-five feet wide. This rink of Canadian dreams stands next door to the soot-blackened frame homestead where Zuke was born, on Metzger Street, downwind from the Algoma Steel plant.

At the back of the yard is a shack, called the "Zukeadome," erected by the parents of Zuke's bantam team fifteen years ago. A Franklin stove breathes fire throughout the winter, providing toasted memories and refuge from the numbing northern chill. Rink records are scrawled on the walls alongside the latest plays Coach Zuke has diagrammed for his players. He invites me into the warmth of the Zukeadome to explain the origins of his winter wonderland.

"The year after we were married, we went skating at a city rink," he recalls. "There were about four hockey games going on and pucks whizzing all over the place. We skated for about twenty minutes and left. As I'm walking back, I looked at all the land I had and said, why can't we have our own rink? I started the next day."

Forty-four years later, it's one of the busiest rinks in Sault Ste. Marie. Zuke posts a schedule for public skating, and hockey sessions for thirteen-year-olds and under, fourteen years and up. He coaches a AAA bantam team that makes his back yard a second winter home. "I sometimes flood three times a day," he boasts with his perpetual grin. "One Saturday we counted sixty-eight different kids who had come over."

With its popularity came the extra burden of juggling rink responsibilities, coaching and working his regular shift at the post office. A decade ago Zuke solved the problem. "I could have worked four more years for a full pension," he chuckles. "I had three jobs and only one paid. I decided to retire from the job that paid. I gave the post office one month's notice and that was it."

There has only been one complaint issued from the tranquil neighbourhood regarding Zuke's winter amusement park. "We had an old couple across the street," he says, pointing to a blue house fifty yards away. "The guy used to get up for work at five in the morning. Late at night in twenty below weather, you could hear that puck hitting the boards for miles. His wife called over and asked us to keep the noise down. So I decided to use a ball. It was the best thing that ever happened. I read a book by the Russian coach Tarasov twenty-five years later. He said the best way to develop shooting accuracy is with a ball. I thought, Holy geez, we've been doing it all along."

One of the Soo's most respected coaches, Zuke has been a student of the game for most of his sixty-eight years. He is a part-time assistant with the junior Greyhounds. But his hockey philosophy is that youngsters develop better skills at play than in a structured environment. "We went to Christmas tournaments in Toronto for two years," Mike says. "There we'd play three games, fifteen-minute periods and that's all the ice time they'd get. On my rink they get five or six hours a day over the holidays and the kids teach themselves. The north always had a smaller population and less competition. What made up for it were the outdoor rinks where kids learned to be creative."

His prime evidence is NHL star Ron Francis, the most famous alumnus of the Zukeadome. "When Ron was bantam age, I said, there's a thirteen-year-old boy that has a hockey mind of a twenty-five-year-old," recalls Zuke. "He was so intelligent, not only in a hockey sense but very mature at that age. Now look where he is. He's going to be a Hall of Famer. It's just great."

Zuke's son Mike played in the NHL for eight seasons with St. Louis and as a Whalers teammate of Francis in Hartford. The younger Zuke possessed superior talent, if not his father's boundless enthusiasm. "When kids would come over to play I'd join in," laughs Zuke, whose hooked nose has been rearranged by at least one high stick. "I'd call my son Michael and say, 'Come on, let's play.' He'd say, 'I can't until I finish my homework.' Usually it's the parent telling the kid to do his homework."

The elder Zuke is a walking, or skating, encyclopedia of Soo hockey knowledge. As a youngster he'd hide in the basement "dungeon" of the old Gouin Street rink to avoid paying admission to senior games. He lined up in three- or four-block-long queues for the ferry to witness the Can-Am battles at Pullar Stadium in Sault, Michigan. His most cherished memory is opening night of the Sault Memorial Gardens in 1949 when the Sault Indians, featuring his brothers Walter and Bill, entertained the Port Arthur Bearcats. "It was something to see. A packed house. They were hanging from the rafters," Mike says, rising to his feet for emphasis. "Every time a Sault player would touch the puck the crowd would start clapping." He continues, re-enacting the game in Meekeresque style. "As they moved through centre ice, the people would stand up, clapping more. When they got over the blueline you couldn't hear anything. They were going mad. Sault lost that night but it didn't matter because the people were so happy to see the new arena. I never heard a crowd holler like that.

"At first the rink was called a white elephant. But it has more than paid a million times in pleasure what everybody has had out of it. It was no white elephant."

It's impossible to place a value on the pleasure that has emanated from

Mike Zuke's back-yard rink. He never had the roaring crowds of the Memorial Gardens. But every winter there are sounds just as precious. "If you could just hear the laughter of the kids on the rink," he says with a smile. "What beautiful music."

The Soo wears its blue collar proudly. Between Mike Zuke's winter shrine and the Memorial Gardens lies Algoma Steel and the St. Mary's paper mill, the city's largest employers. Sault Ste. Marie is Canada's second-largest steel producer with an atmosphere comparable, literally and figuratively, to Hamilton's. There is also a natural wonder to the surrounding region, which is sluggishly emerging from winter hibernation.

The city waterfront is dominated by Roberta Bondar Park and Pavilion, the tent-like amphitheatre and meeting place named for Canada's first woman in space, a native of the Soo. Nearly a century before Bondar's historic mission, her home town took flight as the site of Canada's first professional hockey team.

Sault Ste. Marie entered the International League in 1904 with its cross-river rival Sault, Michigan, as well as Calumet, Portage Lake and Pittsburgh. Players earned thirty-five dollars a week. The first escalation of hockey salaries began when Sault, Ontario, recruited one of the game's early superstars, Newsy Lalonde. George Cowie, a co-founder of the local team, wrote this account of the early days: "During the second season of operation, the club had a lot of injuries. Newsy Lalonde was contacted, and agreed to play. The train, with Newsy aboard, was three hours late and didn't arrive till game-time. He stepped off the train dressed ready to play, including skates. We put him on the ice in the second period and he scored three goals. He was paid the fabulous sum of $40 a week for four weeks."

By 1919 the Greyhound nickname became synonymous with Soo hockey. The local team's trademark was its blazing speed, but gamesmanship was also a motivating factor in its selection. Then, as it remains today, Soo's most intense competition was the Sudbury Wolves. The popular belief is that "Greyhounds" was chosen as a tormenting reminder to their Sudbury rivals that Sault Ste. Marie's team was swifter.

The Greyhounds raced to national prominence in 1924. They were "the best club to emerge from the hinterlands of Northern Ontario," declared the *Globe and Mail*. Led by future Hall of Famer Bill Cook, who won the NHL scoring title three years later with the New York Rangers, Sault Ste. Marie advanced to the Allan Cup final, Canada's senior hockey championship. One hundred "Sooites" paid $23 for the return trip by train to Toronto in support of the local heroes against Selkirk, Manitoba. Despite losing the second game 1–0, Sault Ste. Marie won the two-game total-goal affair 6–3.

A two-hour civic holiday was declared to celebrate the Greyhounds' trium-phant return, and the champions were paraded

through town in distinct Soo fashion. A slag car from Algoma Steel trans-ported the players in a five-ton ladle used for pouring molten metal. The victory also cast the national spotlight on the Soo, the first northern Ontario community to claim the Allan Cup. The *Globe and Mail* commented, "Every man, woman and child in the Soo talks hockey the whole year round. Civic officials, members of parliament, the wealthy and the poor alike."

Allan Cup champion Sault Ste. Marie Greyhounds paraded in an Algoma Steel slag car in 1924

In the Allan Cup's wake came Sault Ste. Marie's first hockey controversy. Toronto and Montreal newspaper reports claimed that George MacNa-mara, the Greyhounds' manager, had applied for an NHL franchise in Detroit. If it was granted, MacNamara would stock his new team with the Allan Cup championship roster. The reports proved to be inaccurate, but they foreshadowed another proposed Greyhounds transfer to Detroit sixty-five years later that rallied the community and marked a critical moment in Soo hockey history.

The Sault Memorial Gardens is an imposing bone-coloured structure on Queen Street in the Soo's business district. It's affectionately called an old barn by hockey connoisseurs but is accorded far greater respect by the archi-tectural community. Built in the Art Moderne style of the late 1940s, the Gardens' façade has been included on the prestigious DoCoMoMo Inter-national Register, which recognizes the finest existing designs of that era. Its smooth curves suggest a grand theatre. Its distinctive centrepiece, the memorial beacon, still beams a nightly signal in commemoration of soldiers who did not return home from World War II. Of the legion of memorial rinks erected across Canada following the war, few if any house such a

Lining up for opening night at the Sault Memorial Gardens in 1950

poignant memorial as the Sault Gardens. Inside the tower's base is an honour roll of Sault Ste. Marie's war dead. Prior to the rink's formal dedication in 1949, Olympic champion figure skater Barbara Ann Scott, one of the first performers at the Gardens, laid a wreath in remembrance of her father, Major Clyde Scott, of the 2nd Canadian Battalion, World War I. Every year since, the Royal Canadian Legion's Armistice Day ceremony has begun here.

Inside the Gardens, the sign over the lockers in the Greyhounds' dressing room trumpets, "Commitment to Excellence, the Tradition Continues." Most Canadian junior franchises boast an impressive list of graduates but few clubs can rival the all-star line-up of Greyhound alumni from the past quarter century. John Vanbiesbrouck and Greg Millen in goal, Paul Coffey, Adam Foote and Craig Hartsburg on defence, Wayne Gretzky, Ron Francis, Charlie Simmer and Rick Tocchet up front. Enforcers? Bob Probert and Chris Simon have cracked their knuckles on the red heavy bag hanging in the room's midsection.

Soon to be included in this élite number is Joe Thornton, a prodigious centre projected to be the NHL's next franchise player. Thornton has perpetuated the Soo's tradition of developing great centres. His physique and style have been compared to those of Phil Esposito and Ron Francis, but his inspiration is another Soo icon, Wayne Gretzky. "When I was drafted

The Rink

by Sault Ste Marie, it was like, wow, Wayne Gretzky played there," recalls the easy-going Thornton. His mentor's influence looms overhead and confronts Thornton squarely in the eye every day at the Memorial Gardens. Gretzky's retired number 99 is draped from the Gardens' rafters. His motivational words are inscribed on the door leading to the ice: "Over ten years with the Oilers I had my share of bad games, but not once did I leave the ice thinking I didn't work as hard as I could. There wasn't a game when I didn't prepare myself the day before, the night before and on the day of the game. I know I put 100 per cent into every game. I didn't cheat myself one time."

"When we walk out, we see Gretzky's message on the door," says Joe, beaming. "It brings a smile to my face because he's a big hero of mine. He was in his prime when I was a kid. He's still in his prime. He'll always be my hero."

A week earlier, Gretzky provided encouragement first-hand by attending a Greyhounds team meal in Detroit. He posed for pictures and inquired about the latest renovations to the dressing room. But the "Great One" was already well-versed on his former team's fortunes. "My buddy Joe Seroski was going for his fiftieth goal," says Thornton. "Wayne wished him good luck on getting number fifty. Joe got it the following game." Thornton is Seroski's Wayne Gretzky. In his first two OHL seasons, Seroski mustered only six goals in fifty-three games. Alongside Thornton he has emerged as one of the most prolific snipers in junior hockey.

Number-one 1997 draft pick Joe Thornton

Thornton has no illusions about matching his hero's unprecedented NHL achievements. His path in Gretzky's footsteps through the Sault has been a valuable rehearsal for the challenges ahead. "We're under the microscope every minute here," he says without complaint. "When you go through the malls, everybody knows who you are. They keep an eye on you, keep you out of trouble. It's a little bit of practice before I get to the NHL."

How will Thornton remember Sault Ste. Marie countless NHL goals and millions of dollars from now? "I'll never forget playing where Wayne Gretzky played," he says, glancing towards Gretzky's banner above. "Two years of my life were here and I had a ball."

In the coach's office formerly occupied by Terry Crisp, who led his team to a perfect 33–0 home record in 1985, and Ted Nolan, who steered his charges to a Memorial Cup title eight years later, Joe Paterson plots the course of the current Greyhounds. On the wall are snapshots from his playing days, one a treasured moment with Gordie Howe when Paterson was a Red Wing. The "Dog Bowl" trophy, made from an overturned silver dog dish, is on display from the Greyhounds' mini-tournament on Mike Zuke's rink.

Today Paterson's Greyhounds lead their division, possess the third-best record in the Ontario Hockey League and are nationally ranked. Nevertheless, the morning newspaper suggests an air of discontent among local fans regarding Paterson. For any coach, dissenting voices come with the territory, especially in the Soo. "It stems from the work ethic of the people, the steel mills and the wood plants. People who work ten- to twelve-hour days," Paterson says. "They have a lot of tradition and past success. This is their big thing. This is their team."

Paterson doesn't need to read the newspapers to gauge fan opinion. During game nights at the Gardens he receives immediate feedback on his work and his players. "The fans are demanding and can turn against your bench quickly," he says without malice. "I've had to turn around and chirp back at them to take the heat off the kids. They're really critical and sometimes too early. The power play comes out and thirty seconds later the fans want a goal or else. In fairness, they pay their money to come to the games. It's a tough environment but it makes the players better in the long run. They know when they move on they're going to be pushed, not only by coaches and management, but also by fans. Go to Toronto and Montreal and everybody knows the demands are great."

The toughest expectations Paterson must deal with are his own. His short-term focus is to lead the Greyhounds back to the Memorial Cup like his acclaimed predecessors. The long-term is Paterson's quest to follow Crisp and Nolan into the NHL coaching ranks. He resides on the city's outskirts to provide a geographical buffer between his coaching job and private life. But even during the low ebbs, Paterson takes solace in the Soo's pure hockey passion. "There are three outdoor rinks on my way home from the Gardens," he says. "A couple of times I have stopped after practice just to watch the kids and to put things back into perspective. When things aren't as good as they should be, or you forget what the game is all about, it's a great feeling to see the kids out there having fun."

A few blocks from the Gardens, at the corner of Queen Street and Andrew Street, is the outdoor rink at Phil Esposito Park. It was dedicated in the Hall of Famer's name in 1981 to acknowledge "his outstanding achievements and contributions to hockey and the recognition he has brought to Sault Ste. Marie." Prior to 1981 it was known as Central Park, the hub of activity for an exceptional gang that included the Esposito brothers, Phil and Tony, and Lou Nanne. "That's where we played all our games in the city leagues," said Nanne, a former player and general manager of the Minnesota North Stars. "The big thing was to make the midget team so we could play inside. We never played indoors through bantam."

For Nanne, a high-scoring defenceman in the Soo, making the team was never a challenge. Surprisingly, it was for Esposito, a future NHL superstar. "I always bug Phil because he didn't make the bantam team our first year," laughed Nanne. "He went home crying. Phil's father worked for Algoma Contractors, which was owned by Phil's uncle. They put a team in the league so Phil could play. By the end of the year, he was good enough to play for us, so the name of our team changed to the Algoma Contractors." Esposito's uncle was also the Chicago Blackhawks' representative in the Soo. The Blackhawks provided financial support and uniforms in exchange for player rights. "We were all owned by Chicago from the time we were thirteen years old," Lou said.

Nanne and the Espositos were raised in the Italian neighbourhoods of Sault Ste. Marie's west end. That area produced NHLers as bountifully as home-made wine. "Matt Ravlich and Jerry Korab's mothers were Italian," said Nanne. "They ended up playing on the same teams as Phil, Gene Ubriaco and myself. I always kidded Chico Maki that he played for us because his name ended in an 'i,' but he was Finnish."

As far back as the thirties, the Soo hockey scene was dominated by Italian immigrants. The roster of the 1938–'39 Northern Ontario intermediate champs sounds like an Italian soccer club: Naccarato, Vernelli, Sanzosti, Luzzi and Deluca were stars of the day. Another was Don Grosso, who played eight NHL seasons with Detroit, Chicago and Boston. Grosso was such an adept forechecker that Jack Adams credited him with influencing the implementation of hockey's centre red line. Grosso returned to Sault Ste. Marie to coach the powerful senior teams of the fifties.

The Soo's demographics were richly spiced with an Italian population that had migrated north in pursuit of employment in construction and at Algoma Steel. "My grandfather helped build the Trans-Canada Highway," said Nanne. "When I left the Soo in 1959 the population was 45,000 and over half were Italians."

The Soo's west end became a vibrant melting pot of proud blue-collar Italian labourers who worked hard and played harder. The accent was on assimilation for second-generation Italians. "Our parents never taught us how to speak Italian," said Nanne. "We were in Canada and our parents wanted us to speak English."

Sport was an effective proving ground for the Ital-Canadians. Whatever the game, the west-end boys dominated. Tony Esposito was regarded as the premier running back in northern Ontario. Nanne excelled in softball and baseball. However, it was their neighbourhood's hockey dominance that left the rest of the Soo red, white and green with envy. "We dominated the Soo for six years," Nanne boasted. "My last year of juvenile we played Ottawa in the Ontario championship. We had 4,500 in the building. I'll guarantee you 500 were cheering for us and 4,000 for Ottawa because locally we always won."

Nanne's mother watched her son play for the first time that night against Ottawa. During the game, Lou delivered a punishing hip check that sent an Ottawa player cartwheeling over his back. The opponent's skate clipped Nanne under the eye, causing a severe laceration. "Somebody told me my dad got up to check on me," Nanne said. "My mother says, 'You're no doctor, sit down!'" The west-end boys came by their toughness honestly.

While playing in Chicago's minor league system in the United States, Nanne became an American citizen. He was captain of the 1968 U.S. Olympic hockey team, an irony not lost on him—as a Soo youngster he revelled in drubbing the cross-border rivals of Sault, Michigan. "We used to kick their ass because they weren't very good," Lou said. "The midgets would play their juveniles to try and make it equal but it never was equal." Nor is the love of the game that Nanne has experienced from both sides of the border. "I tell people in Minnesota that hockey's popularity in my home town is like baseball and football combined in the States."

Pullar Stadium is located on the main drag of Sault, Michigan, on the other side of the International Bridge that spans the St. Mary's River. It was the home of another U.S. Olympic team captain, Taffy Abel. Taffy, an honoured member of the Hockey Hall of Fame, carried the Stars and Stripes in the opening ceremony of the 1924 Olympics in Chamonix, France. He also played on Stanley Cup championship teams with the New York Rangers in 1927–28 and Chicago Blackhawks in 1933–34. The lobby of the antiquated brown brick shrine is adorned with mementoes of one of America's first home-grown hockey heroes. Following his NHL career, he built a hockey powerhouse here fortified with Canadian talent. Team pictures of national amateur champions from Sault, Michigan, are highlighted by the smiling faces of the Zukes, Willie Naccarato and other Canadian recruits. Former NHL linesman Matt Pavelich, a Sault, Ontario, native, was a team mascot. Prior to the opening of Sault Memorial Gardens, the neighbouring Canadians adopted Pullar Stadium as their home rink. This was also the site of the Detroit Red Wings' training camp for five years in the 1950s. "Boofy" Casola, whose son Norm played for the 1996 Grey Cup champion Toronto Argonauts, was a promising Soo netminder invited to the Red Wings' camp at Pullar Stadium. Detroit management told Casola that he would be one of three goaltenders vying for two positions. Flushed with confidence, stemming from the familiar surroundings and his encouraging odds of making the Wings, Casola was the first goalie to hit the ice. He was unaware that sauntering out in his wake were two future Hall of Famers, Glenn Hall and Terry Sawchuk. Fortunately, Casola didn't face a long trip home.

Nearly sixty years after the construction of Pullar Stadium, Canadian and American neighbours continue to share its ice and a spirit of competition as old as Sault hockey. "The Americans and Canadians like to play each other best," says rink attendant Rudy Villarrell. "The Americans usually seem to lead early but the Canadians always come back with a late goal or two. You can still see the friendly rivalry. It's kind of neat. But when tournaments come in from other parts of Michigan, Sault teams always recruit players from Canada."

"You can't live much closer to the United States than this," said sixty-eight-year-old Russ Ramsay, peering out his den window, across the St. Mary's River to Sugar Island less than a mile away on the American side. It's close enough that Ramsay has discovered rifle slugs in his back yard from an American hunter's "friendly fire."

Ramsay is one of Sault Ste. Marie's most distinguished citizens. For eight years he was in the line of fire as a member of the provincial legislature serving as Ontario's Minister of Labour. He's also a local hockey personality who never played the game. "I had rheumatic fever as a child," he said. "My folks wouldn't let me even have a pair of skates." Ramsay channelled his sporting passions into managing teams and writing accounts of their games. By the fifties he possessed a unique portfolio: general manager of both the local television station and the senior Greyhounds, as well as play-by-play announcer. "I had a lot of conflicts of interest," he laughed. "We got a lot of coverage on the sportscasts."

The senior Greyhounds deserved blanket coverage in 1954. Crowds at the Sault Gardens averaged six thousand a night even though there was only seating for four thousand. The current capacity at the Gardens, strictly enforced by the fire marshal's office, is just over 3,900. "It's hard for me to imagine now that we used to draw crowds that size but there was nothing else to do. Senior hockey was the big thing," he said.

Ramsay's Greyhounds were on the verge of immortality in 1954. Instead they are remembered as his greatest hockey disappointment. Sault Ste. Marie topped the northern Ontario standings by twelve points but were upset by their Sudbury rivals in the rubber match of the best-of-five final in the Soo. Later, Sudbury squandered a 3–1 series lead to the Penticton Vees in the Allan Cup playoffs. The Vees, who enjoyed home ice for all seven games, stormed back to defeat Sudbury and successfully represented Canada at the world championship the following year. "I've always maintained that Sudbury was better than Penticton and we were better than Sudbury," Ramsay hypothesized. "It should have been us going overseas for the world's. That would have been monumental."

Gradually, after the Greyhounds' setback in '54, the popularity of senior hockey in the Soo began a downward spiral. "What killed it was 'Hockey Night in Canada,'" Ramsay said. "We played on Saturday nights. When the microwave came in, we started getting 'Hockey Night in Canada' live. People stayed home to watch hockey on TV."

A small room off Ramsay's den is a treasury of Soo sports memories and photos from the past half century. "There are three boys from the Soo," he said, pointing to a picture of Phil Esposito, Matt Ravlich and Chico Maki in Blackhawks uniforms. Ramsay is ubiquitous, posing with visiting stars like Gordie Howe and Red Kelly, as well as Soo native Marty Pavelich during the Red Wings' training camps at Pullar Stadium.

"There's Joe Klukay when he played for the Leafs," said Ramsay of an early NHL star from the Soo. Klukay wasn't the only Toronto connection for the Soo hockey scene. "We had a working agreement with Hap Day's Maple Leafs," said Ramsay, pointing out future Leafs Ed Chadwick, Ron Hurst and Jack Bionda in a 1953–54 Greyhounds team picture.

Joining the Soo in the same era was 1948–49 NHL rookie of the year Pentti

Lund. Lund lost an eye, ending his promising NHL career. "We were the first ones to put a mask on a player," said Ramsay. "Lund finished one season with us and played another but he never was the same."

Every picture tells a story. Ramsay picked up a snapshot of Alan Eagleson smiling with a boyish Bobby Orr in happier times. "I had Eagleson, Orr and Esposito at my cottage that summer," he said. "Phil had just been traded to Boston. Now Phil can be a bit of a whiner at times. All he did that night was lament the fact he was going to Boston. Finally Eagleson says, 'I've had enough of this b.s. I'll make you a bet that you're going to win the scoring championship next year just collecting Bobby's garbage.' The following year Phil lost the scoring title by three points to Stan Mikita before winning it four of the next five years."

An artist's proof of Ken Danby's tribute to Bobby Orr hangs in Ramsay's den. It holds special meaning since Danby, one of Canada's most respected realist painters, is also a Soo native. The Orr painting was presented to Ramsay at a testimonial dinner in his honour on the eve of the 1993 Memorial Cup final in Sault Ste. Marie. The next day Russ was asked to perform the player introductions for the Cup final on the Gardens ice. "I would have paid to do it," he said proudly.

At the back of the Sault Gardens is the Hall of Fame Room where the legends of Soo hockey from Russ Ramsay to Phil Esposito are honoured. Twenty-five years ago, the room was a secondary rink used as a figure-skating ice patch and for "learn to skate" programs. A two-year-old Ron Francis took his fledgling skating steps here. After the 1993 Memorial Cup triumph, it was the site of the Sault Ste. Marie victory celebration. But if the room could talk, its most compelling story would be the Greyhounds' player revolt here in 1978.

Sault Ste. Marie had lofty expectations for its Greyhounds in the 1977–78 season. Sixteen-year-old sensation Wayne Gretzky centred one of the most prolific lines in junior hockey with Paul Mancini and Danny Lucas. Craig Hartsburg was an OHL all star, and over-age goaltender Greg Millen provided solid goaltending. However, by mid-season the Greyhounds were floundering, in danger of missing the playoffs. Popular coach Muzz MacPherson, who had brought Gretzky to the Soo, was relieved of his coaching duties without a successor in place. "We didn't have a coach for two weeks," recalled Millen, now a "Hockey Night in Canada" commentator. "Angelo Bumbacco, who was on the board of directors, was behind the bench during games. He was a nervous wreck and he'd smoke about a hundred cigarettes a game. I ran practices because I was the over-age player. We kept saying, give us Muzz back. We didn't want him fired anyway."

Finally, Paul Theriault, a local coach with the Sault Indians Junior B team, was named as MacPherson's replacement. Theriault was a coach without a team his first day on the job. "We weren't very happy with the coaching decision so we went on strike for a day," said team captain Craig Hartsburg, now coach of the Chicago Blackhawks. "It seems really funny now but one of the beefs we had, besides the coaching situation, was that we wanted new socks. We thought our socks were too tight and were slowing us down."

Current Greyhounds executive John Reynolds was the team's public relations director at the time of the insurrection. He was summoned to the Hall of Fame Room to act as a mediator. "I'm with the players in the back room saying, for Godsakes, boys, don't do anything stupid," said Reynolds. "That afternoon I must have walked fifty miles back and forth between there and the Gardens office. I remember some of the kids being on the verge of tears."

Emotions escalated when the striking players faced off against the Greyhounds' board of directors. "I was the captain and spokesman," said Hartsburg. "As a seventeen-year-old, you tend to say the wrong things at the wrong time. There was a gentleman on the other side of the table who weighed about 320 pounds. He started to roll his sleeves up. My eyes got as big as his forearms when he did that."

Within twenty-four hours, the players' revolt was defused, much to the relief of Greyhounds management and the players. "I think everybody knew it was a one-day thing," said Hartsburg. "I don't think anybody was prepared to do anything longer or more serious than that. We were frustrated and we were going to make a point. I even think we got new socks."

Once the team got back to business under Theriault (pronounced Terry-O), the Greyhounds' vast potential was harnessed. Sault Ste. Marie charged into the playoffs, winning eight of its last ten games. The rookie coach was nicknamed "Wintario." His formula for success hinged on improved physical conditioning and becoming less dependent on Gretzky. "Every time there's a book out on Gretzky, it's written that I benched him," said Theriault, now an assistant coach with Buffalo. "It's bullshit! I cut his ice time down from about forty-five minutes a game to twenty-eight. It helped the team. There were a lot of nineteen-year-olds on the team that, once given the opportunity, played well. Ted Nolan was one of them."

In the post-season, the Greyhounds dispatched a highly regarded Kingston team in the opening round. Next was a showdown with the league-leading Ottawa 67's. The result was a marathon battle undecided until the final minute of the eighth game, a series that is still a conversation piece in the Soo.

As impressive as the Gretzky-led Greyhounds line-up was, the Ottawa 67's, defending league champions, were even more formidable. Bobby Smith had outdistanced Gretzky in the OHL scoring race, playing on a line with future NHLers Tim Higgins and Steve Payne. In the opener, Ottawa threatened to make a mockery of the series with an emphatic 13–3 victory. But the Greyhounds rebounded for a 6–5 decision in Game 2. The two sides dug in for a long, arduous struggle.

Sault Ste. Marie avoided elimination in Game 6 with a 4–3 triumph but still trailed the eight-point series 7–5 heading into the seventh game in the nation's capital. "Nobody gave us a chance," remembered Hartsburg. "We were so cocky in warm-ups we were laughing and barking like dogs because we thought we could win." The Greyhounds did just that, dominating the favoured 67's 6–3 to force an eighth and deciding game at the Sault Memorial Gardens.

"We flew home right after the game on a DC-3. Those were always fun flights," Hartsburg said sarcastically. "That's probably where Gretzky became petrified of flying." Only after arriving back in the Soo did the Greyhounds fully appreciate the magnitude of their victory. "There were so many people at the airport to welcome us," recalled Ted Nolan. "There was a parade of people from the airport into the city. It was like that scene from *Hoosiers*."

"I remember going to the Gardens for practice the next day," said Hartsburg. "There was a line-up all the way around the building to get tickets for the following night." In that line-up, which swelled to 1,500 by daybreak, was one of the Soo's most zealous fans, fifteen-year-old Ron Francis. "The minute the seventh game ended, I told my mom I was headed to the Gardens to line up for tickets," said Francis. "She thought I was nuts but she ended up coming with me. We camped out all night in the freezing weather with sleeping bags. We were allowed to buy eight tickets. I proceeded to scalp seven of them for over fifty bucks apiece. I paid $3.50 or $4.50 for them."

The Soo's frenzied atmosphere raised the ante of this high-stakes showdown. It underscored for players on both sides that more than just a game was at stake. "From the time we landed, we knew we were the bad guys," recalled Jimmy Fox of the 67's. "From the bus, to the hotel, to the rink, the whole city of Sault Ste. Marie was keying on that one game. As a seventeen-year-old, it was the first time I felt pressure. You realize how important games are to a city like the Soo. Then you start thinking, hey, this is meaningful stuff."

The night of Game 8 is still frozen in time for Fox and the 67's, the Greyhounds and Soo hockey fans who filled the Gardens to the brim. "I don't know what the announced crowd was but there had to be eight thousand people in there," said Hartsburg. "There wasn't a stairway you could walk on."

The Greyhounds rode the crest of emotion to a 2–0 first-period lead. It was 3–2 for the home side with under seven minutes to play when the 67's equalized. With overtime looming, towering Bobby Smith drew the attention of three Greyhound defenders. Sudbury native Jimmy Fox, who had just hopped off the bench (à la Paul Henderson in '72) was left uncovered in the slot. Fox converted Smith's pass for the series winner with fifty-one seconds remaining. "I grew up in Sudbury so there always was a little rivalry," Fox recalled. "As a fifteen-year-old I'd played a couple of games for the Wolves, so they didn't like me there anyway. It was a great feeling!"

The defeat marked Craig Hartsburg's final game for the Greyhounds. Although he is a native of Stratford, Ontario, Sault Ste. Marie has become Hartsburg's second home. He met his wife, Peggy, during his junior days here and they return each summer to the family cottage. Hartsburg's legacy at the Sault Gardens is his retired number 4, which hangs from the rafters alongside those of Wayne Gretzky and Ron Francis. "I know a lot of guys

Ron Francis and his hero, Phil Esposito, in 1963

get their sweaters retired in the NHL," he said. "Having my junior sweater retired is extra special because I grew up there. I went in there as a boy and they sent me out a man."

Sault Memorial Gardens has been the home rink of three of the top fifteen scorers in NHL history. Wayne Gretzky was a Greyhounds phenomenon. Phil Esposito was the Soo's first home-grown superstar. As a youngster, Ron Francis idolized Esposito and was mesmerized by Gretzky's junior magic. In sixteen NHL seasons with Hartford and Pittsburgh, the unpretentious Francis has joined his Soo predecessors in hockey's élite class.

"As a kid I always looked up to Espo," Francis

recalled. "Phil came to our school when I was in kindergarten. My teacher, Mrs. Vaillancourt, knew I was a huge hockey fan and took a picture of Phil and me."

Francis stashed away the treasure in a photo album until another encounter with his hockey idol a decade later. "I got to meet Phil again on the day they honoured him in the Soo in 1981," Ron continued. "I went home to get the picture. I had this god-awful orange sweater and brush cut. Phil had his hair slicked back and was wearing a really bad blue polyester suit. When I showed the picture to him, he was in stitches."

The young fan and his idol shared not only the embarrassment of an unflattering picture but the benefits of the Soo's fertile hockey environment. "It has the mentality of a blue-collar town," Ron said. "No matter what you chose to do, you worked your hardest at it. That's the one thing my parents demanded. They didn't have a problem spending money on skates and equipment, but they expected me to put forth an effort every time I was on the ice. That's the mentality I grew up with. I think that's why the Soo has a history of turning out so many players."

Throughout his teenage years, Ron rarely missed a Greyhounds game at Sault Gardens. However, Francis was almost a no-show when it was his turn to don the home-town colours. "I was dead against playing junior hockey," Francis said. "My mind was made up that I was going to Cornell University. The only thing that changed my mind was that Terry Crisp and Sam McMaster [Greyhounds' coach and general manager respectively] sat down and talked to me. They thought I was good enough to play in the NHL in two years rather than five if I went to Cornell. We worked out a deal where they guaranteed four years at the university of my choice if I didn't sign a pro contract."

As Crisp and McMaster had anticipated, the Greyhounds never had to deliver university tuition for the NHL-bound talent. A satisfying fringe benefit of the agreement for Francis was something Cornell could not have matched—the opportunity to play at home before family and friends. "The first time stepping on the ice with the Greyhounds as a local boy was a big thrill," Francis said. "I knew most of the people in the stands. There was a lot of incentive for me to perform well."

On rare nights when Francis's performance didn't meet expectations, the criticism hit close to home, sometimes with humorous consequences. "One night I'd taken a couple of stupid penalties. I'm sitting in the penalty box and I feel this whack across my helmet," Ron recalled. "I looked over my shoulder, and it's my grandfather leaning over the railing. He'd slapped me over the head with his hat telling me to smarten up. As I turned around, the security guards had him. I had to tell them it was okay to let him go."

Ron still receives his most direct feedback from another family member, his younger brother, Ricky. "He'll tell me when I've had a good game and he tells me when I've had an awful game," said Ron. "The beauty of Ricky and other kids like him is that they're brutally honest."

Ricky Francis has a learning disability caused by an oxygen deficit at birth. The resulting brain damage triggered twenty to thirty terrifying seizures daily. "We slept in bunk beds," said Ron. "I remember nights waking up because the beds were shaking from his seizures. He was nine years old when doctors told my parents to put him in an institution."

The Francis family flatly rejected that recommendation. Based on her own research, Ron's mother, Lorita, weaned Ricky off prescribed "miracle" drugs and eliminated dairy products from his diet. Shortly after she introduced high doses of multi-vitamins, the seizures ceased.

Ricky, who bears a striking resemblance to his older brother, shares Ron's passion for sports. "It's been a real common bond for us over the years," said Ron, who had Ricky at his side for Pittsburgh's two Stanley Cup victories. Ricky is an accomplished athlete in his own right, representing Canada in Nordic skiing at the 1997 Special Olympics World Winter Games. "He really worked hard to get where he did," said Ron Francis Sr. proudly. "Team Canada sent a letter asking him to commit himself and he took it to heart. Ron was injured and couldn't play for Team Canada in the World Cup. When Ricky made it to Team Canada, it was just as special. Both sons invited to play for Team Canada—it was a great year."

Like his brother, Ricky Francis is a winner. He captured two gold medals for Canada at the Games. Ron was there to offer encouragement and to make a heart-rending medal presentation. "We were emotional," confirmed Ron Sr. "We're used to Ronnie's success in sports. This was Ricky's Stanley Cup."

Ricky is one of the Soo Greyhounds' most loyal fans, a fixture at the Sault Gardens. Each year as a birthday present, he receives season tickets from his brother. "It's extremely important for him to go there," Ron said. "He knows everybody and socially it's something for him to look forward to."

On his return to the Sault Gardens, following his triumph at the World Games, Ricky was greeted with a tumultuous ovation that rivalled any Ron has ever received. Like his humble sibling, Ricky took it all in stride. He even neglected to mention the ovation to Ron in a telephone conversation the following day. "Later a buddy of mine mentioned that he'd seen Ricky at the Greyhounds game," Ron said. "He told me Ricky came in wearing his medals and it took him a half hour just to get to his seat. Then the whole building gave him a standing ovation. I called Ricky back to ask why he hadn't told me. He said, 'Because you didn't ask.'"

Ted Nolan grew up a few miles east of Sault Ste. Marie, in a distinctly different world than Francis. Nolan, the coach of the Buffalo Sabres, is a full-blooded Ojibway Indian raised on the Garden River Reserve. There, he is known as "Migrating Bird" because he departs each winter always to return the following summer. With every passing year Migrating Bird has brought home more success, respect and, most importantly, inspiration to his people.

Nolan's ascent from Garden River to the Soo Greyhounds and later the NHL, first as a player, then as a coach, is the material of movie scripts and race-relations texts. Like the Sault Gardens' memorial beacon, Nolan's triumphant story sheds light on lessons that should not be ignored or forgotten.

As a youngster, Ted Nolan hardly seemed destined for a pro hockey career. He was a house league player until the age of fourteen, wearing ragged equipment and an inferiority complex. "Playing at the Memorial Gardens for a regular game would have been a thrill," Nolan said. "Making the Soo Greyhounds was for the other guys. It wasn't for us."

The "us and them" attitude was ingrained from an early age on the reserve. Relatives had their self-esteem ripped away in residential schools where they graduated to alcohol and hopelessness. "When I was a kid, I helped dry out my uncles," he said. "Even at six or seven years of age, we had to hold down their arms because they had the shakes. I still remember thinking, when I grow up they're not going to treat me like this. I'm going to show them what we are really about."

Nolan's self-esteem would be tested whenever he visited the Soo. "You'd go to a restaurant and always get served last," he said. "The first time I went to get a haircut, my mom dropped us off. The barber put a bowl over my head to cut my hair. I can still see him laughing at the little native kid coming in." Paradoxically, Nolan related the incidents without indignation. "It was also a great place for us to grow up, but it was a double-edged sword," he said. "I don't hold it against them. We've got to enlighten people and let them know who we are and what we're about. You waste too much time having hatred in your heart."

The acts of racism that stung Nolan were not exclusive to Sault Ste. Marie. Far from it. He was taunted with a myriad of racial slurs on every rung of the hockey ladder, but they subsided in the pro ranks. "We had a brawl one night in Fredericton," he recalled. "One of the players was giving me one of those wahoo war-cry signs. I couldn't get at him. After the game, Jacques Demers came to our dressing room and asked to speak with me. He said, 'That type of behaviour won't happen again.' He apologized for his player. To me that was one of the best things that happened."

For the most part, hockey has been an equalizer, a common bond between "us" and "them," an element of Canadian culture that is shared. "Growing up on the reserve, we had an outdoor rink that my father helped make," Nolan said. "When I was a kid, getting a team from town to come in for an exhibition game against us was a thrill."

The nights he attended games at the Sault Gardens were also special. For Nolan, a Gardens visit was like a trip to the Montreal Forum. A playoff game featuring the visiting Montreal Jr. Canadiens left an indelible imprint. "It was the first time I got to see Gilbert Perreault play," he said. "I was a fan of Bobby Orr and Bobby Hull as a kid. I always wore number 4 or 9. When I saw Perreault play, I switched to number 11. He just seemed to float over the ice."

Nolan didn't suspect that within seven years he would also be playing junior hockey at the Sault Gardens. His relentless spirit and quick fists carried him beyond the house leagues to Junior B in Kenora. Greyhounds management recognized his raw potential and invited him to camp as an undrafted player, an opportunity Nolan was not going to squander.

In preparation, he devised a primitive training regimen that evokes images of Rocky preparing for Apollo Creed. "I never knew about off-ice conditioning," he admitted. "I ran railway tracks for foot speed and walked back on the rails for balance. Then I grabbed an axe. I'd run up into the hills, chop down a tree and run back home. A few days later I got a British .303 rifle. I ran to the top of one of the biggest mountains pumping the gun back and forth to strengthen my upper body. That was my training."

Physically, he was ready for the Greyhounds. Emotionally, he was ill-equipped for the team's demands on him. "They made me move into the city. My home was only fifteen minutes down the road. That was tough," Nolan said. "They also forced me to cut my hair. I was an Indian powwow dancer so I liked my hair long. They didn't, so I had to cut it off. We didn't have enough self-esteem to stand up for ourselves back then. If somebody told my son to cut off his hair now, I'd tell them to cut their head off!"

Nevertheless, Nolan endured the sacrifices and reaped the rewards. It's a source of satisfaction that he is one of the first Garden River products to play for the Greyhounds. In his two junior seasons, he's best remembered as a bodyguard for Wayne Gretzky and for his legendary battles with Behn Wilson and Ed Hospodar. However, Nolan's hockey development created further opportunities that eventually led to an NHL career in Pittsburgh and Detroit.

He's a unique self-made success story. But symbolism woven through his hockey life hints at predetermination. "I'm a big believer in things happening for reasons," he said. "The first game I played in the NHL was at Chicago Stadium. I was a big fan of Bobby Hull and I was playing against a team with an Indian head on its jersey.

"My first NHL head coaching job [Buffalo Sabres] is with a team that has a white buffalo as a logo. In native culture, the white buffalo is very significant. There is a prophecy that when a white buffalo is born, there will be seven years of good luck and prosperity for native people. There was one born in Wisconsin three years ago."

The walls of Nolan's office at the Marine Midland Arena in Buffalo are bare except for a greeting card depicting a white buffalo. It was sent to the Sabres' coach by a native leader. Upon close inspection, Nolan detected two other indigenous symbols, a dove and a wolf, subliminally portrayed among the billowing clouds in the picture's background. His brother recognized a more astonishing image shrouded within the clouds. "The profile right here is exactly of my father," Nolan said, pointing to the top of the picture. "He passed away when I was fourteen years old. I'm taking it to my medicine man to find out what it means."

His native heritage also has a profound influence on his coaching philosophy. "No question, how I coach is how I was raised," said Nolan. "On the reserve, it didn't matter how much money we had, or what position we had. We were all important to our family. We were all equal. That's my philosophy of coaching. I'm not saying fourth-line guys will get as much ice time as first-line guys, but I let them know fourth-line guys are just as important to the team. Making everybody feel wanted and part of it is one of the things I brought from my culture."

Whether it is prophecy, native philosophy or both, the Sabres have reaped the rewards. Nolan inherited a team in the preliminary stages of rebuilding. He was quickly tagged with the "hired to be fired" label all coaches eventually assume. After missing the playoffs in his rookie year, Nolan's Sabres defied the odds, and the season-long absence of star centre Pat LaFontaine, by stampeding to first place in the NHL's Northeast Division in the 1996–97 campaign.

Nolan has yet to introduce another native approach to the NHL that he utilized coaching the Soo Greyhounds. For five years, Sault Ste. Marie had been winless at the Windsor Arena when Nolan resorted to a mystical strategy to try to change that. "Ted told us there was an Indian ritual to get rid of the bad spirits in the rink," recalled Bob Boughner, who has played for Nolan in the Soo and Buffalo. "I remember our team sitting around centre ice during the morning skate in Windsor."

"We have a ceremony with our culture for cleansing our souls, mind and spirit," Nolan explained. "To clean out evil spirits from a building or place of gathering, we burn sweetgrass, sage and tobacco. We did that in Windsor. We cleansed our souls, grabbed the spirit and threw it out. We ended up winning 3–2 that night. I haven't done it in the NHL yet, but I plan to."

However Nolan's coaching acumen is assessed, his record is beyond reproach. To mark the twenty-fifth anniversary of the Soo Greyhounds' major junior franchise, he was a runaway selection by fan balloting as the team's all-time coach. Not surprising, since Nolan took a struggling last-place club to three consecutive Memorial Cup tournaments.

The Greyhounds failed to post a victory at the Memorial Cup in '91 but it hardly mattered to Soo fans. The city and its beloved team were still basking in the triumphant glow of defeating Eric Lindros and the Oshawa Generals in the OHL championship series.

In 1989, Lindros had spurned the Greyhounds when they selected him first overall in the OHL draft. Following a script that he re-enacted in Quebec, Lindros refused to report. The proud hockey city of Sault Ste. Marie was outraged.

Two years later the Greyhounds, stocked with five players general manager Sherry Bassin acquired from Oshawa in exchange for Lindros's rights, clashed head-on with the Generals in the OHL final. The series was laced with the bitter emotion of a blood feud. "We took it very personally," said Nolan. "I could understand if somebody wanted to go to a different league. But if he was going to play in the OHL, as far as I know Sault Ste. Marie is part of the league. As for the excuse about a lack of schooling in the Soo, the year we went to the Memorial Cup, we had twelve university students. Our grade average was 10 per cent higher than the average school mark."

Nolan's coaching savvy would be tested against the Canadian major junior player of the year. Other coaches designated specific players to check Lindros, who had amassed 71 goals and 149 points during the regular season. Nolan tried a different tack, relating to his philosophy of equality among team members. "I said whoever is on the ice is going to check him," Ted recalled. "After the first game, the headlines in the Oshawa paper were 'Greyhounds Use Lindros as a Human Trampoline.' We hit him every time we had a chance. All the players who played in Sault Ste. Marie took a lot of pride playing for the town."

Soo fans ensured Lindros felt their scorn when the series shifted to the Sault Gardens. The atmosphere was bedlam. Pacifiers pelted down from the stands mocking Eric's desire to play in closer proximity to home than Sault Ste. Marie.

The series swung in the Greyhounds' favour in Game 3 when the Soo stormed back from a 5–1 deficit in the third period to post a miraculous 6–5 victory. Oshawa never recovered. Sault Ste. Marie had exacted its revenge,

Ted Nolan (back row, second from left) celebrated the 1993 Memorial Cup title

upsetting Lindros and the Generals in six games. "We gave everything we had," said Nolan with a satisfied grin. "Our goal from the start was to beat Oshawa. We didn't have anything left for the Memorial Cup."

The following year Nolan's Greyhounds claimed their second consecutive OHL title. This time the season would be measured by their success at the Memorial Cup. The Greyhounds were a perfect 3–0 in the round robin only to lose a heartbreaker to Kamloops in the dying seconds of the championship game.

In 1993, the Memorial Cup tournament came to the Sault Gardens. One hundred thousand dollars in renovations spruced up the old building for an anticipated Soo victory party. Spurred on by a delirious home-town crowd, which hadn't celebrated a national championship since the 1924 Allan Cup, Nolan's Greyhounds were third-time lucky. The Soo doubled Peterborough

4–2 to claim its first ever Memorial Cup. "The last twenty seconds there was a mist on the ice," Ted reminisced. "It was magical. The last ten seconds I

could see the players skating in slow motion. To win a Memorial Cup for that city. You don't get that type of opportunity too much in life."

Former Maple Leafs captain George Armstrong had a profound influence on Nolan as a child, and Ted has become the pre-eminent role model for a new gen-

Rabid Soo fans rejoice the 1993 Memorial Cup victory on home ice

eration of native Canadians. Chris Simon has already been enriched by Nolan's example. As a Greyhound, Simon was falling hopelessly into the depths of alcoholism. Nolan, his coach, was there to cast him a lifeline. "He took me under his wing like a younger brother," Simon said. "I was having trouble with alcohol. He'd been through that experience seeing it on the reserve. People said I was a bad apple who would never change. Teddy took that as a challenge. He really wanted to help me. He had a lot to do with me stopping [drinking], along with my family."

Nolan's impact reaches much further. He's already noticed a difference in the self-esteem of youngsters at the Garden River Reserve. "You can tell by the way the kids look you in the eye. Their eyes light up," he said proudly.

For a decade, Nolan conducted hockey camps in native centres across the country. This year he has changed his focus to assist native women with the development of the Rose Nolan Memorial Foundation. It was created in memory of Ted's mother, who was killed by a drunk driver. It's just the beginning. Inspired by the late civil rights leader Martin Luther King, Nolan has designs on leading Canada's native peoples. "To me running a political party or a company isn't any different than running a hockey club. The principles are the same," Nolan said, before outlining his platform. "We have to create jobs, get our self-esteem back, the land

The Rink

issue, work, education. I don't believe in just talking about it. I believe you go to work and show people how good you are."

It's the approach that has carried him from a house-league player on the Garden River Reserve to the coach of the Buffalo Sabres. His philosophy in hockey and life is one every Canadian can identify with. "Give me an opportunity. That's what everybody in life wants, an opportunity."

The beacon's red spotlight greets dusk, signalling another game night at the Sault Gardens. The front lobby is engulfed with the movie-house aroma of popcorn wafting from stands on either side of the main concession booth. The tempting scent is one of Ron Francis's most savoury recollections of the Gardens. "As a kid going to watch games there I'd always grab a popcorn and a soda," he said. "Even when I started playing there, I'd grab a bag of popcorn before the game on my way to the dressing room."

Former Greyhound Steve Sullivan, now a Toronto Maple Leaf, forewarned me of another Gardens trademark. On opposite sides of both bluelines, in sections 5, 12, 6 and 13, there are five rows of seats set on an angle. The irregular seating plan, designed to enhance sight lines, appears to be an architectural gaffe and creates the illusion that the Gardens' stands have buckled in the aftermath of an earthquake.

An hour prior to the opening faceoff, the seats start to fill for tonight's game against traditional rivals the Sudbury Wolves. Dr. George Shunock, a local dentist and Greyhounds majority owner, welcomes early arrivals. "It's a good thing his office is across from the Gardens," jokes his wife, Cathy. "If he gets a cancellation, you know where he's going to be—at the Greyhounds' office."

Eight years earlier, the Soo Greyhounds faced permanent cancellation. Only Shunock's relentless energy and sense of civic duty extracted the local franchise from the jaws of a Detroit suitor. His actions earned him the nickname "Dr. Miracle."

In 1989, the Greyhounds completed one of the most dismal seasons in franchise history. The team finished mired in the OHL cellar. Phil Esposito lost more than $100,000 in two years of absentee ownership. The team's only reward for its ineptness was the blue-chip selection of the midget draft, the rights to the phenomenon Eric Lindros.

Lindros was expected to enhance the Greyhounds' on-ice worth. Instead, the team's newest asset nearly doubled the value of the franchise. Detroit's Compuware (the same group that owns and is moving the Hartford Whalers), fronted by Peter Karmanos and Jim Rutherford, offered one million dollars to Esposito for Lindros and the Greyhounds. The market value of an Ontario junior franchise was closer to $600,000. Esposito agreed to sell.

The transfer of the Sault Ste. Marie franchise would have been immediate except for a critical clause in the city's lease agreement with Esposito. "Thank God for the foresight of the city," praised Greyhounds director John Reynolds. "They had made some concessions with the Esposito group for the arena rental. In return, a local group had the right of first refusal if the club was ever sold. We knew if the Greyhounds moved, we would never see junior hockey again."

George Shunock, a rare Soo native who has never played hockey, took action. "I got twelve guys involved. We raised a million dollars and fabricated a business plan in thirty days," he says. "All of us put our money where our mouths were. All of the guys knew that potentially they could lose their money."

Shunock's group had crossed one major hurdle. There was still the matter of raising capital for the daily operations of the franchise. The Shunock family brainstormed around their kitchen table. George's daughter Lisa proposed a plan to sell three-year season-ticket packages. "She wasn't thrilled with hockey, always in the rinks with her brothers," says a proud father. "Now she's our most avid Greyhound fan."

In the summer heat, on the heels of the Greyhounds' worst season in over a decade, 1,600 three-year season-ticket packages were purchased. It generated sufficient operating capital to ensure the team would be firmly rooted in the Soo.

The month-long struggle to save the Greyhounds unfolded like a sudden-death playoff game, Shunock wearing the home white jersey against Esposito, in villain's black. The editorial pages of the *Sault Star* fuelled a backlash against the hockey legend: "There is good reason for the surprise and anger. The city has gone out of its way to accommodate this team so it remains in the Sault, and its owners, one of them former Sault resident Phil Esposito, have indicated their attachment to the community and their desire to stay here... But when a bundle of money is waved before their eyes, some of the owners and particularly Phil Esposito have shown they feel little allegiance or responsibility to Sault Ste. Marie and they'd appreciate it if the city would step aside and let them sell out to the highest bidder. Sell out is right..."

The resentment against Esposito still lingers. Many Soo residents defiantly refer to the downtown park dedicated in his honour by its original name,

Central Park. When the Esposito brothers were invited to be honorary chairmen of the '93 Memorial Cup in Sault Ste. Marie, they declined rather than confront festering local resentment. While Soo hockey fans have not forgotten Esposito's actions, the local business community has forgiven.

"It's a business. The only thing Phil's group could do was sell it," says Shunock. "They were non-resident owners and it's hard to run a hockey club when you're in Boston, Chicago or New York. In Sault Ste. Marie, people want to be able to walk up to the owner on the street and say, 'George, you know what the hell is wrong with your hockey club. This is what you gotta do to fix it.' It's that local ownership that people can relate to. I get that all the time. They give us hell when the price of popcorn goes up five cents."

Sam Turco has been a season-ticket subscriber at the Gardens since opening day in 1949. We meet during the pre-game warm-up at his choice front-row seat behind the Greyhounds' bench. "It's my ninety-second birthday," he announces proudly. "I'm the oldest hockey fan in the Soo."

Turco wasn't around for those early professional games with Newsy Lalonde at the turn of the century but he hasn't missed many since. "Have you seen the picture of the Allan Cup champs in the slag car in '24?" he asks, referring to the Soo's most famous hockey picture. "I was in the ladle with them. I was good friends with those guys."

Sixty-nine years later, Turco was front and centre in another Soo national championship celebration. "I cried like a baby when they won in '93," he says unabashedly. "They brought me on the ice to help raise the Memorial Cup banner."

Sam has cheered Soo's stars from Bill Cook to Joe Thornton and dined with his favourite Greyhound ever, Wayne Gretzky. Turco retains a grudge against Eric Lindros and admits that he has tangled with a few opposing players over the years. "I got in many a tussle. I got punched a few times and took a hockey stick in the head, but I'm quiet now," he admits. Turco is uniquely qualified to offer a perspective on hockey's place in his home for ninety-two winters. "Take away hockey in this town and you take away our lifeblood," he says. "Algoma Steel is our bread and butter but take away hockey and we've got nothing."

On the first whistle of the season's final meeting between the Greyhounds and Wolves, birthday greetings are conveyed to Sam via the Gardens' public-address system. A thunderous wave of applause cascades through the building as it did a week earlier in tribute to Ricky Francis. The Soo Gardens is a unique community stage that on any given night can shine the spotlight of recognition on a divergent range of its citizenry—a senior citizen, the academically challenged, a native Canadian or a future NHL superstar.

As Turco rearranges the Greyhounds' towels on the railing that separates his seat from coach Joe Paterson, George Shunock presides over the game from his private box directly above. The dentist knows the game and his players like he knows bicuspids and molars. "See Thornton feed that puck," he shouts with delight. "Thornton and Seroski work magic together. They read each other so well."

The Greyhounds take the game's first penalty on a marginal call. "Who's this ref?" Shunock demands. "Is he another NHL trainee? It figures! But we've got five players who can penalty-kill well."

Tonight's attendance flirts with a sell-out. More than 3,600 on a Wednesday evening, which historically isn't the Greyhounds' best night. "The next game is already sold out against Sarnia," Shunock reports.

Business would be even better if not for the limitations of the city and the historic Gardens. "The fire marshal has killed us," George laments, adjusting his Memorial Cup ring. "Our capacity is 20 per cent lower than it was in 1989. We could average five thousand if we had those seats."

Shunock is about to embark on a project to rectify the seating problem. It will rank as his most ambitious challenge since preserving the franchise in 1989. "We need a building that serves as a community centre as well as a rink," he says, using the Centrium in Red Deer, Alberta, as an example. "It will come to the point where we can't survive in this building because our revenues and expenses will cross. We'll be in a Phil Esposito situation. Three years from now we don't want to ask for money to operate the hockey club. We've got to be able to run with it.

"We know the municipalities don't have dollars to spend. We, as businessmen, have to put things together, run it as a business and do something for the community again. It will be an all-purpose facility. We'll get it done."

Shunock and the Greyhounds' board of directors are at the number-crunching stage. They hope to begin building their new ice palace for Sault Ste. Marie within two years, leaving the tradition and historic charm of the Gardens behind.

As the first period concludes with the Greyhounds leading 1–0, I return to Sam Turco to gauge his reaction to the possibility of a new rink. In commemoration of the Greyhounds' twenty-fifth anniversary in the OHL, a new logo was introduced this year that has received mixed reviews. The team replaced its old logo, almost identical to the logo of the Greyhound Bus company, with the cartoon of a snarling helmeted hound. I expect similar resistance to the new rink suggestion.

To my surprise, Turco enthusiastically endorses the new rink proposal. "Yes, I'd like to see a bigger one here," he says. "If there was a building twice as big, we would definitely fill it with twice as many people."

Tonight the Greyhounds are faster than the Wolves. In the second period, the Soo unleashes a barrage of rubber at impressive Sudbury netminder Steve Valiquette. Finally Joe Thornton, warding off a defender with one hand, threads a brilliant pass to Joe Seroski loose in the slot. A split second later, the Gardens' throng rejoices at Seroski's fifty-first goal of the year. "Thornton makes a highlight-reel play like that every night," says Dave Harris of the Greyhounds' front office.

For the remainder of the second period, the Gardens ice appears tilted like some of its seats. The Soo outshoots Sudbury 34–3 in a lopsided twenty minutes of junior hockey.

Early in the final period, a Greyhounds shot glances off a Sudbury defence-man's leg past the helpless Wolves netminder. It is 5–1 for the Soo on their fifty-ninth shot of the game. Mercifully, Steve Valiquette is given the rest of the night off. Although he plays for rival Sudbury, the departing netmin-der receives a standing ovation from the respectful Soo crowd.

Shortly after, George Shunock passes by. You can almost see another Memorial Cup in his eyes. "Our team will be even better in two or three weeks," he says excitedly.

The Greyhounds prevail 5–2, posting a club record seventy-four shots on goal. After the game, coach Joe Paterson wears a satisfied grin. "You've seen a special night in junior hockey," he says. I've already concluded that most hockey nights in the Soo are special indeed, whether at the Sault Memo-rial Gardens or on Mike Zuke's back-yard rink.

10 Memorial Stadium
St. John's, Newfoundland

Scott Russell

We shape our buildings; thereafter they shape us.

—Winston Churchill

OVERTIME OF THE SEVENTH AND deciding game looms, and Bob Cole embellishes the impending drama with a few well-chosen words. "LAST CHANCE FOR CANADA!" Cole booms out, on the coast-to-coast "Hockey Night in Canada" telecast of the Western Conference quarterfinal between the Dallas Stars and the Edmonton Oilers. With his partner, Harry Neale, by his side, Cole is perched high above the ice surface at Reunion Arena and his voice finds its way to an eager audience far away from this hockey rink in north Texas. Earlier, the Ottawa Senators had been eliminated by the Buffalo Sabres. Only the young and surprising Oilers are left to fly Canadian colours in an NHL playoff dominated by American franchises.

Over the course of the next twenty minutes, the Hall of Fame broadcaster will bite off his words in theatrical fashion and tell the story of what has been a brilliant struggle between two valiant teams. Cole will call what he sees and refuse to let his commentary become cluttered with superfluous statistics or unnecessary references to past encounters. He has a great feeling for the value of the moment at hand, an uncanny ability to tap into the building climax. So as Oilers goalie Curtis Joseph dives to rob Joe Nieuwendyk of the Stars, Cole gasps into his microphone, "OH MY GOODNESS!" Then, as Edmonton's Todd Marchant claims the puck and

286

dashes around a stumbling Grant Ledyard at the Dallas blueline, he pauses until the moment is right. His voice rises sharply. "... MARCHANT!" He waits until the act is complete and then he lets it go. "... SCOOORES!" Everyone watching back home knows through Bob Cole that Canada's play-off hopeful will live to fight another day.

He learned his craft at Memorial Stadium in St. John's, Newfoundland. It is a small rink by professional standards and seats no more than three thousand people. Cole can describe the squat, grey building at the corner of King's Bridge Road and Lake Road to a T. The parking lot of the stadium faces onto Quidi Vidi Lake, a stone's throw from the downtown core. "That's where the oldest sporting event in North America is run," Cole reminded me, forcefully. He was referring to the Royal St. John's Regatta, which has delivered the finest in rowing competition to the area since 1824. When you look up from the lake, Memorial Stadium is as unimpressive as a hundred buildings in the immediate area. It's a shed, really, with a standard peak to the roof and bright blue trim on the few windows adorning its outside. It is the rink's inside that Cole insisted on recalling in great detail. In particular, the catwalk, which hangs, perilously, seventy feet above the ice surface. No more than three feet wide, this is the place where he first attempted to do the play-by-play of a local senior hockey game. "They had two broadcast locations but they were being used by two radio stations so I really had no place to go to tape the game," he remembered. "So I climbed to the ceiling, if you will, and I lay on my stomach on the catwalk so that I could see the ice and I did twenty minutes of the game."

The setting for his first broadcast shaped Cole's style forever. Looking straight down to the ice, the movement of the players in the game was all

On the shores of Quidi Vidi Lake, Memorial Stadium opened its doors in 1954

that mattered to his discerning eyes. Unable to refer to notes for fear he might fall, the budding play-by-play man allowed the passionate side of his descriptions to shine through. "It was a beautiful view that I had never seen before," Cole said, with more than a little fondness. "I really

believe to this day that I am more comfortable doing a hockey game from on high because you can see all the holes develop. I feel you can anticipate better." It has been said that Cole can sense when a goal is coming. His greatest ability may be to imbue his delivery with profound urgency so that few of the games he describes appear dull, regardless of the level of play. "I think it is my job to let the fans feel the rink," Cole said. "To bring them from

Bob Cole, the voice of "Hockey Night in Canada," in the stands at his home rink, Memorial Stadium

the bar or the living room, or wherever it is they are watching the game, into the arena." It was his home rink that taught Bob Cole what to do. At Memorial Stadium, the players have changed over the years, but the essential element of fierce competition has not.

Memorial Stadium is the current home of the St. John's Maple Leafs of the American Hockey League. The primary farm club for the parent Leafs in Toronto, this is the first truly professional hockey team to base its operation in St. John's. The stadium, completed on December 27, 1954, is tiny in light of the league's growing demands for revenue. The size of the ice surface is officially listed as 190 feet by 85 feet. That is ten feet shorter than most professional rinks but just as wide. Still, insiders will tell you, "she's a might tighter than that." Seating capacity is 3,765, well below the American League average, and a significant number of the faithful find places in the standing-room sections behind the top row of seats. It seems that every available inch of space on the walls and ceiling has been used to tack on a billboard or hang a banner for advertising. The boards are no longer white but yellow, blue and red from the stick-on placards. "Famous Newfoundland Screech" is just one of a hundred such signs that ring the ice. The pennants of every AHL club dangle from the catwalk and pictures of the Queen and Don Cherry's dog, Blue, hang next to flags, including an ancient Union Jack. The place glitters and sparkles because of the freshly polished glass, and with the lights dimmed just a little, it somehow looks like a Christmas tree that has been laden with a thousand ornaments.

There are a few oldtimers on the ice in the early afternoon. This evening the Leafs are to entertain the Carolina Monarchs in the last regular-season game to be played at the Stadium before the much-anticipated playoffs begin. In the last two rows of blue chairs on the Stadium's east side, a young couple is contemplating the view. Wayne and Laura Carew have made the hour-long trip from Cape Broyle to St. John's to check out the playoff tickets they are considering purchasing. It is not an investment to be taken lightly, because the seats cost $74 for just two games of the opening round of the post-season. "If you wait till the day of the game, the only seats you can get are pretty scrappy," Laura pipes up. She points down to the corner reds and begins to tell the story of the last time they sat there. Wayne cuts in and says his wife was hit by an errant puck off the stick of Jamie Heward, one of the Leafs defencemen. He brushes his finger across the scar the eight stitches have left under Laura's eye, just to verify. "We wasn't too fancy on those seats after that," Wayne decides. "We wanted to see the whole game."

Wayne and Laura have spent countless hours in this and other arenas in the province, he as a player with the Southern Shore Breakers of the Newfoundland Senior League, and she as his greatest fan as well as a devout follower of the game at any level. Perhaps their greatest moments together at Memorial Stadium came in the spring of 1992 when the Leafs battled the Adirondack Red Wings for the Calder Cup, the championship trophy of the AHL. "The people in the standing-room section were three deep," says Laura. "We had to line up for two straight days to get tickets for that series." Wayne provides the typical Newfoundlanders' description of what it was like to be in the Stadium when something was at stake. "She was blocked!" he exclaims. The three words succinctly describe the times when you cannot put another fan into this place even with a shoehorn.

The first artificial ice in St. John's was installed in 1936 at the Prince Rink, which had been constructed in 1867 behind the Newfoundland Hotel. A fire destroyed the city's showcase of sporting life in 1941, leaving the provincial capital without an appropriate and accessible hockey rink. St. Bonaventure College, the Catholic school, had its own facility, the St. Bons Forum, but it was for the use of its student body only. "We didn't get too much ice time," said Bob Cole, matter-of-factly. "In the winter the ponds were frozen and that's where a lot of us learned to play the game, like many other young Canadian boys."

In 1943, a citizens' committee was organized to explore the possibility of replacing the destroyed arena. A site was chosen but plans to begin construction were scuttled because of a wartime shortage of steel. The new rink would have to wait while a much more important endeavour was undertaken. In 1948, post-war optimism led to the committee renewing its efforts to build a suitable venue for hockey. Raising the $300,000 needed for the structure was, however, becoming a huge problem. In June 1949, the year Newfoundland became a province of Canada, the local Lions Club took over the organization of the project.

A citizen, P.E. Outerbridge, provided the impetus to the Lions Club's efforts when he suggested the formation of a limited liability company to build the Stadium. He proposed selling $400,000 worth of one-dollar shares with the help of local radio stations and putting on street dances, carnivals and regattas. It was to be a hockey arena for the people of St. John's built through their collective efforts. With a provincial government loan of $100,000, the Lions Club decided to start construction of the building on land once owned by Bob Cole's father, John, and his uncle, Martin. The property had been a farm adjacent to the lake, not far from downtown, where Cole recalls making hay in August, and now it would be the city's temple of hockey. In 1951, Barbara Ann Scott, Canada's figure-skating darling, laid

A 1952 parade through the streets of St. John's was organized to create public support for a new hockey rink

the cornerstone at an impressive ceremony before a throng of anxious Newfoundlanders. "I was just a little guy at the time, but I remember that this was a big deal that this superstar was going to start things before they began the construction," said Cole. "You knew then it was for real. We knew we were definitely getting a building!"

Even with the foundation in place, the reality of the hockey rink was far from near. Labour and material costs had dramatically increased and

a great deal of work was needed to raise the necessary money. In 1952, local business leaders stepped onto the scene and the Rotary Club formed what was called the Stadium Council. A parade through the streets of St. John's and a placard-waving rally kicked off the fund-raising campaign. At Shamrock Field, the mayor, Harry Mews, addressed many of the community's young people and in evangelical fashion urged them to spread the Stadium gospel to their parents, relatives and school-mates.

The "One Percenters" became an essential building block of the Stadium's success. The organizers had suggested employees of city firms find a unique way to fill the coffers of the building fund. Workers would donate one per cent of their pay cheques to the drive and their employers would match the contributions. This effort was the most im-

The interior of Memorial Stadium was the opposite of most arenas in the early days. The bleacher seats were closest to the ice

portant and consistent factor in the prolonged push towards construction. In addition, giant bingo sessions and concerts were staged. Even the children pitched in by selling lemonade on city sidewalks and eventually handing over the coins to the Stadium Council, which had promised a skating palace.

In the middle of 1953, a dozen years after the Prince Rink had burned to the ground, work began on its replacement. The steel structure of the sides and roof were erected with the youth of the community looking on in amazement. Bob Cole remembers the wonder of seeing what was then a gigantic building take shape in his own back yard. "We would just hang out watching the steel girders and beams going up," Cole said. "There were all kinds of workers that we had never seen before." Many people made a daily routine of visiting the site on the way to and from work or school, monitoring the progress of the building and assuring themselves that all was going according to plan. This was, after all, an arena that had been anxiously anticipated for what seemed like an eternity. Two days after Christmas in 1954 the Stadium, which was dedicated to the sportsmen who had given their lives during the war, opened its doors. The concrete floors shone and the seats were in, leaving a giant bleacher section close to the ice. "Finally it was ready and it was gorgeous," beamed Cole.

The first event was an ice show featuring well-known figure skaters from all over North America. As the final preparations were being made to the artificial surface, Cole was talking with one of the engineers. He confessed that he had stuffed his skates into the back of his car hoping to have a chance to be on the rink before most of his pals. The engineer knew Cole and had noticed his interest, bordering on obsession, with the new building. He agreed to the request, and Bob Cole laced on his blades to enjoy a solitary tour of the Memorial Stadium ice. "I took off on that ice and it was the first thing that had ever happened there," Cole said with pride. "It felt neat that my dad and his brother were kind of connected in years past and that I skated on the ice so soon after it was ready."

The completion of Memorial Stadium brought St. John's into the modern era of hockey. Before its existence there had been, at most, five or six hundred people attending games in smaller facilities around the city. But now there would be thousands, and artificial ice was no longer the luxury of the privileged few. The senior teams would have a huge venue in which to stage battles for the Boyle Trophy, the coveted hardware attached to St. John's hockey supremacy. Minor hockey would grow, not just for the Catholics, who had for so long enjoyed their beloved St. Bons Forum, but also for the Protestants from Bishop Field College and Prince of Wales Collegiate. The Stadium provided a more level playing field for St. John's battle of hockey, which had clearly been based on religious affiliations. "Was it like a palace?" Cole asked, answering his own question with the drama building in his voice. "It was everything. It was like we got the NHL. We were there now!"

Joe and Cathy Slaney, the father and sister of John Slaney, in their barber shop on Merrymeeting Road. John's picture as an L.A. King is on the wall behind

Just above the bustle of St. John's downtown core, where Field Street connects with Merrymeeting Road, sits a little white house. Joe's Barber Shop is like something from another time and place. It has a blue and red candy-cane sign by the front window, and within the comfort of its panelled walls old men slumber in chairs while Joe Slaney and his daughter Cathy snip away at their greying locks. On the old coffee table, in the area where others wait, there are stacks of *Sports Illustrated* and *Hockey News*. Hung on the walls, above the shelves where tonics and powders are stored, are pictures of a young man in a Washington Capitals uniform, in the white,

The Rink

black and silver of the Los Angeles Kings and shaking hands proudly with Gordie Howe. John Slaney's image dominates this peaceful shop where his dad has earned the family's living for twenty-three years.

"I've been everywhere with him," Joe said, not diverting his attention from the head of hair before him. "Russia, Finland, Sweden, Germany, Montreal and Toronto." He is the proud but reserved father of one of the few St. John's boys who has gone on to compete in the NHL. John Slaney played much of his minor hockey at the Brother O'Hehir Rink, which is attached to St. Patrick's School and not far from Slaney's home. In his atom and peewee days, as a member of the Celtics system, John played in the really big tournaments at Memorial Stadium where, as a kid, he had marvelled at the seniors. "It was like the NHL of Newfoundland when you could enter that rink," said John from his temporary home in Phoenix, Arizona. "It could have been one fan or four thousand fans. It was a tremendous thrill for us to play in that rink."

He is finishing out the season with the Roadrunners of the International Hockey League. For Slaney, it has been a bitter pill to swallow in his fourth season as a professional. On "The Rock," hopes have always been high for him. He had starred with the junior Cornwall Royals of the Ontario League and, as one of the brightest rushing defencemen at his level of play, was drafted in the first round by the Washington Capitals in 1990. "Everybody told me he's going to make it one of these days," Joe Slaney recounted. However, the odds of him making it to the big leagues were never really in John's favour, considering the place he had come from. "I truthfully never thought that's where I'd be," he said, referring to the NHL. "There was just no way, coming out of Newfoundland. I said to myself that I'm going to work hard every day and hopefully make good things happen."

The Slaney family makes its home behind the barber shop and John's mother, Helen, was busy cooking up an early lunch in the cluttered kitchen, perfumed by the heavenly smell coming from her stove top. Wiping her hands on a flowered apron, Helen led the way to what she calls her shrine. In a tiny TV room, no more than seven feet wide, a gallery of photos, trophies and memorabilia cram the walls. John Slaney is the subject of every item, and Helen ran her fingers over them as she related the particular significance of each. In the dining room next door are a few more precious keepsakes. One is the photo of the Team Canada Juniors who claimed the world championship in 1991 at Saskatoon. Helen folded her arms and stared at the picture of her son with the Maple Leaf on his chest. In a husky voice she barely whispered, "People in the street still say to me they'll never forget the night that John scored."

Late in the game against the Russians, the score was tied and the gold medal was on the line. Following the face-off in their defensive zone, the Russians had moved the puck around the boards and superstar Pavel Bure was streaking to the attack. At the point, Slaney stayed with the play instead of retreating to the neutral zone as a safeguard. "I said to myself, if I don't stop this I think we're in trouble," he recalled. "I put my full body in front of it and I just had to shoot it as quick as I could. When I shot the puck I hit it full wood, and when it got through I couldn't believe it went in. I didn't know what to think. I couldn't believe that I had scored!"

Both Joe and Helen Slaney were in the stands in Saskatoon and remember their reaction at that moment. "There were four and some odd minutes left and it seemed like two hours," said Joe, the anxious discomfort fresh in his mind. "I was never so proud of him," Helen beamed. "Just to know that Canada was going to win."

The Canadians hung on to win the game and the gold medal with Slaney as the hero. It was the second straight year that a Newfoundlander and St. John's native had made the difference in the championship game. In 1990, Dwayne Norris had clinched a 2–1 victory with his goal against the Czechoslovakians at Helsinki, Finland. Each player had become the talk of Canada's hockey world and, more importantly to them, had become icons back home in Newfoundland. "I guess people who were in bars or sitting at home had one thing cross their mind," Slaney says. "Two Newfies doing it again."

Cathy Slaney remembers being in St. John's and watching her brother's triumph in Saskatoon. "It was very exciting and I still get the chills when I think about it," she said, smiling at the recollection. "The phone here rang until four in the morning with all kinds of people wanting to know all about it." Gifts were dropped off at the Slaneys' door in appreciation of what John had done. Flowers and poems arrived from admiring young women, and young children drew pictures with crayons, depicting the hockey hero's great feat. "My name was spray-painted on the street," said John proudly. "There were chocolates left at the door. I thought it was awesome. Just a great feeling."

After the overwhelming elation of his moment with Team Canada, Slaney returned to the Cornwall Royals to complete his junior career. Since being drafted by Washington, he has played with Colorado and Los Angeles and is working hard at finding a permanent place in the NHL. The glory of his heroics in the gold medal game has been short-lived everywhere but in St. John's, where they remember him with great fondness to this day. Although he had the satisfaction of scoring the goal in Saskatchewan before ten thousand or more fans and millions on TV, he values most what happened to him at Memorial Stadium in early March following the world championships. A special evening of appreciation was held for him at the Stadium where he alone was the main attraction. "I never thought in my whole life that something like this would ever happen for me," he said.

That night there was no game, but every member of the Tier II junior league attended in full uniform to greet a former rival. As Slaney stepped onto the ice, the four thousand fans erupted into delirious applause and the players stood at the blueline banging their sticks on the ice. "I had tears in my eyes because all my old minor hockey buddies that I played with or against were standing there cheering for me," he remembered. "The whole junior league was there and at that moment I felt like I was playing for all five teams."

Helen and Joe Slaney still go down to the Stadium to see the Maple Leafs play or to take in an occasional senior game. They are hockey fans and have always been that way, their interest in the game extending well beyond their own son. "When I'm at the Stadium, I can pick out the hockey boys right away," Helen said affectionately. "There's just something about them." Perhaps it is her familiarity with the players. She has been the president of the mothers' organization of the Celtics Minor Hockey System for years and has watched many of the skaters, who aspire to compete at Memorial Stadium, grow to maturity.

Although he has reached his goal of playing in the NHL and enjoys tremendous status in his home town, there was something special for John Slaney when he played his first professional game at Memorial Stadium as a member of the Portland Pirates. He had a battle with Todd Gillingham, a fan favourite on the St. John's team, and heard a mixture of cheers and boos from the capacity crowd that had come to see his return to familiar ice. "It felt weird not to be on the home team," Slaney reflected. "Still, it was comforting to know that my parents were in the stands to see me play."

With Joe and Cathy still hard at work in the barber shop taking care of the pre-lunch rush, Helen left her "shrine" and returned to the stove to attend to the meal. She was in Los Angeles not long ago to spend time with John and check on the progress of his career. The entire length of the continent separates them now and he lives in very different circumstances. "When I see him with the other boys, they are all dressed up." She shook her head and smiled. "I just can't believe it's him."

For several years Bob Cole has organized a charity golf tournament in St. John's that has brought celebrities from the world of hockey to the island to have some fun and engage in good works. The superstars of the game, such as Gordie Howe and "Rocket" Richard, have made appearances at one time or another, but on one occasion in the early nineties, a relative unknown received an unforeseen response as he stepped up to the tee at the first hole. Alex Faulkner had played for the Detroit Red Wings and the Toronto Maple Leafs for three seasons in the early sixties. His career total of 101 games and 15 regular-season goals was quite modest compared to the other golfers in this particular tournament, but being a Newfoundlander from Bishop's Falls, in the central part of the province, Faulkner was automatically the most revered of all the participants. "He expressed the fear that with all the NHL people there, he wouldn't be recognized," said Cole. "He didn't mind that. Then, when he was introduced, he got the biggest ovation of all."

Faulkner had scored five goals in the Stanley Cup playoffs of 1963 while with Detroit. Three had come against Chicago in the semifinal series, and two of them had turned out to be game-winners. Against Toronto in the final, his two goals had helped secure the Red Wings' only victory, in Game 3, and again one of them proved to be the deciding marker. Although his NHL career was brief, Faulkner holds a special place in the hearts of most Newfoundland hockey fans because he played in the old six-team NHL at a time when it was difficult to earn a spot on a team playing at the highest level of hockey.

In fact, very few Newfoundlanders have played in the NHL over the years. The Maple Leafs had Joe Lundrigan of Cornerbrook in the early seventies, a defenceman who played a total of fifty-two games. More recently, Dwayne Norris of St. John's flirted with a job in the Quebec and Anaheim systems and now plays in the German League with the Cologne Sharks. John Slaney has aspirations to return to Los Angeles and still shows promise as an offensive-minded defenceman. He has 133 games to his credit and 53 big-league points. Once the Canadian junior defenceman of the year, Slaney is the pride of St. John's and has left one of the most significant impressions of Newfoundland on the NHL. The New York Rangers have found regular work for the aggressive Darren Langdon of Deer Lake. Terry Ryan of Mount Pearl and Brad Brown of Baie Verte are valued prospects in the Montreal

Canadiens' development chain. The Belleville Bulls' Danny Cleary of Harbour Grace was chosen in the first round of the June 1997 draft and has become the property of the Chicago Blackhawks.

Alex Faulkner is sixty years old now and still plays four games of hockey a week in the region surrounding his Bishop's Falls home, where he, his wife and family run an extended-care home for seniors. "I play two games in the thirty-five-and-over group that I just barely qualify for," Faulkner teased. "The other two are in the recreation league with the younger kids. I enjoy that because it makes me push myself a little bit harder." He had just come from the bush where he and his son had been cutting firewood and dragging it back to the house by snowmobile. Faulkner's voice almost jumped across the telephone line as he welcomed the chance to reflect on his discovery at Memorial Stadium.

In the mid to late 1950s, he had been playing senior hockey with a team called the Grand Falls Andcos. The Anglo Newfoundland Development Company ran the pulp mill in the community, and many of the players on the team it sponsored were employed there, drawing substantial salaries at the time. In 1958, Faulkner left his job and moved over to Harbour Grace and the Conception Bay C.B.s. Closer to the capital city, his most antici-pated games became those played at the relatively new Memorial Stadium in St. John's. "We'd leave our home Stadium that would accommodate maybe fifteen or eighteen hundred and be just stacked," Faulkner explained. "Then you'd go to St. John's and the people lined up for blocks on end just to see those games. It was amazing."

Rivalry, not money, was the defining factor of hockey at home for Alex Faulkner, and in Memorial Stadium the stakes were that much higher because it had become the showcase arena in the province. "We were small-town Newfoundland and anytime we beat St. John's we loved it," he said. "The small-town thinking is that we were beating the big city slickers." It was the competition between communities on the island that drew fans to the build-ing, according to Faulkner, and not necessarily the level of play. It made for raucous and tension-filled evenings at Memorial Stadium. "In small-town Canada, it's the rivalries between the towns that make the difference as to whether you have a big crowd or not," he estimated. "You could have two towns playing and have four thousand people in the rink. Then you could have Canada's National team come in and play the Czechs and have only a thousand in the Stadium."

In early November 1960, King Clancy of the Toronto Maple Leafs paid a visit to Newfoundland, where he saw Faulkner playing for Conception Bay against St. John's. Clancy was accompanied by former Leaf Howie Meeker, who had been coaching in St. John's at Prince of Wales Collegiate, the United Church school in the capital city. It was Meeker who had called Faulkner to the Leafs' attention. Following the game, one of Clancy's associates phoned Faulkner and asked if he would like to have a try-out with the Leafs. "We were so far removed from the mainstream that playing hockey was a pastime for us," Faulkner said of his opportunity. "The call was far and above anything that I had ever expected. It was absolutely amazing because it wasn't something that I had planned on, or that I had played hockey towards."

When he caught on with the Leafs, Faulkner left Newfoundland for four years and played in Toronto's system at the NHL level and with Rochester of the American League. After being traded to Detroit and his subsequent success in the 1963 playoffs, he had a couple of injuries and decided not to play in the minor leagues again because of his disdain for the endless bus travel. Faulkner returned to Newfoundland and played another couple of seasons in the senior league with the Conception Bay C.B.s before returning to a professional career, in Memphis and then in San Diego of the Western Hockey League. He came home to Newfoundland for good in the early seventies. It was then that he donned the uniform of the St. John's Capitals and played in Memorial Stadium as his home rink. Never was Alex Faulkner more inspired by an arena. Perhaps it was because the Stadium was so revered in his home province. "It's hard to describe how important it was to get to that rink," he said, recalling a childhood spent on the frigid winter landscape near Bishop's Falls. "Coming off the river and outdoor rinks, for us to go into a stadium like that and play . . . it was overwhelming." Even all these years later he remains impressed by the noise and excitement that the building seemed to generate as well as the butterflies he felt as he stepped onto the rink. "I look back on it now and when I think of all those people lined up to get into Memorial Stadium, I just wonder how, when I got on the ice, I could ever play hockey. I guess you just put that thing out of your mind because it was really exciting."

Faulkner is overwhelmingly proud of his home and of the hockey he has played. When it is suggested, however, that he is the most famous player to come out of the province and to have skated at Memorial Stadium, he is beyond being modest. Although fond of the game, he considers it just that— a game—and has no inflated sense of importance about his sojourn in professional hockey. "Whatever profession we are in we want to go to the top," he said. "But I'll tell you this. I did not live my life hoping to go to the National Hockey League."

As our conversation drew to a close, Faulkner sent his regards to Bob Cole and praised his friend: "Of course we have the best broadcaster of all time from Newfoundland in Bob Cole." Even at sixty years of age, he sounded impatient to get his duffle bag loaded up and the stick taped for that night's game. It is only recreational hockey for older fellows but Faulkner brings an infectious youth to his anticipation of the competition. When asked if he still played to win, he did not hesitate in responding. "Anybody that's happy when his team loses shouldn't be involved."

Most lunch hours, Memorial Stadium is alive with big-band music blaring from the loudspeakers as hundreds of skaters circle the crisp, clean ice. The "Seniors' Skate," as everyone calls it, brings retired men and women from St. John's down to the rink in droves for ninety minutes of fellowship and skating. If you watch from the concourse level above the stands, you can barely tell the age of the congregation. Hand in hand, or as singles, they move with a youthful pace more commonly found among teenagers who skate late on Friday nights with their dates at any one of a thousand rinks across the country. One figure does not escape the eye. An extremely tall man, maybe six-foot-four without his skates, is swooping around the rink at what appears to be full speed. With an off-white cable-knit sweater and khaki pants to keep him warm, Jack Reardigan finds the open spaces and moves in and out of the jubilant traffic. Waving to those he leaves behind, the seventy-three-year-old Reardigan's broad and ruddy face beams. What hair he has left is snow-white and has been allowed to grow long over the collar of his sweater. It flows behind him as he moves furiously around the arena. There is no question that when Jack Reardigan is skating, he is in his own personal heaven.

"People ask me when I'm going to give it up," he says with a twinkle in his eye. "I tell them, I'll give it up when anyone down on this rink passes me just once." Reardigan is finished now, and hardly out of breath. There is an unabashed enthusiasm as he greets the others with a loud voice and the charm of a Newfoundlander's heavy accent. "I come down here and every single person who comes through the door knows everybody else," he brags. "It's like going into the church. This is a shrine right here."

Jack Reardigan is the retired chief accountant at Memorial University in St. John's and one of the city's most loved characters of sport. He is the president of the committee that stages the Royal St. John's Regatta on Quidi

Vidi Lake right next door and, as such, holds a special and respected position in the community. It is at this rink, however, that Reardigan has established himself as something of a folk hero and spiritual leader of his generation. For twenty-one years, he played senior hockey for St. Bonaventure College and he holds the record for Boyle Trophy wins by an individual. His name is inscribed on the precious mug sixteen times. For another nineteen years, Jack presided over the heated confrontations on Memorial Stadium ice as the province's most recognizable referee. "I wouldn't say I'm a rink rat but I spend an awful lot of time down here," he says. In many ways, Reardigan is consumed by the nostalgia of the arena and yearns for the type of games that were once played here. "I don't look at hockey much any more and I don't know the names of many of the players. When you look at the competition I refereed down here, it was unbelievable!"

Reardigan played centre for St. Bons when that team enjoyed an undisputed dynasty in Newfoundland Senior Hockey. At one time, there were sixteen consecutive Boyle trophy championships, a whopping twenty-seven in the school's history. Although St. Bons had played their home games from the tiny St. Bons Forum—with an ice surface 139 feet by 60 feet—they also played right around the corner as visitors at Memorial Stadium once it was opened in 1954. When the St. John's senior championship was contested, it was always at the big Stadium, and when St. Bons played for the Herder Memorial Trophy, emblematic of the provincial championship, they did so in the capital city's showcase arena. "We could block this rink every night," Reardigan says matter-of-factly. He drifts into the local dialect, of course, to reveal the fact that attendance was never a problem in the good old days. "St. John's was a great hockey town," he says. "Especially when they saw their own fellas out here and there was somebody to cheer for."

Senior hockey in St. John's and at Memorial Stadium was heavily laced with religious overtones. The clubs were affiliated with schools that have always been based on a denominational system. There were St. Bons, St. Pats and Holy Cross, which were affiliated with the Roman Catholic Church. The Anglican school was Bishop Field College and their team was referred to as the "Fieldians." The United Church school, Prince of Wales College, came to be known as the "Guards." With the players so easily identified by their faith, battle lines were naturally drawn on the ice and in the stands. "It was a religious war," explains Reardigan. "They would pack this place to see St. Bons lose. No one can tell me any different today. We had few supporters and the rink would be blocked—jammed by the other team."

St. Bons had always been seen as the team of the fortunate. They had their own rink attached to the school, and most of the boys who attended and played hockey were from well-heeled families and were headed for professional careers. Don Johnson, a former president of the Canadian Amateur Hockey Association, played for St. Pats and agrees with Reardigan's assessment of the driving force behind senior hockey competition. "I could take you to a hockey game in those days and I knew every player's religion by what team he was playing for," Johnson remarked. "The description of an atheist around here for years was someone who didn't care who won a hockey game at the Stadium."

St. Bons were so dominant and other schools so jealous that one, Prince of Wales College, hired former NHL rookie of the year and Toronto Maple Leaf coach Howie Meeker to come to Newfoundland and run the entire hockey program with the express purpose of knocking off the traditional champs. "The Stadium gave birth to Howie Meeker," Johnson figures. As a result of the new arena's opening, the schools in St. John's, other than St. Bons, now had access to artificial ice and better conditions in which to play. The problem was, they had to go a long way in order to catch up to the Catholic powerhouse. "The local folklore says the city got him to come," remarked Johnson, of Howie Meeker's hiring. "But then the Guards got hold of him and they said they'd pay him more to come and coach the Protestants." Jack Reardigan echoes Johnson's feelings on the matter. "The Guards brought in Howie Meeker to beat St. Bons. There was no other reason," he says.

Reardigan is reserved when talking about Meeker's obvious contribution to the health of the game in Newfoundland. While he agrees that Howie's personality was refreshing and that his expertise strengthened the Guards' system, he laments the change that occurred to the style of play at Memorial Stadium after Meeker's arrival. Only half jokingly, Reardigan blames the one-time NHLer's tactics for ending his playing career. "Meeker came in and changed all the rules. He told his players to never mind the puck, take the man," Reardigan chuckles. "I was a stickhandler and a fairly good skater and nobody hit me. Then when they started hitting, I was around forty years old and I got out."

One of the most remarkable games in the history of Memorial Stadium took place on March 16, 1960. In a best-of-seven final series for the Boyle Trophy, St. Bons was actually trailing St. Pats, their poor Catholic cousins, three games to two. St. Bons had a string of sixteen championships on the line and so there was plenty at stake. The place was "blocked," as the locals like to say. Some estimates say six thousand people or more packed into the place and were overflowing from the bleacher seats close to the ice. Bob Cole was in the broadcast booth, and over the telephone Don Johnson played the tape—still in existence—of his play-by-play: " ... GOT IT OUT TO FORD ON AN ANGLE ... HE COMES IN FRONT AND THE NET IS KNOCKED DOWN ... PLAY GOES RIGHT ON ... "

The commentary is unmistakable—Bob Cole at his best. The crowd sounds immense, as if it were twenty thousand strong in the old Chicago Stadium, roaring with every foray into the goal area. "They told me the next day that bus drivers in the city had their radios tuned to the hockey game so that passengers could listen," said Cole, with pride. "They interrupted the movie at several of the theatres in town and piped in the radio station for the last five minutes of the game. The whole city was the Boyle Trophy." St. Pats, the school run by the Christian Brothers, beat St. Bons 4–2 in that sixth and final game and ended a dynasty on the eve of St. Patrick's Day. Don Johnson remembers being on the ice as the Stadium exploded in celebration of his team's victory. "I know right where that spot is that I was standing on when the final whistle went," he recalled. "I had a feeling that I'd never had and I've never had again. I always felt that I owed hockey a great deal after that."

Jack Reardigan's beloved St. Bons had finally capitulated, and his memories of the game are less vivid after that. He does believe that the loss crippled senior hockey in the city. "They were just waiting for us to lose," he says in justification. "As a matter of fact, when we lost the Boyle Trophy to St. Pats, that ended senior hockey in St. John's. There was nobody to cheer against. St. Pats and the Guards, there was just no interest." As a one-time hero of the most hated team in Newfoundland hockey, Reardigan understands that a dynasty and its longevity can often be one of the most compelling things in the game.

Following the victory by St. Pats in 1960, St. Bons faded from prominence and Howie Meeker's Guards won the Boyle Trophy in 1961–62. It was the first time in recent memory that a Protestant team had been able to capture the title, and an outsider had left an impression on Newfoundland hockey that would forever change the game in the province. "When it came to Howie Meeker, there were no undecided votes. You either loved him or you hated him and it was usually based on religion," Don Johnson said frankly.

Such was the importance of faith and denomination to the fabric of the hockey that was played at Memorial Stadium during that time. In many ways, Howie Meeker brought a breath of fresh air to Newfoundland hockey. He undoubtedly increased the skill level of countless players in the province and had, at one time, been loved by most island fans because of his accomplishments as a Toronto Maple Leaf. It is said that those who played for him at Prince of Wales and with the all-star St. John's Capitals were devoted to him. Still, Howie Meeker had his enemies in the Stadium and there was little he could do to correct that. "The Catholics hated him," Johnson said. "I don't think Jack Reardigan probably had a good word to say about him."

The old referee is a purist in many respects. Reardigan loves skating and the fluid nature of the game of hockey when it is unencumbered by too much physical play. He officiated countless games in his nineteen years of wearing the black and white stripes for the Newfoundland Amateur Hockey Association, including several Herder Memorial Trophy championship matches. Now retired from all aspects of hockey, Reardigan accepts that he was one of the most respected officials in the province based on the important assignments he drew. One he recalls in particular occurred during the Christmas break of 1965 when the Soviet National team, coached by the legendary Anatoli Tarasov, came to Newfoundland for a two-game exhibition tour.

The first of the matches was played at Memorial Stadium in front of a packed house. The Soviets' opposition was a collection of senior league all-stars known as the St. John's Capitals. "It was unbelievable." Reardigan smiles at the memory. "Could these fellas ever skate and stickhandle. I think the only time our guys got in over centre ice was to face off the puck after the Russians scored a goal." The visitors dominated, to be sure, scoring the first sixteen goals of the game and then toying with the local representatives. Loyal until the end, as well as being appreciative of great skill, the Stadium crowd stayed put in spite of the whitewash.

With time running out, a local RCMP officer, George Spraklin, gave the fans a measure of happiness. The tricky forward had been the lone bright light for the home side throughout the game. "One fella could skate with them and that was George Spraklin," Reardigan says. Don Johnson remembered the elation in the building when Spraklin finally beat the Russian goaltender. "It was one of the wildest and loudest cheers I ever heard at the Stadium," he claimed. "When he scored you wouldn't know but they had just won the Allan Cup," Reardigan says. "The crowd just went crazy." The next day in the *St. John's Evening Telegram*, Spraklin's goal was depicted as the defining moment of the game. In a photo, the crowd is seen cheering wildly in the rout the Soviets won by the outrageous score of 19–1.

"Anatoli Tarasov always had a joke with me," said Don Johnson. "Whenever Tarasov would see me somewhere, he'd look at me with a big smile and say, 'Aah … Newfoundland … good … good! Hockey … no … no … no … bad … bad.' And he was right at the time!"

One of the most boisterous incidents at Memorial Stadium took place during the eastern playoffs for the Canadian senior championship in 1973. The series pitted the Barrie Flyers against the St. John's Capitals. The Flyers player-coach was a former NHLer named Darryl Sly, who had also been a member of the world champion Trail Smoke Eaters in 1961. The series promised plenty of emotion—no team from Newfoundland had ever won the Allan Cup, but hopes ran high.

Don Walsh is an off-ice official at Memorial Stadium today, but he was a linesman during the confrontation between Barrie and St. John's in 1973. "It was a brutal, brutal series," says Walsh, shaking his head. It was obvious from the start that the Flyers would attempt to match the aggressiveness of the Capitals in their home rink. Don Johnson had coached the St. John's team and was by this time heavily involved in the administration of Canadian amateur hockey. He had warned his old associate, Darryl Sly, not to try to mix it up at Memorial Stadium. "I told him that they might win every game by a couple of goals," says Johnson. "But I added that they shouldn't try to be tougher than us because we would beat the shit outta them!"

Indeed, the first game in St. John's set the tone for the rest of the series. Not long after the opening face-off, a rugged player from the Capitals, Bobby Lambert, levelled one of the Flyers and the play resulted in an arm injury. Darryl Sly was over the boards immediately and the brawl was on. "The shit hit the fan," Walsh says, wide-eyed. "It was an absolute riot. Coaches on the ice and fans and everybody else." In attendance at the match were three university coaches, Tom Watt from the University of Toronto, Clare Drake from the Alberta Golden Bears and Bob Hindmarsh of the University of Victoria. They were in town to give a clinic the next day in St. John's and bore witness to the slugfest at the uproarious Stadium. "Tom Watt once told me it was the first time he'd seen twenty-two fights on ice all at the same time," chuckles Johnson. "He also said it was the first time he'd seen one team, the Capitals, win all twenty-two!" Watt went on to coach in the NHL with Winnipeg, Vancouver and Toronto but his last coaching position was in the American Hockey League with the St. John's Maple Leafs.

After the game, which they eventually won, the Flyers had learned their lesson and escaped to the relative safety of their dressing room in order to avoid the frenzy of the crowd. Still, they had no faith in their well-being on their exit from the arena that night. "The Barrie Flyers were run out of the Stadium and needed a police escort back to their hotel," said Don Johnson. "They literally locked themselves in the dressing room and refused to come out without a large police force present."

Wagging his head and peering jubilantly over his half-glasses in the press box of the Stadium, a rotund Don Walsh tells the rest of the story with more than a little satisfaction. "From that point on, the whole series was one battle after another," he beams. "They brought in this referee from Goose Bay. He had never refereed a senior hockey game in his life and it was a total fiasco!" With infectious laughter he signals that it did not really matter who won the confrontation because the skirmish was what the fans at the Stadium had come to see—the adventure of the underdog Newfoundlanders sticking up for their rights against the brash and powerful Ontarians. "Barrie won the series but they had pictures of the players coming off the plane in Toronto bandaged up and on crutches," Walsh proclaims. "It looked like the boys coming home from the Second World War."

The Stadium starts to fill up early before the seven o'clock face-off for the Leafs–Monarchs game on this Wednesday evening. When the gates open, the standing-room-only ticket-holders stampede over the concrete floors stained with the black of petrified bubble gum. The loudspeaker plays a lively mix of popular tunes and fiddle music, so as to enhance the maritime atmosphere of the place. Right above centre ice, in a little box marked by the call letters VOCM, Brian Rogers and his broadcast partner, the bright-red-jacketed Tom Ormsby, are getting ready to go on the air.

Rogers is originally from Halifax and grew up idolizing the legendary play-by-play man Danny Gallivan, who was also a Nova Scotian. In broadcasting from this spot, and on the airwaves of Voice of the Common Man, he is following in the footsteps of Bob Cole, the number-one play-caller for "Hockey Night in Canada." "I think he's the best in the business right now," Rogers says of the St. John's native. As he shuffles around the little space, it becomes apparent how spartan the facility really is. There are no chairs or monitors, no spacious table top on which to rest vast quantities of statistics and other notes. It's just a box with a rail to lean on. While standing to describe the action, Rogers and Ormsby have a bird's-eye view of the ice surface right at the centre red line.

"We are fifteen feet above the penalty box, which has made for some interesting fodder in our broadcasts from time to time," Rogers points out. Not far below, the warm-up is taking place. Every slapshot sounds like the crack of a gun, and the profanity of the revved-up players is clearly audible. "It is akin to Chicago Stadium or the Boston Garden," Rogers boasts in proud exaggeration. "The people appreciate this as a little bandbox that makes a lot of noise."

Memorial Stadium is well into its fifth decade of service but only recently has it become the home arena for a professional hockey team. In the 1991–92 season, the Toronto Maple Leafs moved their American Hockey League operation from Newmarket, Ontario, to the Newfoundland capital. The Stadium was adjusted and some small private boxes were added. The bleachers in the lower section were replaced by individual seats and the glass was heightened around the boards. The capacity of 3,765 remains very small by AHL standards and the ability to generate increasing amounts of revenue is strictly limited by the physical constraints of the building. Although it sparkles with fresh paint and immaculate caretaking, the greying upper reaches beyond Bob Cole's catwalk betray the Stadium's years and suggest its eventual replacement by a more modern facility. "You've got a metropolitan area of 250,000 people. Show me one other place in Canada where there's that many people and no civic centre," Rogers argues.

The Leafs have averaged close to capacity yearly attendance in each of the six seasons they have played in St. John's. However, the parent organization in Toronto is reluctant to commit to the city for a substantial period of time because of the lack of a more spacious arena with better prospects for more income. People here fear the eventual loss of the AHL Leafs in spite of the fact that the team has been well received and very successful on the ice. "Black day in Newfoundland and Labrador if this franchise had to leave," Rogers warns. "I just couldn't see the city of St. John's, one of the best-kept secrets in the country, not having a pro hockey team."

While he is all for the city building a new civic centre to house the Leafs, Rogers clearly has an affection for Memorial Stadium because of the memories it has attached to it. Like so many denizens of older rinks across the country, he has attributed a personality to the arena that somehow makes it unique and not easily replaced. "Maple Leaf Gardens is still standing," Rogers points out.

In the McNichols Sports Arena coach's office in Denver, Marc Crawford was filling out the line-up card for the Stanley Cup champion Colorado Avalanche prior to their game with Toronto on Saturday night. A native of Belleville, Ontario, Crawford began his coaching career in nearby Cornwall, in 1989, with the Ontario Hockey League Royals. After two years there, he assumed similar duties with the new AHL franchise in Newfoundland. He had heard all about hockey in St. John's from one of his better players in Cornwall, John Slaney, and was familiar with Memorial Stadium by word of mouth. "I remember the first game we played there. She was blocked!" he said, eager to recall the old expression. "I had never seen so many people in all my life. We watched the pre-game warm-up and we had trouble walking down the hallways. It took us forever to get back to the dressing room."

The inaugural St. John's Maple Leafs of 1991–92. Coach Marc Crawford (front row, fourth from left)

The community easily warmed to their new team in Crawford's first season as coach. The Leafs won thirty-nine of their eighty games and finished second in the Atlantic Division while securing a spot against the Cape Breton Oilers in the first round of the playoffs. One of the coach's lasting memories of the Stadium came when a power failure interrupted the third period of a tight game between St. John's and their rivals. A province-wide ice and snow storm had left most of Newfoundland paralyzed and the frantic contest at Memorial Stadium ground to a halt. "It was amazing being in that building being totally blacked out with just the emergency lights on," Crawford recalled. "The fans were hooting and hollering and having a great time."

and veteran defenceman Joel Quenneville (front row, fourth from right) led the Leafs to the Calder Cup final against Adirondack

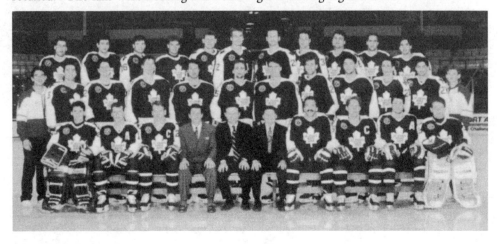

Officials at the rink waited a while before making any decision because the Oilers—who were ahead by a goal—wanted to finish the game then and there. The fans stayed put and started singing to pass the time. "We ended up having to postpone the game and we didn't think we were going to get anyone out of the place," Crawford said. "It really showed me the passion the people had for hockey."

Joel Quenneville, a player-assistant coach with the Maple Leafs that season—he's now the head coach in St. Louis—was patrolling the blueline at the time of the black-out and again the following evening when the final period was replayed with the Leafs trailing 3–2. "We had to play twenty minutes of Game 1—that's all. It was the most amazing game I've ever seen in my life," Quenneville said. "The fastest game I ever saw. For twenty minutes the pace of the game was incredible."

The images of the interrupted game were shown on a "Hockey Night in Canada" telecast as were highlights of the final and overtime periods. From that point, the happenings at Memorial Stadium found a national audience for the balance of the 1991–92 playoff year. The new St. John's Maple Leafs, Newfoundland's first professional hockey team, became a Cinderella story. At home, people lined up for days to buy tickets for the Calder Cup final, which eventually saw the Leafs square off against the Adirondack Red Wings, coached by Barry Melrose of Kelvington, Saskatchewan.

Joel Quenneville remembers the noise the fans made when they entered the building. "We would hear the stampede and knew it was the standing-room-only people running in to get the best location they could," he said. "It was like a herd, a mad dash. It showed you their desire to be at the game and what hockey means to them."

The Calder Cup final between the Leafs and the Red Wings in 1991–92 was an odd one because in the exciting seven-game series the home team failed to win a single game. Adirondack eventually claimed the title by virtue of four victories at Memorial Stadium, while St. John's could not win in front of its boisterous and loyal following. Glenn Stanford is the director of operations for the Leafs and the former rink manager of Memorial Stadium. His opinion is that the physical nature of the building actually worked against his team and in favour of Adirondack. "We had a lot of small forwards and on a little bigger ice surface, our team was able to move around better," he estimated. "They were more suited to playing in this building because they were a little slower and had a tougher defence than we did. It was a very strange series." It was, indeed, the only Calder Cup final that had seen a home team fail so miserably in its own building.

The close call for the Leafs had created enormous expectations on the part of the fans and what followed the spring of 1992 was bound to be anticlimactic. Tickets at the Stadium continued to sell well and the "Baby Leafs," as they are often called, performed superbly to start the next season. By January they were sailing along

in first place in the Atlantic Division. Then a municipal strike by the outside workers closed Memorial Stadium as the rink maintenance staff walked off the job. The Leafs were forced to play four home games on the road in smaller rinks on the island and even borrow facilities on the mainland. They returned to St. John's for a couple of dates but the situation turned nasty. Workers rocked the team bus as the players attempted to get inside Memorial Stadium for a game against Cape Breton. "Oh, it was real ugly," remembered Joel Quenneville. "We were sitting on the bus and we saw these people banging windows. One guy actually cracked a window with his fist right where I was sitting. They were rocking the bus and I thought to myself that it was going over. I'm just glad we got out of there."

The rink maintenance staff at Memorial Stadium went on strike in January 1993, forcing the Leafs out of the arena for three months of the season

The Leafs, who had been adored by the fans in their short history in St. John's, were now cast out of the city, unable to use the storied arena. For three months they had to play their home games in unfamiliar rinks across the eastern portion of the country. Matches were held in Stephenville, Newfoundland; Charlottetown; Saint John; Halifax; and as far away as Cornwall, Hamilton, Montreal and Toronto. The "road warriors" continued to play well, and Marc Crawford was rewarded for his part in holding things together by being named the minor league coach of the year for the 1992–93 season. His feelings about the disruption caused by the Memorial Stadium workers are tempered by an understanding of the people and the place. "I think the decision for us to stay away from Memorial Stadium was probably a good one," he reckoned. "There were some passionate people there involved in a city dispute and they didn't want anything happening in a city building at that point. They would certainly have gone to any ends to make sure it didn't happen."

For his part, Joel Quenneville remembers the inconvenience of the whole episode and admits to feeling a certain homesickness for Memorial Stadium in the midst of an interminable road trip. "It was awful. We were like a travelling circus," Quenneville snorted. "Some days we weren't sure where we were going. We were planning games and ice times by the seat of our pants." In addition, the rigours of life away from home were starting to have their effect. "You just get sick of the guys," he added. "Morning, noon and night you're with them and eventually they start to stink!"

The Leafs finished first in their division that season and had improved on their point total from the inaugural year. However, they bowed out to Cape Breton early in the playoffs, the difficulties with being on the road for so long finally taking their toll on the team. "We were apologized to by many of the guys involved in the dispute after it was over," Marc Crawford said. Still, he understood that some things, like wages and working conditions, were far more important than hockey. "It was almost like when you're playing the game you do things you have to for your own team whether it goes against your nature or not. I had a lot of good friends that worked for the city. They remain good friends even in light of what happened."

Before he turned to coaching, Crawford was a grinding forward with the Vancouver Canucks for parts of six seasons and scored a modest 19 goals and 31 assists in his 176 NHL games. His one-time coach, Harry Neale, says that Crawford was tenacious in his desire to play the game at the highest level. "I kept sending him to the minors because I felt we had to keep more skilled players. In the end we would have been a lot better off if we had kept him and more players like him in the NHL."

He remains one of the youngest coaches in professional sport and has enjoyed tremendous success in his first three complete years in the National Hockey League with the Quebec Nordiques and Colorado Avalanche. In his initial season, he was named the Jack Adams Trophy recipient as the league's coach of the year. The following spring, after the franchise moved to Denver, he captured the Stanley Cup. In many ways, Crawford's ability to excel may have a lot to do with his capacity to understand people. "He was one of the only guys who actually knew or cared what you were going through as a coach," said Harry Neale. In Quebec, Crawford had tutoring in French in order to communicate with the fans through the media. The same commitment can be seen in his attempt to understand the motivations of the people who came to Memorial Stadium to watch his Baby Leafs.

"They were very knowledgeable, very passionate fans and they loved tough, aggressive hockey," Crawford said. "If you didn't compete, then that was the only time you heard anything negative from the crowd. That's the way it should be. People pay good money, hard-earned money, to be entertained, and they want to see a competitive, hard-nosed brand of hockey. That serves everybody well and that's what we tried to be about when we were there."

Crawford spent three full seasons in St. John's and led the team to 125 regular-season victories before he landed an inevitable head coaching job on the mainland with a big-league team. His daughter Kaitlin was born on The Rock and he takes great pride in that connection to the community. As he reflects on Memorial Stadium and its intimacy, as well as the traditions associated with the place, he drifts easily to a discussion of the people in the seats. "In a lot of cities, the important buildings are the city halls and churches and the arena," he said thoughtfully. "The rink becomes an even bigger part of the community's chemistry and the city's lifeline." Crawford used the word passion frequently when describing the fans at Memorial Stadium. "They have such good spirits and good make-ups that you cannot help but feel good about a place like that."

From the press box you have to stand up and lean over the rail in order to see play around the net in the near end of Memorial Stadium. So it is that Glenn Stanford jumps up from his seat in order to witness Greg Bullock's twentieth goal of the season, which puts St. John's ahead of the Carolina Monarchs. The man who acts as the Leafs' top administrator smiles in celebration but knows time is running out. "You would love to, in a new building, keep the atmosphere and closeness of it," he says of the Stadium. "The simple economics of us participating in the American Hockey League means we are not going to be able to do it with this arena for much longer. Toronto has openly said many times that if there is no new rink at the end of our two-year contract, we are done."

Stanford was Memorial's rink manager from 1987 to 1991 and before that he had always been around the place as a fan with a keen interest in Newfoundland hockey. When he assumed responsibility for the arena's operation, he inherited a rollicking old barn known for its peculiar grandstands. "Our building back then was the reverse to any other in North America," he explains. "Your top balcony seats were ten dollars and the three-dollar bleacher seats were next to the glass." The inhabitants of the lower levels of Memorial Stadium came to be known as the "Bleacher Creatures" and were notorious for engaging in parties during the course of the games. On many nights hockey became the secondary attraction. "Those fellas were absolute madness," says Don Walsh, the old linesman. "One night the cops started to crack down and arrested all these people for drinking in public. The police put them all in a big dressing room just down here." He points to the back corner of the rink. "The patrol cars were sent to pick them up. Anyway, somehow the bleacher creatures got out and then they locked the police in!" Walsh laughs uproariously at the tale. Stanford shakes his head as he recalls the challenges he faced. "My first experience as manager in 1987 was calling in the riot squad of the Royal Newfoundland Constabulary so that we could get peace in the building."

The new coach is Mark Hunter of Petrolia, Ontario. A former NHLer who played twelve solid seasons with Montreal, St. Louis, Calgary, Hartford and Washington, Hunter's brother Dale is still starring in the league with the Capitals. In his rookie year with the Baby Leafs, Mark has learned about the professional game in a smaller centre like St. John's. "They know their f—ing hockey," he says, forcefully. "They let me know if I make mistakes and if someone on the ice is cheating they're going to let them know that too."

Hunter loves the intimacy of the Stadium, the fact that the people are right on top of him and dissecting his every strategy. It is old-time hockey to him in a setting that he knew long ago. The posters and pennants add to the charm. Carnation chocolate milk has an advertisement painted on the ice and car dealers flog Chryslers and Dodges on the Player of the Month scoreboard. "First time I walked in I said, 'Wow!' It looks like one of those European things where the players have ads all over their jerseys," Hunter says, with a laugh. He knows it points to the need for change, as St. John's has increasingly grown beyond the capabilities of Memorial Stadium. "They need to get more people into the building in order to meet their costs," he sighs. "It's too bad because it's a grand old building. Glenn Stanford couldn't get one more advertisement on the wall if he tried."

That part is true. Stanford has done everything in his power to make the Stadium suitable for professional hockey. He is limited by the fact that there are only 2,500 seats. At $16.50, ticket prices cannot be raised much higher or many fans will be unable to pay. Corporate sponsors in St. John's have done just about all they can. While several groups have proposed a new civic centre, no one seems to know how much it would cost or who would pay for its enormous expense, which is frustrating for Stanford and the entire Leafs organization. While they love Memorial Stadium, they know it is time to move on. "If we want this type of entertainment in our community, then it is really incumbent on the citizens as a whole to make a new building work." In the end, Stanford recognizes the Stadium's incredible value to the people and to the lifeblood of the city. "It's the link to hockey," he says. "Therefore it is the focal point of the community."

Guy Lehoux has played for this team since its inception. He is the favourite of the Memorial Stadium crowd and the captain of the Maple Leafs. A hard-working defenceman who came here from Disraeli, Quebec, Lehoux played his junior years in Chicoutimi and Drummondville and arrived on The Rock barely able to speak a word of English. At twenty-five years of age, Lehoux has worked hard for everything he has been able to accomplish and has never been close to playing in the National Hockey League. "I'd love to play one game, you know. Even if it's only one game I'd like to make it up there," he sighs, referring to the NHL.

Warren Norris, a native of St. John's, was the only Newfound-lander in the Leafs' line-up in 1996–97

Lehoux is the only Leaf player from "away" to have spent a summer in Newfoundland, and so the people have adopted him as their own son. His commitment to hockey is now matched by his loyalty to the city in which he plays. Outside the dressing-room door, he stands half naked with a towel around his waist and draws back the blue curtain that affords the players some privacy. After the victory by the Leafs, the young fans have come

streaming down to the room looking for his auto-graph. "I was very happy here," he says of his summer. Signing countless pictures of himself and taking time to greet every well-wisher, Lehoux admits this is a great place to play. "Here you meet people and the first thing you know they are asking you to come over for supper next Sunday. They make you feel welcome and at home."

There is only one Newfoundlander on this year's Leafs roster and he has not been there most of the year. Warren Norris of St. John's has just finished his collegiate career at the University of Massachusetts and has only recently joined the team as it drives towards the playoffs. "I think the fans are happy to see a local boy in the Toronto Maple Leafs organization," Norris says, beaming. His brother Dwayne played for the Team Canada juniors that won the gold medal at the world championships in Helsinki in 1990. Everyone here remembers that it was Norris who scored the dramatic winning goal against the Czechs.

Sitting in the dressing room, the younger Norris considers his position with the team and drinks in the joy of playing in a place he has always known. "I was about three years old and I would come to watch Dwayne and Ian, my brothers, play," he says. "I was knee high to a grasshopper but I was kicking around cans on my knees while they were out on that ice playing hockey." Norris is showered and his thick black hair is combed so that it sits neatly above the collar of his dress shirt. He seems older than his twenty-two years because he is a professional hockey player now. Soon he'll receive his Bachelor of Commerce from the university and consider what to do next. For now, he is just happy to talk about this comfortable arena and his memories of it. "I loved being around the rink," he says. "Most times I would put my homework on the back burner to see a couple of hockey games here in St. John's. I'd have to say that I have lived and died hockey since I was a kid."

As a star player for St. Bons, Jack Reardigan had occasion to play against the Fieldians of the Anglican church's Bishop Field College. There was a fiery younger player on that team by the name of Bob Cole. The rivalry between the Catholic powerhouse and the Protestant challengers never lacked intensity in spite of the fact that St. Bons won most of the time. All these years later, both Reardigan and Cole remain as residents of Newfoundland and St. John's. Each has retained an overwhelming love of the game of hockey. To Jack Reardigan, the lunch-time skating at Memorial Stadium is time spent in a hallowed place. He bristles at the thought of some newfangled arena that might replace the charm of the rink he has come to love. "I don't suppose I'll be around when it goes and I hope I never see it happen," he says, resolutely. "This is like a warm living room. You're at home. It's a great feeling."

Bob Cole cannot remember how many Stanley Cup championship games he has called the play-by-play for. He recalls, instead, the acts of greatness on the part of skilled and exciting players. Never one for statistics, Cole prefers the dramatic, the compelling speed and precision of hockey that he once saw from the catwalk of Memorial Stadium, as he first broadcast the game. In the time since, he has defined the wonderful moments of triumph and the pinnacles of careers with brilliant description. Cole has moved beyond the Stadium and seen the game in the grand arenas of Chicago, New York, Toronto and Montreal.

As a younger man, Cole thought of the new rink by Quidi Vidi Lake as a magnificent palace that delivered a better brand of hockey to the residents of St. John's. He remembers describing the simple grey building as "gorgeous." Now on the way to the airport and his next "Hockey Night in Canada" assignment, the Hall of Fame broadcaster concludes there is no reason to be nostalgic about a structure made of bricks and steel. It is time for Memorial Stadium to be replaced, he figures. Only then will the game continue to grow in Newfoundland. "It's sad in a way, but you can't live in the past," Cole reckons. And the metaphor he chooses to expand on this sentiment is fitting for this historic maritime city: "You can't continue sailing the seven seas in square-riggers."

Epilogue

Hockey is the Canadian metaphor, the rink a symbol of this country's vast stretches of water and wilderness, its extremes of climate, the player a symbol of our national struggle to civilize such a land.
—Bruce Kidd and John MacFarlane, *The Death of Hockey*

STANDING IN THE RUSTY-RED CLAY that surrounds tiny Cahill Stadium in Summerside, the old Red Wing Gerard Gallant's final words were simple and effective. "Tell Yzerman hello when you see him." Steve Yzerman, the Detroit captain, had been Gallant's closest hockey friend for many years. The two former linemates had kept in touch faithfully, but it was easy to tell that Gallant, now retired from the NHL and coaching in his native Prince Edward Island, missed his buddy desperately. In a season so critical for Yzerman, the sentiment expressed by a lifelong teammate was telling.

Yzerman himself had become a recurring character to us. Only vaguely had he been associated with the stories uncovered during our excursion to the grass roots of the game. And yet he was there, over and over again. Why didn't we go to the rink in Peterborough, Ontario, where so many great NHLers, including Steve Yzerman, played their junior hockey? We should have recognized the sign when he scored that 3–2 goal for Canada in September to beat the Slovakians in the World Cup. It was a desperate game and deliverance came from a skater who dismissed forever the notion he couldn't rise to the occasion as an international performer.

Here was a rare hockey player—he'd suited up for the same team throughout his glorious professional career. Yzerman had embarked on his fourteenth

year as a Red Wing with more than 500 goals and 1,300 points in his equipment bag. For a decade, he was Detroit's captain and, without question, the essence of his team. We had seen him become an all-star again and witnessed his humble response to a public thanks on national television from the beneficiaries of his charity. In mid-winter, the rink Yzerman had played on as a boy in Nepean, Ontario, was renamed in his honour. In the late spring of 1997, he was saved from his obsession as he finally held the Stanley Cup aloft in Detroit's Joe Louis Arena.

A twelve-year-old Steve Yzerman receiving the MVP award at the Ottawa International Pee-Wee Tournament in 1977

So much had changed over the course of the eight months we travelled to the rinks. Players had been traded, coaches fired, some of the more interesting characters had, unfortunately, passed on. In resigning ourselves to the incomplete conclusion of our yarn, we thought it best to turn to Steve Yzerman. This, after all, had been his year.

We took the trip on the spur of the moment. Who knew what we would find in the city of Nepean, about a fifteen-minute drive from the Macdonald-Cartier Airport in Ottawa? It wasn't even Yzerman's home town—Cranbrook, British Columbia, was where he was born and where he lived until he was ten years old. But we knew there was a Steve Yzerman Arena in this place, and somehow that was fitting because so few active players have their names on one of hockey's living monuments. There is, of course, the arena dedicated to Wayne Gretzky in Brantford, Ontario. Complex Desjardins just outside Rouyn, Quebec, honours Philadelphia Flyers defenceman Eric Desjardins, the rink's most noteworthy graduate. But it is not a common practice to devote a building so sacred to the community before a career is complete and ready for admiration.

The Nepean Sportsplex was opened on June 8, 1973, and it is an edifice that reflects the ambitious country Canada was nearly a quarter of a century ago. Stark and clinically white, its dramatic roof rises to twin pyramid-like peaks. The abundant glass sent piercing light rebounding into the enormous car park on this sizzling summer day. The arena complex is at the centre of a huge athletic park—a lawn-bowling green, baseball diamond and football stadium act as satellites. There was no mention of Yzerman's name as we examined the green and white space-age marquee—only NEPEAN, spelled out in those distinctive letters of the seventies when everything had to appear ultra-modern.

We might as well have entered a shopping mall. Just inside the main door is a gallery for contemporary art and to the left an information kiosk surrounded by plexiglass where it looked as if lottery tickets might be on sale. Outlined in purple and aqua-blue signs on grey poured concrete walls was the directory to the complex: arrows pointing to the swimming pool, the gymnasium, the visual arts centre, the sports medicine clinic, the conference rooms, the administration office, the curling facility, the weight room and finally to the rink and the arena. Still no hint of Yzerman—not even his picture on the wall in the rotunda alongside natives of Nepean who have excelled in sport, such as Olympic medallist Alison Korn of rowing fame.

Down a ramp and through a simple door we found ourselves entering a cavernous room known only as "the rink" to the pedestrians who inhabited the lobby of the Sportsplex. Young figure skaters danced haltingly to the music that blared across the centre redline from a ghetto-blaster balanced on the boards atop the penalty box. A few advertisements hung from steel girders here and there. Stylized pictures of various athletic figures surrounded the ice surface, stencilled on the plain white upper walls. Again no sign that Yzerman had ever been there.

Then we went across the way to the next turn in a faceless corridor lit by the soft glow of fluorescent

Steve Yzerman (top row, second from left) as a member of the Nepean Raiders. Former NHL goalie Darren Pang (bottom row, first on left) was also on the team

light. We opened the blue door, which revealed a bigger hockey rink. More figure skaters and more concrete. To the right, a sharp rise of stands. Room for maybe a couple of thousand to take in a hockey game in black and yellow seats. A couple of banners trumpeting the exploits of a team known as the Nepean Raiders—we knew that Yzerman had played his first junior hockey for them. Then over the near boards we saw it—the only marking on the ice, with the exception of the red circles and lines that define the game's boundaries. At the rink's midway point was a black and red painted rectangle with a simple script, almost like his signature. "The Steve Yzerman Arena."

"The signage goes in next week. The big thing is his name is etched into the ice," Bill Levesque said, over the phone from city hall. Levesque is the director of park planning and development for the City of Nepean and was instrumental in the move to have the arena at the Sportsplex named after Yzerman. The plan was originated more than a year ago by Nepean's mayor, Ben Franklin, who is a sports enthusiast and hockey fanatic. "There are always problems when you try this kind of thing," Levesque noted. "One thing that sticks in people's minds is that you never know how far the person being honoured will go in his or her career, what their accomplishments will be."

It was not a problem for the people of Nepean. The decision taken in mid-winter to honour the Red Wings captain was unanimous. "Nobody said anything that was remotely negative about Steve or the idea," Levesque boasted. "Not even the Toronto Maple Leaf fans." A ceremony marked the occasion before a game Yzerman played against the Ottawa Senators at the Corel Centre in Kanata, not far from Nepean, but the official dedication will be held sometime during the summer when Steve comes home to visit his folks, who still live in the area. With a Stanley Cup ring on his finger, Yzerman will return as the city's most accomplished and revered son. He was born in another province but, as is often the case, he has been claimed by the place where he refined his craft. "We like to take full credit for all of his accomplishments," Levesque readily admitted. "He probably learned to tie his skates in Cranbrook but he learned to use them here!"

The modest community just to the east of British Columbia's Purcell Mountains, midway between Trail and the Alberta border, is where Steve Yzerman first played hockey as a five-year-old. Cranbrook's old rink was made of wood and had enough room for just over a thousand fans to squeeze into its confines. It was a going concern, packed day and night with players of all ages who possessed this one arena to satisfy their huge hockey needs. By the time he left, Steve Yzerman was not yet a teenager and his talent was still in its formative stages. The rink he left behind had, however, played a huge part in what was to become of him down the road.

"Not many years after Steve made it to the NHL I got a letter from the Cranbrook Minor Hockey Association saying they had been following his career," Steve's father told us. Ron Yzerman had moved his family to the Ottawa area in 1975 so that he could assume an upper-level position in the Canadian civil service. Years later, he is struck by the connection Cranbrook insists on maintaining to his superstar son. A request to have Steve's photo for the rink came out of the blue in 1986 or '87 and was readily granted. "We went back to Cranbrook and we stopped at the old arena," the father recalled. "It had a new coat of paint but not much else. There was his picture hanging on the wall inside."

As much as anything, the player can make the rink. Faceless and forbidding sheets of ice develop warmth and personality because of the characters who slice the surface and carve out a story on what starts out as a blank white page. Steve Yzerman is that kind of character. In the first game of the 1997 Stanley Cup championship series, he walked resolutely off the ice after the first period against the Philadelphia Flyers and directly to the "Hockey Night in Canada" camera to be interviewed. He was there early. He was supposed to go to the Detroit dressing room first and take his helmet and gloves off so that the camera could get into position. When Yzerman found out television wasn't ready for him, he snarled. "This is business. There's no time for screwing around!" Then he turned on his heel and rushed into the Red Wings' locker-room. Moments later, he returned, apologizing for his behaviour, and engaged in an interview marked by anxiousness and honesty. Yzerman worked furiously on the tape of his stick's handle throughout.

"He is the most intense kid I've seen in my life," said his bantam coach, Mike Goddard. "He was better than anybody in the city. He had pro written all over him from the time he was thirteen years old." In the Nepean Raiders' minor hockey system, Yzerman had been the captain of every team he played for. As a peewee, he took his team to a provincial championship at home in the Sportsplex against a heavily favoured team from Toronto. The score in the final game was 6–0 and Steve was involved in four of the goals. At the age of fifteen, while playing in the Tier II junior league, he competed against older teenagers—there were even some twenty-year-olds. Yzerman was named the rookie of the year, made an all-star and finished second in league scoring. He was the brightest light the Nepean Sportsplex had ever witnessed. "He really got going in hockey in a serious way right here in Nepean," Ron Yzerman said. "He played so many games and probably had his greatest time right in that arena."

The naming of the rink in Yzerman's honour was a natural as far as his old coach Mike Goddard is concerned. "He is the biggest thing this city has ever had," Goddard estimated. Just as every other person told us, Yzerman had become synonymous with the rink in his home town. Its aspirations were realized in the accomplishments of an honest, hard-working hockey player who has always conducted himself as a member of a team first and foremost. In 1989, Yzerman was the recipient of the Lester B. Pearson Award as the player chosen by his peers to be the most outstanding performer in the league. He is liked and respected at all levels of the professional game, with very few, if any, exceptions.

As the Stanley Cup was extracted from its case with overwhelming care by two men in white gloves on June 7, 1997, everyone standing by in Joe Louis Arena knew it was going to Steve Yzerman first. The final shifts were being played out on the ice a few feet away, but the Detroit captain showed no hint of a smile, only the pursed lips and wide eyes that had always identified him while he was engaged in the struggle. Nothing was going to deter Yzerman now. He had planned this for a lifetime and it was the only feat not yet accomplished. "There were 50 million people who wanted the Red Wings to win the Stanley Cup this year," Mike Goddard reckoned. "I'll bet forty-nine point five million of those wanted it because Steve Yzerman was the captain of the team." When it happened, when the final buzzer went and the Flyers were vanquished, Steve Yzerman awaited his just reward. His father watched him hold the cherished trophy high. "What flashed through my mind was after all the struggles, the ups and downs in the NHL, being cut from the various World Cup teams... I thought, this is real vindication," Ron Yzerman reflected. "Now nobody can say, 'He was a great player but...'"

In the basement of the Sportsplex, one of the Zamboni drivers, Brian Keenan, held the phone out. "It's Steve's brother Chris," Keenan said. "He's the weight room attendant here. You should ask him what he thinks." The younger Yzerman is twenty-five years old and has preferred other sports to hockey. But he is acutely aware of what the game means in Canada and how much the rink is at the centre of life in Nepean. "It's surreal. It's like it's named after another person—the hockey player, not my brother," Chris told us. "We're proud of it but it's hard to get used to."

Soon a bronze plaque bearing a likeness of Steve as well as some biographical information about him will be mounted in the arena's entrance-way. There will be a sign on the scoreclock and of course there will be a picture to let everyone know who the greatest hero of this building is and has been. Most importantly, Yzerman's name is permanently engraved on the ice just as it is, at long last, on the precious Stanley Cup. "In some ways there is a parallel in that it introduces a degree of longevity," Ron Yzerman suggested. "After your playing days, there is a memorial to your abilities. In the case of the arena, it was done on the basis of not only his on-ice accomplishments but his overall persona. In that sense, Nepean recognizes him as a pretty good young man both on and off the ice."

Buildings where hockey is played are a treasure to the Yzerman family. That Steve's name should be associated with the one is an honour. Whether it's in Cranbrook or Nepean doesn't really matter because both arenas contributed, in substantial ways, to Yzerman's greatness. From a community "barn" to a sportsplex in the nation's capital, these places have been his living. The guts of the rink remain unchanged by the years. "It's probably the one element more than any other that has influenced and directed the lives of so many kids," the elder Yzerman concluded. "It's the place that brings the family together more than any other single thing. I think that is still true today."

In the late afternoon at the Nepean Sportsplex, a group of senior citizens gathered to fiddle with crafts and engage in lively conversation. There was a swimming class complete with joking, splish-splashing kids in the enormous pool. Young men and women ran on treadmills and hoisted free weights in the gymnasium. The figure skaters twirled graciously in the Steve Yzerman Arena. We didn't exactly get to "tell him hello" as Gerard Gallant had asked

A rare photo of Steve Yzerman as a goalie, pictured with his younger brother, Chris, not long after Steve turned pro with the Detroit Red Wings

all those months ago. Gallant, no doubt, had done it many times on his own after the Stanley Cup was won. Yzerman had been busy in the arenas of professional hockey making sure his community's gathering place had a fitting title. His gift to the rink that had shaped his life was simple and priceless—his name, and with it a tradition that will endure for generations to come.

Acknowledgments

IN A PERFECT WORLD, WE WOULD have preferred to show our appreciation with an old-fashioned skating party and shinny tournament. The Stannus Street Rink in Windsor, Nova Scotia, would be the ideal venue. Dress up "the old barn" as it was at the turn of the century, complete with a small orchestra in the music loft and bring together the hundreds of Canadians who shared their stories and enriched our journey across the country. There would be an endless supply of hot chocolate and steaming hot dogs at the canteen with complimentary flasks of warmer liquids in the corner seats to beat the chill and embellish the anecdotes. Grace Sutter and Jean Béliveau could swap stories with Elsie Wayne and Mike Zuke.

Instead, we can only hope that this book reflects the communal spirit that Canada's rinks have so uniquely fostered for generations. If we have been successful, it was because of the generous assistance of the following people.

A year ago, veteran sports authority Lou Cauz steered us to Penguin Canada and its publisher, Cynthia Good. Lou's guidance and Cynthia's vision laid the cornerstone for *The Rink*. It is fitting that we found a home here because two other Penguin books, *Welcome Home* by Stuart McLean and Roy MacGregor's *The Home Team*, provided inspiration for our project. Sincere thanks to editor Wendy Thomas, who made the editing process "pain free" for a pair of rookies who had been forewarned that it would be otherwise; Alan Little, who provided a thorough fact check; and Scott Sellers, a New York Islanders fan, for his ardent support.

In Brampton, Ken Giles is the definitive authority on the local scene. His knowledge and photo file were invaluable. Thanks also to Marg Thompson, the Brampton Excelsiors Lacrosse Club, Region of Peel Archives and Carl McCauley for his assistance and access to his files on John McCauley.

I am indebted to Barry MacKenzie, Terry O'Malley, Neta Monson and the entire staff and student body of Notre Dame College in Wilcox, Saskatchewan, for their hospitality and co-operation. Johnny Weisshaar was also an enthusiastic guide.

The Sutter family is just as impressive off the ice as the Viking boys' legacy of hockey accomplishments. Grace and Louis, Darryl, Brian and Gary were double-shifted during my Alberta visit, while Duane was a long-distance resource. I would also like to acknowledge the co-operation of Jack Roddick of the Viking and District Museum, rink manager Ned Kearns and Angela Hanson of the *Viking Weekly Review* for providing photographs and research assistance.

The hospitality was never warmer than in Flin Flon, refuting its reputation as a feared hockey destination. Stew and Normajean Lloyd rolled out the welcome mat and eagerly answered all queries and requests. Lloyd's passionate stewardship of the Bombers' Historical Society facilitated research of the Whitney Forum. Ian Cooper and Pat Jones of the Hudson Bay Mining and Smelting Company were also accommodating hosts. Greta Redahl of the Flin Flon Library did diligent sleuthing to uncover some rare photographic treasures.

An afternoon at Mike Zuke's rink in Sault Ste. Marie left an indelible mark, as did a visit with Ted Nolan in Buffalo. Ron Francis, his father Ron Francis Sr., Greg Millen, Russ Ramsay and Bob MacKenzie all pointed me in the right direction in the Soo. Special thanks to Gino Cavallo and Dave Harris of the Greyhounds' front office, as well as Linda Burtch at the Sault Ste. Marie Public Library and Judy McGonegal at the Sault Ste. Marie Museum.

Windsor, Nova Scotia's love of the game was enlightening. Dr. Garth Vaughn, author of *The Puck Starts Here*, graciously provided the breathtaking photograph that adorns our cover. Every Canadian should visit Howard Dill's farm. His pumpkin seeds are truly magical. They're even growing in my back yard. I am also grateful to the Windsor Hockey Heritage Centre, Chook Smith and Eric Stephens.

Acknowledgments

We deeply appreciate the encouragement of our "Hockey Night in Canada" colleagues. Our association with Canada's Saturday night television institution opened rink doors across the country for our research. We are grateful to Alan Clark, head of CBC TV Sports, executive producer John Shannon and producers Mark Askin, Larry Isaac and Ed Milliken for their support of an outside project. Author emeritus Dick Irvin offered valuable insight and advice while John Garrett, a trusted friend (and an English major, he claims), proofread our copy weekly to keep us on the right track.

Others who offered assistance along the trail are Scott Whitley, Susan Procter, Ted Barris, Billy Warwick, Steve McAllister, John MacKinnon of Canadian Hockey, Mark Piazza of the Philadelphia Flyers and Tony Lasher of the Detroit Red Wings.

I owe special gratitude to my parents, who always took me to the rink, stayed for encouragement and support and have never stopped cheering me on.

Finally, thanks to my wife, Diane, who read every word first with a discerning eye and whose instincts were always right, even when I disagreed. She not only embraced the project but didn't protest when an anniversary getaway took an unexpected detour to the Windsor Rink. And to my daughter, Jennifer, who shares her father's love of writing and hockey and to my son, Justin, who can't get enough of his favourite sport and brought his father back to the magic of the local rink. More than a few times they popped their heads through the office doorway to ask, "Are you finished yet, Dad?" Happily, I can finally answer, "Yes!"

Chris Cuthbert
Brampton
July 1997

I could fill any one of the hockey rinks that I visited with the legions of generous souls who helped me with this project. It was often a lonely pursuit, but I felt warmed in every one of the frozen arenas by the support and understanding of each Canadian I talked with. There is a universal belief in our country that a community's rink harbours much of its soul. More than anything else, I am grateful for that simple and endearing truth.

A great deal is owed to my colleagues at CBC Sports and "Hockey Night in Canada." Both Chris and I appreciated and admired Ron MacLean's and Don Cherry's belief in Canadian hockey at the grassroots level. Alan Clark, John Shannon and Ron Harrison listened patiently and offered suggestions based on experience. The producers Ed Milliken, Larry Isaac, Mark Askin and Jim Hough spend much of their working lives in hockey rinks. Each gave me gentle direction and the friendship that comes naturally with the game. Sherali Najak helped me ask the right questions and cared about the answers. Carol Angela Orchard is a talented partner from another sport. She graciously and expertly did most of the gymnastics work while I lingered in the rinks. John "Cheech" Garrett is the most giving comrade I could hope to know. Hall of Fame broadcaster and author Dick Irvin is an inspiration.

The book could not have been completed without the faith and enthusiasm of Cynthia Good, as well as that of Wendy Thomas who guided me in discovering the right words. Alan Little checked every fact and kept me honest. Jem Bates carried the story through production, and typesetter Laura Brady gave the book the look we had envisioned. Scott Sellers, I could tell, was in our corner of the rink from the very beginning. Research and assistance with photos was readily given by Jane Rodney and Craig Campbell at the Hockey Hall of Fame; Kathy Broderick of Molstar; Chris Schwartz and Scott Courage in St. John's; Steve Tambellini and Ray Picco in Trail; Maurice Robichaud, Peter Walsh and Sean MacLeod in New Brunswick; Donald Beauchamp of the Montreal Canadiens; Nicole Bouchard and Paul Messier in Quebec; Bill Schurman, Bill Semple and Phil Bridges on the Island; and David Langford of the *Globe and Mail*. Steve McAllister and Joanne Martin of the NHLPA could not have been more helpful. Don Meehan talked openly of his boyhood friend, the late Ron Lapointe. Michael Haddad found a document for me that made things clear.

The players, coaches and fans are the main attractions in any rink. Each one of them I contacted was a willing participant. Without this group, hockey's houses have only a superficial charm. Their stories and tall tales would never be told without the people. I will always be in their debt.

Thank you to Elizabeth, Scott and Carrie, my family, who first watched me perform in a hockey rink. Thanks to Steve Stapleton, who showed me the perfect "barn" in our adopted homeland of Prince Edward Island and to my friend Tim Currie, who brought me back to the rink to play the game I love best. My late uncle Jim Koch and I enjoyed our final conversation

Acknowledgments

about a rink where we had both seen the miracle of Bobby Orr at one time or another. I will always remember. Catherine took our kids to the wonder of the open-air ice at Kew Beach alone on many winter nights. She was steadfast and supportive as Chris and I discovered a wonderful game in all the right places.

Scott Russell
Toronto
July 1997

Photo Credits

Photo Credits   331